# CAREER COUNSELING CASEBOOK:
## A RESOURCE FOR STUDENTS, PRACTITIONERS, AND COUNSELOR EDUCATORS

## FIRST EDITION

# The Career Counseling Casebook:
# A Resource for Students, Practitioners, and Counselor Educators

## Edited by:

### Spencer G. Niles
### The Pennsylvania State University

### Jane Goodman
### Oakland University

### Mark Pope
### University of Missouri - St. Louis

## National Career Development Association

Copyright 2002 by the National Career Development Association,
10820 E. 45 Street, Suite 210, Tulsa, OK 74146
Phone (866) 367-6232, E-mail dpennington@ncda.org

Printed in the United States of America
Printed and bound by Royal Printing and Copy Centers, Tulsa, OK

Library of Congress Cataloging-in-Publication Data


The career counseling casebook: a resource for students, practitioners, and counselor educators / edited by Spencer Niles, Jane Goodman, Mark Pope.—1st ed.
    p.cm.
    Includes bibliographical references and index.
    ISBN 1-885333-08-0 (alk. paper)
      1.   Vocational guidance--Case studies. 2. Career development--case studies. I. Niles, Spencer G. 1954- II. Goodman, Jane, 1942- III. Pope, Mark, 1952-

HF5381.C26522 2001
158'.3--dc21

                                200104495

# TABLE OF CONTENTS

# About the Editors

**Spencer G. Niles**, D.Ed., LPC, NCC is Professor of Education and the Professor-in-Charge of Counselor Education at Penn State. He served previously as Professor and Assistant Dean at the University of Virginia. He is the editor of the *Career Development Quarterly* and serves on the editorial boards for numerous other career development journals. He has authored or co-authored over 60 publications and delivered more than 80 presentations related to career development.

**Jane Goodman**, PhD, is Associate Professor of Counseling, Oakland University in Michigan. She is the 2001-2002 President of ACA, and a past president of NCDA. She is the author or co-author of several books, many articles and book chapters, primarily in the area of career development of adults.

**Mark Pope,** EdD, NCC, NCCC, RPCC, MAC, ACS is an educator, consultant, and counselor and is currently an Associate Professor at the University of Missouri - St. Louis in the Division of Counseling and Family Therapy where his specialties include career counseling, addictions counseling, psychological testing, and multicultural counseling. He has written extensively on careers, specifically on the career development of ethnic, racial, and sexual minorities.

# Foreword

This casebook is a project that has been in development for the past couple of years. We think that the result is worth the wait! The book provides a tremendous resource to students, practitioners, and counselor educators seeking to learn more about the practice of career counseling. Leaders in the field have provided their thoughts as to how they would work with the clients described in the cases. As you read the casebook, you will quickly become aware of the fact that the editors have provided diverse cases that "push the envelope" regarding the typical notions of career concerns. The respondents were clearly up to the challenge, and the result is a state-of-the-art career counseling primer.

The casebook represents the most recent in a series of resources the National Career Development Association is providing to help students and professionals enhance their understanding of career development theory and practice. *Experiential Activities for Teaching Career Counseling Classes and Facilitating Career Groups* edited by Pope and Minor, *A Counselor's Guide to Career Assessment Instruments* edited by Kapes and Whitfield, *The Internet: a Tool for Career Planning,* edited by Harris-Bowlsbey, Dikel and Sampson, and the soon-to-be released third edition *Adult Career Development: Concepts, Issues and Practices* edited by Niles are each intended to advance career development theory and practice in the 21st century. The resources complement the already existing NCDA resources related to career counseling competencies and ethical standards that guide practitioners as they help children, adolescents, and adults manage their career concerns more effectively. Of course, each year the NCDA Conference serves as a time for career development professionals to focus on enhancing their skills by participating in workshops, conference sessions, and attending keynote speeches highlighting the latest developments in career interventions.

We trust that you will find the career counseling casebook to be invaluable to you as you move forward in your career.


Roger Lambert
President, 2001-2002
National Career Development Association

# Acknowledgements

We want to acknowledge the important contributions of the many people who helped bring this book to the publication stage. Students at the University of Virginia, the University of British Columbia, Oakland University, and the University of Missouri-St. Louis provided a substantial number of cases. We are extremely grateful to our students for sharing their clinical experiences with us. Obviously, we are deeply indebted to the case respondents for sharing their vast experience and expertise. Collectively, their responses provide a window into the vitality that exists within career counseling. The respondents make it very clear that competent career counselors in the 21st century are sensitive to diversity, draw upon a wide range of theoretical perspectives and incorporate techniques from a broad array of counseling specialties to meet the needs of their clients. It was an honor for us to work on this project with such an elite assemblage of leaders in the field.

Last, but certainly not least, this book would not have been possible without the important contributions of Juliet Miller, Sandra Kerka, Linda Griffin, and Deneen Pennington. They provided crucial input in the editing and production process. They are truly an outstanding group of professionals.

Clearly, this has been a team effort. We hope that you enjoy the results.


Spencer Niles
Jane Goodman
Mark Pope

# INTRODUCTION

The case study method is an established approach for learning how to apply theoretical concepts to real-life situations. In counseling, we often learn much from what our clients have to teach us. Many students consider their practica and internship experiences to be critical in their development as counselors. This book strives to bridge the gap between theoretical discussions and clinical applications by offering readers opportunities for learning about how expert career counselors conduct career counseling. In compiling this casebook we sought to provide readers with numerous examples of case responses representing the breadth and richness of career counseling. In part, this was a selfish endeavor because we each are involved with training students and counselors in the professional practice of career counseling and we felt the need to provide our students with a wide range of case studies. Often, students inquire as to how specifically we might intervene if we were working with a particular client with a specific set of career concerns. In many respects, it seemed too narrow to provide only one response to such student inquiries. To us, there was a need for a resource that would provide multiple examples of how experienced career counselors might assist their clients in resolving their career concerns.

This endeavor also reflects the pride we feel toward the history of career counseling as well as the hope we have for its future. Two decades ago, Crites (1981) noted the challenges confronting career counselors. He stated that career counseling is more difficult than psychotherapy because it encompasses the skills required for providing general counseling in addition to the skills required for practicing career counseling competently. In 1997, the National Career Development Association (NCDA) articulated these competencies by identifying the following knowledge and skill areas as essential for the professional practice of career counseling:

1. Career development theory
2. Individual and group counseling skill
3. Individual and group assessment
4. Information resources
5. Program management and implementation
6. Consultation
7. Diverse population
8. Supervision
9. Ethical and legal issues
10. Research evaluation
11. Technology

The breadth of skills identified by the NCDA competency statement is significant. Although not all competencies identified by NCDA are evident in every case response provided in this book, many of the competencies are used in responding to each person's career concerns. Moreover, the case responses provide readers with a window into the rich tapestry that is the current state of the art in career counseling. In reading the case responses, it is also clear that the field has gone far beyond its initial "growth" stage dating back to the early years of the 20th century.

For much of the last century, career counseling was characterized primarily as "three interviews and a cloud of dust." Many students in counseling and related educational programs were not interested in learning or providing career counseling because they viewed career counseling as a routinized procedure that involved testing clients and then providing clients with the best occupational options emerging from their test results (Heppner, O'Brien, Hinkelman, & Flores, 1996). Although such approaches have an important place in the practice of career counseling, they do not represent the totality of approaches for helping people resolve their career concerns.

In fact, the turn to the new millennium gave rise to an emerging kaleidoscope of career counseling approaches. [These approaches have been described elsewhere (e.g., Brown, Brooks, & Associates, 1996; Herr & Cramer, 1996; Niles & Harris-Bowlsbey, in press) and we refer readers to these sources for more in-depth discussions of specific career theories.] Savickas (1993) reminds us that we can anticipate such developments because new vocational ethics emerge with each new century. It is not surprising, therefore, that career counselors and career theorists should respond to emerging vocational ethics by conceptualizing and implementing new intervention strategies. These developments are necessary to maintain the vitality and relevance of career counseling.

One of the goals for this book is to present readers with specific examples (in the form of case responses) of the vitality that is represented in career counseling today. To the extent that this goal has been achieved, we are indebted to the case respondents. Because they each have a longstanding and deep enthusiasm for the practice of career counseling, they were eager to participate in this project to provide an important service to NCDA and the readers of this casebook. The career development profession has a long history of serving others. In this spirit of service, we want the readers to know that all proceeds generated by the casebook go directly to NCDA's career development fund to sponsor graduate student research awards. Graduate students in counseling and related educational programs will shape the future of our profession. Thus, the contributors to this book were eager to support students' research efforts.

## The Structure of the Book

Given the goals for the casebook, we were careful not to restrain the authors in constructing their case responses. The instructions provided to the respondents are presented in the appendix. These instructions were originally developed by David Jepsen for the "Getting Down to Cases" section of the *Career Development Quarterly*. They provide a useful framework for the respondents and we are grateful to David for his contribution of these guidelines.

In reading the instructions for the case respondents you will notice that we did not require the authors to conform to any particular theoretical approach in constructing their responses. We sensed that many practitioners use integrative approaches in their career counseling, and we wanted case respondents to feel free to draw upon any theory (or theories) they thought was (or were) appropriate in addressing the career concerns presented by their "client." We also did not require respondents to conform to a particular style and format in constructing their responses. Readers will notice that some respondents provide responses in a pithy, outline fashion, whereas others took a more formal approach in their writing style and format, and still others used a conversational style in constructing their responses. One wonders if this variation in style is representative of how the case respondents conceptualized their clients' concerns, how they formulated hypotheses relative to their clients' career dilemmas, and how they might actually approach their career counseling sessions. We did not try to verify this possibility, but pose it as a question worth considering as readers imagine the case respondents working with their clients. Finally, you will notice that there are at least two case respondents for each case. We realize that there are many ways to address each client's career concerns and we wanted readers to get a sense of this by having at least two case responses to compare for each client.

The authors of the case responses also represent a cross-section of professionals. Some are known internationally for their career development research and leadership and others are regional or local leaders known primarily for their highly competent career counseling practice. The authors are also diverse demographically because we think it is important for the case respondents to represent multiple perspectives and diverse groups (while also contributing their unique individual thoughts and perspectives).

The cases were constructed to represent lifespan career development concerns. There are two cases for each developmental level represented. We also sought to bring demographic diversity to the cases so that the "persons" in the cases would reflect the diversity that is evident in our client populations. Although the cases are fictitious, the authors of the cases used their clinical experience as career counselors to help shape the concerns and situations described in each case. Thus, in this way we are also indebted to the many clients with whom we have been privileged to work. Perhaps as much as anything else, this book serves as their legacy to others who will be assisted by the career practitioners who read this book. Finally, it is important that we thank the students at the University of Virginia, University of British Columbia, Oakland University, and University of Missouri-St. Louis who contributed case composites that provided the stimulus for creating the cases.

## Using the Cases

We hope that these case responses serve to stimulate readers to think creatively about how they might go about the task of providing career counseling assistance to their clients. Perhaps the case responses might even serve as a sort of professional smorgasbord from which current and future career counselors can select particular strategies in a systematic fashion. We encourage readers to observe the variety of clients and client concerns presented. Think about how this diversity influences your approach to each client. Consider the degree of overlap between career counseling and general counseling. For many clients presented in this book, their work-related concerns are interwoven with their nonwork concerns. How does this influence your work with these clients? What does this suggest in terms of the competencies required for conducting career counseling? Questions such as these may be useful stimuli for thinking about and discussing the cases.

Students in career counseling courses can be encouraged to critique the responses and offer their own insights as to how they might work with each case. Students could be presented with a case and then work in small groups to construct responses that could then be presented to the larger group. Once the students have had a chance to discuss their responses, they can be given the case responses provided in the casebook. Students can offer reactions to the case responses. What do they like about the case response? What do they think the counselor missed? What did the counselor address that the student missed in conceptualizing the client's concerns?

The case responses could also be used as stimuli for discussing the importance of theory in career counseling. Students can discuss the ways in which theory seems to inform (or not inform) practice. The benefits and costs of the theory-to-practice link can be explored. For example, does taking a singular theoretical approach overly narrow the range of concerns addressed by the counselor? Or, does a singular theoretical approach facilitate more efficient and competent practice? Is theory useful at all in working with clients? Which theories seem most used by the case respondents?

Finally, the case responses could serve as a springboard for future treatment outcome research – something that is sorely needed to advance the profession and to sort the "wheat from the chaff" among emerging career counseling practices. We hope that readers find the book useful in their development as career counselors. If you do, please feel free to let us know how it was useful to you. You have our best wishes as you engage in the life-changing work of career counseling.

## References

Brown, D., Brooks, L., & Associates (1996). *Career choice and development* (3rd ed.). San Francisco, CA: Jossey-Bass.

Crites, J. O. (1981). *Career counseling: Models, methods, and materials.* New York: McGraw-Hill.

Heppner, M.J., O'Brien, K.M., Hinkelman, J.M., & Flores, L.Y. (1996). Training counseling psychologists in career development: Are we are own worst enemies? *Counseling Psychologist, 24,* 105-125.

Herr, E.L., & Cramer, S.H. (1996). *Career guidance and counseling through the lifespan: Systematic approaches* (5th ed.). Glenview, IL: Scott Foresman.

National Career Development Association. (1997). *Career counseling competencies*. Tulsa, OK : Author. Available on Internet at ncda.org.

Niles, S.G. & Harris-Bowlsbey, J. (in press). *An introduction to career development interventions: A competency-based approach.* Englewood Cliffs: Prentice-Hall.

Savickas, M.L. (1993). Career counseling in the postmodern era. *Journal of Cognitive Psychotherapy: An International Quarterly, 7,* 205-215.

# DOUG: THE CASE OF THE YOUNG BULLY

Doug is a 9-year-old African American male in the fourth grade at a local urban elementary school. Doug is a below average student. Although he is at the top of his class in math and science, his reading and writing skills are below grade level. His teacher describes Doug as a likable, outgoing child who causes too many disruptions in the classroom. Although Doug responds well to the adults in the school, he has been referred to the principal several times for bullying other students.

Doug's life outside of school is somewhat complicated. Doug's biological father left home after a divorce when Doug was four and is now incarcerated on an eight-year term for drug-related charges. His mother remarried and moved to another state when he was six, and he has lived with his legal guardians, his grandparents, for the past three years. Although he visits his father every month, he has seen his mom only once since she left. Doug's grandfather is a retired policeman who is not involved much with Doug (he says he already raised his kids). Doug's grandmother is the primary caregiver and has met with school administration and you (school counselor) expressing her concerns about Doug (low achievement, referrals, and lack of friends).

Doug has always lived in a home near or below the poverty line. There is a large extended family in a nearby city, but, since his parents have left, Doug has not seen the other relatives. His grandparents who are in their late 60s do not like to travel.

When prompted, Doug identifies sports as his main interest. He cannot identify anything in school that he really likes besides gym class and being a peer mediator. In casual conversation, Doug talks about being a professional athlete when he gets older. In three individual counseling sessions with you at school, Doug has talked excitedly about his father, but resists any discussion about his mother. He seems ambivalent about his grandparents and struggles to identify any friends in school. Doug explains that he spends most of his time outside of school at the park with people from the middle school.

If you were the school counselor at Doug's school, how would you address Doug's career development needs?

## *Response to Doug: The Case of the Young Bully*
## *Carol Dahir*
## *New York Institute of Technology*

If we were to look at the world through Doug's eyes, what would we see? Poverty, a school program with limited interest to him, the influences of older children, and a future without love and family support. What do we see when we look at Doug? A young boy who is not connected to a plan for school success. A fourth-grader whose academic achievement is erratic. A nine-year-old who does not have a positive male role model in his life who takes an active interest in helping him discover who he is and what he wants. He lives in poverty; his mother is nonexistent. Figures of authority are constantly telling him what he should do; he has no guiding force in his life to help him understand why he needs to think with his head, not his hands. He needs to use his intelligence to strive for his goals, not intimidate those who get in his way.

To work with Doug, we have to try to understand his world. A world in which there exists competing family, community, and school values. This is very confusing to a young boy with too many choices placed before him. Which influences will succeed? What is important to Doug? Where does he go when he dreams? Does he see anything in his world that will help him realize his dreams? More important, does he believe that he can reach his dream?

School counselors working in poverty-stricken urban, suburban, and rural areas encounter many Doug's every day. Sometimes it is hard for us to understand why the Doug's of the world just don't get it! Why don't they connect education to future success? We look into the eyes of children who do not share or understand our family, school, and community values. School counselors face the challenge of helping students meet the expectations of higher academic standards and simultaneously assist students to become productive and contributing members of our society. To do that, we have to see what they see, understand what they understand, and connect them to their dreams.

Social cognitive career theory (Bandura, 1986) reminds us to focus on the interaction of variables. In other words, in the world of an elementary school student, how do gender, race/ethnicity, and social support affect self-efficacy and goals? The primary purpose of career development, especially at the elementary level, is to increase a student's self- and career awareness. The American School Counselor Association's National Standards for School Counseling Programs (Dahir & Campbell, 1997) establish similar goals, expectations, support systems, and experiences for all students. Delivering a national standards-based program ensures that school counselors provide the advocacy and accountability to improve school success in academic, career, and personal/social development for all students. Many students like Doug are often disconnected from the present let alone their futures. When students acquire the attitudes, skills, and knowledge embedded in the career development components of the national standards, they can identify a vision and connect them to their dreams. The national standards emphasize career and academic success for all students, not only those students who are motivated, supported, and ready to learn.

A school counseling program based upon national standards would help Doug to –

- know who he is and where he is going;
- be motivated to achieve;
- develop skills in the planning process;
- establish career goals;
- become involved in career awareness, career exploration, and career experiential activities
- visualize his future; and,
- understand the relationship between his personal qualities, his willingness, and motivation to get an education and his dreams of success.

The three career development standards help ensure that Doug acquired attitudes, knowledge and skills to actively take hold of the present and plan for his future: (1) students will acquire the skills to investigate the world of work in relation to knowledge of self and to make informed career decisions; (2) students will employ strategies to achieve future career success and satisfaction; and (3) students understand the relationship between personal qualities, education, training, and the world of work.

All interventions require addressing his personal/social and academic needs as related to his future. Doug is wise beyond his years and has developed survival skills for success on the streets. Sometimes these behaviors spill over into the classroom. His counselor begins to discover what Doug values. What's important to him? What does he know about himself and how he reacts and responds? Does he readily adapt to the values of everyone who influences him? How does he sort out the conflict between family, school, and community values? Does he have his own sense of self and where he wants to be and how he wants to get there?

We know that Doug likes sports. How can that influence school success and his relationships with his peers? We also know that Doug is a peer mediator. How can he transfer mediation and resolution skills to support good choices for himself? The implementation of the national standards and representative competencies would help Doug to better understand himself, what is important to him, what influences his choices and his decisions. This comprehensive approach would help his counselor better understand his attitude and approach toward life and the world he lives in. It would open the door to provide insight into the world he sees and give us a clearer picture of how we see his world. Doug's counselor would be able to monitor his career growth and development through a variety of interventions and proactive activities.

Group counseling would offer Doug the support from students with similar views of the world but each with a dream waiting to be brought to reality. Individual counseling could result in the creation and monitoring of an action plan. With help from his school counselor, he could see that each step forward is one closer to realizing his dream. Group guidance activities would offer him opportunities for a structured exploratory and learning environment.

Career awareness cannot be separated from the person Doug wants to become. Doug needs a mentor to watch over him and to provide a strong and positive influence at a time in his life that is most impressionable. A missing influence in Doug's life is the connection to family. His school counselor, in a case manager role, could seek resources to help Doug's grandparents find peer support and support among extended family members who might be willing to reach out to Doug.

Making connections is the key – between and among Doug and his counselor, his teachers, his peers, his family, his dreams. School for Doug is a place where he can exert his influence and establish his identity. School becomes the place for Doug to explore, learn, apply, and acquire academic and affective attitudes, knowledge, and skills. Having the opportunity for Doug to participate in a national standards-based school counseling program offers a comprehensive and developmental approach to career development that fills in the cracks so that Doug, and others like him will not fall through. Most important, it offers the venue to help Doug realize his dream.

### References

Bandura, A. (1986). *Social foundations of thought and action: A social cognitive theory*. Upper River, NJ: Prentice Hall.

Dahir, C. A. & Campbell, C. A. (1997). *Sharing the vision: The national standards for school counseling programs*. Alexandria, VA: American School Counselor Association.

## *Response to Doug: The Case of the Young Bully*
## *Amy S. Milsom*
## *University of Iowa*

Doug appears to be a child who I would consider to be at risk for school dropout or delinquency. This impression is based on the combination of factors (i.e., little interest in school, limited support network, poverty status, ethnic minority status, few friends, bullying behavior, urban setting, child of divorce, parental involvement with drugs) that together increase his chances of engaging in risky behavior in the future. I am concerned that he is a child who doesn't feel connected to anyone or anything.

There is, however, a lot of information that we don't know about Doug and his family. For example, what does he do in his spare time with the older kids at the park? What is his relationship like with his grandmother? How much does he study? Does he get help with schoolwork from grandparents? What is the value of education to his family? What do he and his dad talk about when they meet? What are his feelings about his parents? Does he play sports or participate in extracurricular activities? In addition to what we do know about Doug, the answers to all of these questions would also be important in helping us to design career development interventions.

Doug's career development needs must be evaluated in relation to family and culture, as Herring (1998) believed that both can significantly influence career development. For example, Herring suggested that children who are raised by grandparents might be misinformed about career issues because the grandparents may not have current information about careers or the world of work. In addition, Herring believed that it is important to examine and consider some of the family issues surrounding why a child is living with grandparents (in Doug's case, Dad is in jail and mom remarried and moved away) and how those factors might influence career development. Finally, exploring the types of jobs that family members have as well as their expectations about work can provide a basis for designing career development interventions for children (Herring). As discussed above, in Doug's case answers to many of these questions are unknown.

Super's theory (1990) supports the idea that career choice can be influenced by environmental factors (e.g., parent's SES), education, and opportunity. Doug is growing up in poverty. It doesn't appear that he has any positive male role models in his life. His grandfather is a retired policeman but not very involved in his life, his father is in jail and we do not know what type of job he held prior to being incarcerated, and Doug has no contact with other male relatives. Doug also does not appear to be very interested in school. In addition, he is and/or has most likely only been exposed to jobs that he might encounter on a daily basis. Living in an urban setting, therefore, Doug most likely has only been exposed to blue-collar jobs. Because it is common for students to pursue jobs that they are familiar with, Doug may have very limited career aspirations.

As such, career development interventions should be designed to counteract the "negative" effects of the environment in which he lives. More specifically, Doug could benefit from exposure to a wide variety careers. Consistent with Krumboltz's social learning theory of career decision making (Krumboltz, Mitchell, & Jones, 1976), career interventions should be aimed at increasing Doug's awareness of the variety of jobs available to him. In addition, Doug should (if he hasn't already) participate in classroom activities that will help him to identify personal strengths and interests. He may also need help identifying what he likes about peer mediating and recognizing and appreciating his math and science talents. Finally, career interventions that allow him to connect his strengths and interests with careers might help him to understand the connection between academics and careers, possibly resulting in a greater interest in school.

Given that Doug is only in 4th grade, career intervention activities that are experiential and concrete would be most effective. These activities should be designed to help increase his awareness of various careers and to help him begin to understand the types of skills that are needed for certain jobs. Many of the other students in his school would probably also benefit from increased career awareness and exploration, thus, group or classroom activities would be beneficial. Working in peer groups would also allow Doug to improve his interpersonal skills.

Examples of career intervention activities for Doug and his classmates might include having career speakers (especially individuals from ethnic minority groups and/or individuals representing nontraditional careers) or taking field trips to various job sites where the students could interact with workers or equipment. The school counselor could also work with classroom teachers to design career lessons related to each academic subject, again helping students begin to understand the connection between careers and academics. The use of videos or technology-based career intervention activities would also be useful.

Helping Doug to feel more connected to school also seems to be an important goal. In addition to his limited exposure to careers, we know that Doug likes sports and that, typical of boys his age, he has hopes of becoming a professional athlete some day. We also know that he is good at math and science, but he doesn't express any interest in those subjects. I would guess that he has had little exposure to careers in those areas and/or doesn't understand the applicability of math and science ability to other careers. In addition, Doug does not appear to be very successful academically. As a result, he may not feel confident about his academic abilities. Finally, aside from his involvement with peer mediators and participation in gym class, Doug does not seem to be connected to school. Given his experience so far (i.e., not getting along with peers, not achieving academically), it is understandable that he shows little interest in school. Ideally, we need to figure out how to get Doug not only to achieve in school but also to value school. Helping him develop better social skills would also be important in helping him to feel comfortable at school.

To accomplish those goals, Doug could benefit from individual attention and group activities. More specifically, one-on-one help with academic subjects may be effective in improving Doug's grades. Pairing Doug up with an organization such as Big Brother/Big Sister would allow him to develop a long-term relationship with a positive male role model. A mentor could also help Doug to identify and become proud of the things he does well. In addition, involvement with peer group activities or sports could allow Doug to work on social skills and developing friendships with peers.

With support from the grandmother, Doug could be encouraged to participate in extracurricular activities.

The fact that Doug's grandmother has expressed concern about his poor school performance and bullying is encouraging. Eliciting support from the family could be very important. The school counselor would want to help the grandmother to better understand career development issues. In addition, the school could provide support for her and possibly help her to understand things from Doug's perspective. In return, not only could the grandmother provide information about Doug's background, which would help us to better understand his situation, she could also be encouraged to work in conjunction with the school to implement career interventions or academic support strategies at home, and to cooperate with his involvement in extracurricular activities or sports.

In summary, as familial, educational, and environmental factors can greatly influence career development, career interventions should be comprehensive, involving support from school, home, and community (e.g., Big Brother/Big Sister). In addition, as is supported in The National Standards for School Counseling Programs (Campbell & Dahir, 1997), career interventions should be designed in conjunction with activities related to academic and personal/social developmental concerns. Because support from home and community is limited for Doug, it becomes extremely important for the school to provide career intervention. Thus, keeping him in school becomes crucial to his successful completion of career development tasks.

## References

Campbell, C. A. & Dahir, C. A. (1997). *Sharing the vision: The national standards for school counseling programs*. Alexandria, VA: American School Counselor Association.

Herring, R. D. (1998). *Career counseling in schools: Multicultural and developmental perspectives*. Alexandria, VA: American Counseling Association.

Krumboltz, J. D., Mitchell, A. M. & Jones, G. B. (1976). A social learning theory of career selection. *Counseling Psychologist, 6*, 71-81.

Super, D. E. (1990). A life-span, life-space approach to career development. In D. Brown, L. Brooks & Associates, *Career choice and development* (2nd ed., pp. 197-261). San Francisco, CA: Jossey-Bass.

# KELLY: THE CASE OF THE GIFTED STUDENT

Kelly is a 10-year-old white female in fifth grade at a suburban elementary school. She lives with her parents and 6-year-old brother in a predominantly white upper-middle class neighborhood. Kelly's father is an electrical engineer; her mother taught elementary school until Kelly was born, and for the past two years has worked part-time for an educational consulting firm. Her brother is in first grade at the same elementary school.

In third grade, Kelly was identified as a gifted learner after scoring in the 99th percentile on grade 3 achievement tests. In class, Kelly appears bright and quickly grasps material being presented, finding other things to learn about while her peers finish their work. Her teachers have discussed placing Kelly on an accelerated learning program. Although her parents encourage and nurture her learning, they were concerned about the social implications of placing Kelly in advanced classes and instead chose to keep her at the age-appropriate grade level with her childhood peers. They have also resisted having Kelly's IQ tested, as they believe her intelligence should not be quantified but instead fostered through educational experiences in and out of school.

Kelly has had a long-standing interest in animals. Throughout her childhood, Kelly has spent time visiting her grandparents who live in the country and have horses. Kelly learned to ride horses at an early age and continues to do so successfully. She also enjoys playing with her grandparents' three dogs. Her family has two cats and she convinced her parents to buy her an aquarium for her birthday last year. She also enjoys reading stories about animals. During a career day in fourth grade, Kelly met the father of a classmate who was a veterinary assistant. From this time, Kelly was convinced that she wanted to be a veterinarian when she grew up. Kelly often spends more time with and learning about animals than playing with peers, although she does have three or four girlfriends with whom she routinely spends time.

As part of the school's program to prepare students for middle school, Kelly met with her school counselor to discuss classes and the transition. Kelly is excited about the Gifted and Talented program she will be in during middle school, as she understands it from her teachers and parents. Since she sometimes gets bored in school now because she can finish her work while other students need help from the teacher, she is looking forward to being with other kids who won't make fun of her because she is the "smartest in class."

Aware of her interest in becoming a veterinarian, the counselor discusses her career plans. During this meeting Kelly tells the counselor that she is no longer certain about becoming a veterinarian because she thinks only boys take science classes and she is afraid that she will be teased in middle and high school. Although she is sure that she wants to go to college, Kelly does not think that she has what it takes to go through more school to become a doctor. Kelly wants to get married and have a family and live on a farm with many animals, and she is concerned that being in school for too long will get in the way. She is now thinking of becoming a teacher like her mother used to be and her aunt is because it will not take as much time and she can still have time to take care of her children and pets. Her parents have encouraged Kelly's interest in working with animals, and she is afraid to tell them that she has changed her mind because she does not want to disappoint them.

## *Response to Kelly: The Case of the Gifted Student*
### *H. Lori Schnieders*
### *University of Missouri - St. Louis*

*Good judgment comes from experience and experience comes from the opportunities of bad judgment (Patton & McMahon, 1999).*

The process of career planning is a long and winding process and Kelly does not present unlike most preadolescent females. By 10 years of age most children have passed through the Fantasy stage of career development when career preferences typically are linked to a desire for mastery and are moving into the Interest stage, in which enjoyable activities provide the basis for career aspirations (Super, Crites, Hummel, Moser, Overstreet, & Warnath, 1957). Between 6 and 13 years of age, occupations perceived as being inappropriate for one's sex, too difficult given one's intellectual capabilities, and too low level with respect to one's socioeconomic status are eliminated and will not be reconsidered under normal circumstances.

In addition to these factors, as in Kelly's case, the career aspirations of a bright and promising gifted female are often in conflict with expectations that females in rural or suburban environments will help maintain the stable, sometimes conservative, educational, religious and social life of these communities (Kleinsasser, 1986). Clark (1988) suggests that the gifted adolescent girl has the combined burden of dealing with the expectations of traditional female roles and suppressing her considerable intellectual abilities to avoid success and to keep from choosing a nontraditional career field.

Higham and Navarre (1984) suggest that the gifted female adolescent learns to hide her intelligence if it makes her appear different or unfeminine in the eyes of her peers, especially males, which is not inconsistent with what Kelly has expressed to her counselor. Bakken, Hershey, and Miller (1990) report that, although their sample of gifted adolescent girls believed in gender equality in professional and educational roles, the girls' perceptions of relationships are similar to those of traditional females.

Preadolescence and adolescence are complex times when a gifted female experiences personal conflict about sex roles, belonging, and being different (Kramer, 1986). Compounding her own confusion about self and career, the preadolescent female finds that society reinforces social achievement and conformity (Noble, 1987) more than giftedness in mathematics and science (Fox, Benbow, & Perkins, 1983). Family beliefs and cultural values may also condition the school and career decisions that limit the attainment of career goals of the brightest students (Howley, Pendarvis, & Howley, 1988). Additionally family, church, and neighborhood groups often serve as influential, socializing agents to preserve conservative attitudes that adhere very rigidly to sex-role stereotypes (Kleinsasser, 1986). Gilligan (1982) hypothesized that female role relationships are important in strengthening girls' resilience and that girls emulate and are significantly influenced by others. As several studies suggest (Leslie, 1986; Weber & Miller, 1984), the most likely adult role model is their mother, the closest female to them.

With these factors in mind, I would need to explore further with Kelly at what point between fourth grade, when she began to express her initial interest in becoming a veterinarian, and the current interview with the counselor did her perceptions of the role of a veterinarian began to change. It would also be necessary to determine what level of problem identification and problem solving Kelly demonstrates. These factors would allow the counselor to begin strengthening her perception of ability and self as she moves to the middle school when academic decisions will need to be made prior to entering high school. Even though the expectations and support of her family would indicate otherwise, Kelly does not seem to perceive herself as a leader, which would make it desirable to determine what has affected her shift in career decision.

It may be hypothesized that the resistance of Kelly's parents to having her IQ tested or to placing her on an accelerated learning program may have sent an unspoken message influencing Kelly's perception of the social implications of her giftedness. This is evidenced in her statement to the counselor that she is "looking forward to being with other kids who won't make fun" of her because she is the smartest in the class.

In addition to the qualitative data collected through the interview of Kelly, I would administer the What I Like to Do (WILD), second edition, developed by Meyers (Bonsall, Drinkard, Meyers, Nogrady, Organ, & Zinner, 1975), which provides ease of administration as well as content validity (although studies of the validity of the second edition have been limited). Few other inventories are available for the purpose of measuring the interests of children in Grades 4 through 7. The WILD assesses four areas of children's interests (play, academics, arts, and occupations) using 150 pairs of items; the child indicates which of each pair s/he likes more. Asking the child to report what the person likes to read about and to list recent reading is assessed by the additional fifth measure of reading.

A child in Kelly's developmental age group, with the additional impact of giftedness, has clearly given thought to her future and is not too young to benefit from career education and information. At the same time, school counselors should bear in mind that the child should not be pushed into making early occupational decisions. Most 10-year-olds have not made permanent career plans. It is the verbalization of career goals, rather than the commitment to those goals, that is necessary.

As seems to be the case with Kelly, parental influence on children's academic and social interests and patterns as well as on their thoughts about marriage and childbearing seems strong. It should be noted though that parental influence is only one of many pressures on career aspirations. Preadolescent females are discovering and testing out their interests and abilities, and schools should offer them opportunities to develop their interests and become aware of careers that mirror those interests.

It would appear that Kelly has developed an unrealistic view of her chosen careers. Hoyt (1976) argues that elementary children need to understand the variety of work and that people work for different reasons. Hoyt's objectives included making work meaningful, teaching work habits, and teaching decision-making skills. Topougis (1973) included the need to provide children with the opportunity to develop more realistic views of work in his "spiral of career development insights and experiences."

For gifted females who underestimate their intellectual abilities, value career status less than their male counterparts, and accept occupational stereotypes as valid, the vast majority of challenging, high-status career options will be eliminated, as in the case of Kelly.

Hollinger (1985) noted that even multipotential adolescents who rate themselves high on math ability may aim for traditionally feminine careers in art rather than traditionally masculine math or science careers if they identify themselves as also possessing artistic ability.

To counteract the elimination process of childhood, Kelly needs to be encouraged to explore occupations that are congruent with her talents and abilities but perceived to be of minimal or no interest. Information about becoming a veterinarian or teacher as well as other occupations must be complemented by interactions with individuals in these career areas and on-site visits to the workplace if occupational stereotypes and misconceptions are to be overcome (Hollinger & Fleming, 1993). To provide Kelly with realistic views of her career choices as a counselor, I would have her visit and interview a female veterinarian (with a family) and a teacher (outside her family).

Beginning some tailor-made career combination problem-solving activities with Kelly should help her identify and begin to integrate her interests with her skills and abilities. Since she has expressed an interest in combining a full-time career with marriage and a family, the message that combining multiple life roles is indeed possible needs to be accompanied by the information and skills essential for coping successfully with multiple role demands. To this end I would begin using the Project CHOICE (Hollinger & Fleming, 1993) card game. This would allow Kelly and me to begin exploring the integration of these multiple life roles (family, career, volunteering, and unanticipated life events).

Additionally, Kelly needs to begin identifying all that she wants to do and achieve in life and learn how to prioritize those goals, exploring the various ways in which she might time their accomplishments.

In conclusion, Kelly is not unique in her preadolescent struggle with early career choice. Kelly, as other gifted females, would benefit as she moves to the next level of academic selection and career exploration from the following: support of her interests in nontraditional subjects and nontraditional careers; more exposure to math and science concepts; more opportunity to develop problem-solving skills assistance with broadening educational career options; help with identity development; and exposure to options using the strengths she perceives she has, which allows her to interact with others in a variety of settings.

# References

Bakken, L., Hershey, M., & Miller, P. (1990). Gifted adolescent females' attitudes toward gender equality in educational and intergender relationships. *Roeper Review, 12*, 261-264.

Bonsall, M.R., Drinkard, K., Meyers, C.E., Nogrady, M.E., Organ, L.M., & Zinner, E.G. (1975). *What I like to do.* Chicago, IL: Science Research Associates.

Clark, B. (1988). *Growing up gifted: Developing the potential of children at home and at school* (3rd ed.). Columbus, OH: Merrill Publishing Company.

Fox, L.H., Benbow, C.P., & Perkins, S. (1983). An accelerated mathematics program for girls: A longitudinal evaluation. In C. P. Benbow & J. C. Stanley (Eds.), *Academic precocity: Aspects of its development* (pp. 113-131). Baltimore: Johns Hopkins University Press.

Gilligan, C. (1982). *In a different voice: Psychological theory and women's development.* Cambridge, MA: Harvard University Press.

Higham, S.J., & Navarre, J. (1984). Gifted adolescent females require differential treatment. *Journal for the Education of the Gifted*, 8, 43-58.

Hollinger, C.L. (1985). Self-perceptions of ability of mathematically talented female adolescents. *Psychology of Women Quarterly, 9* (3), 323-336.

Hollinger, C.L. & Fleming, E.S. (1993). Project CHOICE: The emerging roles and careers of gifted women. *Roeper Review, 15* (3), 156-160.

Howley, A.A., Pendarvis, E.D., & Howley, C.B. (1988). Gifted students in rural environments: Implications for school programs. *Rural Special Education Quarterly, 8* (4), 43-50.

Hoyt, K.B. (1976). *Career education and the business-labor-industry community.* Washington, DC: Office of Career Education, U.S. Department of Health, Education and Welfare. (ERIC Document Reproduction Service No. ED 146 361).

Kleinsasser, A.M. (1986). Exploration of an ambiguous culture: Conflicts facing gifted females in rural environments. Paper presented at the annual conference of the National Rural and Small Schools Consortium, Bellingham, WA. (ERIC Document Reproduction Service No. ED 278 522).

Kramer, L.R. (1986). Career awareness and personal development: A naturalistic study of gifted adolescent girls' concerns. *Adolescence, 21*, 123-131.

Leslie, L.A. (1986). The impact of adolescent females' assessments of parenthood and employment on plans for the future. *Journal of Youth and Adolescence, 15*, 29-49.

Noble, K.D. (1987). The dilemma of the gifted woman. *Psychology of Women Quarterly, 11*, 367-378.

Patton, W. & McMahon, M. (1999). Comparison of the major theories. In W. Patton & M. McMahon

(Eds.), *Career development and systems theory* (pp. 85-100). Pacific Grove, CA: Brooks/Cole Publishing Company.

Super, D.E., Crites, J.O., Hummel, R.C., Moser, H.P., Overstreet, P.L., & Warnath, C. (1957). *Vocational development: A framework for research.* New York: Teachers College Press.

Topougis, N. (1973) *Career education at the elementary level.* In J.H. Magisos (Ed.), *Career Education.* Washington, DC: American Vocational Association.

Weber, J.A., & Miller, M.G. (1984). Factors related to college women's perception of employment. *Home Economics Research Journal, 13,* 159-166.

## *Response to Kelly: The Case of The Gifted Student*
## *Michael Goh*
## *University of Minnesota*

Kelly impresses me as a bright, thoughtful, and considerate young child. I am more struck by the apparent health of her family upbringing, school experience, availability of parental support, and school resources than by any sense of career dilemma or indecision – at least not any degree of career distress that I would consider needing remediation but more of primary intervention or an opportunity for prevention and education.

It appears that Kelly grew up in a family environment that did not leave her wanting but rather provided for basic needs and perhaps more. Beyond material needs, Kelly further had the attention of her mother who left her job as an elementary school teacher to care for Kelly when she was born and also her to care for her younger brother.

School seems to be an easy and positive experience for Kelly. She has been successful academically and she learns well. Her parents' decision not to accelerate her learning appears to have a positive impact on her social development and identity in that some children may experience anxiety and distress in being removed from familiar peer relationships if they are not ready. This comment is made in view of the parents' sensitivity to knowing when Kelly was later "bored in school" and increasingly self-conscious about being the "smartest in class." It was felt then that Kelly was developmentally ready, both socially and intellectually, to venture into the new surroundings of middle school. This is not to mislead any reader to think that I propose that parents wait for their child to clearly vocalize his/her readiness but more to highlight the point that Kelly's parents, through their actions, appear to be knowledgeable about or at least mindful of Kelly's social and developmental needs.

In terms of Kelly's career development, it may be suggested that because Kelly has experienced both parents working, she was consequently exposed to the notion of career self-concept at an early age. I also consider Kelly to be more fortunate than most children to have her interest in animals, an interest common in many children, translate into a more uncommon experience of being able to access animals, both large and domestic, through her grandparents. She was further able to reinforce her interests on a daily basis via her two cats, her aquarium at home, and unhindered reading of animal stories. What is more admirable is Kelly's ability to consider these interests to be a possible career after the classmate's father presented on career day in fourth grade. I am always intrigued by how early children begin considering the notion of "what I want to be when I grow up" to be more than an essay topic but rather a real life decision. In the case of Kelly, her interest in becoming a veterinarian appears to be serious and informed, albeit cautious. I do not consider Kelly's hesitation about her career choice to be any indication that Kelly has abandoned her plans to become a veterinarian but more reflective of a thinking child who is self-aware and who understands that there are certain social cues that one takes in considering roles in life. This sense of balance on Kelly's part is unclear and only a hypothesis, but may be alluded to in the description of Kelly being equally focused on her time spent learning with animals and her time spent with her three or four girlfriends.

Kelly is both an ordinary and extraordinary kid. Ordinary in the sense that she appears to exhibit the simple pleasures common with children her age with regards to school, friendships, and interests, and there is no evidence that would presently contradict the fact that her personal, familial, academic, and social relationships and development are healthy. If anything, her parents appear to be very affirming and supportive. Kelly's desire to please her parents is understandable and usually normal for children her age.

What is extraordinary about Kelly is not her academic gifts and overall talents but that despite all the affirmation and even reinforcement of her interests, she is still not immune to the powerful messages of gender role socialization that she has experienced. Extraordinary in that Kelly is able to imagine, quite realistically, the possible consequences for her career choice. Kelly worries about being teased for taking classes more attended by boys. She is concerned about her career choice requiring long-term college sojourn and hence interfering with her marriage and family plans, thus jeopardizing her plans for a hobby farm. Her intellect is so keen that she is even able to devise an alternate plan to be a teacher, allowing her to still care for the things she loves – future children and animals. In a sense, the intelligence with which Kelly is so blessed appears to be informing both the breadth and depth of her fears.

Before I embark on my career counseling considerations and other information I would seek about Kelly, I would preface by noting that I do not see Kelly's presenting issue to be a "problem" as phrased in the question. I see career choice as a developmental process within the context of individual, familial, academic, and social influences and in those dimensions, Kelly is not significantly different from other children her age. In fact, Kelly appears to have a good repertoire of personal, familial, and social resources that many of us counselors can only wish for in our clients. Add to that the fact that Kelly is bright, intelligent, and seemingly articulate and we have good prospects for counseling. Although I have noted that Kelly's quick mind can add to the complexity of the case, such talent is by no means detrimental.

Although I utilize various career theories and models in career counseling such as the works of Holland, Super, Lofquist and Dawis, to name a few, Gottfredson's (1981) theory of circumscription and compromise came to mind immediately when reading about Kelly. Gottfredson (1981, 1996) explains how career aspirations develop on the basis of four assumptions: (1) the career development process begins in childhood; (2) career aspirations are attempts to implement one's self-concept; (3) career satisfaction is dependent on the degree to which the career is congruent with self-perceptions; and (4) individuals develop occupational stereotypes that guide them in the career selection process.

The brevity of this response will not allow me to go into the theory in detail but the following are of most interest to me in Kelly's case. According to Gottfredson's (1996) theory, Kelly's growing up experience would best be described as the development of "images of occupations and a cognitive map of occupations" (Gottfredson, 1996, p. 184) along the dimensions of masculinity and femininity of the occupation, the prestige of the occupation, and fields of work. Principles relevant and critical in Kelly's case would be the interplay of what she is learning to be appropriate masculine or feminine occupations and what she learns to be the accessibility of these jobs to her. That is, Kelly's experiences at home, school, and through other media will eventually lead to a focusing or circumscribing of the occupations she will consider depending on her perception of the occupations' compatibility and availability to her. Gottfredson's (1981, 1996) theory suggests that the eventual occupation Kelly chooses, as with most adults and adolescents, tends *toward* a compromise – selecting an occupation that is less than congruent with how she views herself.

From what we know about Kelly so far, we have some insights into what Gottfredson (1981, 1996) describes to be aspects of her social self. That is, how Kelly perceives herself with regard to social status, intelligence, and gender. More accurately, however, the information we have about Kelly is more of a report. What would be important for me as a career counselor is to understand how Kelly perceives these variables *herself* or what has *she* learned. Knowing Kelly's "images of occupations and her cognitive map of occupations" (Gottfredson, 1996, p. 184) would help me determine the extent to which Kelly has learned about gender role stereotypes, the accuracy of her understanding about facts pertaining to the occupation of her interest, and the breadth and depth of her understanding about other fields of work that may still match her interest. Included in this inquiry would be how Kelly's family (including grandparents), school, peers, school counselor, and other sources at large may or may not be contributing to Kelly's notions of gender, occupation, and the field of work.

In addition to knowing Kelly's social self, Gottfredson (1996) suggests that it is also important to know Kelly's private or psychological self such as her values, personality, and family plans. It may be exciting to consider how wonderful it would be for someone with Kelly's genuine love for animals to become a veterinarian but how much do we recognize that Kelly's values and personality are still rapidly evolving and to allow her the space to dream and change her mind, as she pleases. What I think a career counselor can do with Kelly, however, is to ensure that Kelly is (1) provided accurate information about various occupations and career paths; (2) challenged about gender stereotypes; (3) given the opportunity to discuss her marital and family plans without premature decision; and (4) granted access to role models of her desired field(s) of interest to explore how these individuals managed their own careers in light of Kelly's concerns. It is also important to include those with whom Kelly is in contact in this process. Having sometimes considered the fact that perhaps Gottfredson (1981, 1996) emphasizes cognitive and self-concept principles more than most children are capable of, I am struck by how Kelly has the intellectual capacity and wherewithal that I think may be necessary for the theory to work best. On a different note, I am also aware that as Kelly approaches her adolescent years, one has to be cautious about affronting her desire to assert her own identity and to control her own decision-making process.

Having Gottfredson's (1981, 1996) theory as a useful framework for understanding the impact of cultural, social, gender, and other variables on Kelly, the following principles would govern my career counseling relationship with her. First, I think that it is important to allow Kelly to personally express her life story thus far. Second, offer her a basic understanding of the career development process. Third, explore the career dilemmas she faces and why she defines them as such. Fourth, invite her to consider different perspectives for viewing the dilemmas (for example, I have several games and exercises that challenge the notion of gender role stereotypes and also help clients to learn about career decision making), and fifth, especially with her intellect, see how she can, independently or collaboratively with me, consider creative ways to approach her career dilemmas.

In summary, Kelly appears to be a fine young individual who is doing one of the things she does best and that is to think. In this case, she is thinking seriously about her future and about her career plans. Some may feel that such thoughts are too much and too early. My approach is that it is never too early because she is in fact already learning a great amount from her family, school, and relationships particularly with respect to gender role expectations. Given her intellect, self-motivation, and insight, and with Gottfredson's (1981, 1996) theory as a framework for understanding her, I believe that Kelly is best served by my providing a certain amount of flexible scaffolding (to borrow the term from Vygotsky) that will allow her to successfully continue this journey through her cognitive map and beyond.

## References

Gottfredson, L.S. (1981). Circumscription and compromise: A developmental theory of occupational aspirations. *Journal of Counseling Psychology, 28,* 545-579.

Gottfredson, L.S. (1996). A theory of circumscription and compromise. In D. Brown, L. Brooks, & Associates, *Career choice and development* (3rd ed., pp. 179-281). San Francisco, CA: Jossey-Bass.

# GREG: THE CASE OF THE ASPIRING ATHLETE

Greg is a 14-year-old Caucasian boy in the eighth grade. His parents were divorced when he was in the first grade. Since then, Greg has had very little contact with his father. After the divorce, Greg's mother relocated to an upper-class suburban town in the southwestern United States. Greg lives with his mother and older sister (age 21). Greg's father lives in the town where Greg was born, which is two hours away. Greg's other sister (age 20) lives with her father and his second family. Although his parents' divorce was very difficult, no one in the family has received any counseling relative to this event.

Greg's parents are college graduates. Greg's father has a master's degree in school administration and has worked as a secondary school teacher. His father, however, is currently employed as the head of the personnel department for a large company. He changed occupations to increase his salary ("You can't pay the bills on what they pay you as a teacher"). Greg's mother is employed as a high school English teacher. Greg's older sister is a flight attendant. Greg's second sister is in college studying to be a physical education teacher.

Until now, Greg has given very little attention to his career. His major interests revolve around sports. He plays baseball, basketball, and football. He follows the local sports teams as well as the professional sports teams in his area. His heroes are all professional athletes and Greg dreams of being a professional athlete one day. Greg has no other hobbies.

Interpersonally, Greg is a friendly, but shy, boy. Lately, Greg has started to associate with a group of boys in his neighborhood who tend to get into trouble at school. A few have even got into minor trouble (e.g., vandalism) with the law. Greg has not been a disciplinary problem.

In school, Greg has been an average to above average student. He finds history and English are interesting but struggles with mathematics. Not surprisingly, his favorite class is physical education. Greg has a general lack of confidence when it comes to his academic ability. He likes school because it is where he gets to play sports with his friends. Now he is in the midst of having to decide on a high school curriculum of study. Having to think about this has led Greg's mother to become concerned about helping him develop some career goals.

Ideally, Greg's mother thinks he should be a lawyer because they "earn a good living and it is a prestigious occupation." But, Greg thinks it would be "fun" to be a coach. Greg's mother discounts this as an appropriate occupation, telling Greg that he will "never make any money as a coach" and that one day he will be "too old" to be involved in sports. Greg and his father have never discussed what Greg might do "when he grows up." Greg's mother has spoken with the school principal about having the school counselor give Greg some sort of test that will identify his appropriate career options for him. The principal has asked you (the school counselor) to help out.

## *Response to Greg: The Case of the Aspiring Athlete*
### *Norman C. Gysbers*
### *University of Missouri - Columbia*

In reading the Case of Greg, I learned something about Greg's past and current circumstances – the divorce, information about Greg's family, Greg's passion for sports, his school experiences, and his associations with others. I learned that both of Greg's parents value status, prestige, and money. I learned little, however, about Greg as an individual, as an eighth-grade boy who is in the beginning stages of adolescence, other than that he is friendly but shy, has been an average to above average student, and may be associating with the wrong crowd. I also learned that his mother has the stereotyped view that on a given day her son can take a "test that will identify appropriate career options for him."

One concern that I have before I contact Greg is that, according to the case, Greg's mother referred him for help. Working with Greg may be an issue because he did not ask for help, his mother did. In fact I wonder if Greg is even aware that his mother talked with the principal. And, if he is aware, it may be only that he is to "take a test." Thus discussion will need to take place with Greg concerning his willingness to participate in career counseling and other guidance activities. I would talk with Greg's mother first and ask her if she had informed Greg about her request for him. If she hadn't, I would ask her to do so. Assuming there were no problems, I would set up an appointment to meet with Greg.

In my first meeting with Greg I would clarify with him his understanding of the purpose of the meeting, briefly outline for him the process that we would follow if he was agreeable, and begin to explore with him who he is and where he sees himself going. My hypothesis is that during our beginning exploration discussion I would find out that Greg has serious gaps in his knowledge about himself, others, and the world in which he lives. I would probably find out, as the case indicated, that Greg's identity seems to be wrapped up in sports and that, as a result, he is following a "path of least resistance" or "the only path that he knows."

As exploration continues I would explore with Greg his interest in sports and the possibilities this interest presents. I would start with Greg's interest in sports because that is where he is at the present. I may find that one problem may be not what he knows about sports (although his knowledge and understanding maybe very limited), but what he doesn't know about other possibilities. Many years ago, Henry Borow used a phrase to capture this situation. He called it "premature occupational foreclosure." Because Greg apparently has ruled in sports, he may have ruled out many other possibilities, that is, he may have foreclosed on what he knows.

Before I discuss how I would continue to do exploratory work with Greg, I need to explain my approach to individual career counseling. I see it as having six interactive phases all connected to a strong relationship component, the working alliance. These six interactive phases include opening, gathering information, understanding/hypothesizing, taking action, developing goals, and evaluating and closing. I use a holistic perspective of career development (human development) called life career development. It is defined as self-development over the life span through the interaction and integration of the roles, settings, and events of a person's life (Gysbers, Heppner, & Johnston, 1998). According to Gysbers and Henderson (2000), a major goal in using the theoretical perspective of life career development is to assist students such as Greg to identify, describe, and understand the dynamics of their own life career development, to create within them career consciousness, that is, the ability to visualize and plan their life careers. Contained in the concept of career consciousness is the notion of possible selves described by Markus and Nurius (1986). What are possible selves? "Possible selves represent individuals' ideas of what they might become, what they would like to become, and what they are afraid of becoming, and thus provide a conceptual link between cognition and motivation" (p. 954). Why are possible selves important? "Possible selves are important, first, because they function as incentives for future behavior (i.e., they are selves to be approached or avoided) and, second, because they provide an evaluative and interpretive context for the current view of self" (p. 954).

Using the concept of possible selves I would explore with Greg his possible self in sports. I also would explore other possible selves other than those found in the sports world. I probably would use the Self-Directed Search (Holland, 1994) or an occupational card sort as tools of discovery to provide Greg with other possible selves to explore and consider. The goal here would not be to ask him to commit to an occupation but rather to think about possible futures in addition to sports. Such thinking would lead us to consider his current status academically and the type of education he may be required to undertake.

In my work with Greg I would check out my hypothesis about his gaps in knowledge about himself, others, and his present and future worlds as well as be alert to possible family issues (his parents' divorce, his separation from his father, his relationship with his mother). I would not focus directly on these issues, but would be aware that they may surface in our counseling relationship.

Such issues may or may not be related to Greg's current status and future plans although I suspect some of them are. I wonder, for example, if his beginning association with a group of boys in his neighborhood who tend to get in trouble is in part a need to find a support group. It may be his way of reacting to a perceived lack of support at home. I also wonder if his choice of sports is his way of establishing his independence – his mother wants him to be a lawyer but Greg says he wants to be a coach. After all he has some ability and as Greg stated "it would be fun to be a coach."

As I continue to work with Greg, Krumboltz's Learning Theory of Career Choice and Counseling (Mitchell & Krumboltz, 1996) provides me with a way to focus on understanding Greg and respond to his career choice issues. Krumboltz suggests that special abilities play a part in occupational preferences. As individuals grow and develop, two kinds of learning take place. The first is instrumental learning. In Greg's case, he participates in sports. He does well and his "self-talk" is positive about himself in sports. The second type is associative learning. Again in Greg's case, he is associating with others who do well in sports as he does and he receives positive messages. As a result of these learning experiences, Greg draws conclusions and makes generalizations about sports in general and he being involved in sports occupationally. Action ensues and Greg states he is interested in sports and in becoming a coach.

In dealing with the specificity of choice that has ensued from the experiences Greg has had, Krumboltz's theory suggests that individuals such as Greg need to expand and extend their capabilities and interests and not make decisions on only what they know based on limited life experiences. Thus my work with Greg would emphasize expanding and extending Greg's vision. I would acknowledge his interest in sports but at the same time help him consider other possibilities.

Because Greg is in school we have the opportunity to work developmentally with him. Due to his limited life experiences, his lack of knowledge about educational career possibilities, I would make sure Greg was knowledgeable about our schools' comprehensive guidance program (Gysbers & Henderson, 2000). I would ask him to participate fully in guidance curriculum activities where he will have the opportunity to explore various career and educational possibilities. Periodically, I would meet with him to process what he is learning. In our individual sessions I would check to see how he is internalizing the information. These individual sessions would also give me the opportunity to see how other aspects of his life are unfolding. The individual sessions become a vehicle to support Greg.

In addition to Greg's work in the guidance curriculum, I would start him on an individual career plan. Some of our individual sessions would focus on helping him integrate information about himself together with career and educational information into an individual career plan that he could use throughout his years in school. Once a year I would meet with Greg and his mother to review his plan and talk about next steps educationally and occupationally. My goal in having him develop a plan is not to force him to make early career decisions, but rather to ensure that he makes no academic decisions that might close doors to opportunities that he might later wish were open (Orfield & Paul, 1993).

## References

Gysbers, N.C., Heppner, M. J., & Johnston, J.A. (1998). *Career counseling: Process, issues, and techniques*. Needham Heights, MA: Allyn & Bacon.

Gysbers, N.C., & Henderson, P. (2000). *Developing and managing your school guidance program* (3rd ed.). Alexandria, VA: American Counseling Association.

Holland, J.L. (1994). *Self-directed search*. Odessa, FL: Psychological Assessment Resources.

Markus, H., & Nurius, P. (1986). Possible selves. *American Psychologist, 41*(9), 954-969.

Mitchell, L.K., & Krumboltz, J.D. (1996). Krumboltz's learning theory of career choice and counseling. In D. Brown, L. Brooks, & Associates, *Career Choice & Development* (3rd ed., pp. 233-280). San Francisco, CA: Jossey-Bass.

Orfield, G. & Paul, F.G. (1993). *High hopes, long odds: next steps*. Indianapolis, IN: Indiana Youth Institute.

## Response to "Greg: The Case of the Aspiring Athlete" Using a Developmental Career Counseling Approach
### Juliet V. Miller
### National Career Development Association

### A Framework for Career Counseling

When I first started career counseling, I felt confused about how to understand and work with clients. Through graduate studies, reading, and supervision, I had learned about career development theory and research. Although I found this fascinating, I needed to bring the key elements of several theories together into a framework that could be used to organize information about clients, to identify gaps in my understanding of clients, and to set specific sequential goals for my work with clients.

I found it helpful to develop a diagnostic framework that I use in working with clients on vocational issues. I have incorporated concepts from several career theorists (Holland, 1992; Super, Savickas & Super, 1996) in the framework and used statements of career development goals for various developmental levels (Kobylarz, 1996).

My framework includes a comprehensive description of the client's current vocational situation including abilities, interests, educational achievements, self-concept, decision-making style, emotional state, work values, gender role attitudes, degree of career salience, current relations with family, friends, and others, and physical health. Also, I am interested in a developmental history including racial/cultural background, health history, family background, friends and guides, early interests and abilities, early vocational goals, and school and other achievement patterns.

In my work, I am trying to help the clients become involved in the process, discover their vocational identifies, reduce both inner and outer barriers to the expression of that identity, and set short- and long-term career goals.

### My Initial Image of Greg

Before my first meeting with Greg, I review the information given in the case description using my diagnostic framework. Here is a summary of how I organize the case information prior to meeting with Greg.

*Developmental level.* Greg is 14 years old and in the 8th grade. He is in the exploratory stage of career development so I would not expect him to be able to state a specific occupational goal that is based on an accurate view of self.

*Race/cultural.* He is Caucasian and lives in an upper-class suburb in the southwestern U.S. He has not always lived in this neighborhood and may have lived in a different type of neighborhood earlier in his life.

*Interests, general ability, special talents, and achievements.* He is very interested in sports including baseball, basketball, and football. His favorite subjects are history and English but he has trouble with math. I want to learn more about Greg's interests and life achievements.

*Self-concept.* I have some concern here because Greg is shy and lacks confidence in his academic ability. I know that this will affect the quality of his career development over time.

*Decision-making style*. Although I need to learn more, it seems that Greg is somewhat uninvolved in making his own decisions. I note that friends are influencing him somewhat negatively and that his mother rather than Greg has requested counseling.

*Emotional state*. Greg is friendly but shy. Although not a discipline problem, he is spending time with a group of boys who are getting into trouble. His family has experienced emotional upheaval with no chance to process feelings. He has limited contact with his father. I want to know more about how he feels at this point in his life.

*Work values*. Financial success seems to be the primary work value to both his father and mother. His father a presents negative image of the occupation of teaching. I am not clear what Greg's values are.

*Level of career salience*. How important is career to Greg? Until now he has given very little attention to his career but this is not developmentally inappropriate. I want to explore this with him.

*Peer relationships*. He is selecting friends who are getting into trouble. Greg is not a discipline problem. I want to explore these relationships to determine whether they are satisfying to Greg and whether he wishes to have other more positive connections in his life.

*Health background*. I know nothing about Greg's physical and emotional health background. I need to learn more.

*Family background*. His parents were divorced when he was in first grade. Although it was a difficult divorce, family members did not receive counseling to help them process their feelings. He has little contact with father. The siblings are split between the mother and the father. His parents value upward mobility and higher education. Both parents are college graduates.

*Mentors/guides*. I know little about this. I would like to know whom Greg admires, and how these role models can give us clues about Greg's vocational identity.

When I have used the framework to organize what I know about Greg, I summarize my initial impressions:

- Greg does not feel very involved in career planning.
- Greg's vocational identity at present centers on doing something related to sports, namely he wants to be a coach.
- Greg's mother wants him to consider being a lawyer. This is based more on her work values of prestige and financial reward than on a specific understanding of her son's unique interests and talents. She is not pleased with Greg's interest in coaching because his occupation does not meet her work values.
- Greg's mother has requested that he come for counseling to take some tests. I have no sense of how Greg feels about seeing me.
- Greg has experienced a difficult separation of his parents and has not been given specific support in processing that loss.
- Greg is selecting friendships that may work against his goals.

### Initial Interview: Closing the Gaps in My Image of Greg

I open the initial counseling session with an open-ended question such as, "Tell me what brought you here today." I listen carefully to what Greg says. For example, imagine how different these possible responses that Greg might give are: "My mother sent me," "I want to learn about how to become a coach," "I need to decide what to take in high school," or "The principal said you could give me some tests." I would spend time working with Greg on whatever response he gives to my opening question.

As we talk about issues that are most important to Greg, I will also seek to clarify some of the gaps I have in my understanding of Greg. Specifically, I want to better understand how Greg feels about himself and what his general emotional tone is. I want to know much more about Greg – what are his interests, achievements, and heroes? I want to know how his family members and friends are influencing him. My goal is to engage Greg in talking about the things that are most important to him while I listen for information that I need to better understand him.

## Plan for Career Counseling

I feel that it is important to set some goals with the client by the end of the initial counseling session. Although these goals may be tentative, they do provide motivation for the client. It is especially important to start with goals that mesh with the client's most immediate perceived needs. Although I do generate a comprehensive list of counseling goals, I will propose specific goals to Greg based what I have heard from him during the session. Based on the initial information I have about Greg, here are some possible career counseling goals:

- Help Greg develop a positive relationship with me.
- Help Greg feel more positive about himself.
- Help Greg find supportive counseling to resolve issues around his parents' divorce and absence of his father.
- Encourage Greg to feel empowered about his own life.
- Help Greg connect with his vocational interests, abilities, and values that have been evidenced throughout his life.
- Design some vocational exploration experiences for Greg.
- Help Greg's mother and father understand which career-related developmental tasks are most appropriate for Greg at this stage of his life.
- Help Greg understand how career goals relate to curriculum choice.
- Help Greg understand the type of educational choices he will make in the next few years and their effect on long-term career goals.

## Career Counseling Strategies

*In-school counseling.* I would continue to meet with Greg to help him become clearer about who he is vocationally. If he is interested, I might administer an interest inventory but would do this only this in combination with other career exploration strategies. I would also encourage him to talk to friends, teachers, coaches, and family members to get their perceptions of his strength and interests.

*Referral and support.* My initial sense is that Greg will need some support in processing feelings, developing more positive peer relationships, and finding positive male role models. As a counselor in a school, I may be limited in the amount of time that I have to help Greg. I will suggest out-of-school counseling resources to him and his mother, and help them understand that it is important issues to address these issues since career closely relates to his feelings about himself.

*Help him find a male mentor.* Greg has limited access to his father and his mother is not supportive of his stated career choice. For these reasons, it seems particularly powerful to help Greg connect with a male mentor. A natural choice would be one of his coaches. The goal is not to finalize the career choice but to help him learn more about the reality of his stated occupational interests and to find a supportive guide

*Career exploration experiences.* I would help Greg use several methods of exploring his vocational interests. These might include reading about careers, joining teams or clubs at school, or volunteering in his community. He could also talk to people in specific jobs such as coach, lawyer, and other areas that we discover. A computer-based career planning system could also help him to identify career families of interest and relate school subjects to career families.

*Meet with Greg's mother and/or father.* Greg is living in a difficult family context. Ideally, I would meet with both his father and his mother. My goal would be to help his parents understanding Greg's current needs and identify career development tasks that are the most important for a 14-year-old.

# References

Holland, J.L. (1992). *Making vocational choices: A theory of vocational personalities and work environments* (2nd ed.). Odessa, FL: Psychological Assessment Resources.

Kobylarz, L. (1996). *National career development guidelines: K-adult handbook.* Washington, DC: National Occupational Information Coordinating Committee.

Super, D.E., Savickas, M.L. & Super, C.M. (1996). The life-span, life-space approach to careers. In D. Brown, L. Brooks, & Associates, *Career choice and development* (3rd ed., pp. 121-178). San Francisco, CA: Jossey-Bass.

# MARIA: THE CASE OF THE ARTISTIC 10TH GRADER

Maria is a 15-year-old 10th grade student. She is a Hispanic American living in a predominantly Caucasian, suburban middle-class neighborhood. Maria is "normal" in intelligence but reports that she dislikes school. She associates with a group of girls who are often in trouble with the police. It is your impression, however, that these friendships are superficial. Recently, some of the girls in her circle of friends have been arrested for drug possession (marijuana). Maria is not hostile or disrespectful. She, however, routinely hands in schoolwork late, if at all.

In most classes, Maria is Artistic, but she enjoys art class (especially painting) and being in the school band (she plays the flute). She dislikes math and science. Her mother is employed as a teacher's aide in a local elementary school and her father is employed as a car salesperson in a local dealership. Maria has two younger sisters ages 12 and 14. Maria takes a significant role in caring for her two younger sisters. Her parents count on her heavily for this responsibility.

Maria's current plans are to finish high school but she has not made plans for what she will do beyond that point. She stated that she would probably marry and raise a family "someday." Her parents have asked you to help her "make a good career choice." She agrees to meet with you to discuss her career plans.

## *Response to Maria: The Case of the Artistic 10th Grader*
## *Richard J. Noeth*
## *ACT, Inc.*

I believe that the "Case of Maria" presents at least two significant opportunities for career counselors. One is the application of career counseling interventions to assist Maria in assessing her current situation and planning for her future. The other might incorporate (assuming that these are not present in the school) programmatic interventions that enhance the academic, social, and career success of minority students in a predominantly majority environment.

### Initial Image

I picture Maria as a young women who manages significant family responsibilities; has a congruent (but perhaps narrow) set of interests and preferences; has given some thought to her future; has not yet sorted out her school, family, and social responsibilities; and is possibly a person who might perceive – both given her academic and social activities and because of her cultural background and the different cultural background of the majority of her classmates – limited academic, social, and career opportunities.

### Information Seeking

There is a considerable amount of information (much of which already exists) that would help to assist Maria in her career exploration and decision-making activities and possibly outside of this realm as well. I would view this information in three interdependent categories: (1) academic, (2) family-social, (3) and career-related. Initially, I would further examine the notion and bases that describe Maria as "normal" in intelligence. Specifically, I would look at her grades, teacher comments, and standardized test score information. I would also talk with her teachers across the range of subjects – making sure to include those subjects she is reported to both like and dislike. My objective here would be to understand ability versus performance, language skills, any academic performance patterns (or lack thereof) over time, and to gain any additional insight from those professionals who have had substantial interaction with Maria over the course of several school years. I would also want to talk with Maria about her own reactions to school. I would want to learn more about the subjects she likes and dislikes and the reasons for these choices. Also, given how well she seems to have handled her other responsibilities – it would be important to know why she does not hand in schoolwork, either on time or at all.

The next set of information I would seek would revolve around Maria's family-social life and responsibilities. For example, Maria seems to take a "significant role" in the care of her two younger sisters (ages 12 and 14). Given the proximity in age of her sisters and the working hours of her mother (a teacher's aide with likely the same time requirements as Maria), it would be helpful to know what is (and should be – recognizing important cultural mores) expected of Maria in this role and what impact these expectations have on the other aspects of Maria's life (e.g., time for homework, time for other outside-of-school activities, time to develop other friendships, etc.). I would also want to affirm the statement regarding the strength of relationship (i.e., "superficial") that Maria has with her friends and whether these are her friends by design or default (possibly a school cultural/sorting factor that could be explored).

Finally, I would want to explore further the depth of Maria's interests and enjoyment regarding painting and music. How long have these been the case, are they supported by additional outside-of-school activities, what related reinforcements exist within these activities (e.g., recognition, self-expression, potential social network, etc.)? Also, are there related activities that would be of interest to Maria in terms of things that she would like to engage in? Who and what have influenced these interests and are they interests and activities that Maria would see herself undertaking after her high school years are over in future education and work settings?

## Career Counseling

I believe that a multifaceted approach to career counseling might work well with Maria and I would propose such an approach to her. By this I mean an approach that would look independently and then interdependently at the (1) academic, (2) family-social, and (3) the career aspects of Maria's life as they exist now and might exist in the future, and how their relationship might influence the path she sets for herself.

I would suggest to Maria that each of these three areas is important to examine now as they help define who she is as a person as well as set the stage for the roles she will undertake in the future. It would be important to convey to Maria that although she is able to assess how she functions within each of these roles now, it will be useful and important to see how these roles relate to each other and how they may be affecting her functioning in the other aspects of her life and the future implications of these role relationships. I would then talk with Maria about why it is important now to begin to focus with great specificity on her values, interests, and abilities as they relate to future education and work. This is a time when Maria can begin to formulate some tentative hypotheses and plans about her future, try out some of these potential plans in various ways, examine what barriers (perceived or otherwise) might exist in her path, and begin to take steps across all stages of her life that will move her in reasonable and desirable future directions.

Given the preceding background, specific career counseling methodology would employ several interrelated activities: individual counseling sessions where much of the preceding would be explored and discussed, with specific goal-setting objectives (e.g., regarding homework, relationships, family responsibilities, self-reliance, educational and career plans, etc.); career interventions to include an interest measure (preferably the computerized Self-Directed Search with accompanying materials); career exploration tasks (e.g., computerized job searches, job shadowing); educational exploration tasks (e.g., Peterson's computerized college, college major, and financial aid search package); and a scheduled set of time-by-activity goals to meet in accomplishing the preceding. An overlay to these career counseling activities would be the fact that Maria is a female Hispanic American attending school in a majority Caucasian culture and that many of the expected real or perceived barriers need to be explored and dealt with – including educational and career expectations both within and outside of the school (e.g., from Maria's family), the opportunity for various kinds and levels of involvement both academically and socially within the school, and the need for strong support systems to enhance the likelihood of success for Maria.

## Theoretical Models

It is no surprise that several theoretical models of career development might fit the case of Maria. The model, however, that I would employ in working with Maria is the Social Cognitive Career Theory (SCCT) as described by Lent, Brown, and Hackett (1996). Viewed as a "new evolving theory" by Zunker (1998), SCCT fits many of the issues surrounding Maria and her situation. Included would be the application of Bandura's (1986) "triadic reciprocal," which focuses on personal and physical attributes, external factors, and behavior. I see the interaction of these three factors as integral to counseling dialogue with Maria as her understanding of their interrelationship will help Maria to better understand her own academic, family-social, and career roles both now and in the future.

I further think that the notions of self-efficacy, expected outcomes, and goals can overlay much of the counseling discussion with Maria in terms of how she views her own behaviors across the academic, family-social, and career areas. I also believe that the SCCT focus on gender and ethnicity in terms of influential factors, and the choice process in terms of anticipated and expected behaviors (not necessarily directly career related) are appropriate to Maria's case. Certainly the application of a values, interests, and abilities structure to both educational and work planning fits with the SCCT and is likely enhanced by it. Finally, I see considerable appropriateness in the SCCT approach to opening up the career exploration process and the presentation that barriers can be assessed and plans made to neutralize them.

## Programmatic Issues

Although this response has focused on the case of Maria, it is important for career counselors to think in broad, programmatic interventions as well. The setting is a predominantly Caucasian high school where the case involves an Hispanic American student and also refers to at-risk students (i.e., the superficial friends of Maria). Thus, activities that celebrate multiculturalism and diversity within the entire school community will both stimulate awareness as well as break down perceived (and perhaps real) barriers for all students. Small group activities that incorporate team-building skills (e.g., the Outward Bound model), days that celebrate diversity, and classes that focus on cultural differences as well as similarities are good examples of programmatic interventions. More specific activities might include early awareness college planning nights for both students and parents. Programs that focus on college planning, college major and career considerations, test preparation, and financial aid are important interventions for minority students and their families. Finally, specific programs geared toward the needs of at-risk students that involve skill building, workplace readiness, and real-life work experiences are ways to further enhance the success potential of these individuals.

## References

Bandura, A. (1986). *Social foundations of thought and action: A social cognitive theory*. Englewood Cliffs, NJ: Prentice Hall.

Lent, R.W., Brown, S.D., & Hackett, G. (1996). Career development from a social cognitive perspective. In D. Brown, L. Brooks, & Associates, *Career choice and development* (3rd ed., pp. 373-416). San Francisco, CA: Jossey-Bass.

Zunker, V.G. (1998). Career counseling: Applied concepts of life planning (5th ed.). Pacific Grove, CA: Brooks/Cole.

## Response to Marie: The Case of the Artistic 10th Grader
### Alicia Andujo
### Long Beach City College

Maria, a young 15-year-old Hispanic woman appears to be going through the stage in life know as adolescence. In particular, it appears that she is experiencing "peer pressure" from friends at school to conform to values and beliefs that are in direct conflict with the values and beliefs held by her immediate family. Of key importance is Maria's sense of identity confusion (Erikson, 1968). Additionally, she appears to lack self-esteem and holds a limited vision of herself.

From a cultural standpoint, Maria may be experiencing stress as she learns to navigate living within a bicultural world. As Hispanics, Maria's family seems to regard highly the values of "respect and loyalty." These values, although honorable, can be a source of conflict for many teenagers as time with friends and involvement in extracurricular school activities must often be sacrificed in the name of loyalty to family. For a young Hispanic female such as Maria, a tightrope is walked daily as she continually thinks and makes choices based on the values of two cultures.

In terms of academic ability, Maria seems to have the potential to succeed academically if provided with the proper guidance. Her interest in art classes as well as her involvement in band indicates to me a young woman of promise, one who is searching for a sense of direction in relation to her path in life. Her association with a group of young women who are known to have prior arrest records for illegal drug possession indicates that Maria is in need of immediate assistance at this critical time in her life. Maria is fortunate in that her parents care enough about her future that they have asked for professional assistance.

In developing an educational career plan for Maria it would be important to acquire information such as a grade history report as well as results from any standardized tests completed in school. In addition, I would question Maria regarding her level of interest in art and music and would seek knowledge from her regarding any other interests and hobbies. I would want to know why she dislikes math and science and would be particularly interested in learning how she perceives her skill ability to be in math.

In terms of social support systems, I would question Maria regarding her level of comfort at school. Specifically, I would be interested in knowing whether she feels any sense of alienation from the mainstream population at school due to her ethnic background. Additionally, I would be interested in knowing whether she perceives support and encouragement for the pursuit of higher education from her teachers and parents.

Finally, I believe it would be important to meet with Maria's parents. In speaking with Maria's parents I would hope to obtain knowledge of their level of acculturation as well as insight into their desired wishes for their daughter's future.

In order to develop an educational and career plan I would ask Maria to complete a career assessment inventory such as Holland's (1977) Self-Directed Search in order to validate her interests. Additionally, a values card sort activity would cause Maria to begin the process of thinking critically about the relationship between values and future career satisfaction.

Based upon the results generated from these assessment activities, I would meet with Maria to explore in depth her expressed interests in relation to matching occupations, school subjects, and college majors. Our discussion would focus upon an area Maria would be interested in exploring further. For example, if Maria's career assessment inventory confirmed an interest in the area of art, I would explore with her options regarding taking art classes as part of her school curriculum. Additionally depending upon the resources available at school in relation to art class offerings, I would share information with Maria regarding the possibility of taking classes at a local community college or community recreation and arts center.

Using the results from her career assessment inventory, Maria would be encouraged to investigate occupations of interest utilizing one of the many computerized career information programs readily available today. To strengthen her sense of self-esteem and to enlarge her vision of career opportunities for women in the workplace, I would encourage Maria to participate in an organized mentor program such as Girls, Inc., an offshoot of the organization formerly known as Girls Clubs (separate from the Boys Clubs organization). My hope would be that, through participation in a mentoring program, Maria to be matched with a Hispanic female role model who could work with her at enlarging her vision of opportunities available in the world of work.

Finally, I would set up a meeting with Maria and her parents. At this meeting I would review my educational and career plan for Maria and share information regarding the college admissions and financial aid process with the family. It is my strong belief as a counselor that information regarding the college admission and financial aid process should be shared with students and parents at every opportunity regardless of the level of interest. This is particularly of great importance in working with students from lower socioeconomic backgrounds as often the pursuit of a college education is seen as unaffordable by their families.

In relation to a career development theoretical model I would utilize Donald Super's Life-span Model (Super, 1980). This model seems appropriate to use in working with Maria as it centers on self-awareness and the development of self-concept in relation to career choice. At the age of 15, Maria is clearly at the exploratory stage of Super's model of development. Primary tasks for her at this stage include participation in activities that will increase her level of self-awareness in relation to her personality traits, interests, skills, and values.

Through participation in mentoring activities such as job shadowing and volunteer or paid work experiences, Maria can move toward what Super (1980), calls the "crystallization" phase. During this phase she can begin to formulate ideas about careers and work environments that may be appropriate based upon knowledge of self. With increased knowledge in these areas Maria can make tentative decisions with regards to academic course selection and possible career paths.

From a cultural standpoint I would employ a directive structured approach in counseling with Maria. My choice of approach is based on research that shows that many ethnic minority groups desire a structured relationship in which the counselor is cast as an expert, giving advice and solutions to problems (Sue & Sue, 1990). In addition, my choice of including Maria's parents in the discussion of the design of her educational and career plan demonstrates a sense of respect for her parents, which is a value of great importance in the Hispanic culture.

Overall, Maria appears to be a typical adolescent who is questioning her role in society at large. She is fortunate in that her two parents care enough for her that they have sought advice from a counselor with regard to the development of an educational and career plan. The Self-Directed Search career assessment inventory along with activities such as occupational research, mentoring, and job shadowing should serve to assist Maria with a preliminary exploration of career occupations and work environments. It is important to keep in mind that Maria is only 15 years of age and according to Super's (1980) Life-Span Model at the stage where career exploration is the primary task at hand. In working through this stage and the suggested activities Maria can begin to move in the direction of selection of a vocational preference. As a counselor I would make certain to inform Maria and her parents that the process of selection of a vocational and or career goal is a lifelong process and that she has taken the first step.

# References

Erikson, E.H. (1968). *Identity: youth and crisis*. New York: Norton.

Holland, J.L. (1977). *The Self-Directed Search*. Palo Alto, CA. Consulting Psychologists Press.

Sue, D.W. & Sue, D. (1990). *Counseling the culturally different: Theory and practice* (2nd ed.). New York: Wiley.

Super, D.E. (1980). A life-span, life-space approach to career development. *Journal of Vocational Behavior, 16*, 282-298.

# JOSÉ: THE CASE OF THE FARMER'S SON

José is a 15-year-old, ninth grader with a problem. His terrible grades in language arts and social studies are only compensated for by his good grades in art and physical education. He spends his time before and after school helping out on his family's small farm. He spends what little free time he has playing baseball or drawing. He had an opportunity once to use a computer design program, which he enjoyed very much.

José is from a Mexican American (Chicano) family; he has a large extended family in the U.S. His parents were both born in the United States, but his grandparents came from Mexico and retired there when they had the opportunity. José speaks a little Spanish, but does not identify strongly with Mexico or the Hispanic culture that is so important to his parents.

José's school has a required career development class in the ninth grade that asks students to begin to make choices about their curriculum for high school and to start the "employment/education development plan" required by the school district. José has been acting out in this class, telling jokes, drawing, and refusing to develop his plan. The teacher referred him to the counselor in hopes of finding our what was behind this behavior.

José tells the counselor that he is planning on dropping out of school when he is 16, so all this planning is "just silly – a waste of everyone's time." He is planning on working his father's farm and sees no need for more school. José has an older sister who is finishing high school this year, planning on getting a job in the local department store, and hoping to marry her high school boyfriend this summer. He also has an older brother, a high school sophomore, from whom José is somewhat, alienated, who is a good student and is hoping to get a scholarship to the state university.

José says that his parents do not have any opinions about his future, that they say it is his decision. His father, however, has warned him that the farm may not provide enough income to support two families. When the counselor asks José about his dreams for his future, he says that dreaming is for girls and fools that "real men" just work and provide for their families.

## *Response to José: The Case of the Farmer's Son*
### *Consuelo Arbona*
### *University of Houston*

José, a 15-year-old ninth grader, is having difficulty thinking about and planning for his future. Even though José states that after he leaves school at age 16 he will work in his parents' farm, this plan does not seem to be the product of a well thought-out career decision-making process. The conceptual framework guiding my interpretation of José's vocational difficulties is Super's (1990) career development theory. In terms of interventions, I will also incorporate aspects of Krumboltz's (1996) learning theory of career counseling and Holland's (1997) theory regarding career interests.

According to developmental career theory (Super, 1990), José's lack of a firm and well thought-out career plan is consistent with his age and the developmental tasks in which he is expected to be engaged. At age 15, José is expected to be in the Growth and Exploration stages of career development. The primary tasks in these stages involve developing a realistic self-concept and exploring the world of work. However, José's attitude in the career class indicates that he lacks career maturity, that is, he does not seem to be ready to engage in the career tasks appropriate for his age. He lacks planfulness as well as an exploratory attitude regarding occupations and educational opportunities. Furthermore, his joking around, drawing, and plain refusal to work on his "employment/education developmental plan" suggests that there may be powerful personal reasons for José to avoid, and even to sabotage, the process of exploring himself and the world around him. His comment to the counselor that "dreaming is for girls and fools and that *real men* just work and provide for their families," could be a defensive stance rather than a proclamation of a "macho" ideology or worldview. José may be hiding behind this "macho" facade (that, ironically, reflects mainstream stereotypes of Hispanics) to avoid issues that seem to be threatening for him.

With these ideas as guiding hypotheses, in my first meetings with José I would explore the reasons that motivate him to avoid engaging in career planning activities. I believe these issues need to be resolved to some extent before José will be ready to engage in career development activities such as completing interest and aptitude inventories, exploring the world of work, and trying to match his interests with specific occupations and training activities. In this process, important areas to explore include José's family relations, sense of personal identity (including issues of race, ethnicity, and social class), history of academic achievement, and exposure to the world or work. Following, I will discuss how issues in these four areas may impinge on José's career development. I must warn the reader that the ideas presented in this case discussion are simply hypotheses that I have formulated based on the limited information that I have about José. I stand ready to discover, in the process of working with him, that these hypotheses may only be figments of my imagination.

José is the youngest of three siblings, and he is a second-generation Mexican American immigrant (grandparents were born in Mexico, where they currently live, and he and his parents were born in the United States). Even though José reports that his parents do not have any opinion about his future, except to warn him that the farm may not provide enough income for two families, I would explore this issue further. For example, I would like to know to what extent José actually talks with his parents about his school and work plans. Is it that his parents offer no opinions or is it that José is not interested in them? José reports that he plans to leave school when he is 16; however, both of his siblings are planning to complete high school and his brother plans to attend college. This suggests that the family, at the very least, does not discourage school completion. One way to go around José's dismissal of family influences is to ask him, regardless of what his parents say, what he thinks they really would like for him to do in terms of school and work. My goal here is to explore to what extent José's attitude toward school is motivated by a desire to rebel against the family, part of which could involve following a different path from his siblings. Another possibility is that José feels responsible for his parents. The older sister is planning on marrying and moving on. His older brother is planning to go on to college and probably pursue a white-collar profession. José may feel pressured by the fact that he is the only child left to stay around and help his parents with the farm. In exploring these issues it will be important to learn about the role models José has been exposed to and what are the expectations that he thinks others in the family have of him. If I were to discover that José feels responsible to stay on the farm to help his parents, I would encourage him to think about other ways in which he could help his parents in the future, in case the plan with the farm does not work as he expects.

According to career development theory (Super, 1990), formulating and implementing a sense of self are important aspects of the career decision-making process. I believe that one's sense of self or identity is embedded in the interpersonal, social, and cultural contexts in which one participates (Josselson, 1992 cited in Blustein, 1994). In order to understand José's sense of self and to assist him in forming an identity in the career realm, the counselor needs to consider, and help José explore, the familial, sociocultural, and socioracial (Helms & Cook, 1999) factors that influence his core beliefs, values, and perceived attributes (Blustein, 1994). For example, I believe it is important to explore with José to what extent issues related to racial and ethnic identity are salient for him as he forges a sense of self and a career identity (Helms & Piper, 1994). José's lack of identification with Hispanic culture, which is important for his parents, could be motivated by adolescent rebelliousness. Another possibility, however, is that José experiences himself as different from his parents. He may be more acculturated than they are in terms of language and behaviors typical of youngsters his age, and does not feel comfortable in the context of more traditional Mexican values and behaviors. If, at the same time, José does not feel accepted in mainstream society, he may have developed an oppositional identity. Research findings with African American and Mexican American adolescents have indicated that minority adolescents often construe a sense of ethnic/racial identity in opposition to the values and beliefs embodied by the school, which leads them to reject attitudes and behaviors conducive to school achievement, because they equate them with acting White (Matute-Bianchi, 1986; Ogbu, 1992). The extent to which José has developed an oppositional ethnic/racial identity that is reinforced by his peer group may help explain his lack of interest and achievement in school as well as his feelings of alienation from his brother. José may interpret his brother's academic success as a way of selling out and leaving the family to become like "them," White and middle class.

Issues of race, ethnicity, and the experience of discrimination are sensitive topics. Because these issues may be involved in some way in José's vocational difficulties, I believe they need to be explored. To facilitate this conversation, I would share with José some personal experience as a Hispanic in this country. If José is working with a non-Hispanic counselor, it would also be important that this person acknowledges his or her race in some way (Helms & Cook, 1999), to communicate to José that issues related to race and ethnicity are acceptable topics. One way to initiate the exploration of ethnic and racial identity issues is asking José to what extent he thinks that being Mexican American, including the way he looks (visible racial issues), affects him in school now and how these issues are likely to influence his job opportunities in the future. If José shares experiences of discrimination, in addition to providing empathy for the likely feelings of sadness and anger that these experiences are likely to elicit, I would explore with him alternative ways to cope with the discrimination that he has experienced.

It is also important to keep in mind that José may have internalized negative stereotypes of Mexican Americans. He may believe that he is not smart and that he has no chance of making it in the academic and occupational world (in other words, he may have a low academic self-concept and lack self-efficacy regarding academic and career planning related tasks). Also, I would be sensitive to the possibility that José could hide behind issues of race, ethnicity, and discrimination as excuses to avoid taking responsibility for himself. One way to deal with these attitudes, if they were present, would be to help José become aware of how he may have internalized some of society's negative views of Mexicans and Mexican Americans and encourage him to consider how he could plan for the future in a way that validates his sense of being Mexican American, distinct from both the Mexican culture of his predecessors and the mainstream culture where he lives.

José's difficulties with schoolwork may also influence his attitudes toward career-related activities. Educational issues constitute the bedrock of career development and choice (Arbona, 1996). The concept of career and career planning make sense only to the extent that one perceives availability of choices and, in today's world, availability of choices is predicated on educational attainment (Betz, 1994; Richardson, 1993). From this perspective, José's lack of interest in career planning is consistent with his low grades and his plans to drop out of school at age 16. He is experiencing success in art and physical education, areas that are not valued academically as much as language and social studies, the areas in which he is failing. I would explore José's academic history. Has he always been a poor student? Or, is his lack of academic achievement a recent phenomenon? What are his study habits like? To what does José attribute his lack of academic success and to what extent does he believe that his friends devalue doing well in school? In addition to helping José explore his motivational strivings and sense of ethnic/racial identity, I believe it will be crucial for José to participate in academic enrichment activities, such as tutoring and study skills, so that he improves his grades and feels motivated to stay in school. As his counselor, I would take a very active role in identifying available resources in the school and community, as well as encouraging and helping José to connect with these services

Another contributing factor to José's lack of attitudes and behaviors indicative of career maturity may be lack of exposure to the world outside of his rural community. It is difficult for José to think about work or training possibilities, if he is not aware that any exist. Visits to postsecondary institutions and information about sources of financial aid will help José visualize that postsecondary training and work outside the farm could be real possibilities for him. Because of his lack of planfulness and knowledge of the world of work, initially it may be more to have José explore a specific field that appears to be of interest to him (e.g., computer design, commercial art, engineering technology applied to farming), to help him develop some awareness of the need to plan, rather than to guide him to narrow his choice to one occupational preparation program (Super, 1990). This exploratory process will allow José to connect some of his interests and abilities with a specific occupation. Once José becomes engaged in the process of planning for his future, then I would encourage him to complete interest inventories (Holland, Fritzsche, & Powell, 1994) to further explore himself and the world of work. Because the expression of interests is based in part on past experiences, I would encourage José to discover new interests as he learns more about himself and the world of work (Krumboltz, 1996).

In summary, José's lack of attitudes and behaviors indicative of career maturity may be related to family issues, ethnic/racial identity issues, academic difficulties, and lack of exposure to the world outside his community. Initially, my goals in working with José would be to help him explore family and racial/ethnic identity issues that may impede him from engaging in career development activities and attend to his academic needs to increase his motivation to stay in school. Once José becomes engaged in the career planning process, I believe that the career interventions available in the field (Brown & Brooks, 1991; Spokane, 1991) to help students explore themselves and the world of work (e.g., books, the Internet, films, and actual visits to training and work sites) will be useful in enhancing José's career development.

## References

Arbona, C. (1996). Career theory and practice in a multicultural context. In M.L. Savickas & W.B. Walsh (Eds.), *Handbook of career counseling theory and practice* (pp. 45-54). Palo Alto, CA: Davies-Black.

Betz, N.E. (1994). Basic issues and concepts in career counseling for women. In W.B. Walsh & S.H. Osipow (Eds.), *Career counseling for women* (pp. 1-41). Hillsdale, NJ: Erlbaum.

Blustein, D.L. (1994). Who I am?: The question of self and identity in career development. In M.L. Savickas, & R.W. Lent (Eds.), *Convergence in career development theories: Implications for science and practice* (pp. 139-154). Palo Alto, CA: Counseling Psychologist Press.

Brown, D., & Brooks, L. (1991). *Career counseling techniques*. Boston, MA: Allyn & Bacon.

Helms, J.E., & Cook, D.A. (1999). *Using race and culture in counseling and psychotherapy*. Boston, MA: Allyn & Bacon.

Helms, J.E., & Piper, R.E. (1994). Implications of racial identity theory for vocational psychology. *Journal of Vocational Psychology, 44*, 124-138.

Holland, J.L., (1997). *Making vocational choices: A theory of vocational personalities and work environments* (3rd ed.). Odessa, FL: Psychological Assessment Resources.

Holland, J.L., Fritzsche, B.A., & Powell, A.B. (1994). *Technical manual for the Self-Directed Search*. Odessa, FL: Psychological Assessment Resources.

Krumboltz, J.D. (1996). A learning theory of career counseling. In M.L. Savickas & W.B. Walsh (Eds.), *Handbook of career counseling theory and practice* (pp. 55-80). Palo Alto, CA: Davies-Black.

Matute-Bianchi, M.E. (1986). Ethnic identities and patterns of school failure among Mexican-descent and Japanese-American students in a California high school: An ethnographic analysis. *American Journal of Education, 95,* 233-255.

Ogbu, J.U. (1992). Understanding cultural diversity and learning. *Educational Researcher, 21,* 5-14, 24.

Richardson, M.S. (1993). Work in people's lives: A location for counseling psychologists. *Journal of Counseling Psychology, 40,* 425-433.

Spokane, A.R. (1991). *Career intervention.* Englewood Cliffs, NJ: Prentice Hall.

Super, D.E. (1990). A life-span, life-space approach to career development. In D. Brown, L. Brooks & Associates, *Career choice and development* (2nd ed., pp.197-261). San Francisco, CA: Jossey-Bass.

## *Response to José: The Case of the Farmer's Son*
## *Joseph G. Ponterotto and Dhruvi Kakkad*
## *Fordham University - Lincoln Center*

### Some Initial Reactions and Perceptions

To summarize some salient aspects of the case very briefly, it appears that José is a young adolescent with academic strengths in art and physical education and with academic difficulties in language arts and social studies. Apparently, José has extensive (by "traditional" American standards) responsibilities in the family business, working both before and after school on the farm. His interests in baseball, drawing, and computers reflect some of his abilities and are not atypical of American adolescents in the 1990s. It appears that José has a large extended family encompassing three generation levels and multiple acculturation levels. We might hypothesize that José and his siblings are more acculturated to U.S. "mainstream" society than are his parents, who in turn are likely more acculturated than the grandparents.

The impetus for an assessment of José stemmed from a teacher who perceived him as "acting out" during the career development class. Apparently, José believes that his career plan is already set – working on the family farm – and he need not participate in futuristic career planning.

### Additional Impressions and Questions

Responding to a brief case description is always difficult given the lack of detail presented. One must also refrain from stereotyping the client based on sociocultural factors such as race, ethnicity, geographic region, or gender. Naturally, our initial reaction to the case vignette is that we need more information to truly understand José's situation from both a personal and career development perspective. Particularly, we would like to gather more information in the areas of career interests and expectations, academic experiences, and family relationships. Let us explore these areas.

## Career Interests and Expectations

Does José like working on the farm? What does he think and how does he feel regarding the prospect of working on the farm full-time? A number of hypotheses can be explored here:

1. José loves the farm work and sees no need to consider other options.
2. Given his older brother is a good student and hoping to go to college maybe he feels the need to support financially the family immediately, and further believes there are not funds for him to pursue college as well?
3. Maybe he would like to consider attending college (or pursuing art or physical education [sports?] through other avenues) but lacks the self-efficacy, exposure, or perceived teacher or family support to consider such options at this time.
4. Perhaps there is pressure for someone in the family to run the farm (despite his father's perception of farm income limits) and José sees himself as the logical or expected choice given his sister's and brother's current plans.

Though we need to refrain from stereotyping, it is not uncommon for 15-year-olds from economically disadvantaged backgrounds (though we are not fully clear about the family's financial situation) to have some apathy toward futuristic career exploration. Furthermore, we wonder whether there may be a gap between José's career expectations (the family farm) and aspirations. We would want to explore José's current or past career aspirations, even if he does not see them as realistic at this time.

## Academic Situation

How "terrible" are José's grades in language arts and social studies? Is he in danger of failing? Furthermore, how talented is he in art and physical education? What about math and science, that are not touched upon in the vignette? What have José's previous schooling experiences been like up to this point? Does he like school? Is he comfortable there socially? Is he popular with and connected to peers? With whom or what is his primary connection/identification at the present time? What is the economic and racial/ethnic background of the school body – students and staff? Is José a minority there in terms of being Chicano or representing a farm family?

## Family Situation

A good amount of exploration is needed in terms of family dynamics. Apparently, José "has a large extended family," which is not uncommon for many Mexican American families (Falicov, 1996). Where is the immediate and extended family located? In the Southwest, with closer proximity to the grandparents now retired in Mexico? Or perhaps in the Northeast, Midwest, South, or Southeast where there is a growing number of Chicano families? How close emotionally is he to cousins, el padrino (godfather), and other relatives? What is the family's religious and or spiritual persuasion? Are indigenous models of healing and religion practiced? How close is he to his grandparents who have now moved back to Mexico? What role did (do) they play in his personal and academic development and to what extent does he miss them and have contact with them? Why does he feel "somewhat alienated" from his older brother? What is his relationship like with his older sister, father, and mother?

Given the salience of machismo and marianismo in immigrant and multi-generational Mexican American families (Casas et al., 1995), how do José's father and mother view their roles? Though the case description states that José does not identify strongly with his cultural group, we wonder what gender-role socialization may be happening at home. How do his parents feel about his talents in arts, for example? Though José believes "his parents do not have any opinions about his future," he may be referring to spoken opinions rather than to subtle modeling common to all families.

Our experience working with immigrant and first-generation Mexican American families in the west (California), east (Pennsylvania) and south (Tennessee) is that the extended family is often a great source of support, strength, and sense of connection (see also Falicov, 1996). Therefore, we would want to explore further José's relationship with both immediate and extended family members (see Fouad, 1995).

Another important issue to explore with José is his sense of ethnic identity and his evolving acculturation level. Is he currently exploring or struggling with his sense of ethnic identity? How does this identity exploration (Phinney, Lochner, & Murphy, 1990) interact with the demographic makeup of his school environment and the ethnic attitudes of other students and the teachers? Understandably, issues of acculturation and ethnic identity are closely linked to career development (Arbona, 1995; Leung, 1995).

The vignette notes that he "speaks a little Spanish, but does not identify strongly with Mexico or the Hispanic culture that is so important to his parents." Therefore, can we assume that he and his parents are at different acculturation levels? What about his siblings and relatives? Intergenerational acculturation conflict can cause quite a bit of stress for the family (Roysircar-Sodowsky & Maestas, 2000) and this issue would need to be explored.

## Theoretical Foundation and Initial Treatment Plan

An important assumption that underlies our case analysis is that José's academic, peer, and personal (including family) issues are closely interconnected. Theoretically, the foundation for our case conceptualization and treatment plan is Sue, Ivey, and Pedersen's (1996) theory of multicultural counseling and therapy, which we believe transcends all existing theories of personal and career counseling and development. We supplement Sue et al.'s theoretical foundation with recent developments in Social Cognitive Career Theory (SCCT; Lent, Brown, & Hackett, 1994; Hackett & Byars, 1996) and Holland's (1985) career development model.

The more recent Sue et al. (1996) theory is particularly relevant to our case given the reality of a growing multicultural society in the 21st century. Furthermore, though SCCT and the Holland theory were developed initially by middle class White American psychologists studying mostly White subjects and clients, we believe the models have cross-cultural relevance and coalesce well with Sue et al.'s (1996) framework. Given the space confines of this case response, and acknowledging that the reader is likely familiar with SCCT and Holland's model, we review briefly only the major propositions of the newer Sue et al. (1996) theory.

Sue et al.'s (1996) theoretical formulation holds that worldviews are culturally established, that the counselor and client often bring divergent worldviews to the counseling process, and that both the worldviews of the client and counselor need to be explored. Furthermore, the theory holds that both counselor and client possess multiple cultural identities (e.g., racial, ethnic, religious) that need to be acknowledged and explored in counseling. An inherent goal for Sue et al. (1996) is the acknowledgement of a sometimes racist and oppressive society, leading to the need for both institutional intervention on the part of the counselor and client empowerment for organizational change.

## Proposed Treatment Plan

Though our initial treatment plan is dependent to some degree on the responses to the many questions we raised earlier, it would likely include the following considerations:

1.  We would want to explore with José both his feelings about seeing the school counselor, and his thoughts about how the counselor could be of assistance. We might like to explore with José his perceptions of how working with a counselor would be interpreted by his family. We would consult with Mexican American community leaders and counselors to learn more about Mexican American farm life in the area.

2.  Assuming that José and his family are supportive of continuing counseling and that referral to a bilingual Mexican American counselor (ethnic-specific role model) is not deemed necessary, we would explore in time the questions and hypotheses raised earlier. Drawing

from the Sue et al. (1996) model that emphasizes client empowerment and institutional intervention, we might see if the family or farm community would like the counselor's (and school's) assistance in any way.

3. To help José explore his interests and values and the world of careers, we might administer in time a few career assessment tools. The Self-Directed Search (SDS), Strong Interest Inventory (SII), Myers-Briggs Type Indicator (MBTI), and Career Beliefs Inventory (CBI) may prove useful and interesting to José. Our choice of these possible measures stems from their natural link to our theoretical base – Sue et al. (MBTI), Holland (SDS, and in part the SII), and SCCT (CBI) – and our own comfort and experience in using these particular instruments with high school students. Furthermore, given his artistic talent, we might help José develop family career genograms (Ponterotto, Rivera, & Adachi-Sueyoshi, 2000), that will encourage his interaction with extended family members and his exploration of ethnic identity issues.

4. Feeling connected somewhat to peers and school may be important to José's future academic success. Though he has extensive farm responsibilities at present, we wonder whether José might be interested in joining a school computer, art, or sports club. Of course, we need to consider the views of those who may be central to José's future planning, for example, his mom and dad, grandparents, and godparents.

## Summary

As most cases, the story of José is complex and inclusive of many variables that need to be considered collectively for a comprehensive career assessment, among them academic ability, interests, and self-efficacy; career exposure, aspirations, and expectations; family acculturation levels and gender role expectations, extended family connectedness and educational/career influence; and possible institutional or community bias toward Chicanos.

## References

Arbona, C. (1995). Theory and research on racial and ethnic minorities: Hispanic Americans. In F.T.L. Leong (Ed.), *Career development and vocational behavior of racial and ethnic minorities* (pp. 37-66). Hillsdale, NJ: Erlbaum.

Fouad, N.A. (1995). Career behavior of Hispanics: Assessment and career intervention. In F.T.L. Leong (Ed.), *Career development and vocational behavior of racial and ethnic minorities* (pp. 165-192). Hillsdale, NJ: Erlbaum.

Hackett, G., & Byars, A.M. (1996). Social cognitive theory and the career development of African American women. *Career Development Quarterly, 44*, 322-340.

Holland, J.L. (1985). *Making vocational choices: A theory of vocational personalities and work environments*. Englewood Cliffs, NJ: Prentice Hall.

Lent, R.W., Brown, S.D., & Hackett, G. (1994). Toward a unifying social cognitive theory of career and academic interest, choice, and performance. *Journal of Vocational Behavior, 45*, 79-122.

Leung, S.A. (1995). Career development and counseling: A multicultural perspective. In J.G. Ponterotto, J.M. Casas, L.A. Suzuki, & C.M. Alexander (Eds.), *Handbook of multicultural counseling* (pp. 549-566). Thousand Oaks, CA: Sage.

Phinney, J.S., Lochner, B.T., & Murphy, R. (1990). Ethnic identity development and psychological adjustment in adolescence. In A.R. Stiffman & L.E. Davis (Eds.), *Ethnic issues in adolescent mental health* (pp. 53-72). Newbury Park, CA: Sage.

Ponterotto, J.G., Rivera, L., & Adachi-Sueyoshi, L. (2000). The career-in-culture interview: A semi-structured protocol for the cross-cultural intake interview. *Career Development Quarterly, 49*(1), 85-94.

Roysircar-Sodowsky, G., & Maestas, M.V. (2000). Acculturation, ethnic identity, and acculturative stress: Evidence and measurement. In R.H. Dana (Ed.), *Handbook of cross-cultural and multi-cultural personality assessment* (pp. 131-172). Mahwah, NJ: Erlbaum.

Sue, D.W., Ivey, A.E., & Pedersen, P.B. (1996). *A theory of multicultural counseling and therapy.* Pacific Grove, CA: Brooks/Cole.

# NANCY: THE CASE OF THE ASPIRING NEUROSURGEON (OR "GYM" TEACHER)

Nancy is a 16-year-old Italian American urban high school student who responded to most of the counselor's questions with "I don't know." She came to the counselor at her parents' request apparently willingly; however, she appeared uncommitted to the process, stating that she knew she wanted to be a neurosurgeon or a gym teacher.

Her responses to some of the questions in the initial history hinted that there had been some serious problems in her childhood, but she was unwilling to talk about those, stating that they had nothing to do with her career decisions. Nancy's parents have indicated to the counselor that as a child she had seizures, but these have ceased, the latest being six years ago. They say the doctors tell them that there is no reason for her to believe that they will recur. Nancy did, however, spend some time in the hospital as a young child. She is the third child in a family of four, and the only girl. Her two older brothers are in college, the younger still in middle school. One of her older brothers is studying to be a computer information specialist; the other is still undecided about his future goals. Her parents seem willing to allow this indecision with him, although they are pushing her to be more decisive.

Nancy's mother is a full-time homemaker, although she is a certified elementary school teacher and taught for five years before her children were born. Her father is an engineer for an automotive supply company. Neither of their parents had a college education. Nancy's maternal grandmother is also a full-time homemaker; her maternal grandfather, now retired, worked in a factory on the assembly line. Nancy's paternal grandmother is a teacher and her paternal grandfather is a bookkeeper.

Nancy's grades were average. Her scores on aptitude and achievement test scores hovered around the 60th percentile. She has never had any particular academic problems; neither has she had any outstanding successes. Further, all of her grades are consistently Bs, with few Cs or As – even in the sciences. Her attendance has been excellent, although she says she is often uninterested in her classes. She stated that it was "easier" to come to school than to deal with the hassles of absenteeism. Nancy acknowledged that this information was true but stated that she was prepared to work hard in college so as to get into medical school. If she "failed," she said, she could be a teacher.

Nancy's only part-time jobs in high school were baby-sitting for her younger brother and helping her next-door neighbor with some yard work. Neither of these was of any particular interest to her. She is not involved in any high school activities, nor does she have any particular hobbies. She does not read for recreation except perhaps some magazines designed for the teen girl market. She stated that she spends her free time watching television or "hanging out" with her friends. She has no special boyfriend, but does date and go to parties, mostly in groups.

Nancy's scores on the Strong Interest Inventory were generally low and flat, though they did confirm an interest in medical areas and teaching. Her Holland code is SI. Her Myers-Briggs code is ISTP.

## Response to Nancy: The Case of the Aspiring Neurosurgeon (or "Gym" Teacher)
### JoAnn Harris-Bowlsbey
### Career Development Leadership Alliance

### Image and Desirable Additional Information

After multiple readings of this case, the persistent image gained of this student is that of a person whom you might easily overlook because she appears to have so little energy invested in or commitment to any specific interests or goals. From the picture presented, therefore, it appears that she has a low self-concept, low internal locus of control, low career maturity, low commitment to any specific direction, low motivation to explore, a deficit of vocational exploration experience, and possibly irrational career beliefs.

There are a number of areas in which additional information would be helpful in getting a broader picture of Nancy's background and possibilities. These areas include the following:

- *The reason the counselor called her in.* Was it routine, or did some event precipitate the interview?
- *The relationship she has with her parents and her siblings.* Does she see either parent, or anyone else, as a role model? Are her grades and career possibilities compared to those of her brothers? Is there any family attitude that the career options of females are different from those of males? Are her parents pressing for career decisions? Is she rebelling against parents in any way? What are their expectations of her in terms of educational and vocational goals? Is this a loving, caring, supportive family unit?
- *The details of the early childhood health situation.* What was the nature of the condition that resulted in seizures and a hospital stay? Is this problem truly at an end? What effects, if any, did this experience have on Nancy and on the family?
- *Details of Nancy's high school educational experience.* Has she taken the courses she really needs to support the vocational goals she is proposing, especially the possibility of being a medical doctor? What have been her grades in college-preparatory courses, especially math and science? Since she is earning Bs, doesn't seem to spend a lot of time studying, and has aptitude and achievement scores at or around the 60th percentile, what kind of academic rigor does her school offer?
- *Financial resources of the family.* Even if Nancy has sufficient academic background to seriously consider being a medical doctor, is this realistic from a financial point of view, considering that this is a one-income home with other children in college simultaneously?

## Theoretical Basis for Considering the Case and Possible Interventions

I would consider Nancy from both Holland's and Super's theoretical perspectives. Applying Holland's theory would lead the counselor to these kinds of implications:

- Nancy has a low flat profile of interests because either few activities were presented to her in early childhood that would become grist for forming interests, or few or no activities in which she did engage were positively reinforced. Either or both of these conditions could account for the fact that her interest profile is undifferentiated, though it is moderately consistent.
- Nancy is not currently ready to make a well-informed vocational choice for the above reasons.

From Super's theoretical perspective, the counselor could draw these kinds of implications:

- For some reason that we do not currently know, Nancy has a low, and possibly poor, undifferentiated, and abstract self-concept. Thus, she is not ready to make a vocational choice since she would be unlikely to make a good translation from what she knows about herself to how she might use those characteristics in satisfying work.
- Though we do not have the results of an inventory that measures career maturity, it is likely that Nancy's is low in all aspects – awareness of need to plan ahead, decision-making skill, knowledge about the world of work, knowledge about career in Super's broad definition of that word, and specific knowledge about the tasks, entry requirements, and satisfactions of occupations whose names she mentions. Thus, from this perspective as well, she is not ready to make informed choices.
- It is likely that some very basic ingredients of career maturity – such as engaging in vocational exploratory behavior, developing strong internal locus of control, acquiring role models, and learning decision-making skills – were not developed in childhood.

It would be unwise in this case to attempt to bring early closure to making some specific vocational choice. Rather, as Super advocated, the counselor will need to try to make up for some lost time and undeveloped skills by becoming an "engineer of experience." Through interviewing, the counselor needs to gain information about any activities, course work, volunteer experiences, or daydreams that might give some clues to possible interests. Any kinds of assignments, including course work, paid employment, volunteer work, school activities, job shadowing, or use of computer-based systems or websites that could increase Nancy's knowledge of world-of-work options would be highly desirable. It would also be desirable to find out why Nancy is mentioning the particular occupations that she is – because parents are encouraging them, because she doesn't really know much about them, or because they represent some characteristics or values that are important to her. Investigation, either by using an instrument or by detailed interviewing, of possible negative career beliefs that might serve as obstacles could provide some clues. Interviewing with Nancy and with her parents, separately, might provide information about family dynamics that have contributed to Nancy's present indecision. While all of this is going on, it would be wise to encourage Nancy to take a solid college-preparatory course as a base for whatever she may later decide, to help her evaluate what she does learn by suggested exploration, and to assure her that she does not have to know all of the answers at this time.

### Possible Contributing Factors or Influences

There are insufficient data to support any specific influences or factors that bear on this case. The counselor should, therefore, be aware that some of these could pertain: the fact that Nancy is an Italian-American, her attendance at an urban school in which she may not feel motivated, a possible attitude on the part of her father that higher education and career are less important for women than for men; the possibility that she is compared in a negative sense to her brothers; the way-out possibility of sexual abuse; the possibility that her mother is not supportive of women playing significant roles outside the home; and the possibility that the childhood health problems resulted in some emotional damage if not malingering physical damage.

## *Response to Nancy: The Case of a Very Normal Person*
### *Kathleen Mitchell*
### *City College of San Francisco*

If Nancy's counselor asked her "what are you interested in?" or "what do you want to do?" then Nancy's response of "I don't know" is very appropriate. For interests to be developed, one must be curious. Flat scores on the interest inventory do not reveal Nancy's indecision. On the contrary, the scores reveal that Nancy has not had an opportunity to be curious. Nancy's life has been punctuated by events that have postponed her curiosity and consequently prevented her from developing interests.

For the first 10 of her 16 years, Nancy experienced the uncertainty of seizures. Doctors populated her world during those years. No doubt her parents were driven to protect her from normal childhood experiences because of an overriding anxiety caused by the thought that a seizure could strike at any time. Presumably Nancy was frequently absent from the social and cognitive experiences of school because of her medical condition.

Considering Nancy's concentrated exposure to the medical field for so many years, it is no wonder she expressed the intent to be a neurosurgeon. Likewise, gym class was most likely a class where Nancy could do well. Perhaps the gym teachers she encountered were especially kind and considerate of her medical vulnerability. That kindness may have influenced Nancy's desire to be a gym teacher.

Because parents who have children with a disability worry about the child's future, and especially a future without them, the parental push on Nancy to become decisive about a career direction is understandable.

For Nancy to develop a willingness to explore and to develop interests, she must be taught to be curious again. Nancy has not had the opportunity to be surprised or to be struck by a sense of wonder. Messick (1979) recognized that the challenge of education, especially during the elementary and secondary years, is to introduce appropriate elements of surprise, contradiction, paradox, or doubt to help develop a sense of curiosity. In all likelihood, Nancy did not have opportunities to develop her curiosity about the world. Her world was centered on hospitals, doctors, and parental protection. Day (1982) recognized that curiosity must be taught for exploration to take place. Because Nancy's educational experiences were interrupted by her health restrictions, she did not have guidance in learning how to explore and to discover.

Necka (1989) found that deliberately performed exercises and techniques might stimulate curiosity. However, Day (1982) stated that teachers must recognize when a child is too anxious to become curious. Jones (1979) found that fear of failure overshadows learning curiosity. Therefore, a counselor assisting Nancy to be curious must first assess Nancy's anxiety level.

Day (1982) found that teachers frequently incorrectly identified children who had scored high in anxiety as children who were curious. When he interviewed the teachers more thoroughly about their observations, Day found that anxious children asked many questions, but they were not interested in the answer. Children exhibiting curiosity, on the other hand, would quietly listen to and reflect on answers given to their questions. Likewise, counselors can at times overlook client anxiety. Bradbard, Halperin, and Endsley (1988) found that anxiety blocks curiosity and exploration. These researchers found that one cannot be anxious and curious at the same time.

Asking Nancy to discuss her concerns and fears about the future might assist a counselor to identify Nancy's level of anxiety about her future. Referring Nancy to appropriate resources to assist in addressing the sources of her anxiety would be appropriate. Directing Nancy to identify her interests is not useful. She has had no adequate opportunity to explore interests much less to develop them. The intervention most useful to Nancy is one that would teach her to be curious. By developing her curiosity, Nancy will be better able to transform her curiosity into an interest.

Mitchell, Levin, and Krumboltz (1998) found that the Curiosity 4A was an effective intervention to assist clients to become curious. This curiosity exercise guides people through four steps to develop and explore curiosity. The four steps are attend, ask, anticipate, and act. A counselor using this exercise as an intervention with Nancy would explain that the purpose of the exercise was to assist her to develop her curiosity. The counselor would instruct Nancy to take a walk down a familiar street and to notice and record what she sees.

Lenox (1985) quoted Merlin Pryce, a co-worker of Sir Alexander Fleming, the person who discovered penicillin: "What struck me was that he didn't confine himself to observing but took action at once. Lots of people observe a phenomenon, feeling that it may be important, but they don't get beyond being surprised – after which, they forget." Lenox also noted that students are generally taught to see but not to observe. He recommended that teachers teach students to record their observations. He advised that teachers should help students "develop as a discoverer."

The purpose of the "attend" step, therefore, is to ask Nancy not only to observe her surroundings, but to record what she saw. The counselor should encourage Nancy to pay special attention to and be sure to record in a notebook those events, interactions, sounds, and sights that surprised her.

In the "ask" stage, the counselor should guide Nancy in how to ask questions about what she observed. The counselor should instruct Nancy to ask two or three "how" and "why" questions about her observations.

Isaacs (1930), who was credited with first researching children's "why" questions stated that "our goal is to guide the child to ask 'why' to learn, not to answer." Additionally, Pyszczynski and Greenberg (1981) found that the more surprised a person is, the more willing he or she is to ask "why."

Asking "why" encourages people to develop curiosity, to learn, explore, seek surprises, and discover and invent (Mitchell et al. 1998). The purpose of this step, therefore, is to teach Nancy to engage her curiosity in order to learn and to explore. The counselor might give Nancy the following example to demonstrate how to ask "how" and "why" questions:

> Let's say you observe the sun reflecting off a stained glass window. Some questions might be: "I wonder how the artist decided to put those colors together?' "How does someone get an inspiration for a stained glass window?" "Why does the sun seem to reflect off of certain colors and not off the rest?"

The next step is "anticipate" or guess. Within this step, Nancy will be encouraged to guess at the "how" and "why" questions she composed about her observations. Loewenstein (1994) found that guessing combined with feedback increased curiosity. He also found that guessing at an answer encourages a person to stay engaged with the object to discover the accuracy of the guess.

During this step, the counselor could work with Nancy to compose guesses to the questions she raised. To avoid overwhelming Nancy, the counselor might encourage Nancy to pick one question she asked and guess one answer. The counselor could use the following example:

> Let's recall our stained glass window question. We asked: "How does someone get an inspiration for a stained glass window?" We might begin to guess at the answer with a response such as, "someone who is inspired to create a stained glass window must really love color and light, and want to express the beauty of the two through the creation of a window." Another guess might be "maybe the artist was inspired by a visit to a place of worship or to a sacred place."

In the "act" step, Nancy should be encouraged to list one or two steps she could take to look into some of her observations. Mayes (1991) found that the very act of exploring, whether or not solutions or new discoveries emerge immediately, often engages a person's curiosity. The counselor could give the following example to introduce Nancy to the "act" step:

> Let's go back to our stained class window example. If we generated a list of actions we might take to investigate our guesses about how an artist becomes motivated, the list might contain the following: visit a stained glass window store and talk with the proprietor; go to an art gallery or museum that features stained glass windows and engage the curator in a discussion; try to track down an artist who made a stained glass window and discuss how the artist became inspired; search the Web to learn more about the topic or check a book out of the library.

The counselor should encourage Nancy to choose one action and to complete as much of it as she can. Taking action to investigate an area of curiosity, no matter how small the step, will provide the counselor and Nancy an opportunity to discuss how Nancy learned and discovered.

Meeting with Nancy while she takes each step is an opportunity for the counselor to be encouraging and to ask Nancy about the surprises she encountered along the way. Asking Nancy to discuss how she was surprised and how she learned from the 4A experience will provide the counselor an opportunity to discuss with Nancy how interests are developed. The counselor can introduce the statement that taking action on curiosity develops interests (Mitchell et al., 1998).

Piaget recognized that curiosity is necessary for the growth of knowledge (Camp, 1986). Nancy's childhood was interrupted because of her health. Her curiosity was postponed but not lost. For Nancy to learn about her interests, she must first learn to become curious. It is from the actions she takes while being curious that Nancy will develop interests. Counselors are teachers and guides. Nancy will require a patient adult who will guide her to reengage her curiosity and to transform her curiosity into interests.

Rachel Carson (1956), a renowned environmentalist and visionary, set out to teach her grandson to become curious about nature. From her adventures with her grandson, Carson recorded this passage in her memoirs:

> I sincerely believe that for the child, and for the parent seeking to guide him, it is not half so important to know as to feel. If facts are the seeds that later produce knowledge and wisdom,

then the emotions and the impressions of the senses are fertile soil in which the seeds must grow. The years of early childhood are the time to prepare the soil. Once the emotions have been aroused – a sense of the beautiful, the excitement of the new and the unknown, a feeling of sympathy, pity, admiration and love – then we wish for knowledge about the object of our emotional response. Once found, it has lasting meaning. It is more important to pave the way for the child to want to know than to put him on a diet of facts he is not ready to assimilate (p. 56).

# References

Bradbard, M R., Halperin, S.M., & Endsley, R.C. (1988). The curiosity of abused preschool children in mother-present, teacher-present, and stranger-present situations. *Early Childhood Research Quarterly, 3*, 91-105.

Camp, C.J. (1986). I am curious-grey: Information seeking and depression across the adult lifespan. *Educational Gerontology, 12*, 375-384.

Carson, R. (1956). *The sense of wonder*. New York: Harper & Row.

Day, H.I. (1982). Curiosity and the interested explorer. *Performance and Instruction, 21*, 19-22.

Isaacs, N. (1930). Children's "why" questions. In S. Isaacs (Ed.), *Intellectual growth in young children* (pp. 291-349). London: Routledge.

Jones, R.S. (1979). Curiosity and knowledge. *Psychological Reports, 45*, 639-642.

Lenox, R.S. (1985). Educating for the serendipitous discovery. *Journal of Chemical Education, 62*, 282-285.

Loewenstein, G. (1994). The psychology of curiosity: A review and reinterpretation. *Psychological Bulletin, 116*, 75-98.

Mayes, L.C. (1991). Exploring internal and external worlds: Reflections on being curious. *The Psychoanalytic Study of the Child, 46*, 3-36.

Messick, S. (1979). Potential uses of noncognitive measurement in education. *Journal of Educational Psychology, 71*, 281-292.

Mitchell, K.E., Levin, A.S. & Krumboltz, J.D. (1998, July). Planned happenstance constructing unexpected career opportunities. Workshop presented at the meeting of the National Career Development Association, Chicago, IL.

Necka, E. (1989). Stimulating curiosity. *Gifted Education International, 6*, 25-27.

Pyszczynski, T.A., & Greenberg, J. (1981). Role of disconfirmed expectancies in the instigation of attributional processing. *Journal of Personality and Social Psychology, 40*, 31-38.

# Response to Nancy: The Case of the Aspiring Neurosurgeon (or "Gym" Teacher)
## An Interpersonal Path to Career Exploration
### Thomas V. Palma
### Cleveland State University

Nancy acknowledges personal factors that appear manifest by career indecision. Although traditionally career counseling was seen as distinct from personal counseling, contemporary views challenge that notion (Betz & Corning, 1993; Super, 1988) recognizing that affective and social factors are essential to the provision of vocational guidance (Schultheiss, 2000). This response will examine the presenting information and empirical data in advocating an interpersonal approach to the provision of career counseling services.

## Background Information and Assessment Data

The presenting information suggests that there are endogenous and exogenous factors that have influenced Nancy in her attempts to establish a vocational or personal identity. The "serious problems" and "seizures" in childhood have been readily acknowledged, yet the parents and the child dismiss the relevance of such issues. Furthermore, little weight appears to have been afforded the cultural dynamics present within the home.

The client's academic performance and tests of intellectual achievement are unremarkable, but may have been moderated by psychological/emotional concerns. The latter may be supported by her lack of motivation to excel in academic or social settings. Notwithstanding, there is little to suggest that intellectual ability will prove to be a substantive barrier in Nancy's effort to secure a satisfying and rewarding career.

Measures of vocational interest may also suggest that Nancy is experiencing psychological/emotional difficulties. Average or below average interest in any occupational dimension was indicated on the Strong Interest Inventory (SII). This has been associated with depression/altered mood, family or peer pressure, poor self-esteem, chronic indecision, role conflict, or limited occupational knowledge (Harmon, Hansen, Borgen, & Hammer, 1994; Hansen, 1992). Furthermore, the "SI" profile is of medium consistency. This may indicate a tendency to mirror the career aspirations of her parents.

The client's quiet, reserved, and observational demeanor is consistent with an "ISTP" personality (Myers & McCaulley, 1985). Despite such confluence, Myers-Briggs Type Indicator (MBTI) scholars regard her personality type as nontypical of professionals in teaching and medicine. This lack of clarity in her career decision making may be a function of her personality. Healy and Woodward (1998) found that Introverts (I) may lack the supports necessary to evaluate or guide decision-making or to establish realistic vocational aspirations. Perceptive (P) personalities were also found prone to anxiety/depression and to demonstrating a lack of resolve for career decision making. The aforementioned factors appear borne out in Nancy's lack of social activities and limited levels of vocational exploration in youth and adolescence.

Given that career exploration is essential to effective vocational decision making and career satisfaction (Holland, 1985; Blustein, 1992), the therapist must help develop and reinforce a milieu that will encourage such exploration. Research consistently has found that self-efficacy (Blustein, 1989; Luzzo, James, & Luna, 1996), and secure attachments (Blustein, Prezioso, & Schultheiss, 1995) were associated with career exploration. Furthermore, the research highlights the importance of family and relational factors in the career development of women (Crozier, 1999; Lucas, 1997; O'Brien & Fassinger, 1993).

## Case Conceptualization

This case appears well suited to an interpersonal therapeutic approach (Sullivan, 1968) that employs elements of Gottfredson's Theory of Circumscription and Compromise (TCC: Gottfredson, 1981, 1996) and Social Cognitive Career Theory (SCCT; Lent, Brown & Hackett, 1994, 1996). An interpersonal approach recognizes the importance of child-parent relations in the establishment of one's "self" and one's interpersonal relationships later in life. Furthermore, it is that image of "self" (i.e., appearance, abilities, personality, values, gender, etc) and image of various occupations that inform the selection of a career. Individuals select a career in which they perceive themselves competent to perform (self-efficacy) and that meets their short-term (outcome expectancy) and long-term (personal goals) needs.

Nancy appears to be a reserved young woman who has a desire to succeed, yet may lack the knowledge or capacity to formulate a vocational plan and move toward it. Her moderately consistent profile and lack of congruence between expressed interests and personality type would suggest that her view of self may be externally mediated/prescribed. Given the "serious problems" encountered in youth, she may have become disproportionately reliant upon authority figures and her ability to explore and interact with peers may have been restricted. Interactions with many medical personnel and the reactions of others as a result of her problems may have evoked feelings of helplessness/incompetence. The resulting stress could have compromised parental capacity to nurture her at a level sufficient to establish a secure parent/child attachment.

The cultural components in the home may also have influenced her view of "self." The patriarchal (i.e., male breadwinner, female housewife) home environment provided Nancy a gender-stereotypical view of womanhood. The pressure for her to decide upon a career path, while providing her brother flexibility in his selection, suggests that women's careers were considered of lesser importance. The lack of validation for personal thoughts and feelings she may have experienced did little to facilitate introspection or the ability to solve problems. To avoid anxiety, she may have adopted the view of "self" prescribed by her family and her social environment.

Nancy's expressed vocational interests appear largely congruent with an externally constructed view of self. Her career aspiration to become a neurosurgeon may have emanated from admiration for the medical personnel who cared for her in youth or from the suggestion of someone she perceives as strong/knowledgeable. If she foresees failure in an effort to secure a medical degree, she expects to become a teacher. This compromised occupational choice is the same vocation pursued by her mother and grandmother. The marked discrepancy between these occupational paths suggests that her perceptions of "self" are imprecise, her impressions of the abilities and skills required of either profession are inaccurate, or both. Although the SII indicated interests in social and investigative professions, this self-report instrument merely reflects rather than informs her "self" image.

Her parents appear to provide little guidance to her in the selection of a career, thereby reinforcing occupational aspirations that may be outside their daughter's interests or abilities. Although Nancy might recognize that her parents and other social forces have influenced her career interests, she appears largely unaware that her actions have contributed to the career indecision. Her limited social encounters and preoccupation with nonacademic content in such encounters afford little opportunity for the introduction of information that would be dissonant with her socially constructed view of self. The avoidance of dissonant ideas, or what Sullivan (1968) might refer to as anxiety, is an interpersonal style that shapes her environment. Therefore, SCCT theorists would suggest that Nancy is an active agent in the creation of structures that are psychologically and behaviorally limiting.

## Therapeutic Approach

A calm, nurturing, and deliberate therapeutic demeanor is congruent with the client's needs to establish trusting relationships and to understand appropriate levels of investment in her own future.

The counselor must demonstrate the aim of helping Nancy with what "she desires," rather than merely demonstrating compliance with the directives of her parents. This is central to modeling a "self" that recognizes the internal as well as social needs in one's life. Such modeling would be in marked contrast to the behavioral patterns she seems to have adopted. Upon establishing substantial rapport with the client, the therapeutic relationship can be an effective tool to identify interpersonal patterns that reinforce helplessness, insecurities, and career indecision (e.g., how her behaviors in session communicate her limitations or seek direction from others). The therapist must be willing to address those actions and thoughts that are aimed at avoiding anxiety and that compromise her ability to form a personal and vocational identity.

Initial steps must include a medical consultation to address the seizures and potential medical issues present in the client's life. A psychological evaluation to assess dysthymia, anxiety, or other psychological factors is also warranted. These steps and the review of prior medical and psychological records will allow the therapist to ascertain the integrity of the information provided by the client and her parents. Such information will reveal the developmental influence of physiological/medical difficulties or the psychological distress that could accompany past traumatic event(s) (e.g., witnessing or experiencing violence/abuse, etc.).

Within-session strategies must appreciate the client's lack of experience and/or reluctance in expressing internal thoughts and feelings. The presentation of a theoretical model of helping and employment of didactic exercises consistent with that model will facilitate discussion of elements central to Nancy's view of "self." By framing the discussion as an academic exercise, the therapist can moderate the level of anxiety experienced by the client when communicating personal experiences or family dynamics. These exercises may include an occupational card-sort, journaling and picture drawings. As anxiety is decreased and trust enhanced, the sessions must address the "serious problems" she encountered in childhood and their relative congruence to such descriptions from external (parental, medical) sources. The relative congruence of client and other perceptions will aid in revelation of the client's self-image. These concepts of "self" and levels of interpersonal skill may become evident in Nancy's descriptions of her family and social life.

The aforementioned exercises will likely reveal the degree to which environmental factors have influenced Nancy's actions and choices. As such, the framework is set for a discussion of her desire to become a neurosurgeon or a gym teacher. Inquiry around the appeal of either profession will highlight the marked dissimilarity of the occupations. The therapist can encourage the client to learn more about either profession by directing her to resources that outline descriptions and academic competencies/credentials required of each occupation.

Although Nancy may have limited awareness of her motivations for pursuing either profession, discussion of skills/abilities and educational requirements will disclose some of the motivational elements associated with these vocational interests. More specifically, the client's self-efficacy, occupational expectations and goals would become apparent. Through increased awareness of these constructs associated with TCC and SCCT, the therapeutic relationship may spur the client's exploration of a wider range of occupations. The therapeutic process must also encourage the client to interact with environments / pursue activities that will reinforce these more adaptive perspectives and behaviors. Environmental resources that reinforce career exploration include:

- *Shadowing Programs.* Immersion in vocational environments parallel with those in which the client has expressed interest. Such programs provide for vicarious learning of tasks/skills necessary for success in a given profession. The professional/ tradesperson at a worksite may provide opportunities and encourage Nancy in the performance of occupation-specific tasks.
- *Mentoring Program.* Pairing Nancy with a mentor from a distinct socioeconomic and/or cultural background will assist the client in considering her own values and interests in the establishment of a personal and vocational identity. Furthermore, the mentor can encourage Nancy to attempt activities that are outside of those in which she feels competent.

- *Community Volunteer Program.* Involvement in an activity in which she can demonstrate some leadership capacity or independence. Her involvement with other young adults will allow for peer reinforcement of competencies/abilities/skills that she will exhibit.

Over time, the identified interventions would facilitate career exploration and the identification of occupational aspirations and expectations that more congruent with her abilities/skills and view of "self." Through such congruence, Nancy is more capable of effective decision making and career satisfaction.

## References

Betz, N.E., & Corning, A.F. (1993). The inseparability of "career" and "personal" counseling. *Career Development Quarterly, 42,* 137-142.

Blustein, D.L. (1989). The role of goal instability and career self-efficacy in the career exploration process. *Journal of Vocational Behavior, 35,* 194-203.

Blustein, D.L. (1992). Applying current theory and research in career exploration to practice. *Career Development Quarterly, 41,* 174-184.

Blustein, D.L., Prezioso, M.S., & Schultheiss, D.P. (1995). Attachment theory and career development: Current status and future directions. *Counseling Psychologist, 23,* 416-432.

Crozier, S.L., (1999). Women's career development in a "relational context." *International Journal for the Advancement of Counselling, 21,* 231-247.

Gottfredson, L.S. (1981). Circumscription and compromise: A developmental theory of occupational aspirations. *Journal of Counseling Psychology, 28,* 545-579.

Gottfredson, L.S. (1996). Gottfredson's theory of circumscription and compromise. In D. Brown, L. Brooks & Associates, *Career choice and development* (3rd ed., pp. 179-232). San Francisco, CA: Jossey-Bass.

Hansen, J.C. (1992). *User's guide to the Strong Interest Inventory* (rev. ed.). Stanford, CA: Stanford University Press

Harmon, L.W., Hansen, J.C., Borgen, F.H., & Hammer, A.L. (1994). *Strong Interest Inventory: Applications and technical guide.* Palo Alto, CA: Consulting Psychologists Press.

Healy, C.C. & Woodward, G.A. (1998). The Myers-Briggs Type Indicator and career obstacles. *Measurement and Evaluation in Counseling and Development, 31,* 74-85.

Holland, J.L. (1985). *Making vocational choices. A theory of vocational personalities and work environments.* Englewood Cliffs, NJ: Prentice Hall.

Lent, R.W., Brown, S.D., & Hackett, G. (1994). Toward a unifying social-cognitive theory of career and academic interest, choice, and performance. *Journal of Vocational Behavior, 45,* 79-122.

Lent, R.W., Brown, S.D., & Hackett, G. (1996). Career development from a social-cognitive perspective. In D. Brown, L. Brooks & Associates, *Career choice and development* (3rd ed., pp. 179-232). San Francisco, CA: Jossey-Bass.

Lucas, M. (1997). Identity development, career development, and psychological separation from parents: Similarities and differences between men and women. *Journal of Counseling Psychology, 44*, 123-132.

Luzzo, D.A., James, T., & Luna, M. (1996). Effects of attributional retraining on the career beliefs and career exploration behavior of college students. *Journal of Counseling Psychology, 43*, 415-422.

Myers, I.B. & McCaulley, M.H. (1985). *Manual: A guide to the development and use of the Myers-Briggs Type Indicator*. Palo Alto, CA: Consulting Psychologists Press.

O'Brien, K.M., & Fassinger, R.E. (1993). A causal model of the career orientation and career choice of adolescent women. *Journal of Counseling Psychology, 40*, 456-469.

Schultheiss, D.P. (2000). Emotional-social issues in the provision of career counseling. In D.A. Luzzo (Ed.), *Career counseling of college students: An empirical guide to strategies that work*, (pp. 43-62). Washington, DC: American Psychological Association.

Sullivan, H.S. (1968). *The interpersonal theory of psychiatry*. New York: Basic Books.

Super, D.E. (1988). Vocational adjustment: Implementing a self-concept. *Career Development Quarterly, 36*, 351-357.

# CHARLIE: THE CASE OF THE PROTECTIVE POET

Charlie is a 17-year-old African American high school senior. He attends a vocational-technical school in a large city and has taken courses in carpentry because his father had advised him to, saying he "needed to learn something practical" so that he could support himself when he turned 18. Charlie's father works as a truck driver and he is away more than half of every month. Charlie's mother works as a cashier at a local grocery store. Charlie is an only child and feels that he must protect his mother who is not in good health.

Charlie has worked as a bag boy at the same grocery store as his mother ever since he turned 16 years old. Charlie has always felt like a loner. He spends much time by himself at school. During his free time Charlie can often be found at Miller's Pond, where he daydreams about writing poetry and acting. Charlie thinks, however, that he is terrible at both activities and states that people usually ridicule his poetry and laugh at his dreams of becoming an actor. Charlie does not want to be a carpenter. He would like to do something that is meaningful to him, but he does not know what that would be, and he thinks that he is "not smart enough to ever amount to anything." His father has stated that he expects Charlie to be on his own when he turns 18 years old in six months. Charlie is worried about his mother and what he will do when he is on his own. He has come to see you to get some help figuring out "what would be a good job" after high school.

## *Response to Charlie: The Case of the Protective Poet*
## *Tyrone Holmes*
## *T. A. H. Performance Consultants, Inc.*

### Introduction

The case of Charlie is a fairly common one in the field of career counseling and development. It involves a young man who is seemingly at a crossroads where he must make several decisions that will have a significant impact on his life. A somewhat troubled young man who lacks self-esteem and will likely find the decision-making process difficult.

In order to effectively communicate recommendations and strategies relative to Charlie's current situation, this case analysis will be broken into three sections. In the first section, Assessment, I will discuss how I would facilitate an initial counseling session with Charlie. Of particular importance is the information that must be gathered relative to Charlie's situation.

In the Treatment section, I will introduce my Career Empowerment System and how it can be applied to address Charlie's career issues. Discussion will include the identification of specific interventions and activities that can be used to meet counseling goals. I will conclude by discussing the long-term implications of Charlie's concerns as well as the impact of contextual issues such as race and socioeconomic status on the career development process.

### Assessment

During my initial session with Charlie, I would begin by helping him understand the counseling process and his role in it. I would make sure he felt comfortable about the actions we would be taking and use this discussion to help build the foundation to an effective counselor/client relationship. My primary goal during this time would be to collect additional information relative to Charlie's career concerns. I would attempt to gain insight in several areas. First of all, I would be quite concerned about Charlie's current level of self-esteem and self-efficacy relative to his interest in poetry and acting. His statement that he "is not mart enough to ever amount to anything" is troubling.

I would want to get at the roots of these feelings because enhancing his self-concept would likely be one of our primary counseling tasks.

I would further probe Charlie's interests in poetry and acting. He seems to be an artistic personality type (Holland, 1992). This would indicate that he has a preference for unsystematic, expressive activities where his creative interests can flourish. The artistic personality type also tends to be averse to routine, structured activities such as those found in the field of carpentry. I would attempt to understand the nature of his interests and how they may conflict with his current area of study.

Most important, I would seek to understand what Charlie truly wants. It is stated in the case that he needs help figuring out "what would be a good job." Although certainly important as a presenting problem, I sense that there are other issues that Charlie might wish to address. These include his relationship with his parents, clarifying his interests and how they can be expressed in the workplace, dealing with the pressure that he is expected to be on his own within the next six months, and adapting to a field of study that may not hold his interest. It would be important for us to get at his feelings regarding these issues before we decided which counseling tasks to focus on.

## Treatment

Based on the information presented in the case, I believe there are three primary counseling tasks to be addressed relative to Charlie's career development. These include enhancing his self-esteem and career-related self-efficacy; expanding his self-knowledge and knowledge of the world of work; and helping him to identify and pursue both long and short-term employment possibilities.

One way to help Charlie effectively address these tasks is through the utilization of the author's Career Empowerment System. This system represents a comprehensive approach to career and life development. It is designed to help one think about personal and professional success in a synergistic way and to help individuals characterize and achieve that success for themselves.

The Career Empowerment System has four modules: Defining Success, Developing a Plan for Success, Preparing for Success, and Maintaining Successful Attitudes. During the first module, clients clarify what success looks like for them. It helps to bring about greater self-knowledge relative to one's interests, values, and skills – knowledge that can be applied in the career decision-making process.

The focus of the second module is on goal setting and planning. Once clients have a vision of what success looks like for them, they can set goals and create plans for achieving that vision. This module helps clients to set effective goals, identify potential barriers to these goals, and create career plans. It also helps clients to develop effective decision-making skills.

Module three is the most involved of the four components. It introduces the E.R.I.C. approach, which helps clients prepare for the world of work in four areas. *E*ducation and experience involves determining the education, training, and work background necessary to attain the client's short- and long- range goals. *R*epresentation refers to the client's portrayal of self to others. It involves resume preparation, job searching, and interviewing that maximize their chances for success. *I*nformation refers to world-of-work knowledge and helping clients tap into the various sources of occupational information. *C*ollaboration involves helping clients to establish a strong career network of colleagues, mentors, and protégés. Utilizing the E.R.I.C. approach, a client like Charlie can prepare to meet the vision of success that he has created for himself.

The final module focuses on the attitudes and mental mindsets necessary for personal and professional success. It emphasizes the fact that any individual is much more likely to achieve his or her goals with a positive mental attitude, an internal locus of control, and strong career self-efficacy.

It is with this final component that I would begin an intervention with Charlie. Clearly, his self-esteem and career-related efficacy are somewhat low. Through basic questioning, I would attempt to understand how this has come about. In order to enhance his esteem and particularly his efficacy in specific career areas, I would adopt the approach offered by Bandura (1977) in his social learning theory and further refined by Hackett and Betz (1981) in their discussion of self-efficacy in women.

Bandura (1977) defines self-efficacy as one's perceived level of effectiveness in relation to specific tasks. What makes this construct so important is that it significantly influences psychological functioning and behavior. For instance, people like Charlie who feel they are incapable of effectively completing certain tasks will typically limit their career mobility and restrict their career options. They tend to give up more easily, procrastinate and may avoid making career decisions altogether.

Bandura (1977) offers an approach to enhancing self-efficacy that can be applied with Charlie. He states that by providing encouragement, assisting with performance accomplishments, providing role models, and helping to reduce performance anxiety, a client's self-efficacy can be enhanced.

With Charlie, it would be important to provide him with encouragement and to help him create environments where he could receive supportive feedback and interact with positive role models. Because successful performance accomplishments can greatly enhance self-efficacy, I would also attempt to put Charlie in situations where he could practice various career skills such as goal setting, decision making, job searching, and interviewing. This would allow him to achieve small wins and ultimately to build his confidence.

Charlie also needs to gain more self-knowledge relative to his interests (what he likes to do), values (what he hopes to gain from doing this), and skills (what he is good at). I would help him create a personal vision statement consisting of what he wants to do and the type of life he wants to live. Specifically, I would use both a values card sort and skills card sort to help Charlie clarify what is important to him and what skills he is motivated to use.

I would also help Charlie learn more about the world of work and how he can find the greatest occupational fit for his interests, values, and skills. We would do this by initiating an occupational information search on two levels of inquiry: understanding what he needs to know about various occupations and identifying means of obtaining this information. I would make sure that Charlie could effectively utilize three types of occupational information media. These include passive sources such as books and periodicals; interactive sources such as interviews with experts, computers, and the Internet; and actual work experience.

During this time, we would begin to identify short- and long-term employment possibilities for Charlie using a variety of means such as newspapers, job banks, personal contacts, and the Internet. I would impress upon Charlie that his short-term choices might not reflect his long-term professional objectives. He is in a situation where he may need to simply work for the time being at any available job as he continues to enhance his credentials. Our sessions would likely include discussion on effective decision making as well.

## Conclusion

It is important to note that Charlie's circumstances are not unusual for young African American males in our society. As a counselor, one must consider the unique issues and concerns that someone in Charlie's position might face. Much has been written about these issues, that can include a constrained economic opportunity structure (e.g., higher unemployment, limited occupational representation, fewer career choices), impaired self-concept, parental disassociation, loneliness, academic frustration, identity crisis, discrimination, poverty, and a lack of educational opportunities (Cheatham, 1990; Hawks & Muha, 1991; Holmes, 1997).

Likewise, Brown, Minor, and Jepsen (1991) identified several differences between the career development needs of African Americans and Caucasians. They state that more African Americans report needing assistance in obtaining job information and actual employment; believe the usefulness of occupational information should be improved; lack the information needed to make effective career decisions; believe there is significant workplace discrimination; and are more likely to take a job because it is the only one available.

Several strategies have been proffered for facilitating the career development of African American clients. These include enhancing self-concept, helping individuals to become more internally directed, enhancing knowledge about job opportunities, clarifying client aspirations, and helping clients to effectively engage in a eurocentrically-based society (Zunker, 1998). Strategies such as these and the approaches suggested in this case analysis could be instructive when working with African American clients like Charlie.

## References

Bandura, A. (1977). *Social learning theory*. Englewood Cliffs, NJ: Prentice Hall.

Brown, D., Minor, C.W., & Jepsen, D.A. (1991). The opinions of minorities about preparing for work: Report of the second NCDA national survey. *Career Development Quarterly, 40,* 5-19.

Cheatham, H.E. (1990). Africentricity and career development of African Americans. *Career Development Quarterly, 38,* 334-346.

Hackett, G. & Betz, N.E. (1981). A self-efficacy approach to the career development of women. *Journal of Vocational Behavior, 18,* 326-339.

Hawks, B.K. & Muha, D.G. (1991). Facilitating the career development of minorities: Doing it differently this time. *Career Development Quarterly, 39,* 251-260.

Holland, J.L. (1992). *Making vocational choices: A theory of vocational personalities and work environments* (2nd ed.). Odessa, FL: Psychological Assessment Resources.

Holmes, T.A. (1997). *Culturally responsive career services for African Americans: A comprehensive model*. Paper presented at the meeting of the National Career Development Association, Daytona Beach, FL.

Zunker, V.G. (1998). *Career counseling: Applied concepts of life planning* (5th ed.). Pacific Grove, CA: Brooks/Cole.

## *Response to Charlie: The Case of the Protective Poet*
### *Kenneth B. Hoyt*
### *Kansas State University*

### Images of Charlie

I have numerous impressions of Charlie as a result of reading the case information. For example:

1. He appears to be a very insecure person with a poor self-concept.
2. My impression is that he has probably done nothing with his life so far that has brought him happiness and/or a meaningful feeling of accomplishment.
3. Charlie appears to be amenable to help – if it is offered to him in the right way.
4. Charlie does not see himself as one of those "smart" youth headed toward a 4-year college degree after graduating from high school.
5. Charlie appears to be more dependent on remarks – positive and negative – made by his parents regarding his future than he is in formulating such self-concept remarks for himself.

## Other Information to be Sought

To gain a more complete picture of Charlie, I would need additional information in a variety of areas. For instance, I would like to learn more about Charlie's abilities and his school performance. To acquire information about the former, I would administer the General Aptitude Test Battery (GATB). Information about Charlie's school performance (e.g., grades, attendance, high school rank) would provide important data for formulating a sense of Charlie's strengths and future educational options. Related to this, understanding Charlie's aspirations (if he has them) for postsecondary education as well as his parents' aspirations for Charlie's postsecondary education will provide useful insights into what thoughts Charlie might have about his future. It would also be helpful to learn more about his current relationships with his peers. This information helps provide information about Charlie's interpersonal skills as well as his self-concept. Finally, I would administer the Self-Directed Search (SDS) to learn more about Charlie's personality types and education and work environments that might provide potential direction for Charlie.

1. Do Charlie and/or his parents have *any* aspirations with reference to *any* kind of postsecondary education?
2. Charlie's rank in his high school class.
3. Description of current peer relationships experienced by Charlie.

## Plans for Career Counseling with Charlie

In working as Charlie's career counselor, I would develop the following plans for career counseling:

1. Be sure he understands the need for *some* kind of postsecondary education if he ever expects to get a good job in the primary market.
2. If Charlie persists in plans to enter the labor market directly upon leaving high school, be sure he understands such things as (1) the need to practice good work habits in every job he finds; (2) the need he can expect to find calling for him to change jobs frequently; and (3) the nature of his own *work values* and his need to find some way of practicing them in every job he holds.

## Direct Interventions

In my direction interventions with Charlie, I would attempt to do the following:

1. Help Charlie learn about the wide variety of kinds of postsecondary education beyond those available in four-year colleges; help him think about the kind he things may most appeal to him; help him find out how to gather more information from those institutions in which he appears to have some interest.
2. Help Charlie think about things he might want to do in his leisure time that would bring him some feelings of personal enjoyment and satisfaction. Include a discussion of how he may practice both poetry and acting as volunteer leisure time activities; encourage him to make contact with local groups that present theater pieces and see if he can find *some* kind of volunteer activity needed by this group (even if it is backstage with no formal recognition by the audience).
3. Encourage Charlie to continue to hold strong personal interest in both poetry and in activities taking place in theaters. At the same time, make sure he understands that very few persons can make their living through these activities – that his interest here will probably best be met by how he chooses to use his leisure time.

### Theoretical Models Used – Rational Behavior Model

Given the case information provided for Charlie, it is clear that contextual factors will play an important part in his career decision-making process. My initial reactions to how they might be influential in Charlie's career development are:

1. I strongly suspect Charlie's parents have no serious aspiration that Charlie would attend and graduate from a 4-year college. They appear to be looking for him to seek employment immediately after leaving high school.

2. Socioeconomic factors are almost sure to make it tough for Charlie to seek some kind of postsecondary education rather than seeking immediate employment. It appears likely he will probably have to be one of those students who works at a part-time job 20-30 hours per week.

3. I doubt if Charlie has many contacts, at this time, with other persons who are enrolled in various kinds of postsecondary education. It will require some kind of systematic effort to reduce his ignorance in this area. It will not be easy to motivate him toward seeking any kind of postsecondary education, and, in the long run, we may have to settle simply for his ability to secure and hold secondary labor market jobs; but I would not settle for that if any other path can be found.

### Summary

In summary, I am saying it appears that the best counseling help that could be made available to Charlie would be serious consideration and eventual choice of *some* kind of post-secondary education offered at the sub-baccalaureate level.

On the surface, he appears to be neither bright enough, wealthy enough, or his family supportive enough for Charlie to think that a 4-year college decision would be the best one for him to make at this time. At the same time, we certainly would not like to see him dumped in one of the 21+ million low pay/low skill/low secure jobs expected to be available during the 1996-2000 period in the secondary labor market. Since 80+ percent of students in postsecondary sub-baccalaureate programs appear to be holding part-time or full-time jobs while enrolled, this is a pattern into which Charlie should be able to fit rather easily. I see no other alternative that looks as good right now.

# MARK: THE CASE OF THE SEARCHING COMMUNITY COLLEGE STUDENT

Mark is a likable 18-year-old white man of average appearance who recently graduated from high school in a small Midwestern town. During the summer prior to entering 12th grade, Mark was involved in a car accident and has been paralyzed from his waist down since then. Because of this accident, and because he wanted to stay close to home for another year, Mark decided to attend the local community college. He is currently enrolled in his first year of community college and plans to go to a large, prestigious university in the eastern United States next fall. His father is a well-known scientist employed by the local university. His mother is a music teacher in a local middle school. Mark has no siblings.

Mark stated that he decided to attend college when he was in the first grade. He noted that he always felt that his father wanted "a famous son" and that he feels as though, in some ways, he is competing with his father. In fifth grade, Mark won a prize in his school's science fair and since then he has devoted considerable time to science competitions in which he has been quite successful. He considers himself to be an authority on numerous scientific and technical topics. Mark values being exact and precise. When he cannot resolve problems through scientific reasoning he experiences significant anxiety. Mark notes that he "hates to make mistakes."

During high school, Mark was involved in several extracurricular activities. He participated in the drama club and was on the school newspaper staff for three years, rising to the position of editor in his senior year of high school. He reported that serving as editor was the best experience of his high school career.

Given Mark's strong academic record, high college entrance examination scores, and interest in science, he had thought that majoring in physics at a prestigious university made sense for him. Recently, however, he began to question that decision. In addition, he has heard that many college freshmen have difficulty adjusting to a large university setting and he is anxious about how he would fare in such a situation. He has enjoyed the relaxed atmosphere of the community college but worries that he will not be prepared for more rigorous academic requirements when he transfers to a four-year institution. He is also concerned about accommodations and his ability to "get around." He has the uneasy feeling that he will make the wrong choice about his future. He wonders if he should transfer or remain at his community college for another year and live at home. Also, he is unsure about what his major should be when he transfers. He requests your help in making these decisions.

## *Response to Mark: The Case of the Searching Community College Student*
### *R. Rocco Cottone*
### *University of Missouri - St. Louis*

I am very pleased to be able to respond to the case of Mark, the case of the son with paralysis below the waist. I feel I am able to respond as a counselor with special training in rehabilitation. Also, I am able to respond as a father of a son with a very serious disabling condition. My son will most likely be bound to a wheelchair by his early teens and may not live far into his 20s.

The image I have of Mark is complex. I see a young man who is lucky to have his life and to be able to consider a potentially rewarding professional career. I also see a young man who must address both the physical and social demands of a disabling condition. I would definitely want more information about his physical limitations and how they translate to functioning in everyday activities. I would also want detailed information about his social network, especially his extended family and close friends. Of greater importance, I would want to know about his mother's view on his career aspirations. What are her thoughts about his future, and what is the nature of his relationship to his mother? We know about the relationship to his father – he views his father as wanting a "famous" son and he also views his father in a competitive light. In this case, I might ask Mark's permission to have his parents come to an early career counseling session to assess the nature of their relationship to Mark, their relationship to each other, and any family dynamics that might influence Mark's decisions about choosing a college, a major, and a career. I would be especially mindful of any observed disagreement between the parents related to Mark's future, because Mark's confusion may be a direct result of conflict in the social context. I would also want to know where Mark's best friends are going to school and his plans related to his friendships. People do not make educational and career decisions in a social vacuum.

My curiosity about his social network is actually quite theory centered and not just a result of curiosity about his personal life. I believe strongly that social systems – our networks of social relationships – strongly influence decisions; what we think and do are strongly affected by the social and cultural influences that direct us. Career decisions are no different.

Specifically related to his relationship with his father, it is true that some father-son relationships are strained, and young men may in fact have fathers who are controlling or overbearing. On the other hand, it is also true that some sons may believe their fathers to be controlling or overbearing when, in fact, the father's expressions of interests really reflect best wishes for the son. Some sons may misinterpret a father's attempt to guide as a demand for a specific action. These issues would have to be addressed with Mark, and having observed the father-son interaction, the counselor might be able to accurately reflect the father's position on the matter. For my son, what is important to me is that he is able to find his place, his niche, with happiness and with as little frustration as possible on matters related to his limitations. I hope to be his advocate as well as his guide, but I respect that he will have to make many decisions without my direct influence and he will have to face many challenges over which I will have little control. It is also important to respond to the influence of the mother – to see only the father-son issue is to be blinded by stereotype. Mothers can be controlling, overbearing, and competitive, too! His mother may be influencing him in ways that are subtle to the marital relationship. Maybe she experiences a need to have her son close to home, for example, to balance marital imbalance.

Mark will need career guidance. Since he is really undecided about his career direction, some basic career guidance seems appropriate – for example, assessment of interests and exploration of vocational options (given his limitations) seems very appropriate. Interest assessment might be very helpful, because he may be given normative data about how his interests align with those in possible occupations of choice. Interest assessment may open his eyes to options he has not considered.

He will need to make an informed decision about what college to attend. He should be encouraged to visit and to apply to several schools. It is hoped he will have a choice among several schools. He will need to know what support on campus is available to an individual in a wheelchair. Is the campus fully accessible? Are there others in wheelchairs on campus? What barriers will be encountered? What health care facilities and services are available? Are there aides? What living arrangements accommodate special needs students? He is a young man with special needs, and an environment that will meet those needs while maximizing his educational opportunity, will be essential. Assurance that he will have physical and social support regardless of his choice will be imperative. For Mark, a wise educational or career choice will be a choice of good "fit" socially and physically.

In counseling Mark, theoretically I will be guided by "a systemic theory of vocational rehabilitation" (Cottone, 1986, 1987; Cottone & Cottone, 1986; Cottone, Grelle & Wilson, 1988). A systemic theory of vocational rehabilitation posits that career decisions and career success, assisted through the rehabilitation process, are highly dependent on social processes and social fit. "System theory" is a theory of relationships (see also Cottone, 1992). So a systemic theory of vocational rehabilitation is a theory about how relationships affect rehabilitation processes and outcomes. It is a comprehensive theory that predicts positive outcomes based on the degree of positive relationships and social fit within a context supportive of constructive/productive vocational behavior. Based on a Systemic Theory of Vocational Rehabilitation, several predictions can be made.

First, it can be predicted that Mark's satisfaction with a choice of colleges will depend highly on the degree to which his physical disability can be accommodated and what relationships derive from the disability-related services provided on campus. Some very prestigious campuses have large populations of individuals with physical disabilities and provide special housing and assistance. The relationships involved in such assistance, and the social network that derives from such a setting, will have powerful positive effects. Such effects will manifest themselves in what will appear to be a positive attitude in Mark and "self-esteem." Mark should avoid a college where he stands out in a deviant sense; he should find a place where others in his situation have found acceptance. He will adjust to the new environment to the degree he has social and physical support.

Second, his career indecision is not unusual. It is, paradoxically, an enviable circumstance. He has many choices due to his intelligence. Some individuals with serious physical limitations have fewer choices, due to cognitive or perceptual limitations. He should be guided to a college and a curriculum that is broad-based in the freshman and sophomore years. A broad-based general education curriculum would provide him with an opportunity to sample many academic disciplines. Also, a facility that can provide follow-up career guidance will be valuable. A decision about a major will not be easy. It will be a decision that is best made considering his abilities, physical requirements, and social factors. For example, he developed some interests in journalism in high school. Certainly, he should explore the work and the career path of an "editor." Are the physical demands consistent with his limitations? What prior jobs or experiences are required to achieve the status of "editor," and are they feasible given his impairments? Likewise, since he has scientific interests and abilities, are there possible options that would blend such skills and interests? Mark should not be forced to make a decision about a major until there has been full exploration in his early college years. He will need to make a wise choice, because disabilities do limit the options.

Third, it can be predicted that his worries about the rigors of college will probably subside with success in his chosen environment. Certainly, his concerns should be addressed in counseling. He should be encouraged to consult successful individuals with a similar rehabilitation profile, and the career counselor should assist in identifying such individuals.

Fourth, the issue of staying near home is not just a career decision. It will be influenced greatly by his family and friendship relationships. These relationships must be addressed in counseling related to a college choice. As mentioned earlier, the relationships to the mother and father are critical. It would be ideal if the parents were in agreement on a path for Mark, or at least would communicate that they will accept his decision regardless of their agreement with his decision. The family issues will need to be incorporated into the career counseling process. It is hoped that Mark's choices will be attractive social choices and not those derived by a desire to escape an uncomfortable circumstance. Social repulsion can have as powerful an influence on a career as social attraction. It will be important to explore what he is trying to avoid socially as well as what he is hoping to encounter. If, for example, he is trying to make a choice to avoid the wrath of his father or mother, that would be less predictive of success than a career choice made because there is the promise of "good fit" socially and occupationally.

This is a complicated case. It challenges the counselor to address physical impairments as a limiting occupational factor. It requires the career counselor to be adept at assessing social factors as well as vocational factors in guiding Mark through the rehabilitation process. It requires an in-depth understanding of disability and resources available to those with limitations. It is a case that makes career counseling a challenging yet rewarding profession, because, as with Mark, individuals with disabilities have special needs requiring special counseling skills.

## References

Cottone, R.R. (1986). Toward a systemic theoretical framework for vocational rehabilitation. *Journal of Applied Rehabilitation Counseling, 17*(4), 4-7.

Cottone, R.R. (1987). A systemic theory of vocational rehabilitation. *Rehabilitation Counseling Bulletin, 30*, 167-176.

Cottone, R.R. (1992). *Theories and paradigms of counseling and psychotherapy.* Needham Heights, MA: Allyn & Bacon.

Cottone, R.R., & Cottone, L.P. (1986). A systemic analysis of vocational evaluation in the state-federal rehabilitation system. *Vocational Evaluation and Work Adjustment Bulletin, 19*, 47-54.

Cottone, R.R., Grelle, M., & Wilson, W. (1988). The accuracy of systemic versus psychological evidence in judging vocational evaluator recommendations: A preliminary test of a systemic theory of vocational rehabilitation. *Journal of Rehabilitation, 54*(1), 45-52.

# *Response to Mark: The Case of the Searching Community College Student An Eclectic Integrative Model*
## *Keith B. Wilson and Mark Fleming*
## *The Pennsylvania State University*

There are many considerations one has to scrutinize when addressing Mark's career counseling issues. Mark's case is made more complicated because he is a person with a disability, which in fact, has a backdrop that is in addition to issues that people who are able-bodied encounter on a daily basis. Equally important with Mark is that his disability is acquired. As a result, the emotional issues regarding adjustment not only to the disability but to the long term effects of the disability must be addressed when planning career counseling for him. Because Mark has a disability, we would like to *briefly* define the appropriate terms to use illustrating concerns about Mark's case relative to having a disability:
1. Disability – Any physical and/or mental impairment.
2. Handicap – Any architectural (e.g., no cut-a-way sidewalks for wheelchair users) or attitudinal (e.g., people with disabilities do not want to work) barrier that may be present.
3. Acquired Disability – A disability that is not present at birth but rather attained at some point in the person's life
4. Congenital Disability – A disability that is present at birth.
5. Able-bodied Individuals – People who are not identified as having a physical disability.

We will examine Mark from an eclectic integrative approach. Since all theories have both strengths and weaknesses, we will integrate two theories to assist Mark in making a career decision. The eclectic integrative approach is consistent with the philosophy of rehabilitation counselors (professionals who assist people with mental and physical disabilities). Thus, we will be examining Mark from a more holistic stance and using strengths of learning and trait and factor career-counseling theories. As defined, a social learning approach affirms that a person will express a preference for a course of study, an occupation, or the tasks and consequences of a field of work if the individual has been positively reinforced for engaging in the said activities. In addition, social learning theory attempts to: (1) encompass a total process, not just some phase of the process, (2) seeks to explain developmental career aspirations based on some concepts of the trait and factor approach, (3) allows the influence of economic and sociology variables, and (4) clarifies the role of the evolution of decision-making skills.

Another approach we will apply to Mark's case will be the trait and factor approach. The trait and factor approach conceives that the individual possesses a pattern of traits – such as interests, aptitudes, achievements, personality characteristics – that can be identified through objective means, usually psychological tests, inventories, and the profile to represent the individual's potential. Because people with disabilities may have certain obvious limitations, the trait and factor approach is considered optional because of the matching that is required when working with a person who has a disability. By matching, we are referring to matching (mental and physical abilities) what the client can do with the vocation he/she would like to pursue. Because rehabilitation counselors (persons who work with people with disabilities) view a disability as only a part of the entire person, it is important to include an eclectic approach to assist Mark in addressing the many challenges (e.g., personal, professional, environmental, and discriminatory) he will encounter because of his disability. Included in the eclectic integrative approach is helping Mark to recognize the often hindering attitudes of able-bodied individuals, whether unconscious or conscious, often manifest as barriers to people like Mark who have an overt disability.

Based on the presenting information, our first impression of Mark was that of an academically motivated (high college interest scores and strong academic record), confused (not sure about his college major when he transfers to a prestigious university) person with skills in the sciences (won science fair in fifth grade and successful in subsequent science fair competitions), and arts (drama and editor of high school newspaper), who is concerned about his ability to "get around" if and when he transfers to a larger four-year institution. Although much of what Mark is experiencing deals with obvious developmental issues that most graduating high school students experience, when coupled with adjusting to his new disability, he has particular concerns that may potentially cause him not only psychological stress, but also stagnation with the career decision process.

While we attempt to investigate Mark's possible career concerns from an eclectic integrative model, we would like to learn more about Mark's relationship with his mother. From the information presented, we do not know if Mark's mother is supportive of his decision to pursue, for example, majoring in physics. Since Mark tends to have an aptitude in both the arts and social sciences (drama/writing) and hard/natural sciences, it would be interesting to learn why he is not considering a career as a journalism major. Although the client has been very successful in competing in past science fairs, it is not clear if he is happy and/or enthusiastic for pursing a career science. In contrast, the client did report that serving as editor "was the best experience of his high school career." Based on these observations, we wonder whether the client would rather pursue a career in the sciences because of: a) the parental influences are encouraging the client to seek vocations that are considered prestigious and b) whether the father feels like a "loser" because he is not satisfied with his career in science. Mark's father is a well-known scientist employed by the local university. However, it is not clear what is meant by "well-known." We would also solicit Mark's father to explain what "a famous son" means. It appears from the case illustration that being "famous" (wish for son) is elevated higher than being "well-known" (farther). If so, living up to such expectations may be difficult to accomplish. Inquiring about the parental influences is consistent with the social learning theory approach.

Perhaps socioeconomic factors may also play an important role in the client deciding to major in physics, once he transfer to a larger, more prestigious university. It seems apparent that the client has aptitudes in both the arts and hard sciences. However, based on the information given, Mark only enjoyed being editor of the school's newspaper his senior year in high school. It is not uncommon for high school students to prefer careers based on the earning potential of the vocation. In Mark's' case, we would like to inquire about his work related values (e.g., money, doing a good job). Based on the social learning concept of knowledge acquisition from the parental environment, the client may be experiencing an internal dilemma between seeking a vocation as a physicist that pays more over a vocational that pays less, but gives him more personal satisfaction. Also, consistent with the social learning theory, it is tenable that the client is receiving more positive reinforcement to seek vocations that may have "high" status and pays well from the parental milieu. Again, the possible internal dilemma is supported by the case illustration of not only confusion by the client, but no statements about the client enjoying his science activities. Asking the client abut his work values may lead to more insight regarding careers he may not only be competent in, but enjoy as well. One way of helping Mark connect to these values is by having him use the DISCOVER system, a nationally recognized tool used in many career placement centers that helps students learn about their interests, values, skills, and experiences in an effort to help them make more informed career decisions.

As with any new client who is seeking career counseling services, we would propose that the client take one or two career counseling inventories to verify his interest and values. Specifically, we would recommend that the client take the Strong, the Values Scale, the Self-Directed Search, and/or the Myers-Briggs to help him connect at a deeper level to his skills, abilities, interests, and values. Administering some sort of assessment is warranted because the client is afraid "he will make the wrong choice about his future" and also "he is unsure about what his major should be once he transfers." Because the client has a disability (paraplegic), interest inventories may also function to assist him with integrate into the world of work, via higher education. For example, because the client is a paraplegic (limited use of lower extremities), it will be important for him to eliminate vocations that will require him to use his lower extremities as a primary part of a particular job. While federal laws require for some employers to make reasonable accommodations for people with disabilities, the client may eliminate some vocations from consideration because of educational requirements, physical requirement, and earning potential of the job.

In keeping with the eclectic integrative approach, we would also recommend testing that would assess the client's functional limitations. Basically, these tests will determine what the client is able to do physically and mentally. From the information presented in the case illustration, it is not clear whether the client has little or not use of his lower extremities. In assessing the physical abilities of the client, it would be inappropriate to assume that the client has *no* use of his lower extremities. Generally, the word *paralyzed* is ambiguous and can mean several things to a client who is a paraplegic.

It is with the assessment(s) to assess the functional limitations of the client that we would then move toward the trait-and-factor approach. Using the trait and factor approach, we would begin to match the clients' abilities with the requirements listed for each job that he would like to pursue. We would then assist the client with developing a list of possible vocations that he would like to pursue once enrolled at the four-year university he is planning to attend. Although the matching process between abilities of the client and job requirement is not perfect, we believe that social learning trait and factor theories will be an excellent start to assist the client with his career concerns.

Finally, because Mark is obviously experiencing "significant anxiety" "when he cannot resolve problems through scientific reasoning," we would recommend that he see a therapist to work through some of the anxiety apprehensions. Although speculative, we believe Mark is experiencing significant anxiety because his father is a perfectionist and is requiring him to be a perfectionist as well. Again, this speculation is supported by the many connections between the fathers' occupation, personality types that are associated with his father's occupation, his father desire to have a famous son, and Mark's feeling like he is competing with his father. Therapy can also help Mark work through his adjustment to his disability and how understanding the disability might be affected not only his outlook for the future, but how he thinks others, particularly his father, view his disability.

While we did attempt to address Mark's concerns through an eclectic integrative model, we do realize that other pertinent information and theories may apply to assist Mark in the evolution of his career development.

# FRANCES: THE CASE OF THE STRUGGLING SENIOR

Frances is a 19-year-old female high school student, receiving special education services, preparing for graduation from a large urban school district. She faces many choices and is reluctant to make decisions without seeking advice from a great many people. Help from home is nearly nonexistent.

Frances was born in Romania and came to the USA in 1988. She has learned English as a second language, but has been identified as learning disabled (LD.) Her IQ falls within the low normal range. Frances has been receiving special education services for reading and math skills. She has epileptic seizures and is taking medication (Tegretol) to control them. She has not had a seizure at school. Frances is a heavy-set girl with a broad and open face, of average height and a shy demeanor. She will be graduating from high school and is facing choices about further schooling, work plans, and finances. It seems to be slightly overwhelming to her. Frances has a good work ethic but is very dependent on others.

As Frances prepares for graduation, she needs to make many decisions regarding her immediate and long-range futures. She has always been highly dependent on others when engaged in decision making. Frances would ask several teachers and counselors as well as many support or custodial staff about class choices or other decisions she faced. Frances' father passed away about one year ago. Her father had been the decision maker for the family and held the family tightly in his grip. He was a very conservative man and did not allow his wife or daughters much freedom or choice. Since his passing, the two sisters and mother initially closed ranks to the outside world but are just beginning to try out some new things. For example, Frances could not have a driver's license but now mother will allow her to take lessons, for example. She is considering college as one alternative as well as going directly into the work force and gaining some real-world experience.

Frances has not yet held any sort of job, nor has her mother. She has not been allowed to baby sit nor do any other type of adolescent endeavor. The family has always done things together, as a group, including grocery shopping. This has hindered Frances from striking out on an individual enterprise. Her reliance on others is a roadblock as well. Although Mother is willing to allow driving lessons, there will be no car or singular driving for Frances. Public transportation is unavailable in Frances' environment.

Frances also harbors dreams of attending expensive postsecondary schools in a state far away. She has done little exploration regarding these schools except to hear people mention them. She has recently applied to a local community college; however, she knows little of this school but that many students from her high school attend there after graduation. She has yet to identify a career direction. The special education team is working diligently with Frances to prepare her for graduation.

Frances is LD with a low normal IQ (94). She receives support in reading and math through the special education consultant but has no special education classes. Vocational training and work experience were refused when presented as options at Individual Education Plan meetings. Frances has some difficulty distinguishing what is a practical reality for her. She remains highly dependent on others, yet expresses a wish to be independent. She is beginning to make a few decisions for herself (the community college application) but was unable to enlist her mother's cooperation in completing the FASFA form.

Frances' reading and math skills are about two years behind grade level. She is maintaining a 2.494 grade point average in regular education classes. She is strong in study skills, reading comprehension, and math computation. Frances is weak in word analysis, reading vocabulary, and math concepts and applications.

Frances has expressed a desire to become independent; however, she remains very much dependent on her mother and sister. She is aware she is an adult in the legal sense but still very much a child in her ability to deal with the world and adult responsibilities. She is beginning to emancipate herself but recognizes the need for a great deal of guidance and assistance in naming and attaining her life and career goals. She relies on adults and has difficulty forming peer relationships.

Frances is anxious to please others and has experienced very little freedom or independence. She is delayed in her ability to set life and career goals. She lacks the greater world knowledge to formulate a realistic picture of what her future could look like. She is concerned with the opinions of others almost to the exclusion of her own feelings. She experiences times of emotional fragility. Her health concerns may also be a drawback to some career areas.

Frances has received strong support from school throughout her high school years. Much has been done for her because of her reluctance to do for herself (take chances). She has not developed many strong feelings regarding the world of work or her place in it. Again, she is anxious to please others at cost to herself. She has no work experience to draw from so the possibilities are wide open for Frances to experiment. It seems she is chronologically advanced to be at this stage of career awareness and exploration.

Frances functions at a much lower age than her 19 years. She is at a career awareness and exploration stage and behaves much more like a fourteen or fifteen year old. With little job experience, personal interactions (except with adults), or freedom, Frances has a great deal of growing and investigation to do. Attendance has been excellent at school, even when she found the experience challenging. It could be expected the same would hold true for her working. Frances enjoys and seeks adult company. She is averse to joining her peers. She has made few friends with the other students and those friends are largely her sister's friends. This will influence her career options.

## *Response to Frances: The Case of the Struggling Senior*
### *A Developmental View in Context*
### *Ellen P. Cook*
### *University of Cincinnati*

The description of Frances is essentially a photograph of a being in motion. In responding to the case, I must allow my imagination to elaborate how a flesh-and-blood Frances might experience her life. My response inevitably reflects the limitations set by my own perceptions and by the clarity of this singular photograph.

In any counseling, counselors must generously acknowledge the strengths of their clients and their own weaknesses as a helper. I must remember when working with Frances that I have little professional experience with individuals from her cultural background, or those with her type of disabilities. In real life I would rely on colleagues for consultation or referral if needed. I am also a parent of a child with complex disabilities, a role that could prove to be either a strength or weakness (or both) in working with Frances. I must be especially vigilant about how I use my personal experiences to understand her life. She is not the person my daughter is, nor am I Frances' mother. In actual practice I would use a combination of personal consultation, supervision, and/or counseling to help me sort through this issue, again keeping the possibility of referral in mind.

Where do I start with Frances? From the information provided in the case example, I know much more about how others see Frances than how she sees herself and her possibilities in the world. She is seen as overly dependent on others; vocationally immature in terms of her readiness to make those provisional decisions expected of high school seniors; restricted in life experiences and social relationships; and challenged to some extent by her disabilities. I have no information about career relevant interests, abilities, and values, but her description suggests that these personal attributes may be relatively undifferentiated. It sounds as if she is simply not ready to make a well-reasoned decision at this time.

As with any client, I must first try to understand the context of Frances' life thus far and how she experiences it. This understanding can stimulate thinking about what she needs to make preliminary decisions shaping her adult life. Themes central to understanding Frances concern her family life as conditioned by cultural and gender-based experiences and her statuses as an immigrant and a disabled person. The speculations to be presented here are, of course, only hypotheses to be confirmed in actual sessions with Frances. My approach is primarily developmental (e.g., Super, Savickas & Super, 1996) in nature, drawing heavily from social cognitive theory (Lent, Brown, & Hackett, 1996).

The first theme to be explored is lessons learned within her family of origin. Frances grew up in a household where her father apparently maintained tight control over the (female) members of the family. A patriarchal pattern of family power is quite common all over the world, although there are wide variations in how this power is sanctioned and exercised (Lips, 1993). It is possible that Frances and her mother and sister regarded her father's autocratic behavior as normative in their cultural background, and thus their (submissive) response as also normative. What Americans may define as overly dependent, Frances and her cultural cohort may define as typical and even preordained by genetics (i.e., "the way women and men were created to be").

Frances has probably been exposed to divergent models for female behavior from the media, school, discussions with peers, and so on. However, her exposure may be quite superficial because of her father's tight reins in the past and her limited peer interactions. I should be aware that models of independent women choosing satisfying life and career roles might seem foreign or conflictual to her.

Alternatively, her family's relationship patterns may be idiosyncratic even within her cultural context. Her father's domination might reflect a pervasive emotional, physical, and/or sexual abuse of all or part of the family. If so, Frances might have been a target, especially if her father viewed her as "defective" because of her disabilities. She might also have been traumatized by observing abuse of her mother or sister. When abuse is part of the picture, healing from its effects can be a long and slow process, and can complicate resolution of career issues.

Whatever the nature of her father's domination – cultural, gender based, abusive, or some combination of the three – Frances has probably experienced years of reinforcement within her family for what we label as dependent behavior. She may, in fact, not view this behavior pattern as problematical. Despite her family's tentative experiments with broadening their world after her father's death, family members may view such dependent behavior as desirable for her in particular, whether because of her sex, age, or disabilities. She may be expressing interest in more autonomous life patterns to please school personnel or to imitate her peers, without any real understanding of the emotional consequences of these choices. Anything that Frances chooses to do now, other than remain at home full time, could challenge her family's familiar mode of functioning to some extent. These issues could further complicate her career development.

A second theme that must be explored is the personal meaningfulness of her statuses as an immigrant and a disabled person. For unspecified reasons, Frances's family emigrated to the U.S. when she was about eight years old. How and why this transition took place probably had an important impact on her life: Did her family see themselves simply as escaping a worse fate, or more optimistically as moving toward a better job or sociocultural environment? Did they move here alone (perhaps strengthening their isolation as a family unit), or did family, friends, or ethnic community members welcome them? Were her parents fearful or hopeful about their lives yet to unfold in the U.S.? This life transition might be expected to have shaped her view of the world, and of her own future in it, as either full of exciting possibilities or rife with potential dangers.

Geographical and cultural uprootings pose challenges to anyone, but perhaps did so particularly for Frances because of her disabilities. There is little information about her disabilities: their precise nature and impact on her educational process; when her disabilities were identified by her school and when she began to receive supportive services; the degree to which her disabilities might be expected to influence her range of career opportunities and subsequent job performance. Children identified with disabilities may have restricted opportunities for career exploration because of their disabilities, and may develop negative worker self-concepts because of others' views about their capabilities

(Kosciulek, 1998). We do know she was able to learn English as a second language and to progress through the school curriculum with some assistance – notable successes in light of her language, cultural, and physical or learning obstacles.

To complete the picture of Frances, what personal strengths and challenges characterize Frances and her career development thus far? Frances was able to survive what must have been a frightening and confusing new world when she emigrated as a child. Whatever personal qualities enabled her to adjust then will be instrumental now to her future career success. Her work ethic is described as strong and her attendance record at school excellent despite her difficulties there. She is able to relate positively to adults and willing to solicit their help. She wants to emulate successful peers. She has a desire to be independent, although it is not clear what independence means to her. Frances has an on-going close relationship with her family. This family support can potentially provide a secure base for her career exploration. It appears that Frances and her family are beginning to stretch the boundaries of their home life now that her father is dead, so this may be an ideal time for her to begin exploring possibilities for herself. Finally, as suggested by her previous behavior with adults, she is likely to be motivated to please me, which may help her undertake difficult tasks in the course of counseling.

As a career counselor, I am particularly concerned about her self-concept, her specific self-efficacy beliefs, and the skills she can utilize to master the career development tasks of growth and exploration now facing her. I hypothesize that Frances may have a predominantly negative view of herself that will impede her ability to find a satisfying and satisfactory place for herself in the world of work. She might be expected to see herself as "dependent" or "helpless," an "outsider," "unattractive" by American standards of adolescent attractiveness, "damaged", and perhaps "dumb" as well. Her life experiences since childhood have probably impeded the development of her confidence in her ability to perform academic, social, or career tasks well. She wants to be like her classmates, may not understand how and why she is not like them now, and may not believe that their popularity and life opportunities are possible for her after all.

My career counseling with Frances would have two purposes common in career counseling: (1) understanding how Frances currently sees herself and her possibilities, and (2) assisting her to expand her occupational self-concept and awareness of congruent options through exploratory activities. These purposes would be particularly complex to accomplish with Frances because of the unique context of her life thus far. I hope to enable her to expand her life horizons while she affirms core cultural values (cf. Fouad & Bingham, 1995). To understand Frances now, I need information about messages about herself as a woman she absorbed from her family and cultural context (see Gysbers, Heppner, & Johnston, 1998); what being "independent" and "adult" means to her; real versus inaccurately imposed limitations posed by her disabilities and "emotional fragility"; what social skills with her peers she currently does and does not possess; the types and limits of interpersonal support available to her from home and other sources (e.g., neighbors or extended family). Frances may need to work on clarifying and modifying her self-perceptions before she implicitly uses them as a foundation for her career decision making. Consultation with school personnel and an expert on disabilities could provide invaluable information. Frances might find it affirming her status as a young adult to participate in these discussions, perhaps considering with me ahead of time what questions she herself might ask to explore her options.

In jump-starting Frances' career exploration, our starting point needs to be her level of career maturity (pre to early adolescence) rather than her chronological age (late adolescence to early adulthood.) Consistent with the planful and progressive nature of career decision making, I must consider what immediate steps she can take to expand her world and personal confidence. Such steps must challenge yet support her emergent sense of personal agency and enthusiasm for her possibilities.

Enlisting her family's support for her career development is likely to be crucial for Frances. Family consultation and counseling appears to be a high-priority career intervention for this client. There are some indications in the case description that her mother may currently oppose Frances' active career exploration. Some of her mother's ambivalence about Frances' evolution into independence might reflect a fear of the potential consequences for Frances and an uncertainty about how to help her effectively. Family sessions could provide essential information about how the family perceives Frances, explore and resolve complex feelings, and may also encourage other members' own tentative steps *toward* an expanded life as well. A family intervention may also help the family realign as a unit after the death of the family head.

Frances needs to discover interesting possibilities for herself through exploration and reality testing. In light of her willingness to consult with adults and her need to improve interpersonal skills, carefully planned assignments involving interactions with others are likely to be most valuable. For example, I would explore with Frances what resources for information and support currently exist in her environment (e.g., church, neighborhood, extended family) and how she might draw on them for information and guidance. She can also begin to expand her peer relationships and skills through challenging and safe activities fostering development of interests (e.g., classes at a local YMCA or volunteer activities). A career exploration group or class offered at a local community college or women's center might also be considered. Family members might even plan some exploration they could do together with Frances, and later provide support for her solo efforts. Throughout the counseling process, I would consider ways of structuring my role to offer her flexible support that could later be provided by individuals within her own environment.

With development of a more positive sense of herself, an ongoing support base within her own world, and awareness of how to explore new possibilities through assuming tolerable (and exciting) risks, Frances should be in a much better position to face her future with optimism and self-confidence.

## References

Fouad, N.A., & Bingham, R.P. (1995). Career counseling with racial and ethnic minorities. In W.B. Walsh & S.H. Osipow (Eds.), *Handbook of vocational psychology* (2nd ed., pp. 331-365). Hillsdale, NJ: Erlbaum.

Gysbers, N.C., Heppner, M.J., & Johnston, J.A. (1998). *Career counseling: Process, issues, and techniques*. Boston, MA: Allyn & Bacon.

Kosciulek, J. (1998). Empowering the life choices of people with disabilities through career counseling. In N.C. Gysbers, M.J. Heppner, & J.A. Johnston, *Career counseling: Process, issues and techniques* (pp. 109-122). Boston, MA: Allyn & Bacon.

Lent, R.W., Brown, S.D., & Hackett, G. (1996). Career development from a social cognitive perspective. In D. Brown, L. Brooks, & Associates, *Career choice and development* (3rd ed., pp. 373-421). San Francisco, CA: Jossey-Bass.

Lips, H.M. (1993). *Sex and gender: An introduction* (2nd ed.). Mountain View, CA: Mayfield.

Super, D.E., Savickas, M.L., & Super, C.M. (1996). The life-span, life-space approach to careers. In D. Brown, L. Brooks, & Associates, *Career choice and development* (3rd ed., pp. 121-178). San Francisco, CA: Jossey-Bass.

# Response to Frances: The Case of the Struggling Senior
## John Patrick
## California University of Pennsylvania
## Donald Thompson
## Troy State University-Montgomery, Alabama

Frances is a 19-year-old female Romanian émigré who presents with multiple disabilities. Although she experiences epileptic seizures, it appears that her seizure activity has been greatly reduced with the use of medication (Tegretol). She has been assessed as learning disabled and with a low normal IQ (94). Frances continues to be heavily dependent on family members and adults when engaged in decision making. She has had difficulty forming and maintaining peer relationships. Additionally, Frances has not been encouraged by family members to become independent. She often displays passivity, a willingness to please others at cost to herself, and emotional frailty when handling normal functions of living. This is suggestive of a poor self-concept.

As a high school senior, Frances is confronted with the inevitable developmental task of choosing to attend postsecondary education or entering into gainful employment. It is quite evident Frances is not yet ready to make such a meaningful vocational decision. Though she maintains a "C" average, Frances has been diagnosed as being two years below grade level in reading and math with specific difficulties in word analysis, reading vocabulary, and math concepts and applications. Frances has no work experience, has minimally participated in exploration of the world of work, and thus has no defined career direction. Though she expresses the intent to matriculate at a local community college, she knows little of the school for which she has applied. Clearly, Frances is in need of further career exploration and improved career decision-making skills.

Perhaps the most compelling thing to consider in career counseling with persons with disabilities is to utilize a career development theory that takes into consideration the vocational challenges experienced as a direct result of the disability. For Frances, an improved self-concept, expanded career awareness, and development of career decision-making skills are the vocational challenges that she is experiencing. Szymanski, Hershenson, Enright, and Ettinger (1996) have identified developmental approaches to career counseling as inclusive of the vocational challenges inherent in the career development of persons with disabilities and thus serve as an appropriate theoretical orientation to career counseling. This is the approach that we will take when career counseling with Frances.

Super (1980) has stressed the importance of the self-concept in career development. A critical feature in helping Frances develop a healthy self-concept is to understand how she views her disabilities. How has Frances incorporated these disabilities into her self-concept? What is her understanding of her functional limitations? Are her disabilities likely to change over time? How has Frances adjusted to multiple disabilities? Before meaningful work can begin on answering these questions, it would be strongly suggested to consult with Frances' physician to provide information with respect to the course of the epilepsy and any functional limitations placed on her that are relevant to career planning. Often persons with disabilities underestimate their physical abilities and cognitively distort their perceptions as to the type of work activities that they can perform and/or career aspirations that they can realistically achieve.

With respect to her identified learning disability, it would be prudent to revisit how this diagnosis was made. Frances came to the United States as a young child, where she has learned English as a second language. Ascher (1990) notes that the assessment of bilingual students through the use of standardized educational and psychological tests may be suspect. The reliability and validity of tests may be undermined by language differences and administering an English language test to non-

English proficient students will assess only English language proficiency, not a subject domain. In many cases the test scores underestimate learning capacity.

Lewelling (1991) states that bilingual students often become proficient in communication skills within a short time after immigration. Often these students are mainstreamed quickly into regular classrooms where they encounter difficulties understanding and completing schoolwork in the more cognitively challenging English needed for successful performance in academic subjects. Cummins (1981) found that non-English speaking immigrants schooled in English since their arrival to Canada took approximately 5-7 years to achieve comparable grade norms on achievement tests as compared to their native-speaking peers. Schwarz and Burt (1995) note that other conditions including limited educational experience, lack of effective study habits, native language interference, or mismatched learning and teaching styles may account for perceived appearance of a learning disability.

It is not clear from the information given if these considerations where ruled out when the initial assessment of Frances' learning disability took place. Instead of relying solely on achievement and intelligence tests that yield little prescriptive information, Frances would benefit from a multiple assessment that includes an interview in her native language (if appropriate) so as to provide information about her previous learning experiences in English and in her native language as well as insight into her functioning in her first language. Schwarz and Burt (1995) indicate that a portfolio assessment in which measurements of learner progress in reading and writing are considered along with attendance data, writing samples, autobiographical information, and work on class assignments would provide more useful information. Ascher (1990) recommends that ascertaining how well one can master new learning and skills with the assistance of a teacher or computer will yield pertinent information in diagnosing a learning disability. If after this assessment Frances is indeed diagnosed with a learning disability, then the challenges placed by this condition will need to be incorporated in future career counseling activities.

At some point in the career counseling process it will be necessary to involve the family. From all appearances it seems that Frances' family is overprotective of her and may be unwilling to let her "fend for herself." It would be useful to explore with the family their attitudes toward Frances' disabled status and concomitant work expectations. In the few times that Frances has attempted to make independent decisions, the family has sabotaged her efforts (i.e., Frances can take driving lessons but won't be allowed to obtain a driver's license, her mother refuses to assist her in filing financial aid papers). What is it that family members fear if Frances becomes more independent? We would want to explore these issues with the family, as they are major impediments to her career development.

It is our contention that much of the overprotectiveness shown to Frances by her family may be culturally driven. In many Eastern European countries, persons with disabilities are not afforded the same status as non-disabled persons. In these countries persons with disabilities are actively discriminated against with few accommodations made to ease functions of daily living. Additionally, Romania was in severe civil unrest during the 1980s. It is known that children who were severely disabled (especially HIV-positive children) were allowed to die or live under inhumane conditions, predominantly in orphanages, throughout Romania during this time period. Given these realities, it would seem that their overprotectiveness of Frances may have been a survival mechanism. In order for Frances to develop a healthy self-concept and make meaningful career decisions, it will be necessary to explore with the family ways for them to let go and allow Frances to become more independent and assertive in planning for her entry into competitive employment. Specifically, the family can be active in this process by allowing Frances to engage in career counseling and transition planning while in high school. They can also encourage her attempts to act independently and make decisions in everyday functions of living. They can also assist Frances by reinforcing social skills, as poor social skills are a leading cause of unemployment for students with disabilities (Beale, 1999).

Frances is in the earliest stages of career development during which career awareness, that is the development of knowledge, values, preferences, and self-perceptions that an individual draws upon in the course of making career-related choices, is being formed (Herr & Cramer, 1992). Salomone (cited in Morningstar, 1997) finds it useful to include in a career intervention at this stage of development, activities that further understanding of self, the relationship between self and the world of work, the career decision-making process, implementing career and educational decisions, and finally adjusting to the world of work.

In furthering an understanding of self, Frances would certainly benefit from participating in activities that focus on identifying her values, needs, interests, abilities, aptitudes, skills, and temperaments. She should also be encouraged to participate in structured experiences that help to build self-confidence and self-esteem (Trenholm, 1994). Learning to handle frustration, understanding that there are multiple approaches to any vocational or educational challenge, and being persistent would be useful for Frances to acquire. Trenholm makes the point that many adolescents with disabilities are dependent, hesitant to undertake new experiences, and often react negatively to past failures, thus leading to poor educational and career choices.

In furthering career exploration, Francis would benefit from participating in career exploration programs that enhances her understanding of the world of work. Given the resistance by the family in allowing Frances the opportunity to drive and engage in part-time employment, the use of a computer-assisted career guidance system, such as DISCOVER, would be useful in furthering her knowledge of the world of work and meet with less resistance from family members. The DISCOVER program enables individuals to progress sequentially or on demand modules that describe the world of work, allows for self-assessment, finding and learning about occupations, making educational choices, and career decision making. It is likely that use of a computer-assisted career guidance system would allow Frances to make more effective career choices.

If Frances and her family will agree, active participation in activities that provide meaningful work experiences would also be useful. Job shadowing, externships, internships, and part-time employment would further her understanding of the world of work.

In summary, Frances is a young woman who is contending with epilepsy and possibly a learning disability. Her family is overprotective and she is dependent upon family members and adults to make life decisions for her. She appears to have a poorly formed self-concept and has participated only minimally in career awareness and exploration activities. Employing a developmental approach to career counseling, the primary focus of our interventions is to work with Frances in improving her self-concept, to explore the world of work more actively, become better able to make career decisions, and to enable family members to become less protective of Frances and encourage her to become more independent as she makes the transition from high school to either postsecondary education or work.

## References

Ascher, C. (1990). *Assessing bilingual students for placement and instruction* (ERIC/CUE Digest No. 65). New York: ERIC Clearinghouse on Urban Education, Teachers College, Columbia University. (ERIC Document Reproduction Service No. ED 322 273)

Beale, A.V. (1999). Career planning guidelines for parents of students with mild disabilities. *Clearing House, 72*(3), 179-181.

Cummins, J. (1981). *The role of primary language development in promoting educational success for language minority students: A theoretical framework*. Los Angeles, CA: National Dissemination Center.

Herr, E.L. & Cramer, S.H. (1992). *Career guidance and counseling through the lifespan.* (4th ed.). New York: Harper Collins.

Lewelling, V.W. (1991). *Academic achievement in a second language.* (ERIC Digest 73). Washington, DC: ERIC Clearinghouse on Languages and Linguistics, Center for Applied Lingusitics. (ERIC Document Reproduction Service No. ED 329 130)

Morningstar, M.E. (1997). Critical issues in career development and employment preparation for adolescents with disabilities. *Remedial & Special Education, 18*, 307-320.

Schwarz, R., & Burt, M. (1995). *ESL instruction for learning disabled adults.* (ERIC Digest). Washington, DC: Adjunct ERIC Clearinghouse for ESL Literacy Education, Center for Applied Linguistics. (ERIC Document Reproduction Service No. ED 379 966)

Super, D.E. (1980). A life-span, life-space approach to career development. *Journal of Vocational Behavior, 16*, 282-298.

Szymanski, E.M., Hershenson, D.B., Enright, M.S., & Ettinger, J.M. (1996). Career development theories, constructs and research: Implications for people with disabilities. In E.M. Szymanski & R.M. Parker (Eds.), *Work and disability: Issues and strategies in career development and job placement* (pp. 79-117). Austin, TX: PRO-ED.

Trenholm, J. (1994). Career development for individuals with learning disabilities: A process approach. *Guidance & Counselling, 9*, 15-19.

# ARIN: THE CASE OF THE UNDECIDED QUARTERBACK

Arin, a 19-year-old African American gay male, presents for career counseling during the second semester of his sophomore year in college. He is the second of four children and grew up in a large city in the western U.S. In his initial appointment he states that he has not given much serious consideration to "life after college" and that he feels "confused" about his career goals. As the starting quarterback for the university's football team, Arin had always thought he would play professional football. An injury and lackluster performance in the past season, however, have left him feeling less confident about his ability to achieve this goal. He reports feeling "overwhelmed" and "doubtful" that he will be able to identify a suitable occupational alternative to professional football.

Arin has a high grade point average (3.6 out of a possible 4.0) and has taken a wide variety of courses without declaring a college major. He is very personable and reports interests in math, literature, and music (he has played the piano since elementary school). He is also very involved in community service and is a mentor for two junior high school students.

From his comments, it is clear that Arin has high expectations for himself. He now feels very anxious because he is not sure what he wants to do. Arin's parents are educators. His mother is employed as a high school math teacher and his father is employed as a high school principal. Arin reports that he took the Self-Directed Search in high school and remembers that he scored highest in occupations in the Social and Investigative categories. His goal for career counseling is to identify an occupation that can give him a level of satisfaction similar to what he experienced as an athlete.

## *Response to Arin: The Case of the Undecided Quarterback*
## *Jeffrey P. Prince*
## *University of California at Berkeley*

The case of Arin is a rich example of the complex challenges that confront career counselors of young adults. Although Arin's situation is comprised of a combination of issues unique to him, his questions and doubts also exemplify some common themes critical to the career development of traditional-age college students. In the following response, I will highlight these themes. In addition, I will address some of the specific issues Arin is facing and offer some suggestions for intervention. First, I will discuss some possible goals for counseling, along with the theoretical models I would follow. Next, I will highlight what appear to be the central issues for Arin and will provide examples of questions and interventions I might use. Finally, I will comment on the overall structure of the counseling process itself.

### Establishing Counseling Goals

His stated goal for counseling is "to identify an occupation that can give him a level of satisfaction similar to what he experienced as an athlete." However, a number of additional pieces of information would be important to gather before we agreed upon this or any other preliminary goal for counseling. Specifically, I would want to clarify any additional expectations for counseling, discuss any previous counseling experiences, and learn more about how he came to seek counseling at this particular time (e.g., was he self-referred, or referred by a coach, parent, or college advisor?). This information would help to assess his level of motivation for counseling and to identify particular attitudes that may help or hinder our establishing a working a relationship. Then we could proceed to evaluate the degree to which his stated objective is appropriate or achievable as a preliminary goal.

An initial step would be to discuss directly Arin's stated counseling goal. I would try to demonstrate empathy for his situation and acknowledge the difficulty in suddenly doubting his competence and direction. However, I would also question whether "identifying an occupation" is the remedy. I would point out that he has a number of decisions ahead of him, that selecting an occupation may be one of them, but that there are other, intermediate decisions and tasks as well. College students often feel pressure to choose an occupation or career before they have enough experience or readiness to do so. In fact, Arin's first choice appears to be choosing a college major that could later lead to a number of different career decisions. Helping Arin to separate these decisions could help to reduce some of the "overwhelmed" feelings he is experiencing.

However, in addition to the typical developmental academic and career issues confronting a college sophomore, a number of complex issues are raised in Arin's situation. Each could provide a focus for career counseling: his sexual orientation, his racial identity, and his role as a student athlete. Since all of these issues concern Arin's identity development, they are not independent of one another. However, for the purpose of highlighting how each might contribute to his dilemma, I will discuss each separately.

## Central Issues

### Sexual Orientation

Arin is described as a gay male, but no detail is provided about the possible impact of his sexual orientation on his career situation. It is not uncommon for a discussion of a college student's sexual orientation to be left out of the career counseling process. This may be due to the generally invisible nature of sexual orientation or to discomfort on the part of the client or the counselor. Nevertheless, sexual identity can be a critical variable to an individual's career development. I would hypothesize that Arin's sexual identity is inextricably linked to his racial identity and his identity as an athlete.

I might begin by gathering more information about Arin's history of sexual identity development – specifically the degree to which he has personally and publicly integrated his gay identity. I would ask such questions as: When did he first acknowledge to himself and others that he was gay? To what degree is he connected to social and emotional supports that affirm a positive gay identity? How do his parents and siblings react to his being gay? Answers to such questions would help me assess the degree to which he is comfortable and proud of his sexual orientation and to understand how his development as a gay man has affected his past and current career decisions and goals. For example, I would explore when he first came out (publicly acknowledged himself to someone as a gay man), and how this process affected his life, academically and otherwise. It is common for individuals to begin exploring their sexual orientation during their undergraduate college years (Evans & Levine, 1990). However, confronting social stigma, risking rejection from friends or family, and establishing new support systems and relationships can sometimes disrupt an individual's academic progress (Rhoads, 1995; Prince, 1995). It is conceivable that Arin's recent lackluster athletic performance, decreased confidence, and lack of focus relate to a recent exploration of his sexual identity. I would also explore the extent to which his level of self-confidence and his limited exploration of interests, values, and skills may be due to negative cultural stereotypes about gay men. For example, are his doubts about finding a suitable profession partially due to concerns about employment discrimination or to beliefs about barriers to certain career opportunities?

Effective career interventions for gay men often involve going beyond traditional career development interventions (Pope, 1995). With Arin, for example, I might focus upon connecting him to environments and people who would affirm his sexual orientation. The goal would be to provide support for managing the stigma and isolation that accompany most gay men as they approach various tasks of career development. I would suggest, for instance, that he investigate campus support groups for undergraduate gay men and social and political student organizations focused on lesbian, gay, and bisexual concerns. In addition, I would try to connect him with gay male role models and mentors in both athletic and non-athletic career fields so that he could begin to widen his awareness of career options and challenge any stereotypic beliefs that may be limiting his goals. In time, I might also direct him to print and Internet-based career resources that identify and describe the degree to which particular businesses, organizations, and graduate programs offer "gay-friendly" policies and practices.

### Racial Identity

As an African American gay male, Arin is managing a dual minority status. I would discuss with him the pressures as well as strengths that he experiences as a result. For example, does he feel torn between identifying as an African American man versus a gay man as he seeks out support systems and clarifies his values and needs? Also, has he experienced discrimination not only from the majority culture, but from either group toward the other, and how has this influenced his career aspirations or his perceptions of barriers to success? I would try to help Arin to articulate how membership in each group may have influenced his exploration of interests, values, and skills. I would also attempt to highlight the strengths he has built from managing a dual minority status within a majority culture. In other words, I would explore how his racial identity development has influenced his career identity development in ways similar to those described for his sexual identity development. In doing so, I would aim toward clarifying his values as they relate to his family, culture, or religion and examine any conflicts they present to him. For example, does his possible rejection of an athletic career cause conflict with his parents' aspirations for him? Does he experience conflict in defining what would be a successful lifestyle or career as he considers his family's values or religious beliefs? In addition, I would help Arin evaluate the extent to which he might find support from African American student organizations, and particularly from connections with other gay, lesbian, or bisexual African American students.

### Role as a Student Athlete

Even if Arin's injury heals, his performance improves, and he reconsiders a career in professional sports, he could benefit from exploring alternate career paths nevertheless. He needs to prepare for his career direction whenever his athletic career ends, whether that be at graduation or at some later time. Like many student athletes, he has not explored a broad range of career options to this point, even though he appears to have interests and skills in a range of Social, Investigative, and Artistic domains. The role of counseling, therefore, might be to encourage him to explore a variety of academic and career options and to clarify the values, needs, interests, and skills that are important to him. To do this, I would first try to identify what specifically he found satisfying as an athlete. I would also attempt to point out the strengths he has already developed as an athlete: the skills, abilities, and personal characteristics that are transferable to other career fields and to the career decision-making task itself. In addition, I would explore what motivates his athletic aspirations and discuss specific experiences he has had as a gay male athlete. Given the homophobic environment of the typical campus athletic department, I would question how he managed to cope with overt or covert discrimination from peers and coaches. I would also explore how these experiences may have affected his self-confidence and career goals. For example, did he cope by pleasing others for external validation and keeping his sexual identity secret? If so, at what cost? Role models of gay-identified professional or student athletes are not common, so it would be difficult to connect Arin with supportive individuals or mentors in similar circumstances. However, should he decide to stay in an athletic career, he may need additional support such as ongoing or intermittent counseling, or a close relationship with a coach, athletic advisor, or ally who is gay supportive.

## Counseling Process

I have outlined several of Arin's issues in isolation from each other for the purpose of highlighting the possible significance of each. However, the course of counseling would involve addressing these themes concurrently and gradually over the course of time. I would attempt to create a safe and welcoming environment to encourage him to discuss issues that he might find sensitive or that he may not have expected to discuss in the context of career counseling. Early in counseling, I would focus on developing rapport and gaining his confidence. For example, I would attempt to demonstrate an understanding of the three issues outlined above, through carefully crafting questions that demonstrated I had some expert knowledge of these concerns. My office environment might also encourage his trust through books, artwork, or other objects that reflect my multicultural and gay affirmative values.

I would be cautious about introducing career testing tools with Arin; their use has come under increased scrutiny for use with individuals of socially oppressed groups (Betz, & Fitzgerald, 1995). I would be interested in evaluating further his Holland type and exploring his personality and values in some detail. However, before suggesting he complete formal assessment tools, I would investigate carefully his past experiences and current attitudes with testing. For example, he may have had negative experiences or may have current fears of being labeled or inappropriately classified by instruments designed primarily on White, heterosexual samples. If we did proceed with assessments, I would select them cautiously, to ensure the items are not heterosexist (Prince, 1997) and that reference samples are culturally relevant. Also, during the interpretation, I would rely on him to confirm the accuracy of scores, rather than allow him to assume the instruments automatically reflected the truth.

No one theoretical model fully accounts for the range of interventions I have proposed for Arin. However, my work with Arin would draw primarily upon three theoretical approaches: (1) self-efficacy theory (Lent, Brown, & Hackett, 1994), to evaluate how his past experiences and his current beliefs may influence his self-confidence, career aspirations, and goals; (2) developmental theory (Super, 1990) to assess how he has confronted the developmental tasks and challenges of a college student and to target goals appropriate to his developmental level; and (3) person-environment fit theory (Rounds & Tracey, 1990) to evaluate his need for information about himself and about career and academic options and to prepare for decision making. In combination, these theories offer a broad platform for framing how his sexual identity, racial identity, and his identity as a student athlete might influence his career development and decision making.

## References

Betz, N.E. & Fitzgerald, L.F. (1995). Career assessment and interventions with racial and ethnic minorities. In F.T. Leong (Ed.), *Career development and vocational behavior of racial and ethnic minorities* (pp. 263-279). Mahwah, NJ: Erlbaum.

Evans, N., & Levine, H. (1990). Perspectives on sexual orientation. In L.V. Moore (Ed.), *Evolving theoretical perspectives on students: New directions for student services*. (pp. 49-58). San Francisco, CA: Jossey-Bass.

Lent, R.W., Brown, S.D., & Hackett, G. (1994). Toward a unifying social cognitive theory of career and academic interest, choice, and performance. *Journal of Vocational Behavior, 45*, 79-122.

Pope, M. (1995). Career interventions for gay and lesbian clients: A synopsis of practice knowledge and research needs. *Career Development Quarterly, 44*, 191-203.

Prince, J.P. (1995). Influences on the career development of gay men. *Career Development Quarterly, 44*, 168-177.

Prince, J.P. (1997). Career assessment with lesbian, gay and bisexual individuals. *Journal of Career Assessment, 5* (2), 225-238.

Rhoads, R.A. (1995). Learning from the coming-out experiences of college males. *Journal of College Student Development, 36,* 67-74.

Rounds, J.B. & Tracey, T.J. (1990). From trait-and-factor to person-environment fit counseling: Theory and process. In W.B. Walsh & S.H. Osipow (Eds.). *Career counseling: Contemporary topics in vocational psychology* (pp.1-44). Hillsdale, NJ: Erlbaum.

Super, D.E. (1990). A life-span, life-space approach to career development. In D. Brown, L. Brooks & Associates, *Career choice and development* (2nd ed., pp. 197-261). San Francisco, CA: Jossey-Bass.

# Response to Arin: The Case of the Undecided Quarterback
## Elizabeth Toepfer-Hendey and Jack R. Rayman
## The Pennsylvania State University

### Initial Impressions and Suggested Inquiries

Arin presents as a bright and involved college student who is overwhelmed and anxious about identifying career goals due to a "shattering" of his dreams to become a professional athlete. Career counselors working in university settings often counsel students dealing with the range of factors related to Arin's career dilemma. However, in Arin's case, as with any other student, plans for career intervention will be specific to his unique needs and subjective experience. The following information would be sought to clarify the nature of Arin's career concerns in order to focus the career intervention.

Areas that would be helpful to learn about include his developmental stage, affective experience, and interrelated factors that contribute to his personal and career development. Arin reports that he feels "overwhelmed," "doubtful," and "very anxious." As a 19-year-old sophomore, his anxiety may be related to tasks specific to his developmental stage. Arin is most likely in the exploration stage of his career development process (Super, 1957) and is navigating individuation in early adulthood. Further information about his personal and career identity, such as his current relationship with his family, could reveal what has influenced his current concerns. Is he experiencing pressure, conflict, or support from his family regarding his current situation? If so, how is he managing the situation? Have feelings about the current situation led him to reconsider a future and identity for himself that is different than his or his family's expectations? Further questioning could reveal what issues are underlying these emotions and if planned, career interventions might also include discussion of family issues and anxiety management techniques.

Investigating specific components of Arin's identity would be particularly helpful in planning interventions. It is clear that an important part of Arin's identity has been as an athlete. Further information about whether Arin is attending a NCAA Division I, II, or III university, if his injury is career threatening, and the type of feedback received from coaches and teammates regarding his athletic abilities would help the counselor to assess the realistic nature of Arin's career dream. Arin has "always thought he would play professional football" and fully investigating his identity as an athlete would be helpful. When did Arin begin to identify himself as a professional athlete and has he had other career dreams for himself? Have Arin's career development and career decision-making skills been delayed or underdeveloped due to an early exclusive identity as an athlete? Finally, what components of athletics have been most satisfying to him?

Arin's experiences as a gay African American male may also influence his career development. Understanding Arin's racial identity development and how this has shaped his experiences of the world and vision of possible career options is crucial. From a middle class and educated family, what types of African American role models has he had? Has he perceived racial discrimination and has this influenced his perceptions of career opportunities? Are Arin's interests in athletics a true reflection of his preferences, or do they reflect a culturally stereotypic perception of high-paying occupations open to African Americans? In addition, Arin's feelings about his sexuality and how this has influenced his self-identity would be crucial to investigate. At what stage is Arin in his sexual identity development? Has Arin "come out" to family and peers or is he "passing" as a heterosexual in some component of his life? Has he experienced or witnessed the homophobia of others and has this influenced his career exploration, decision making, or career choice? What is his experience in the African American community as a gay man? Investigating how his development as an African American man has been shaped by the sex role expectations of his family, culture, and environment may also be useful. Understanding Arin's racial and sexual identity status and development would allow the counselor to plan interventions that would match his individual and sociocultural career development needs.

Finally, other major areas of inquiry would be to ascertain Arin's awareness of his own abilities, interests, values, decision-making style, and knowledge of the world of work and the career planning process. Arin has apparent abilities in athletics, academics, music and social activities and his high expectations may indicate past success in these and other areas. Further investigation into his interests, abilities, and other attributes could be gained through discussion of previous satisfying and meaningful courses, experiences, work, and volunteer activities. A discussion of his decision-making style would inform interventions that would further his career planning and decision-making skills.

## Career Counseling Plans and Interventions

Arin's goal for career counseling is to "identify an occupation that can give him a level of satisfaction similar to what he experienced as an athlete." He has come to counseling as a second-semester sophomore and is not only experiencing stress related to a disappointing athletic experience, but is possibly feeling pressure to quickly choose a major. One goal for counseling would be to encourage Arin to engage in career exploration behaviors, such as self-assessment, exploration of the world of work, increasing the use of decision-making strategies and job-seeking skills, and linking self-awareness with knowledge about the world of work. Other goals would be to assist Arin in identifying a range of occupations that may lead to satisfaction and to identify a major that will allow him to move toward these occupations.

Plans for career counseling would include processes and activities that would address the three phases of career counseling as outlined by Spokane (1991): beginning, activation, and termination, as well as tasks specific to the career development paradigm (Rayman, 1993). In the beginning work with Arin, attention to developing the counseling relationship and establishing trust and support would occur in conjunction with clarifying expectations, offering structure and information about the process of career counseling, and contracting regarding planned activities. Holland (1985), among others, has indicated the importance of assessing difficulties in decision making in order to plan interventions. Completing "My Vocational Situation" (MVS) (Holland, Daiger, & Power, 1980) may help Arin to identify possible difficulties in making career decisions, including the need for information or training, lack of vocational identity, and personal or environmental barriers. Self administered and hand scored, the MVS would allow the counselor to quickly assess Arin's career decision making needs, involve Arin in the process, and provide a simple framework for more extensive discussion regarding the career decision-making process.

During the beginning work with Arin, plans and strategies should be informed by the interaction of personal and environmental factors influencing Arin's career development. Super's (Super, Savickas, & Super, 1996) life-span, life-space developmental approach highlights the need to consider Arin's developmental stage and current and future life roles. Arin is in the exploration stage of career development, which corresponds with separation and individuation in early adulthood (Chickering, 1969). In order to support Arin's development as an adult, sensitivity to his needs for autonomy as well as connection to his family and peers should inform career counseling interventions.

Cultural and individual values and needs regarding autonomy and connection should be assessed and respected. Delayed career development can be a risk factor for athletes (Murphy, Petitpas, & Brewer, 1996) and his decision to become an athlete early in life may have precluded continued exploration in a wider range of career fields. However, Arin's continued involvement in activities outside of athletics (academics, music, volunteer opportunities) provides evidence that exploration of other interests, and perhaps life roles, has occurred. Encouraging Arin to continue already begun self-assessment and exploration of career and life roles through school, part-time work, and leisure activities could address his developmental identity needs by assisting him in defining valued roles.

Attending to cultural, social, and individual differences that influence Arin's and the counselor's expectations and attitudes toward counseling is crucial. The counselor's and Arin's racial and sexual identity status would guide the level of involvement in the counseling session and type of intervention (Helms, 1990). Discussions about Arin's identity as an African American gay athlete could provide valuable information about his racial and sexual identity status. His exposure to career role models, cultural influences, and discrimination experienced as a gay African American male may have affected his perceptions of career options. Information about the impact of Arin's "outness" on his identity development, social support network, and career exploration behavior would also inform the counselor about planned interventions. If Arin is experiencing difficulty in accepting himself or dealing with the reactions of others, it may be that the career counseling work should be conducted in conjunction with or be proceeded by individual personal counseling to assist in this process. However, even if he reports comfort with his identity (which we will assume for this case study), continued sensitivity to the impact of social variables related to this issue and his career development is important. Continued attention to Arin's needs related to his sexual and racial identity throughout the counseling process will be essential.

Arin expressed that he has "not given much serious consideration to 'life after college'" and it may be helpful to explore his career and life aspirations. A fantasy exercise focusing on career and lifestyle "daydreams" (Spokane, 1991) could assist Arin in increasing his self-awareness and identifying his lifestyle and career goals, while providing an avenue for discussion of perceived limitations or conflicts.

This technique may unearth feelings about his "loss of a dream" to become an athlete. The counselor could attend to and empathize with his reactions, feelings, and thoughts about a possible change in his dreams and concerns that the career intervention process will require some work. This might lead to Arin feeling increased anxiety, and when appropriate, it would be helpful to continue the "activation" stage of career counseling and encourage self-assessment and career exploration.

To foster self-understanding and to broaden his perspective about other career options, assessing Arin's attributes, such as his interests would be warranted. Utilizing John Holland's (1985, 1996) typology the counselor could encourage Arin to broaden his career exploration. Arin's previous experience of taking the Self-Directed Search (SDS) indicates that he may have some knowledge about Holland's theory. Arin's results on the SDS, as well as his reported interests, academic courses, and volunteer activities, provide evidence that he may have stronger interests in the "Social" and "Investigative" categories. However, he appears to have had difficulty making the link between how interests relate to careers. Helping Arin to understand how his current interests, in combination with his preferred abilities, may link to the world of work may be facilitated by having Arin complete another inventory that categorizes interests into the Holland typology. The Strong Interest Inventory (SII) (Harmon et al., 1994) would be a viable choice.

The results of the SII would allow Arin to further understand how his interests correspond with individuals already correspond to his Theme Code. He would also be able to explore how his Theme Code relates to his parents' occupations and examine how his interests and satisfaction in athletics are congruent with his range of interests. His results on the SII would also be discussed in relation to the values, decision-making styles, his previous SDS scores, and other information that he has discussed to this point.

Studies of the use of the SII with African Americans have shown general comparable validity and counseling implications (Lattimore & Borgen, 1999; Fouad, Harmon, & Hansen, 1994), with some limitations. For example, Arin's experiences as an African American gay male would be important to consider throughout the assessment and "activation" process. Fouad, et al. (1994) suggest that African Americans may be cautious or suspicious about the assessment process. To assist Arin, the counselor could speak with him directly about these concerns, explain the use of the SII as a means for exploration, and share with Arin information about the numbers of African/Americans in the norm sample. In addition, the counselor must be aware that between and within differences by race on the SII and in Holland's typology may influence the results. For example, on the SII, African American men and women have been found to like religious activities more than other races (Harmon, Hansen, Borgen, & Hammer, 1994). African Americans have also been found to be over-represented in the Social category and underrepresented in the Investigative category (Holland, 1979). It would be important to discuss with Arin if the Social category feels "true" to him or if it is more likely a reflection of his socialization that only certain occupations may be available to him as an African American.

The use of the SII may also be combined with other exercises that could assist Arin in his self-assessment. For example, a values exercise, such as a ranking list, may facilitate his understanding of the influence of his own and other's values. The Myers-Briggs Type Indicator (1985) could assist him in understanding his personality style and its relation to the world of work. Completing an exercise such as SkillScan (1993), a card sort exercise that categorizes clients' preferred and transferable skills, could assess Arin's self-perceived abilities.

As Arin's self-awareness grows, the counselor could encourage him to investigate the world of work more actively. For example, assigning a homework assignment such as identifying three to six occupations to investigate in the Occupational Outlook Handbook (1998) and discussing how they match what Arin now knows about himself would be helpful. A personable and socially oriented person, Arin could also investigate the relationship between majors and identified occupations by conducting informational interviews with individuals in the workforce. Assisting him in identifying and interviewing individuals who may share his African American heritage and/or sexual identity might also be of benefit. Rehearsal within a session of information-gathering techniques would facilitate Arin's skills and provide the opportunity to discuss any concerns related to the process. As Arin gathers information and continually links what he learns about careers and majors with what he knows about himself, assessment of decision-making strategies, conflicts, and barriers to decisions and occupational options would continue. Assessing and perhaps enlisting family and peer support in the career exploration tasks might be helpful in assisting with barriers and conflicts that might arise.

As Arin continues in this process, decisions regarding a future career path and a possible major are likely to emerge. As "termination" of career counseling begins, Arin may make a decision regarding his major and may have identified several possible career paths. The counselor may now want to speak with Arin about continued experiential exploration regarding his career goals. For example, discussing the benefits of internships or part-time work experiences would encourage Arin to continue to develop his career exploration and implementation skills. Discussing with Arin his short-term goals for exploration, discussing resources and support networks to be used and other future plans would all be helpful to Arin in his ongoing career development. Finally, reviewing with Arin the career decision-making skills and strategies that he has learned in career counseling would facilitate recognition of skills that he can continue to use to further his personal career development throughout life.

# References

Chickering, A. (1969). *Education and identity*. San Francisco, CA: Jossey-Bass.

Fouad, N.A., Harmon, L.W., & Ansen, J.C. (1994). Cross-cultural use of the Strong. In Harmon, L.W., Hansen, J.C., Borgen, F.H., & Hammer, A.L. *Strong Interest Inventory: Applications and technical guide*. Palo Alto, CA: Consulting Psychologists Press.

Harmon, L.W., Hansen, J.C., Borgen, F.H., & Hammer, A.L. (1994). *Strong Interest Inventory: Applications and technical guide*. Palo Alto, CA: Consulting Psychologists Press.

Helms, J.E. (Ed.) (1990). *Black and white racial identity: Theory, research, and practice*. New York: Greenwood.

Holland, J.L. (1979). *Professional manual for the Self-Directed Search*. Palo Alto, CA: Consulting Psychologists Press.

Holland, J.L. (1985). *Making vocational choices: A theory of careers* (2nd ed.). Englewood Cliffs, NJ: Prentice Hall.

Holland, J.L. (1996). Exploring careers with a typology: What we have learned and some new directions. *American Psychologist, 51,* 397-406.

Holland, J.L., Daiger, C.D., & Power, P.G. (1980). *My Vocational Situation*. Palo Alto, CA: Consulting Psychologists Press.

Lattimore, R.R. & Borgen, F.H. (1999). Validity of the 1994 Strong Interest Inventory with racial and ethnic groups in the United States. *Journal of Counseling Psychology, 46,* 2, 185-195.

Murphy, G.M., Petitpas, A.J., Brewer, B.W. (1996). Identity foreclosure, athletic identity, and career maturity in intercollegiate athletes. *Sport Psychologist, 10*(3), 239-246.

*Occupational outlook handbook, 1998-1999*. Bureau of Labor Statistics, U.S. Department of Labor (1998). Indianapolis, IN: JIST Works.

Rayman, J.R. (Ed.) (1993). *The changing role of career services*. San Francisco, CA: Jossey-Bass.

Spokane, A.R. (1991). *Career intervention*. Englewood Cliffs, NJ: Prentice Hall.

Super, D.E. (1957). *The psychology of careers*. New York: Harper and Row.

Super, D.E., Savickas, M.L., Super, C.M. (1996). The life-span, life-space approach to careers. In D. Brown, L. Brooks & Associates. *Career choice and development: Applying contemporary theories to practice* (3rd ed., pp. 121-178). San Francisco, CA: Jossey-Bass.

# KATHY: THE CASE OF THE EXPLORING ENVIRONMENTALIST

Kathy is a 20-year-old junior at a large Midwestern university. She was the youngest of three children and was raised by her mother who had divorced her father when Kathy was 18. Her mother said that she was just waiting for the youngest one to get out of the house before she filed for divorce. She attended an urban parochial high school in the Midwest.

She has come to the university's career center to get some help in making a career decision. During her first session with the career counselor, Kathy talks about a number of occupations she has considered. She likes to write and has thought about working as a journalist or a researcher. She is also very concerned about the environment, but she is not aware of any occupations that would allow her to be involved in environmental issues. She also likes working with children and elderly people and wants to know how she can tie these interests into her career. She has considered the possibility of going to law school because it seems like a "smart thing to do."

Her struggle to make a career decision is also reflected in the difficulty she has experienced in selecting an academic major. After "trying out" several possibilities, Kathy decided to major in history and French. She is not involved in any extracurricular or community activities.

Kathy presents herself in a confident way. She is very talkative and animated and seems at ease throughout the session. Her primary concern is identifying what career would be best for her and she does not make reference to anything beyond her interests. Toward the end of the first session, she asks you about how you got into counseling because it is another occupation that interests her.

## Response to Kathy: The Case of the Exploring Environmentalist
### Expanding the Context
### Darrell Anthony Luzzo
### National Career Assessment Services, Inc.

It has always been a challenging exercise for me to provide a response to cases that are presented in a narrative format. Without the opportunity to engage in first-hand interactions with a client, I find it difficult to form concrete images of the client's presenting issues and concerns. I believe the role that nonverbal cues (e.g., body language, inflection of voice) plays in the communication of a client's needs and concerns is vital to the therapeutic relationship. As such, proposing plans for the provision of career counseling services to a client whom I have never met seems premature (to say the least). Nevertheless, I realize that the scope of this exercise is to simply provide a snapshot view of the strategies and techniques that have become a part of my career counseling repertoire based on previous clinical experiences with clients and theoretical and empirical foundations of vocational psychology. Therefore, despite the challenge of forming impressions of someone about whom I know very little, I offer the following response to the case of Kathy, the exploring environmentalist.

### Initial Images of Kathy

One of the initial images I formed about Kathy as I read her case is that she seems to be the type of client with whom establishing a therapeutic relationship should be relatively straightforward. In my work with clients, I have discovered that developing a strong therapeutic relationship often plays a major role in determining the overall effectiveness of the career counseling experience. Because Kathy sought career counseling services on her own accord and seems animated about participating in the counseling experience, it seems likely to me that developing therapeutic trust, establishing a working alliance, and making a commitment to achieve specific therapeutic goals will naturally emerge from early counseling interactions with Kathy.

A second image I formed about Kathy after reading her case is that she seems genuinely interested in narrowing her career options. Although it appears that Kathy may believe there is only one true occupation/career in the world that will bring her satisfaction and success, she also seems to approach the career exploration and planning process with an understanding that she possesses multiple work-related interests. As such, I would expect Kathy to identify her primary goal of career counseling to be narrowing her options to a few career areas/occupations that are worthy of more sustained exploration.

The other initial impression I made about Kathy was based less on the information provided in the case summary and more directly associated with a personal bias I have regarding the impact that the divorce of one's parents can have on many facets of one's life – including (but certainly not limited to) career decision making. Although I cannot be sure based on the limited information provided in the case study description, it seems at least probable that Kathy may have been affected by the recent divorce of her parents.

## Additional Information to Learn about the Client

When providing career counseling services, I almost universally focus my early work with clients by engaging in a process that I refer to as "expanding the context." What this essentially refers to is my desire to join the client in constructing a more complete picture of her or his background and life experiences. If I were to engage in career counseling with Kathy, I would begin by expanding the context of her current life/career situation. I would start this process by asking Kathy to talk about the influence of family relationships on her career decision making. As alluded to earlier, I would be sure to inquire about the effect the divorce of Kathy's parents has had on her life.

I also would want to talk with Kathy about previous paid and unpaid work experiences, including any volunteer work that she has done. Because she is not currently involved "in any extracurricular or community activities," it also would be important to talk with Kathy about the role of leisure and nonwork activities in her life. It's hard to imagine someone with absolutely no extracurricular or community involvement; therefore, it seems important to determine why this might be the case.

As part of the expansion of the context, I also would want to ask Kathy about the importance of culture in her life. This would include a discussion of the roles that spirituality and racial/ethnic identity play in her life as well as a discussion of the core life values that she possesses. I would want Kathy to discuss her perceptions regarding her role as daughter and sister as well as her thoughts regarding what it has meant to grow up as a girl. I also would want to talk with Kathy about her early career dreams and interests.

## Plans for Career Counseling: The Importance of Theoretical Foundation and Collaboration

Early in my professional career I probably would have found myself desperately wanting to "solve" Kathy's present dilemma in a very focused fashion – maybe even trying to work with Kathy to discover (or possibly even create) that one perfect career for her to pursue. Odds are that I would have tried to figure out the occupational field that offered Kathy the most direct link between her interests and values and the world-of-work. I might have focused exclusively on her apparent artistic and social interests and tried to help her identify the "ideal career." It is not that there is anything unethical about wanting to help a client determine careers that might be congruent with her or his self-concept, but over the years I have learned that there is much more to the career counseling process than matching an individual's vocational self-concept to specific occupations.

As I alluded to earlier, I believe that it is critical for career counselors to establish a strong therapeutic relationship with their clients. My early work with Kathy would be focused on establishing a therapeutic environment in which Kathy would feel safe, supported, and free to discuss issues in an honest, open manner. Similarly, I would endeavor to be genuine with Kathy, "in the moment," and committed to collaborating with her in developing counseling goals and determining appropriate strategies to be used for accomplishing those goals.

Without knowing the additional contextual information that I would have explored in my first session with Kathy, it is difficult for me to outline the precise counseling strategies that I might propose for Kathy's consideration. However, it is likely that I would work with Kathy in a very collaborative fashion to accomplish at least three major tasks: (1) determine the outcome(s) of our work together that she would like to accomplish; (2) increase Kathy's self-awareness (i.e., vocational self-concept) regarding her work-related interests, abilities, and values; and (3) consider the role of contextual factors in Kathy's career decision making and assist her in preparing for and incorporating those contextual factors into her career development. In carrying out these three tasks, I would be operating from a theoretical model that incorporates ideas forwarded by Charles C. Healy (1990), Donald E. Super (Super, Savickas, & Super, 1996), and the recently developed Social Cognitive Career Theory (SCCT; Lent, Brown, & Hackett, 1996).

In determining what the specific goals of our work together might be, I would want to serve as a collaborator in helping Kathy to identify those outcomes she would like to accomplish. Several years ago, UCLA professor Charles C. Healy (1990) outlined a process by which counselors and clients work together to determine the goals of counseling treatment and the methods/strategies that will be used to achieve those goals. I have found this perspective to be particularly effective in working with college students. They often appreciate the opportunity to maintain a sense of control over and responsibility for the career counseling process. Because Kathy is motivated to participate in career counseling, it seems likely that she would appreciate the opportunity to collaborate in the process of outlining counseling goals and expected outcomes.

Based on the limited information provided in the case study, it also seems likely that Kathy would benefit from increased self-awareness (i.e., vocational self-concept) regarding her work-related interests, abilities, and values. For many years, Donald E. Super and his colleagues have discussed the importance of implementing one's vocational self-concept when making career decisions (Super, Savickas, & Super, 1996). Assuming that Kathy would agree, I would invite her to consider a variety of methods that might be used to provide her with increased self-awareness. I would be sure to inform Kathy of computer-assisted career guidance (CACG) systems that might be used to provide an evaluation of work-relevant interests, abilities, and values. I also would provide Kathy with brief descriptions of the several paper-pencil inventories that are available for self-evaluation of interests, abilities, and values. I would want to create a context wherein Kathy could select for herself the particular inventories that she wants to complete and the particular method (computer vs. paper/pencil vs. clinical assessment) she wants to use.

It would also be important for me to teach Kathy about the career decision-making process. I believe that we offer clients a valuable service by providing them with information about the career decision-making process itself. In fact, I consider one of my primary duties as a career counselor to be a teacher, directly instructing clients on the various factors that ought to be considered when engaging in the career exploration and planning process. My goal is to teach clients the process of decision making so that they can apply relevant principles of decision making to future career decisions as well as to other aspects of their lives.

The other broad goal that I would expect Kathy to agree to incorporate into our work together is to consider the role of contextual factors in her life and evaluate their influence on career decision making. Without the benefit of additional interaction with Kathy, it is difficult to know which contextual factors are most meaningful to her. Nevertheless, I would hope that Kathy would agree to the value of considering previous life experiences, perceived educational and career-related barriers, and her current life situation when making career decisions.

Much of the recent research emanating from the Social Cognitive Career Theory (Lent et al., 1996) – particularly the emphasis on perceived barriers to career goals and the importance of self-efficacy and outcome expectations – also is important to integrate into career counseling. I would want to talk with Kathy about the particular challenges that she has overcome in the past. Throughout that discussion, I would be sure to focus on prior successes that Kathy has experienced in overcoming previously encountered barriers. I would then encourage her to identify barriers that she may encounter in the future and determine ways that she might overcome – or at least successfully cope with – such barriers when they arise.

## Concluding Comment

Working with clients to foster their career development is something that I consider a true honor and privilege. It is something that is almost sacred in nature, as clients share with me a part of themselves and trust me with the challenge of collaborating with them to arrive at what I hope are personally satisfying and rewarding decisions. As such, I would hope that my interactions with Kathy would be useful to her not only at this stage of her career, but throughout her life – serving as a blueprint for other important life decisions that she will be making in the future.

## References

Healy, C.C. (1990). Reforming career appraisals to meet the needs of clients in the 1990s. *Counseling Psychologist, 18,* 214-226.

Lent, R.W., Brown, S.D., & Hackett, G. (1996). Career development from a social cognitive perspective. In D. Brown, L. Brooks, & Associates, *Career choice and development* (3rd ed., pp. 373-416). San Francisco, CA: Jossey-Bass.

Super, D.E., Savickas, M.L., & Super, C. (1996). A life-span, life-space approach to career development. In D. Brown, & L. Brook, & Associates, *Career choice and development* (3rd ed.). San Francisco, CA: Jossey-Bass.

## *Response to Kathy: The Case of the Exploring Environmentalist*
### *Michael E. Hall*
### *The Pennsylvania State University*
### *Elizabeth R. Beil*
### *The Johns Hopkins University*

### Theoretical Lens

A three-fold clarion call has sounded. There is a need for collaboration between various psychological specialties (Slaney & Russell, 1987), for convergence of career theory (Savickas, 1994), and for a contextual approach to the practice of career counseling (Vondracek & Kawasaki, 1995). From our experience as counseling psychologists in a career center (Hall) and a counseling center (Beil), we offer a response to the case of Kathy. We describe an approach to career counseling where the contextual factors of family and gender are considered primary, rather than secondary influences. Developmental-systems and feminist theories as well as women's career psychology models inform their case conceptualization.

The developmental frame will be provided by essential concepts from Okun's (1984) integrated developmental-systems approach. Fintushel and Hillard (1991) will be relied upon for the feminist/gender view whereas Betz and Fitzgerald (1987) and Gottfredson (1996) will guide the women's career psychology perspective.

## Impressions

The information from the initial counseling session forms an emerging image of a sociable young-adult woman, one who is pleasant and eager to please. Kathy's engagement of the counselor hints of psychological openness, perhaps curiosity. In the familial sphere, there is evidence for characterizing her family as a "launching-center family" (primary task: letting go of the oldest child) or a "middle-aged-parents family" (euphemistically referred to as "empty-nest"). Kathy's observation that her mother has been anxious for Kathy to leave the home and her parents' recent divorce may be evidence of the separation-individuation tasks associated with this stage of family life. For example, as her mother ventured ahead once her youngest child left home, Kathy may have acutely experienced rejection and abandonment, threatening the secure attachment base that Blustein, Prezioso, and Schultheiss (1995) find critical to tame the anxiety that accompanies career exploration.

Given that Kathy's parents' divorce occurred as she was emerging from adolescence, her sense of self may have been negatively affected. For example, it appears as though Kathy's mother stayed in an unsatisfying relationship until Kathy graduated from high school. Influenced by exposure to marital and/or family conflict, Kathy may have become resigned to the unhappy arrangement and adopted her animated style as a response to family tension.

Kathy presents with many stated interests, but apparently with little experience "trying out" her interests in the world. Gottfredson (1996) reminds us that constructs such as masculinity-femininity and occupational prestige help form the self-concept, and that individuals are likely to consider occupations conforming to their perception of sex roles and prestige. In fact, these concerns may be weighted more heavily than may interests alone. Therefore, it may be critical for gender-role identity to be incorporated in Kathy's developing career aspirations.

## Case Planning

The aforementioned impressions are viewed as markers of a readiness for beginning career counseling with positive expectations. Taken together, the impressions suggest that Kathy's quest for career specification may benefit from assistance with separation-individuation, as well as consideration of the impact of her parents divorce and her gender identity on her career identity. McDaniels and Gysbers' (1992) seven-phase model of career counseling will be used for the purpose of case planning. In conceptualizing career counseling as a two-phase process, Hall and Beil's case conceptualization includes only the initial three phases of McDaniels and Gysbers' model.

| *Initial Phase* | *Action Phase* |
|---|---|
| 1. Therapeutic alliance | 4. Acquisition of work world information |
| 2. Problem identification | 5. Action plan development |
| 3. Exploration of self | 6. Choice implementation |
| | 7. Evaluation/ renegotiations |

## Initial Phase

The goals of the initial phase are to establish the counselor-client working relationship, to increase self-awareness, and to set realistic intervention outcomes for the action phase of counseling. These goals will be achieved by pursuing the following two objectives: (1) the explication of Kathy's personal decision-making style, and (2) exploration of the familial and gender context of Kathy's career identity. The initial counseling session would have concluded with the counselor and Kathy agreeing that "to find a best career," it will be useful to initially look at how, in general, she makes educational/career choices, and also to identify some of the major influences on those choices.

## Decision-making Style

While continuing to build the working alliance in the second and possibly the third sessions, the following questions will be used to guide the exploration of Kathy's decision-making style.

1. How did you choose this college; select history and French as your majors?
2. What other majors did you consider and what caused you to switch from them?
3. What positive and negative experiences have you had with writing/journalism; with problem-solving/research?
4. How do your skills, values, and personality preferences relate to your three career aspirations?

## Family/Gender Influences

As an entrée to the contextual dimension of Kathy's career dilemma, the counselor will offer that a more in-depth understanding of her decision-making style may aid her discovery of a "best career." To operationalize this idea, it will be suggested that it may be informative for Kathy to review the impact of some of the major factors that have shaped her recent educational/career choices. The next group of questions will be used to elucidate the family and gender contexts of Kathy's career identity.

1. Was your choice of college influenced by either or both parents, and if 'yes,' to what extent?
2. How was your choice of a college or course of study affected by your parents' divorce?
3. What do your parents and sibling(s) do for a living and do they like it?
4. What have you learned from your mother (and sisters, if any) about the meaning of work for women?
5. What career options and barriers are you expecting to encounter because of your gender?

## Assessment

To further delineate the influence of the contextual factors of family and gender on Kathy's career decision making, use will be made of the genogram technique. Based on the premise that the family of origin exerts a significant influence on one's attitude and perception about the world, there is a substantial literature describing how this family therapy technique has successfully aided clients in systematically exploring interactions with family members (Brown & Brooks, 1991). When applied to the career domain, this graphic depiction of the occupations of family members is expected to facilitate the identification of key models influencing Kathy's occupational perceptions. Exploration of the implication of the genogram will be critical to raising Kathy's awareness about familial and gender influences on her career aspirations.

She will be asked the following questions, categorized by the essential variables identified during the problem identification phase. These questions will be used to aid Kathy in determining the sources and status of her work and career perceptions, roles, and goals.

*Values.* (1) What are the core values retained by the family? (2) Does the family have a general career mission (e.g., health care, politics/government)? (3) How do your values fit with those espoused by the family?

*Work.* (1) How does the family address family relationships, leisure, and work? (2) What are the career patterns that emerge as you look at your family's genogram? (3) What unfulfilled aspirations are members living out through the children and grandchildren?

*Gender.* (1) What role(s) did each person assume in the family? (2) What attitudes and behaviors were reinforced (were discouraged) for females, for males? (3) Who were the most powerful models of womanhood other than family members?

*Decision Making.* (1) How were decisions made in the family? (2) Are there generational myths or misperceptions about work/careers? (3) What boundaries or limits on career choices or change have been established?

## Action Phase

As a result of the self-exploration and the consideration of familial and gender-related influences, it is anticipated that the initial phase of counseling might conclude with Kathy viewing the quest to translate her interests, academic majors, and co-curricular experiences into a career aspiration as a *process*. In a fourth and/or fifth session, it would be posed that given her gregarious temperament and learning-style preferences, Kathy continue her career exploration by engaging in a series of experiential learning activities (i.e., co-ops, externships, internships/ co-ops, volunteerism, and summer work). This would be contrasted with the more passive interventions (e.g., talk-counseling, accessing printed or audiovisual occupational information). A list of developmentally appropriate activities in which she would participate during her junior and senior years would be formulated. In addition to the counselor, Kathy will be referred to the offices of experiential education and the alumni career network to identify potential sites (in industries related to the environment) where she could research, write, or otherwise inform others about environmental issues.

Kathy would be expected to participate in the action phase with greater confidence, even with her level of career uncertainty, given an increased awareness of the contextual aspect of her career identity. She will, for example, be guided to select a mentor who can help her ongoing assessment of the effects of sex-role stereotyping. Should Kathy's uncertainty revolve around the issues associated with traditionally male-dominated fields or roles, then it will be important for the counselor to help Kathy mobilize a strong system of support, including female role models, mentors, and supportive faculty. This may be especially useful if the familial context mirrors societal sex-role stereotypes.

As an alternative, it may be useful to consider Betz and Fitzgerald's (1987) observation that the process of women's career choice historically has suffered from the underuse of abilities. In extending Kathy's interests, her abilities can be assessed as well. Perhaps through the use of an instrument such as the Self-Directed Search or the Strong Interest and Skills Confidence Inventory, assessment results could be used to aid Kathy in identifying the transferable skills she may have developed, but not considered thus far in her articulation of a career direction. Her facility with French, for example, may suggest not only an interest, but also a talent in learning language. This could lead to exploration of language-related careers with children or the elderly.

## Conclusion

Practitioners from two different types of counseling centers joined forces to illustrate how approaching the case of Kathy from a multitheoretical perspective has the potential for facilitating the design of a career intervention plan where contextual dimensions are considered as primary features of the presenting issues. The case plan described supports the notion from feminist theory that for many women external factors weigh powerfully and can exert great influence on decisions. "Because of the mutually formative nature of family relationships, a divorce after twenty or so years of marriage profoundly alters the patterns of interconnection and thus shakes the roots of each member's self-perception" (Fintushel & Hillard, 1991). Thus, the proposed intervention strategy is likely to be among the most efficacious because it respects the development and systemic aspects of Kathy's individual experience (Ivey & Ivey, 1999).

## References

Betz, N.E. & Fitzgerald, L.F. (1987). *The career psychology of women*. Orlando, FL: Academic Press.

Blustein, D., Prezioso, M. & Schultheiss, D. (1995). Attachment theory and career development: Current status and future directions. *Counseling Psychologist, 23*, 416-432.

Brown, D. & Brooks, L. (1991). *Career counseling techniques.* Boston, MA: Allyn & Bacon.

Fintushel, N. & Hillard, N. (1991). *A grief out of season: When your parents divorce in your adult years.* Boston, MA: Little, Brown.

Gottfredson, L. (1996). Gottfredson's theory of circumscription and compromise. In D. Brown, L. Brooks & Associates, *Career choice and development* (3rd ed., pp. 179-232). San Francisco, CA: Jossey-Bass.

Ivey, A.E., & Ivey, M.B. (1999). Toward a developmental diagnostic and statistical manual: The vitality of a contextual framework. *Journal of Counseling & Development, 77,* 484-490.

McDaniels, C. & Gysbers, N.C. (1992). *Counseling for career development: Theories, resources, and practice.* San Francisco, CA: Jossey-Bass.

Okun, B.F. (1984). *Working with adults: Individual, family, and career development.* Monterey, CA: Brooks/Cole.

Savickas, M.L. (1994). Convergence prompts theory renovation, research unification, and practice coherence. In M.L. Savickas & R.W. Lent (Eds.), *Convergence in career development theories: Implications for science and practice* (pp. 235-257). Palo Alto, CA: Consulting Psychologists Press.

Slaney, R.B., & Russell, J.E.A. (1987). Perspectives on vocational behavior 1986: A review. *Journal of Vocational Behavior, 31,* 111-173.

Vondracek, F.W., & Kawasaki, T. (1995). Toward a comprehensive framework for adult career development theory and intervention. In W.B. Walsh & S.H. Osipow (Eds.), *Handbook of vocational psychology: Theory, research, and practice* (2nd ed., pp. 111-141). Mahwah, NJ: Erlbaum.

# FERRIS: THE CASE OF THE RELIGIOUS MATHEMATICIAN

Ferris is a 22-year-old single male of European American descent who recently graduated from college with a bachelor's degree in mathematics. He had decided to take a year off before he began a graduate program in mathematics. After having a difficult experience as a teacher in a volunteer program he came to the career counselor. He was hoping to gain direction and find a job that he enjoyed until he could begin his doctoral program. Ferris had joined the volunteer teacher program out of a sense of mission. He is very active in his religious organization, one that promotes "good works" as a central part of its mission.

When Ferris first came to the counselor, he had already applied for numerous positions teaching music. He completed the assessment and job search portions of DISCOVER, which indicated the occupational codes Realistic and Artistic. He received "very similar" scores on mathematician and music teacher. He expressed a great passion for music as well as math and was very conflicted as to which path to follow. He was also questioning how much either path would fulfill his spiritual need to serve humankind, a need that was growing in importance for him, as he became more involved in his religious work.

Ferris stated that his parents were accepting of any path that he wanted to follow. Although they shared his concern for making a difference in the world, they believed that there were many ways to do so. Ferris is not as sure as they that any of his potential paths would lead him in this direction. Indeed, one thought he has had is becoming a religious leader. But he is worried that this path will not lead to enough intellectual challenge for him.

Ferris has always been a good student; his high school grade point average was 3.9, and he maintained a 3.6 in a very demanding undergraduate mathematics degree program. He tells you that he enjoys an intellectual challenge and gets bored when things are "too easy." He has pursued mathematics because it is fun and has been challenging. He has always been able to master the content, but it has sometimes required a lot of hard work, an aspect he enjoyed. He also tells you that he originally became a math major because an admired teacher suggested he consider making it a career. He has never really fantasized about any particular line of work and resists doing so when you suggest it during your sessions.

When queried about other options he has considered, he tells you that he never really thought much beyond school. He says that, with the length of time it takes to get a PhD, he felt that he did not need to "think about that yet." His knowledge of the world of work is scanty. He was surprised that you found 40 different mathematical careers on the Internet.

Ferris has had the same steady girlfriend for the past eight years; they started dating in their freshman year of high school. She is pursuing a degree in nursing and says she is supportive of any decisions he chooses to make. He knows, however, that she would like to get married, and he does not feel he can do so until he completes his formal education. He says that is another tug away from the doctoral program.

## *Response to Ferris: The Case of the Religious Mathematician*
### *Lee Richmond*
### *Loyola College, Maryland*

Obviously a very bright young man, Ferris enjoys being challenged intellectually. He is "passionate" about music and has applied for jobs teaching, though he has had a "difficult" time teaching math, another subject about which Ferris is passionate. More is unknown than known about Ferris. It is unknown whether Ferris merely enjoys music, and is truly gifted with musical ability. And if he is gifted, it is unknown whether his gift is vocal or instrumental or both.

Ferris has an interesting Holland Code: Realistic and Artistic. Although music is an occupation congruent with people who are artistic, mathematics is congruent with people who are the investigative type. Realistic people like to work with things. Does Ferris? Without an intervening Investigative in the Holland Code, and none was mentioned, Realistic is somewhat inconsistent with Artistic. People with high scores on the Realistic scale have personality characteristics that are far more practical, concrete, and conforming than are the characteristics of people who score high on the Artistic scale.

Additionally, little is known about the spirituality of Ferris. His "spiritual need" to serve humankind is undefined in the narrative. His uncertainty about whether math or music would meet his spiritual need to serve shows a certain naiveté in Ferris, or perhaps, a rigidity about spiritual matters. It is unknown how Ferris defines spirituality. If spirituality is defined as something that connects us to the transcendent, surely both music and higher mathematics have been means for people to do this for thousands of years. In fact, the very search for meaning in work is a spiritual quest. In the terminology of Mathew Fox, it is humankind's quest to connect our work to the Great Work of the Universe. In the theory of L. Sunny Hansen (1997), finding meaning in work is finding work that the world needs doing. Surely both music and math fill that bill.

On the other hand, if Ferris defines spiritual work as religious work, the picture changes somewhat. Ferris has thought of being a "religious leader" but questions whether that occupation is intellectually challenging. In reality, intellectual challenge depends on what one does as a religious leader. Again, Ferris shows a degree of naiveté. One can pastor a congregation, but one can also teach religion in seminaries. Theology is hardly an easy science, and metaphysics poses a conundrum to the best of philosophers. Comparative religion intrigues the intellect. None are subjects for intellectual slugs. Furthermore, there are occupations that combine religion with sacred music. It is obvious that Ferris needs more in-depth information about all three fields – religion, music, and math – than he currently has.

Not only does Ferris need to search occupations, he must also search himself. Since most people sometimes think in the future tense, it is somewhat odd that Ferris has never, even as a child, fantasized or daydreamed about future jobs. Either he never thought ahead, or he does not remember doing so. He majored in math because someone else, his teacher, told him what to do. Furthermore, he can't exactly decide what to do about his girlfriend who seems quite decisive and wants to marry soon, when he sees it best to wait. Ferris seems to have difficulty thinking in concrete terms and in making decisions. Is this fact? Very little is revealed about Ferris the person, and one knows nothing about his relationships, except that he has had "accepting" parents who offered scant direction to him, and a single steady girlfriend since he was probably 15 years of age. How sociable is Ferris? No mention is made of siblings or friends. And as little as is known about Ferris's intentions, less is known abut his thoughts and behaviors, and still less about his feelings. What does Ferris feel?

It is important for the counselor, as well as for Ferris, that much more become known about Ferris. To accomplish this, Adlerian theory will be helpful. Ferris should resonate to counseling based on Adlerian thought because his interest in doing service corresponds with Adlerian emphasis on social interest.

Eliciting stories from Ferris about early memories will give both client and counselor a key to lifestyle analysis and self-understanding. Once Ferris becomes aware of his life themes, he can decide how to construct his life projects. At some point, one might incorporate the process theory of Anna Miller-Tiedeman (1999), which contends that Ferris is the architect of his own career. He need only use his Lifecareer compass – his experience, intelligence, and intuition to synthesize what he has learned about himself and apply it to his search.

Tiedeman's (1997) concept of Lifecareer, or living life as career, will probably be a new idea to Ferris who needs to think more holistically. He does not know where his girlfriend fits into his life and he is thinking in either/or terms. Get married or go to grad school, which? When one thinks more holistically, one thinks of career not only as job, but as work, leisure, learning, and family. It becomes a lifestyle issue. Ferris's question is a broad one. He is really asking how he can live his life in such a way that he can practice his faith, render service to humankind, engage his intellectual talents, satisfy his interests in mathematics and music, have a satisfying relationship, earn a living, and possibly raise a family. In other words, career counseling for Ferris involves helping Ferris not only find work, but find meaningful work, and harmony within himself and his world. To do this, the issues of interest and ability are essential, but so are issues that relate to connections and values. Ferris is struggling to connect his spirit to work in such a way that what is deepest within himself unites with what is greatest outside of himself. However, he cannot verbalize this. He knows this only intuitively. His dearth of information and confusion about the world of work and what needs to be done to achieve his goal force him to a standstill. Thus, he thinks about taking a year off. Intuitively he knows that he doesn't know.

Ultimately, Ferris needs to study himself, improve his scanty knowledge about occupations and how to search them, and then synthesize the information that he has so that he can maximize his talents and use them in his life-career, which encompasses more than his job. So for Ferris, lifestyle analysis, integrative life planning, and "soulwork" are in order. Because there are psychological issues involved, there are instruments that can assist the counselor. In addition to Ferris's Holland code, and his high intelligence that is known, it is useful to measure Ferris's values, personality type, and social needs. Instruments like Career Anchors, the Neo-PIR, the FIRO-B, along with a Spiritual Transcendence Scale may be of interest to Ferris and might help him synthesize information about self and work. As a client, Ferris allows the counselor to utilize everything he or she has ever learned about career development and choice.

## References

Firo-B ™ (1996). Self-scorable booklet and answer sheet. Palo Alto, CA: Consulting Psychologists Press.

Hansen, L.S. (1997). *Integrative life planning; Critical tasks for career development and changing life patterns.* San Francisco, CA: Jossey-Bass.

Miller-Tiedeman, A.L. (1999). *Learning, practicing, and living the new careering.* Philadelphia, PA: Accelerated Development.

Schein, E.H., (1990). *Career anchors.* San Francisco, CA: Jossey-Bass Pfiffer.

## *Response to Ferris: The Case of the Religious Mathematician*
### *Helen H. Kim*
### *University of Virginia*

On the surface, Ferris is coming in for job placement rather than for career planning. He wants to decide if he should teach math or music. However, he is also caught in a more complicated dilemma between his religious obligation and his academic/professional passion. He indicates his interest in math and music, which marks his Investigative and Artistic types and carries high consistency on Holland's RIASEC (1992). Ferris also is very clear about his passion for math, which provides him with intellectual stimulation, abstract, creative, and analytical problem solving and academic challenges. Although the subject is rigorous and demanding, he seems to feel validated by the fact that he can "master" it. Clearly, he also considers math to be "fun" and is very explicit about how and why it is enjoyable. Math is clearly meaningful for him. In contrast, when he presents his spiritual need to fulfill his mission to serve humankind, he seems to be fulfilling a duty rather than a passion. Ferris seems to be grappling with his desire to accept his academic vocation after a year of making room for his religious calling. In his attempt to fulfill his duty, he volunteers to teach. And even after a bad experience, he still decides to teach for a year before returning to graduate studies in math.

By teaching math or music, he is able to pursue his passion and to fulfill his duty. However, teaching is a Social occupation, which entails interest in helping others personally, socially, academically, and/or spiritually and requires strong social and interpersonal skills. The Social environment may not be congruent with his Investigative and Artistic inclinations. This incongruence may be related to the "difficult experience" in his volunteer teaching. Similarly, being a religious leader requires a Social personality type, and neither teaching nor religious leadership may provide enough intellectual stimulation for Ferris. I can also hypothesize that he may be seeking to "give" and serve the way his own religious leader and his admired teacher may have modeled for him. Is it possible he is emulating those role models who gave to him and he is following in their image?

At this point, his indecision on whether he should teach math or music seems moot since we have not determined if he even has the genuine desire, let alone the ability or skills to teach: DISCOVER generated Realistic and Artistic occupational codes. Although Realistic code is consistent with Investigative type, it leaves more unanswered questions about Ferris related to his codes: How does he spend his leisure time? What work experiences does he have? What are his abilities and skills? What are his interests, activities, and skills outside of math? There are other pieces of information that could shed more light on Ferris: How is he interested in music? Does he have any musical ability? How does DISCOVER assist in temporary job seeking and did Ferris gear his answers toward this job search and negate his vocation in math? He seems to have supportive social support or is it really? What is his decision-making style? Why teaching and not other service-oriented jobs such as service for at-risk youths, elder care, or Peace Corps? Is he identifying with his admired teacher? Which socioeconomic status level does he fall into and how does that affect his career decisions?

It is also very interesting how Ferris views his girlfriend. He describes her as "another tug away from the doctoral program." He seems to construe his religious duties and interpersonal obligations as obstacles to his vocation in math. Clearly, there is a parallel process between his two obligations in relation to his career goal.

At this point, Ferris does not have appropriate information about the world of work to choose a specific career. But developmentally, it is not surprising that Ferris is unable to see his career goals. In accordance with Super's vocational developmental stages (Super, Savickas, & Super, 1996), Ferris falls appropriately into the Exploration stage where he has tentatively decided to pursue math: The decision is narrowed down, but not yet finalized. In addition, he is a logical thinker and would obviously have difficulty fantasizing or going beyond what is sequentially next in line, graduate school. I would imagine he will come together on which area of math and what kind of career in math in due time. Besides, visualization and imagery techniques would be ineffective with cognitive clients like Ferris. In addition, being in the Exploration stage lends itself to the Implementation tasks where he is completing his training for future vocational preference.

The exploration stage can also be seen as a transitional phase in vocational development. Ferris' hiatus and decision to trying out teaching math or music before entering grad school may be a moratorium (Marcia, 1989) or transition (Super et al, 1996), when exploration of possibilities occurs without making a full commitment to anything in particular. His struggle to find out which area he wants to teach is not the primary issue, although it may be the most immediate.

Sharf (1997) asserted that a client like Ferris, being an Investigative type, may be challenged by unanswered questions about his career path and may opt to be independent in approaching his problem. Although his initial decision to enter the field of math was swayed by someone else, this someone was a trusted person who may have known Ferris enough to guide him in this direction. Nevertheless, as indicated by his passion for the discipline, the guidance seems so far to be an appropriate one.

As Ferris' counselor I would begin by assessing the contextual factors and would utilize a developmental lens to work with him. It would also be useful for me to serve as his partner in his investigation and will be conducive for me to provide a setting for critical thinking and intellectual stimulation (Sharf, 1997). I understand Ferris from his contextual influences, which are religious convictions and obligations, age and developmental variables, gender, and relationship status. His religious identity or self-concept seems most poignant in this moratorium as he strives to fulfill his mission by teaching, a job he has not explored nor with which he had positive experience. Being 22 and having just graduated from college leaves Ferris in much transition to becoming an adult, graduate student, prospective husband, and spiritual manager. With all these transitional processes occurring, he may not feel the immediacy in pinpointing a long-term goal beyond entering and completing his doctoral training in math.

Typically, he may see his girlfriend's nursing career as giving and serving as woman's role. A teacher, not a university professor, is in a female-dominated field and he may consider the profession too feminine. His long-term relationship with his girlfriend also serves as another significant transitional point to explore. His interpretation of her expectation as a "tug away" from his own goal may be a source of pressure and not support.

Most immediately, I would caution Ferris about relying solely on the DISCOVER results but invite him to consider the results and to explore what his own self-assessment looks like. I would examine his decision to teach and assist in exploring his cognitive structuring for wanting to take a year off to do this. I would utilize paradoxical intervention (Weeks & L'Abate, 1982) and ask why not two years or three or more? I would also explore his religious duty to serve humankind and what it would mean for him to become a religious leader. We would initially clarify his "mission" and strategize other alternatives to teaching to serve that mission if he comes to the conclusion that teaching either math or music is a good fit now.

As for his long-term goal and career decision, information on the world of work will be appropriate at this time. I would invite him to review the 40 different mathematical careers to narrow them down to a handful of possibilities to help him specialize/focus his program of study when he enters graduate school. This may facilitate a move into the Implementation substage of Exploration stage of vocational development (Super et al., 1990). Additionally, I would validate his developmental process and provide support as he cultivates his own sense of self and understands his life roles, which are crucial as he shifts and spirals toward career maturity (Sharf, 1997).

In continuing to undertake his life roles, Ferris' relationship with his girlfriend is also a crucial factor as a 22-year-old straight man in this society considering not only his career but also his interpersonal development. However, without further collection of data about their relationship, it is difficult at this point to speculate on an intervention in that arena.

In addition to gathering more client data about Ferris, it is essential to consider the contextual element of transition in his spiritual, professional, and personal development. Finding an appropriate personality and environment fit in how he can serve his mission, continue his passion in math, and realize his matrimonial plans seems just as important.

## References

Holland, J.L. (1992). *Making vocational choices: A theory of vocational personalities and work environments* (3rd ed.). Odessa, FL: Psychological Assessment Resources.

Marcia, J.E. (1989). Identity and intervention. *Journal of Adolescence, 12*, 401-410.

Sharf, R.S. (1997). *Applying career development theory to counseling* (2nd ed.). Pacific Grove, CA: Brooks/Cole.

Super, D.E., Savickas, M.L., & Super, C.M. (1996). A life-span, life-space approach to careers. In D. Brown, L. Brooks, & Associates, *Career choice and development* (3rd ed., pp.121-178). San Francisco, CA: Jossey-Bass.

Weeks, G.R., & L'Abate, L. (1982). *Paradoxical psychotherapy: Theory and practice with individuals, couples, and families*. New York: Brunner/Mazel.

# JANINE: THE CASE OF THE UNEMPLOYED SURVIVOR

Janine is a 22-year-old, white female who is self-identified as "queer." She appears for her initial appointment dressed casually, wearing a torn leather jacket, jeans and sneakers with four piercings – ears and nose. Her hair is blond with orange streaks and somewhat disheveled. She is the youngest of three from an intact Midwestern suburban family. She appears to be somewhat nervous and ill at ease. She indicates that she is not currently employed, but is interested in coming to the community college to take courses that will assist her in developing career-related skills. She is somewhat unclear about her direction, but indicates a strong interest in art and graphic design. A discussion of her high school experiences reveals that high school was an extremely difficult experience with the exception of art classes. She reports that she "had a lot of trouble paying attention and doing the work" which resulted in an extremely low GPA. She was not evaluated during school for learning disabilities or attention deficit hyperactivity disorder (ADHD). An initial assessment of basic academic skills indicates limitations both in reading and written expression. It is not possible to know whether the assessment is reflective of her limited preparation at the high school level or is indicative of an underlying learning or developmental disability.

Janine left home in another state at 19 to escape a situation she felt was abusive and has very limited contact with her parents. She currently is Sharing living space with several friends. Further discussion reveals two prior hospitalizations following suicide attempts. Janine was diagnosed with bipolar disorder during her second hospitalization and is currently taking medication that has stabilized her moods. She has participated in a computer-training program through the state rehabilitation program, but has failed to keep several positions obtained through a temporary service due to the slower pace of her work. She reports an immediate need to find work, as well as pursue an educational program that will allow her to obtain her objective of living independently.

Later, Janine revealed that her awareness of potential career directions is extremely limited. Although expressing the desire to work in the art field, she has almost no realistic knowledge of what types of careers might build on artistic interests and skill and is equally uninformed about the necessary education or training required. When asked to imagine herself at work and then to describe what she sees, she is only able to articulate "working in an office where the people are nice." Based on her prior, limited work experience, she knows that she does not want to work in food service settings and expresses considerable doubt as to her ability to be successful at a "regular job."

Although she feel strongly that additional education is important, she reports a high level of anxiety about returning to school and is discouraged about the length of time that earning a degree will take, since she feels she can attend only part time. She has been referred to a special program at the community college that will support at-risk students with tutoring and other accommodations if required and has been scheduled for continuing contact with the counseling department to explore both career and personal issues.

When asked what she meant by self-identifying herself as "queer," she states that being queer is a state of mind. She says that it is about being different and throwing that in the face of "straights." She offers that it is sexual too, but that she sleeps with both men and women, but especially women because that really challenges the status quo.

## Response to Janine: The Case of the Unemployed Survivor
### Lynn Haley-Banez and Stuart F. Chen-Hayes
### Fairfield University

#### Our Image of Janine
Janine appears to be artistic, creative, challenging the status quo, fearful of academic or career failure, and a likely survivor of emotional, physical, and/or sexual abuse who may be in a victim

mode (Herman, 1992). Clarity is needed regarding Janine's multiple cultural identities (Arredondo, 1999). For Janine, salient cultural and contextual variables (Astin, 1985; Herr & Niles, 1998) for a successful career-counseling plan include the intersections and interrelationships between age, ethnicity, gender, sexual orientation, social class, and disability in her career and educational her-story/history.

A culturally competent career counselor would refrain from using terms with adverse connotations and consequences (i.e., negative and nonconformist) to ensure that the client's lived experience and values are not demeaned. Instead, a counselor interested in social justice (Chen-Hayes, in press; Haley-Banez & Garrett, in press; Lewis & Arnold, 1998) would advocate for Janine. The emphasis from a career counseling advocacy perspective includes emphasis on a person-situation fit (Herr & Niles, 1998) that celebrates her employability skills, strengths, and potential successes as opposed to focusing on potential failures or deficits.

For example, Janine might fit well into some aspects of today's corporate advertising and marketing model that has "capitalized" on alternative appearances and counterculture as a way to sell products and services. In addition, in work environments that promote and encourage creative expressions in both employee output as well as their personal appearance, she would find a welcome home in such diverse areas as landscape design, computer graphics, the alternative press, or other arenas that showcase a combination of design, creativity, and technology applications. Her avant-garde look would therefore be seen as a plus. Swadener and Lubeck (1995) conceptualized youth and family members as being "at promise" as opposed to being "at risk." Janine deserves to have her career counselor advocate for her and against a pathologizing assessment in favor of her potential in the world of work.

Other information we want about Janine to put her strengths and concerns in context:
- Contextual specifics: ethnicity, social class, religious/spiritual identity, her story of emotional/physical/sexual abuse and how she has/has not healed from that; her support system; family of origin, family of choice (i.e., dating, relationships, social support), her gender/gender identity and the roles that she sees nontraditional
- How has Janine experienced the roles of women/girls in the world of work?
- What were the precipitating factors in her prior suicide attempts? How does she perceive her diagnosis at one time as bipolar? What is her family history/herstory of abuse/trauma? Is there a family history of depression?
- What, if any, relationship would depression or ongoing unresolved trauma/violence have with her slow work pace?
- Has she been tested for learning disabilities?
- Were the medications helpful? Were the medications affecting how quickly she's able to work/process information?
- What does she love about herself or see as her personal and career/work strengths?
- What do her friends do for work and what do they say are her career strengths?
- Who are her sheroes/heroes and what does this say about her career possibilities? ·
- What does she do for fun and how does she incorporate fun into work?
- What did her parents/siblings do for work and what messages did she receive from her family of origin/family of choice about work and careers?
- What are her hopes and dreams?
- What are her computer/technology interests/competencies?
- What are her beliefs about how others perceive her?
- How does she cope with setbacks and disappointments?
- Who has the power in her life? Who has used power inappropriately against her? How can she heal and use power in healthy ways to find her life's work/love?

## Our Plan for Successful, Culturally Competent Career Counseling

We would start with a culturally sensitive framework addressing Janine's multiple cultural identities (Arredondo, 1999). Next, we would develop a career counseling plan using Guerriero and Allen's, (1998) process career counseling model to assist Janine in developing critical thinking skills and strengths related to her career counseling search across the following stages: foundation, assessment, feedback, goal-setting, resolution of resistance, and follow-through.

The use of key questions (Guerriero & Allen, 1998) would be developed to promote advocacy and social justice in Janine's life through career counseling. Janine could benefit from being taught how to empower herself and how to challenge issues of oppression (Lewis & Arnold, 1998) that she may have internalized or been targeted for by external forces (heterosexism, ableism, sexism, trauma and violence) that have adversely affected her school and work performance. Next, we would work to assess specific areas related to unanswered questions around Janine's past mental health issues (suicide attempts, medications, prior diagnoses), and ask what worked for her in her past and what did not. Building on her strengths, we would utilize a developmental model specific to lesbian, bisexual and gay persons (D'Augelli, 1994; Gelberg & Chojnacki, 1996) and adapt each level of the model to a career counseling context. D'Augelli's (1994) model helps to assess where a lesbian, bisexual, or gay person is on six levels: exiting heterosexual identity; developing a personal lesbian, bisexual, or gay identity; developing a lesbian, bisexual, or gay social identity; becoming a lesbian, bisexual, or gay offspring; developing a lesbian, bisexual, or gay intimacy status; and entering a lesbian, bisexual, or gay community. Each of these developmental tasks may be central to Janine's past, present, and future educational and career success.

In assessing the particular issues related to her life as a "queer" woman, we would want to take advocacy roles to challenge any internalized or externalized heterosexism (Chen-Hayes, in press; Haley-Banez & Garret, in press; Gelberg & Chojnacki, 1996) that she may have faced in work or family settings in the past or that she could anticipate in the future. We would want to coach Janine about the power of interrupting oppression and creating ally relationships (Gelberg & Chojnacki, 1996; Lewis & Arnold, 1988) with heterosexuals willing to challenge heterosexism, men willing to challenge sexism, and so forth in both in her personal life and in her work setting to create optimal functioning.

## Direct Actions, Interventions, and Advocacy to Challenge Oppression and Promote Career and Educational Success

Janine would need a variety of services related to career success. We would coach her how to use computer-assisted career interest inventories initially (i.e., DISCOVER, SEEK). Once she has developed an idea of what she wants to do, we would assist her in developing skills for building effective resumes, job search skills, interviewing skills, and how to manage workplace heterosexism (Gelberg & Chojnacki, 1996). We would also want to have her tested for learning disabilities and we would collaboratively discuss her prior mental health issues and her perceptions of the accuracy of those diagnoses as a survivor of abuse and trauma (Herman, 1992).

We would encourage Janine to use the Internet and in-person interviews to meet with other lesbian, bisexual, and gay persons in informational interviews about their jobs, the necessary skills, and dealing with workplace heterosexism (Gelberg & Chojnacki, 1996). In addition, we would use cognitive-behavioral strategies such as modeling, role-plays, and disputation of negative thoughts to assist her in challenging her thoughts about not being successful in a "regular" job. We would ask Janine to talk about her life using circularity as a metaphor, as she appears not to fit a "linear" model of living or being. We would encourage her to notice her own world-view and what workplace(s) would be affirming of her nontraditional ways of being.

## Theoretical Models in Career Counseling

Astin's (1985) sociopsychological career choice and work behavior model is especially useful to look at the importance of women's career development being placed in multiple contexts, and it would be critical to work with Janine as a queer woman on the interplay of workplace oppressions, particularly heterosexism, sexism, and ableism (Arredondo, 1999). In addition to helping her build her own skills, we would utilize Gelberg and Chojnacki's (1996) mentoring model of career counseling for allies Gelberg and Chojnacki (1996) delineate the gay, lesbian, and bisexual allies model as having the following stages; awareness, ambivalence, empowerment, activism, pride, and integration. Janine could learn to find heterosexuals in her work environment who would support her identities, in addition to potential lesbian, bisexual, and gay colleagues. Lastly, the theme of advocacy and coaching Janine, as a queer woman, in social justice and social action strategies throughout her search would be a cornerstone of our work, as described by Arredondo (1999), Chen-Hayes (in press), Haley-Banez and Garret (in press), Herr and Niles (1998), and Lewis and Arnold (1998).

## Summary

There is nothing negative about Janine, but plenty that appears to be nonconforming. We would posit that it is best to see Janine as "at promise," to challenge the pathologizing of the term "at risk" (Swadener & Lubeck, 1995). Our approach would be to affirm Janine's differences in career counseling and work collaboratively to help her build on her strengths and challenge others' attitudes toward her sexual orientation, her personal style, and potentially, her disability(s). At the same time, it is crucial to see how Janine perceives herself in the world as either a survivor or victim of abuse. We would want to know how she was targeted as a girl and as a woman, and a queer person with bisexual behavior, and as a student who did not achieve her potential in high school. What effects have these had on her identities now as she seeks to change/grow in education and in the job market, and what will be keeping her stuck? How can she resist the forces of fear and develop success? Using advocacy and social action models, the future is bright for career counseling with Janine.

# Response to Janine: The Case of the Unemployed Survivor
## Wei-Cheng Mau, Steven Grimsley, and Carissa Sherwood
## Wichita State University

Our initial impression of Jeanine is that she has been confronted with developmental issues related to autonomy/independence, sexual identity, and career identity. Janine's case present an excellent illustration of how career and personal identities are often interwoven and overlap, which validates their need to be attended to and integrated into career counseling (Anderson & Niles, 1995). We will discuss how these identity issues relate to her current difficulties in life and how they affect her career decisions. Suggestions on how to assist Janine are offered.

Janine's immediate concern is that she needs assistance in career-related skills, and she want to find work and attend college to escape from an allegedly abusive environment. We believe what masks her initial concerns are hurt, anger and self-doubt, which are critical and need to be addressed before and throughout the career counseling sessions. Janine seems to have many internal and external obstacles. Some obstacles are self-imposed, whereas others are inherent in the environment. Janine's self-imposed obstacles include low self-concept, occupational self-efficacy, and dysfunctional beliefs. External obstacles likely to present challenges to Janine include a lack of education, low socioeconomic status, being a woman, and her sexual orientation. The goals for Janine are to help her identify her obstacles and her irrational thought and behaviors when these obstacles present themselves, and then discuss the consequences of her actions.

Behaviorally, Janine seems to believe that the only recognition she ears from others is by acting out in socially unacceptable ways. She displays this inappropriateness through her overt behaviors when she throws her sexuality and beliefs "into the faces of straights." Her personal appearance accentuates and reinforces the negative reactions from the general "heterosexual" population, which may place here at a disadvantage in particular social settings.

Cognitively, Janine appears to approach most of life's situations without an overall plan. We must question Janine's effectiveness as a problem-solver and effective decision-maker. We question her ability in these areas based on her desire to work in the field of art without having any working knowledge of how that world operates, what is available, and what types of training she will need to be successful.

Janine has been employed and dismissed from several positions. It is our belief that these positions did not match her interests or skill level. When asked to imagine herself at work, her imagery led her to state that she wanted to work in an office where the people were nice. Her response suggested that she may not have a realistic sense of the world of work and that she has not prepared herself to effectively deal with difficult people in the workplace.

On the other hand, she may have encountered discrimination and hostility from her previous jobs, which have led her to desperately seek a friendlier working environment. Janine obviously sees herself as a person who is incapable of coping with the normal demands life places upon a person This feeling of incapability may have been learned as a result of several job losses, trouble paying attention, poor grades in school, and her self-doubt that she will ever be able to participate in a "regular job." Her perception about and attitude toward the world of work may have severely inhibited her career options. This distorted perception and Janine's ineffective decision-making approaches deserve some attention when working with her.

Affectively, concerns arise out of Janine's diagnosed depression and the high level of anxiety associated with returning to school. We suspect that her episodes of depression may have been a result of an abusive situation and a feeling of hopelessness she incorporated into her philosophy of life while living in a hostile environment. She seen herself as uneducated, "queer," and perhaps as a person whose current situation lacks any sort of permanence. She seems to be angry at society for its view of her, and she may have generalized her anger toward the entire heterosexual community. This kind of anger is likely to be projected onto the counselor, who she may perceive as an enemy like other heterosexuals (Croteau & Thiel, 1993).

In working with Janine, we would need to be honest about our own biases and prejudice toward sexual identity issues (Sue & Sue, 1999). Suring our initial visits with Janine, it would be critical to establish a positive and effective working relationship. Given the difficulties and discrimination she may have encountered, we believe there will be a great deal of mistrust and skepticism on her part regarding our ability to help her. Even more so, because of her sexual identity, she may see us as part of the establishment, which is unwilling or unable to see her point of view. We would need to convey respect and unconditional positive regard to her without being judgmental. Furthermore, we would need to work with her so that she could apply these core conditions to her relationships with others socially and professionally.

Once Janine is comfortable, we would want to ask her if she would allow us to visit with the other helping people in her life. Since she is on medication for bipolar depression, we would want to consult with her psychiatrist to ensure all was okay with her medication and recovery because of her previous bouts with depression and hospitalization. If the medication had the bipolar depression under control, it would be helpful to explore situations in which depression for Janine occurs.

In addition to medication, Janine would benefit from personal counseling on a regular basis. Based on her condition, a cognitive-behavioral approach, such as rational-emotive imagery, may be appropriate. Janine could imagine herself in a situation that she finds extremely depressing. As she imagines the situation and feels herself becoming depressed, we would ass her to keep the situation as it is, but reevaluate her feeling regarding the situation. In fact, we would work with her to perhaps learn to be disappointed with the situation without becoming depressed. Once she feels comfortable with this type of imagery, it is something that could be done outside of our visits as homework. It could even be generalized to other situations where irrational emotions dominate Janine's ability to function.

Once Janine's personal problems are under certain control, her career concerns can then be addressed. First and foremost, it would be necessary to have her tested for Attention Deficit Disorder and for a possible learning disability. If any of these were confirmed, special accommodations would need to be arranged to ensure her success in college. The extent to which her needs in academic advising, financial assistance, and other areas that nontraditional students are likely to have need to be assessed as well.

To address her career concerns, we suggest a number of assessment devices. These assessments would provide additional insight into her strengths and weaknesses as well as possible sources of dysfunctional thought and career attitudes. Her career interests can be assessed using instruments such as Strong Interest Inventory (SII) or Campbell Interest and Skill Survey (CISS). After examining her general interest, we would pay special attention to the artistic scales, since she expressed a strong interest in this area.

Both SII and CISS assess academic comfort. This information would help Janine understand how comfortable and successful she feels she would be in a formal, traditional academic setting. Janine's fears of returning to school may be helped by coming to understand the information provided by this special scale. Since it provides information regarding a person's comfort in a formal education setting, each discomforting issue could be evaluated in terms of the event, the beliefs Janine holds for each event, and thus the consequences for those beliefs. If any of the beliefs are unfounded, they can be debated and challenged. It may even be helpful to place Janine into group counseling or some sort of self-help group. An excellent example of a group in which to place Janine would be that of other returning students who might have similar anxieties about returning to school. This would provide her with a network of people who understand first hand how she feels.

We would also be interested in Janine's self-reported skills. This could provide information about how she sees her strengths, as well as allow us to examine possible gaps between her assessed strengths and her perceived strengths. This kind of assessment is important for Janine because she has so little knowledge regarding her abilities. In fact, the assessment that determined she had reading and writing difficulties may not have addressed her mathematic abilities, musical talent, interpersonal or intrapersonal skills, spatial abilities, or her relationship to her environment as a whole. A skill assessment test, such as the CISS or the Ability Explorer (Harrington & Harrington, 1996), would give us a picture regarding other areas in which Janine may be able to function at her maximum capacity. By focusing on her areas of strength, perhaps, she would be able to relate her strengths to some "regular job." It is with this factual proof that Janine could dispute her misguided belief that she is incapable.

To understand Janine's current thinking on careers and her self-imposed obstacles that may have limited her career options, diagnostic tools such as the Career Thoughts Inventory (Sampson, Peterson, Lenz, Reardon & Saunders, 1996), the Career Beliefs Inventory (Krumboltz, 1991), or the Career Decision-Making Self-Efficacy (Betz & Luzzo, 1996) would help both the counselor and Janine identify, challenge, and change negative thinking that is a detriment to her ability to effectively solve career problems and make career choices. Once she understands these dysfunctional thoughts, she will be able to work on resolving them.

Even though Janine wants to do something with the world of art, it would be wise for her to assess the rate of return for her investment. Working in the field of art or graphic design would likely require extensive education, apprenticeship, and credentials. If this is true, she would want to be aware of this in advance and prepare herself for this journey. Nevertheless, by taking the CISS, she will open up many other opportunities that may be more viable, especially since her goal is to quickly become self-supportive and independent.

Another possibility for Janine, since she has been diagnosed with bipolar depression, would be to have her placed on a 504 plan. This plan could be worked up to ensure that necessary steps be taken to help her successfully complete school. The 504 plan could establish tutoring for Janine, assist with reading and writing, and perhaps adjust the work requirement for her so that she could be successful.

Addressing issues relating to Janine's sexual orientation, we would like to know her current feelings about being a lesbian and how they affect her feelings of worth. Assessing her sexual identity from a developmental perspective may help her clarify the confusion she is currently experiencing while helping her work toward possible integration of a fragments self (Cass, 1979; Levine & Evans, 1991). Once Janine can clarify her identity, she must change her approach to others in regard to how she present herself. Counselors need to be sensitive to the values and lifestyles of the lesbian community and avoid using language that reflects heterosexual assumptions. Janine needs to explore ways that can help her deal with discrimination and that do not lead to furthering the public's misguided stereotypes of homosexuals.

Last, may university and college settings have gay and lesbian groups that regularly meet. Involvement with other people like her could help her understand how other people are coping with similar obstacles and difficulties. This way, Janine would be able to establish herself with a more positive group identity. If a campus group were not present, then finding a gay and lesbian community center or another available support group would be important. Most local bookstores offer free newsletters, newspapers, or magazines that are published for the gay and lesbian community; a myriad of resources is published in these different media.

Once Janine has worked through her personal and career issues with us, it is our hope that she will be able to feel empowered and realize that events in life can occur as a result of her actions or even independently of her. If the events are independent of her, she needs to think about each situation and evaluate all of the possible responses she could provide and then act deliberately.

In reviewing the entire counseling process, Janine should have become more aware of her skills and interests, available occupations, and the educational requirements for each. She has explored with us her irrational thoughts and behaviors that have interfered with employment as well as in her own personal life. With this knowledge, she should be able to determine if in fact, she still wants to be in an occupation that requires artistic abilities. If she does, she will at least have the knowledge with which to make an informed decision. She will also have the tools with which to positively approach problem solving and deal with the eventual discrimination she will encounter as a woman and a lesbian.

## References

Anderson, W.P. & Niles, S.G. (1995). Career and personal concern expressed by career counseling clients. *Career Development Quarterly, 43*, 240-45.

Betz, N.E. & Luzzo, D.A. (1996). Career assessment and the career decision-making self-efficacy scale. *Journal of Career Assessment, 4*, 413-428.

Cass, V.V. (1979). Homosexual identity formation: A theoretical model. *Journal of Homosexuality, 4*, 219-235.

Croteau, J.M. & Thiel, M.J. (1993). Integrating sexual orientation in career counseling: Acting to end a form of the personal-career dichotomy. *Career Development Quarterly, 42*, 175-179.

Harrington, J.C. & Harrington, T.F. (1996). *The Ability Explorer*. Chicago, IL: Riverside Publishing.

Krumboltz, J.D. (1991). *Career Beliefs Inventory*. Palo Alto, CA: Consulting Psychologists Press.

Levine, H. & Evans, N.J. (1991) The development of gay, lesbian and bisexual identities. In N.J. Evans & V.A. Wall (Eds.), *Beyond tolerance: Gays, lesbians and bisexuals on campus* (pp. 1-2). Alexandria, VA: American College Personnel Association.

Sampson, J.P., Peterson, G.W., Lenz, J.G., Reardon, R.C. & Saunders, D.E. (1996) *Career Thought Inventory*. Odessa, FL: Psychological Assessment Resources.

Sue, D.W. & Sue, D. (1999). *Counseling the culturally different: Theory and practice* (3rd ed.). New York: Wiley.

# Response to Janine: The Case of the Unemployed Survivor "Caqueer" Counseling
## Mary Z. Anderson and James M. Croteau
## Western Michigan University

Janine is a 22-year-old white woman, self-identified as "queer," and currently unemployed and living with friends. She has limited career knowledge or experience, and a history of academic difficulties in high school. She has expressed a desire to take community college classes and develop career-related skills. She also feels an immediate need to find employment. Financial compensation and a good interpersonal work situation seem to be the most important outcomes she currently seeks from employment. Though Janine has limited information about the art field, she is highly interested in that field and has had past success with art classes. She is anxious about taking community college classes, pessimistic about career success, and uneasy in the counseling situation. Historically, Janine reports an abusive family situation that she left 3 years ago. She has had two previous psychiatric hospitalizations following suicide attempts, is diagnosed with bipolar disorder, and is taking medication to stabilize her mood. In terms of social support, she is living with friends, is likely to have some support from her relationships with other women, and may have support within the larger queer-identified community. She is also enrolled in the "at-risk" student program at the community college for tutoring, counseling, and other support.

The place in the case example where Janine seems the most self-confident is her description of her queer identity and what that means to her; thus we suggest an approach that recognizes the strength and value of Janine's sense of being different, being queer. Such an approach must be built on a theoretical perspective that explicitly considers contextual as well as personal career development variables and must incorporate current knowledge concerning career development of sexual minority persons.

Social Cognitive Career Theory (SCCT; Lent, Brown, & Hackett, 1994) has been proposed as particularly useful in conceptualizing the career psychology of socially marginalized populations such as sexual minority persons (Bieschke, Eberz, Bard & Croteau, 1998; Croteau, Anderson, & Distefano, 2000; Fassinger, 2000; Morrow, Gore, & Campbell, 1996) because the role of contextual influences, including both internal and external barriers to optimal career development, is explicitly considered. Within this framework there are three major determinates of career-related behavior: (1) self-efficacy beliefs, or the sense of one's ability to perform career-related behaviors, (2) outcome expectations, or the anticipation that a career-related behavior will lead to a desired outcome, and (3) contextual factors (e.g., gender socialization) that influence development of self-efficacy beliefs and outcome expectations as well as the translation of those beliefs and expectations into successful career behavior.

According to SCCT, career interests develop through learning experiences that begin early in life and provide opportunity for the development of self-efficacy beliefs and outcome expectations in career related activities. In Janine's case, we can speculate that her learning experiences are likely to have been limited due to her particular context, i.e., her personal history with abuse and psychiatric issues as well as social norms concerning her gender and/or sexual orientation. Although we do know the relative influence of these contextual factors, both the general- and the lesbian/gay/bisexual- (LGB) specific career literature explicitly addresses gender as a primary contextual factor and provide potentially useful guidance in conceptualizing Janine (e.g., Fassinger, 1996; Lent et al, 1994; Morrow et al, 1996). Many sexual minority people experience interest in gender-nontraditional activities early in life, whereas families and society tend to encourage gender-traditional and discourage gender-nontraditional activities from a very early age (e.g., Chung, 1995; Croteau et al., 2000, Fassinger, 1995, 1996; Morgan & Brown, 1991). Janine's interest in art – a female-typed field – may have been shaped by having had early opportunities for positive art-related experiences. She may have had little opportunities for experiences in less gender-traditional areas despite potential early interest in those activities. Further, depending upon the details of her history with abuse and bipolar disorder, Janine may have had limited opportunities to develop self-efficacy and positive outcome expectations in any career area.

SCCT further suggests that translation of interests into educational and career choices is also shaped by self-efficacy and outcome expectations. Janine's history of success in art classes and her recent difficulty succeeding in a series of temporary "regular" work positions may have shaped Janine's sense of self-efficacy relative to artistic versus "regular" work. It may also be that she sees art, but not "regular" occupations, as an area that would be supportive of her queer identity. In other words, Janine's negative outcome expectations about "regular" work may be due to perceived limits in the occupational opportunity structure for queer people.

A recent review of the vocational psychology literature identified five themes that are important to consider in working with sexual minority career clients (Croteau et al., 2000). With respect to Janine's case, the most salient of these appears to be the role of sexual minority identity development in career development. Other LGB-unique career concerns that may also be important for Janine include the influence on career development of workplace discrimination, sexual identity management, and societal messages about gender and sexual minorities on career development. We also see that intentional and effective affirmation of queer identity will be crucial in the counseling relationship.

In general, sexual minority identity development models outline a process of acquiring a positive identity as a LGB person that begins with realizing one may have a minority sexual orientation, proceeds through unlearning negative notions about LGB people, and ends with internalizing and integrating a new positive identity as LGB. (See McCarn and Fassinger, 1996, for a promising recent model and Reynolds and Hanjorgiris, 2000, for an overview of identity models). In the 1990s, a new possibility for identification emerged with the development of the queer movement. In this movement, LGB, transgendered, gender nontraditional, and other socially marginalized people have formed communities and identities expressly inclusive and affirmative of a range of "differentness" (Alexander, 1999; Atkins & Marston, 1999). The limited developmental cues provided concerning Janine suggest that she is in the pride stage of sexual minority identity development (Cass, 1979). Her description of what she means by queer clearly indicates an open pride-filled self-identification, a sense of separation from "straights," and an active confrontation of the status quo by "throwing" her queer identity "in the face of straights." The pride stage of development is crucial to the full rejection of socially prejudicial notions of sexual minorities and the internalization and integration of a positive identity as a sexual minority person. If Janine is in this important stage of identity development, then mistrust and even anger toward a counselor perceived as part of the "status quo" is likely.

In working with Janine, it will be critical for the counselor to take care to behave in an LGB affirmative manner. The counselor should seek to demonstrate a valuing of the pride stage experience, as well as actively acknowledge the reality of anti-queer oppression and the importance of anger in the face of that oppression. Many authors have made numerous suggestions for affirmative career counseling and most include attention to the counselor's own awareness and development in regard to sexual orientation issues (Croteau, et al, 2000). If Janine is in the pride stage and the counselor is heterosexual, it will be particularly important for the counselor to have done significant self-exploration work on his/her issues with sexual orientation and with being LGB affirmative (see Gelberg & Chojnacki, 1996). The aforementioned problem with the subtitle of this case is a good illustration of how a counselor can slip into attitudes that support the oppressive status quo; such attitudes with need to be recognized and worked through.

Janine's trust in the counselor-client relationship will also be furthered by an approach that respects and prioritizes her immediate concerns. Thus, early sessions should be focused on assisting Janine with her concrete needs for securing needed financial resources and beginning her coursework in a successful manner. In terms of financial resources, we recommend helping Janine (1) accurately assess her financial needs, (2) generate and explore a variety of avenues for meeting those needs (e.g., part-time employment, student financial aid, work-study, educational loans), and (3) select and implement effective financial strategies. With respect to coursework, we recommend the same general approach of assessing needs (e.g., where is she with course selection, enrollment, establishing herself within the academic support program, etc.) and then generating and selecting strategies based on those needs.

In the longer term, Janine appears to need assistance with career exploration and decision making. Given her apparent lack of exploration of her own career interests, we recommend a process of interest exploration that allows for considerable dialogue between counselor and client about sources of interests or the lack thereof. Techniques such as a vocational card sort might be especially effective in raising Janine's consciousness in regard to past learning experiences. As Janine makes interest choices in the process of a card sort, the counselor could ask questions that help her explore whether early gender messages limited opportunities to develop self-efficacy and outcome expectations in gender nontraditional areas. Asking open questions about how she has come to know each of her interests or disinterests could lead to greater awareness of other possible contextual factors such as the family abuse, bipolar disorder, or other as yet unidentified influences that may have served as barriers to interest development. Further, asking questions about the relationship between being queer and her expressed interest can help Janine begin to explore her perceived opportunity structure and develop accurate perceptions of career opportunities and obstacles for sexual minorities. From information gained in these discussions, Janine and the counselor can determine whether Janine would benefit from further learning experiences with a broader array of interest areas or whether she is ready to learn more about how to translate her current interests into educational and world of work options. We anticipate that resolution of Janine's career concerns will involve explicit consideration of her past experiences with discrimination and affirmation around her queer identity, as well as her expectations about discrimination and affirmation in future workplaces. Assessing the level of LGB/queer affirmation in potential employment settings and making choices about how to manage her queer identity in the workplace will be important issues to discuss as Janine begins to translate career interests into educational and career choices. Finally, given Janine's history, the counselor should continue to assess, monitor, and respond to Janine's level of functioning and suicidal potential.

We have attempted to employ SCCT and LGB affirmative career perspectives to shape our suggestions for career counseling that affirms and makes central the notion of differentness or queerness, instead of marginalizing or pathologizing such difference. As we discussed and planned our response to this case, our language became instructive as our tongues twisted around the similar sound of "career" and "queer." Soon out of our tongue-twisted mouths came the phrase "caqueer" counseling. It is crucial for Janine's career counselor to believe in the positive power of Janine's "in your face" challenge to "straights." The title "caqueer counseling" is meant to be just a bit "in your face." It is meant to challenge career counseling, particularly any counseling that has become too status quo, to follow the lead of queer communities and give "differentness" a place of central value.

## References

Alexander, J. (1999). Beyond identity: Queer values and community. *Journal of Gay, Lesbian, and Bisexual Identity, 4*, 293-314.

Atkins, D., & Marston, C. (1999). Creating accessible queer community: Intersections and fractures with dis/ability praxis. *Journal of Gay, Lesbian, and Bisexual Identity, 4*, 3-21.

Bieschke, K.J., Eberz, A.B., Bard, C.C., & Croteau, J.M. (1998). Using social cognitive career theory to create affirmative lesbian, gay, and bisexual research training environments. *Counseling Psychologist, 26*, 735-754.

Cass, V.C. (1979). Homosexual identity formation: A theoretical model. *Journal of Homosexuality, 4*, 219-236.

Chung, Y.B. (1995). Career decision making of lesbian, gay, and bisexual individuals. *Career Development Quarterly, 44*, 178-190.

Croteau, J.M., Anderson, M.Z., & Distefano, T.M. (2000). Lesbian, gay, and bisexual vocational psychology: Reviewing foundations and planning construction. In R.M. Perez, K.A. DeBord, & K.J. Bieschke (Eds.), *Handbook of counseling and psychotherapy with lesbian, gay, and bisexual clients.* (pp. 383-408). Washington, DC: American Psychological Association.

Fassinger, R.E. (1995). From invisibility to integration: Lesbian identity in the workplace. *Career Development Quarterly, 44*, 149-167.

Fassinger, R.E. (1996). Notes from the margins: Integrating lesbian experience into the vocational psychology of women. *Journal of Vocational Behavior, 48*, 160-175.

Fassinger, R.E. (2000). Applying counseling theories to lesbian, gay, and bisexual clients: Pitfalls and possibilities. In R.M. Perez, K.A. DeBord, & K.J. Bieschke (Eds.), *Handbook of counseling and psychotherapy with lesbian, gay, and bisexual clients,* (pp. 107-132). Washington, DC: American Psychological Association.

Gelberg, S. & Chojnacki, J.T. (1996). *Career and life planning with gay, lesbian, & bisexual persons.* Alexandria, VA: American Counseling Association.

Lent, R.W., Brown, S.D. & Hackett, G. (1994). Toward a unifying social cognitive theory of career and academic interest, choice, and performance. *Journal of Vocational Behavior, 45*, 79-122.

McCarn, S.R. & Fassinger, R.E. (1996). Revisioning sexual minority identity formation: A new model of lesbian identity and its implications. *Counseling Psychologist, 24*, 508-534.

Morgan, K.S. & Brown, L.S. (1991). Lesbian career development, work behavior and vocational counseling. *Counseling Psychologist, 19*, 273-291.

Morrow, S.L., Gore, P.A., Jr., & Campbell, B.W. (1996). The application of a sociocognitive framework to the career development of lesbians and gay men. *Journal of Vocational Behavior, 48*, 136-148.

Reynolds, A.L. & Hanjorgiris, W.F. (2000). Coming out: Lesbian, gay and bisexual identity development. In R.M. Perez, K.A. DeBord, & K.J. Bieschke (Eds.). *Handbook of counseling and psychotherapy with lesbian, gay, and bisexual clients.* (pp. 35-56). Washington, DC: American Psychological Association.

basic career exploration and choice. Naturally, these paths are not mutually exclusive, but it is important to arrive at an intentional, cooperative decision about where to begin counseling. If Barbara opts for the first path, I would want to help her to produce a neatly drafted resume that effectively showcases her potential. In view of her apparently limited experience in the work world, I would discuss with her the consequences that a messy draft could have on her job search.

I would also engage her in a discussion about the unconventional, first person style of her resume. My suspicion is that this style reflects a personally valued aspect of her work personality, namely, her artistic side. I would encourage Barbara to share her resume with a few knowledgeable, "safe" others, such as mentors, law professors, or her internship colleagues. I would then help her to process, and consider how she might wish to respond to, the feedback she receives from them. The aim would not be to pressure her to change her self-presentation style, but rather to gather data that could better inform her job search strategy. Such information may enable her, for example, to consider the sorts of employers who might value her style or to fine-tune the ways in which she presents herself to employers.

In addition, I would explore other aspects of Barbara's job search, such as her network of job contacts and her job interview behavior. Various resources, such as self-help guides, could be drawn upon to assist her resume writing and other job search tasks. I would also discuss with Barbara my view of career development as an ongoing process, help her to anticipate and prepare for possible set-backs regarding job search and entry, and invite her to return for further counseling assistance, should the need arise in the future.

My response to this first possible scenario might not depart all that dramatically from that of career counselors who work from several other theoretical orientations. However, should Barbara opt to pursue the second scenario (i.e., broader career exploration), my approach would more clearly be derived from SCCT's basic tenets. Offering the rationale that it may be useful to select among the widest possible array of options, I would recommend assessment activities aimed at clarifying Barbara's talents, values, and interests. These activities could take several possible forms. For example, we might review Barbara's pattern of interests and attainments in academic, leisure, and career-relevant contexts, relying on self-reports as well as performance feedback from her internship supervisor and, possibly, important others (e.g., teachers, employers). We might also use a modified vocational card sort to identify existing occupational interests, together with options that may have been foreclosed due to unrealistic self-efficacy or outcome expectations (see Brown & Lent, 1996). Considering Barbara's artistic bent, creative methods – such as narrative/story-writing or guided fantasy exercises – might be used to help her to clarify her values and to envision potentially satisfying career options that might otherwise be overlooked.

Alternatively, adapting procedures described by Brown and Lent (1996), we might employ formal aptitude and needs/values measures, tied to explicit occupational classification systems, to help identify options that Barbara may find satisfying (because they correspond well with her values) and at which she might be successful (because they are congruent with her skills). Fields that are suggested on the basis of value, aptitude, and interest assessment would be targeted for further discussion. It may be useful to explore, for example, what she knows about these different options, how she has acquired this information, and what factors form the basis of her choice of corporate law.

These assessment activities would likely produce a broadened list of occupational options that are worth exploring further. Mindful of her considerable investment in law school and her satisfaction with her internship experience, I would be particularly inclined to help her identify legal specialization options that would allow her to capitalize on her current training while also enabling her to express valued parts of her work personality and to receive outcomes that she values. Once this expanded list of options has been identified, Barbara would be encouraged to gather information on each of them, using such sources as print materials, the Internet, and hands-on experiences, such as job shadowing and personal interviewing (the latter of which could also serve as a basis for increasing her network of potential job contacts). As is typical of most approaches to career counseling, efforts would be made to assist her in integrating information about her self and about the world of work in arriving at a decision and a subsequent course of action.

Parenthetically, it is important to observe that Barbara's expressed and previously measured interests do not include the enterprising/business-type theme that is prominent in most law specializations, including corporate law. However, social and artistic interests – Barbara's primary interest themes – are common secondary or tertiary interests among lawyers. Data gleaned from her Myers-Briggs type and from her internship experience also paint a picture of a socially aware individual, who may prefer harmony over conflict, be a good team player, and enjoy activities that directly affect people's lives. Review of such data, which are already available, may be sufficient to assist her to think more expansively about her options (e.g., branches of the law that might involve a more direct, helping role) and to gather information aimed at learning what different types of lawyers do and how their values (e.g., altruism vs. compensation) might be fulfilled. Even if Barbara ultimately decides to stick with her choice of corporate law, such information-gathering and self-reflective activities may help her to develop more realistic outcome expectations, consider particular occupational niches within corporate law that might suit her well and, hence, form a more solid base for career choice and adjustment.

Finally, as implied earlier, an SCCT-based approach would also recognize explicitly social-contextual aspects of Barbara's career decision making, such as gender- and culture-based considerations. For example, we might explore such questions as, how might her family or friends be likely to respond to particular career options in which she is interested? What roles do dual-career relationships or multiple role planning play in her thoughts about her career future? What messages has she internalized about what careers are appropriate for her? What barriers (e.g., social, cultural, racial, financial) does she anticipate encountering in her career pursuits? In addition to identifying possible barriers, I would expect to help Barbara to prepare for barriers she believes she will be likely to encounter. I would also want to help her to build a maximally helpful support system composed of individuals on whom she can count for ongoing career assistance (e.g., encouragement, advice). These barrier-coping and support-building aspects of SCCT have preventive and developmental aims – that is, they are intended to prevent or minimize future impediments to Barbara's work entry and to empower her as an active agent in her own career development.

## References

Brown, S.D. & Lent, R.W. (1996) A social cognitive framework for career choice counseling. *Career Development Quarterly, 44*, 354-366.

Enns, C.Z. (2000). Gender issues in counseling. In S.D. Brown & R.W. Lent (Eds.), *Handbook of counseling psychology* (3rd ed., pp. 601-638). New York: Wiley.

Hackett, G., & Byars, A.M. (1996). Social cognitive theory and the career development of African American women. *Career Development Quarterly, 44,* 322-340.

Lent, R.W., Brown, S.D., & Hackett, G. (1994). Toward a unifying social cognitive theory of career and academic interest, choice, and performance. *Journal of Vocational Behavior, 45,* 79-122.

Lent, R.W., Brown, S.D., & Hackett, G. (1996). Career development from a social cognitive perspective. In D. Brown, L. Brooks, & Associates, *Career choice and development* (3rd ed., pp. 373-421). San Francisco, CA: Jossey-Bass.

Ponterotto, J.G., Fuertes, J.N., & Chen, E.C. (2000). Models of multicultural counseling. In S.D. Brown & R.W. Lent (Eds.), *Handbook of counseling psychology* (3rd ed., pp. 639-669). New York: Wiley.

# *Response to Barbara: The Case of the Uneasy Lawyer*
## *Rhonda Paul*
## *Wayne State University*

I have been asked to respond to Barbara on the basis of background information provided in a case format. My comments will include impressions of Barbara, additional information to be sought about Barbara and her current situation, plans for career counseling to include direct actions and interventions, and theoretical and contextual framework used to form the basis of my career counseling strategy.

## Image/Impressions of Barbara

Barbara, a 25-year-old recent African American female law school graduate, is seeking career counseling for resume writing assistance in an effort to acquire a position in corporate law. After reading about this case, I formed various impressions about Barbara. She strikes me as a person who is insecure and feels the need to give the appearance of being self-assured. Barbara also appears to be a very expressive and creative individual. This was demonstrated by the manner in which her resume was constructed. My guess is that her family income is low and she is the first in her family to go to college.

## Conceptualization of the Case

Barbara's issues, on the surface, appear to be simple, but I believe there are other underlying issues that are more complex and deserve careful consideration. Although resume writing is her reason for counseling, she reports that she is uncertain about pursuing a corporate law career. Her apprehension may stem from the fact that she has had very little exposure to the legal field and does not know what to expect.

Additionally, Barbara placed in the bottom half of her law school class. Because of this, she may have internalized low self-efficacy beliefs about her ability to become successful as a lawyer. Furthermore, the outcomes she may have expected from pursuing a law career may not be as positive as they once were.

Barbara's results from career inventories taken in college also provide some insight as to why she may be having second thoughts about pursuing a career in corporate law. Her Holland code from the Self-Directed Search (Holland, 1985) of social, artistic, and realistic (SAR) appears to be incongruent with her expressed interest of corporate law. This code is also inconsistent as well. Her realistic trait may represent her experiences growing up on a farm, rather than a career personality characteristic. Her Myers-Briggs Type Indicator code of ESFJ indicates that she is an individual who is helpful, sociable, personable, caring and sensitive to the needs of others. (Myers & McCaulley, 1985). Her preference code coincides with her desire to "help people." Perhaps a legal environment within the public sector would be more congruent with her work personality.

Her decision to pursue law may also have been influenced by her cultural or racial background. In the African American community, law is considered a "protected" career field. Law, along with education, social science, medicine, is also perceived by many African Americans as being a career field that is stable, provides a needed service to the Black community and less racially biased (McCollum, 1998). As a consequence, African Americans have traditionally gravitated to law as a career. At the same time, African Americans tend to avoid certain career areas such as those in the business world because they perceived them as being more discriminatory (Evans & Herr, 1991, cited in McCollum, 1998). Thus, Barbara's reluctance to pursue corporate law could be due to her perception of a relatively small opportunity structure and a considerable amount of discrimination in Corporate America.

## Additional Questions

Due to the limited information given about Barbara, I would attempt to address several questions.

### Traditional
1. How did Barbara make the decision to pursue law?
2. When did she decide to pursue law? Was it in high school or college?
3. Has Barbara held other jobs? If so, were any of them related to law?
4. Did Barbara take the bar exam? If so, did she pass it?
5. Were her positive experiences as an intern an indication of her desire to work with the less fortunate or her interest in law?
6. What was Barbara's academic performance in college?
7. What were Barbara's strong and weak subjects in high school and college? What were Barbara's SAT and LSAT scores?
8. Was her academic performance in law school a reflection of her lack of motivation to pursue law?
9. Did career counseling and test interpretation accompany her scores on the Self-Directed Search and the Myers-Briggs? If so, how were her scores interpreted?
10. Did she consider other careers which more compatible with her codes? If so, why were other options discarded in favor of law?

### Cultural/Contextual
1. Is Barbara making assumptions about her capabilities based on her academic performance in law school?
2. Were there any other experiences in law school that may have discouraged her?
3. What influence did her family have on her decision to enter law school?
4. What is the educational background of her parents?
5. Does Barbara have a steady boyfriend? If so, are there plans for marriage?
6. What messages has she received about careers considered appropriate for women and African Americans?
7. What are the academic and career interests of her siblings?

## Plans for Career Counseling and Assessment

### General Framework for Overall Assessment
The theoretical framework for my counseling approach would be derived from Super's perspective on self-concept implementation in career development, Holland's theory, and Bandura's social cognitive theory. I would also incorporate assessment and career counseling interventions that take into consideration cultural background and social environment. Reference would also be given to Fouad and Bingham's (1995) "Culturally Appropriate Counseling Model" and Cheatham's (1990) "Heuristic Model of Students' Career Development."

After obtaining answers to the questions listed above, my next priority would be to determine whether Barbara's most pressing concern is to revise her resume and devise a job search strategy, to explore possible career alternatives within the law field or whether to make a total career change. If Barbara's primary objective is to revise her resume and find a job, then I would provide feedback as to how her resume could be improved, assistance in developing job search skills, practice in developing interview techniques, and help in assessing background and skills. If we determine that Barbara's objective is to pursue work environments within the legal field, I would first explore her career knowledge and reasons for wanting to pursue corporate law.

## Cultural/Contextual Approaches

I would work with Barbara with the intention of determining how cultural, familial and societal expectations have shaped her career situation. Specifically, I would employ the following procedures:

1. Assess Barbara's stage of racial identity. The racial identity of Barbara could influence her career behavior and have implications for the career counseling process (Carter & Cook, 1992; Parham & Austin, 1994).
2. Explore what she meant by "helping people." I'd be interested in whether this statement was more a reflection of her commitment to her community or race as a whole, or her interest in helping individuals.
3. Put emphasis on the importance of role models and networking. I would also assist her in establishing contacts with African American women in various specialties of law.
4. Administer the Career Counseling Checklist (Ward & Bingham, 1993). This instrument would provide useful information about Barbara relative to contextual, cultural, and familial issues.
5. Explore her perceptions of barriers. I would also employ counseling strategies designed to strengthen her ability to overcome obstacles and deal with racism and sexism effectively.
6. Explore her bicultural stress associated with various work environments. I would also assess her ability to function biculturally in the work world.
7. Seek to determine her primary sources of identity. Theoretically, the self-concept of African American women consists of at least four self-referents: psychophysiological self-referent, afro-self-referent, Euro-self-referent and the myself referent according to Brown-Collins & Sussewell, 1986; (cited in Gainor & Forrest, 1991). African American woman make career decisions depending on which self-referent is stronger (Gainor & Forrest, 1991). As Barbara's counselor, I would explore each aspect of her self-concept in an effort to determine which self-referent she considers most relevant to career decision making.
8. Conduct a gender role analysis (Brown, 1986) where her views about women in various life roles would be explored.
9. Assess the acculturation level of Barbara. This information would give me an understanding of her worldview. It would also provide a framework for approaching the career counseling process.

## Traditional Approaches

Traditional approaches would consist of the following:

1. Assisting her in identifying career resources and finding a satisfactory work environment within the legal field.
2. Guiding Barbara into occupations within the legal field that are more congruent with her personality and interest (i.e. government, politics, civil rights).
3. Assisting her in exploring and developing efficacy beliefs so that she may be more apt to consider a wider variety of options.
4. Assisting her in building her self-confidence and determination by guiding her through positive self-talk.

If the goal of career counseling is to initiate a career change, I would recommend that Barbara continue counseling over a longer period of time. In addition to the procedures listed above, the career plan would involve the administration of a battery of career inventories including the Strong Campbell Interest Inventory (Harmon, Hansen, Borgen, & Hammer, 1994); Career Barriers Inventory (Swanson & Tokar, 1991); Role Salience Inventory (Nevill & Super, 1986); Work Values Inventory (Super, 1970); Career Maturity Inventory (Crites & Savickas, 1995); African American Acculturation Scale (Landrine & Klonoff, 1994). Test interpretation would be conducted with consideration given to gender and racial/cultural bias.

## Summary

In summary, the approach I would use with Barbara would be a combination of traditional and nontraditional strategies, incorporating cultural/contextual perspectives. In essence, my counseling strategy would consist of an integration of career counseling and multicultural counseling. The length of the counseling relationship would depend on its overall purpose.

## References

Brown, L.S. (1986). Gender role analysis: A neglected component of psychological assessment. *Psychotherapy: Theory, Research, Practice, Training, 23*, 243-248.

Brown-Collins, A.R., & Sussewell, D.R. (1986). The Afro-American women's emerging selves. *Journal of Black Psychology, 13*, 1-11.

Carter, R.T., & Cook, D.A. (1992). A culturally relevant perspective for understanding the career paths of visible racial/ethnic group people. In H.D. Lea & Z.B. Leibowitz (Eds.) *Adult career development: concepts, issues, and practices* (2nd ed., pp. 192-217). Alexandria, VA: National Career Development Association.

Cheatham, H.E. (1990). Africentricity and the career development of African Americans. *Career Development Quarterly, 38*, 334-346.

Crites, J.O. & Savickas, M.L. (1995). *Career Maturity Inventory*. Odessa, FL: Psychological Assessment Resources.

Evans, K.M. & Herr, E. (1991). The influence of racism and sexism in the career development of African American women. *Journal of Multicultural Counseling and Development, 19*, 130-135.

Fouad, N.A., & Bingham, R.P. (1995). Career counseling with racial and ethnic minorities. In W.B. Walsh & S.H. Osipow (Eds.). *Handbook of vocational psychology: Theory, research and practice* (2nd ed., pp. 331-365). Hillsdale, NJ: Erlbaum.

Gainor, K., & Forrest, L. (1991). African American women's self-concept: Implications for career decisions and career counseling. *Career Development Quarterly, 39*, 261-272.

Harmon, L.W., Hansen, J.C., Borgen, F.H., & Hammer, A.C. (1994). *Strong Interest Inventory: Applications and technical guide*. Palo Alto, CA: Consulting Psychologists Press.

Holland, J.L. (1985). *Making vocational choices: A theory of careers* (2nd ed.). Englewood Cliffs, NJ: Prentice Hall.

Landrine, H., & Klonoff, E.A. (1994). The African American Acculturation Scale: Development, reliability and validity. *Journal of Black Psychology 20*(2), 104-127.

McCollum, V.J. (1998). Career development issues and strategies for counseling African Americans. *Journal of Career Development, 25*(1), 41- 51.

Myers, I.B., & McCaulley, M.H. (1985). *Manual: A Guide to the development and use of the Myers-Briggs Type Indicator*. Palo Alto, CA: Consulting Psychologists Press.

Nevill, D.D., & Super, D.E. (1986). *The Salience Inventory Manual: Theory, application, and research*. Palo Alto, CA: Consulting Psychologists Press.

Parham, T.A. & Austin N.L. (1994). Career development and African Americans: A contextual reappraisal using the nigrescence construct. *Journal of Vocational Behavior, 44*(2), 139-154.

Super, D.E. (1970). *The Work Values Inventory*. Boston, MA: Houghton Mifflin.

Swanson, J.L. & Tokar, D.M. (1991). Development and initial validation of the Career Barriers Inventory. *Journal of Vocational Behavior, 39*(3), 344-361.

Ward, C.M. & Bingham, R.P, (1993). Career assessment of ethnic minority women. *Journal of Career Assessment, 1*(3), 246-257.

# PRISCILLA: THE CASE OF THE WANDERING HIKER

Priscilla is a 26-year-old Caucasian woman and a single mother of two children ages 3 and 5. She has an associate degree in biology and lacks 35 hours for a bachelor's degree (also in biology). She has worked in a variety of jobs (mostly clerical), of which none lasted more than two years. She was laid off from her most recent position as a secretary in a large legal firm.

Priscilla has been on unemployment for the past 6 months, but her benefits have expired. Priscilla is experiencing severe financial difficulties, which she expresses a strong desire to over-come. She has talked about returning to school to complete her degree but has never done anything to make that a reality. Priscilla has a long history of assuming dependent/caretaker roles in her personal relationships. Her current partner is a 35-year-old man, who recently was court-ordered to enter substance abuse treatment.

Priscilla enjoys gardening and hiking. Her favorite memories as a child are spending time on her grandfather's farm. Often, she would spend several weeks there during the summer months. Priscilla describes her grandfather as her "hero" because he "worked hard every day, didn't complain, and was both gentle and strong." Priscilla's father is a recovering alcoholic who is self-employed as a lawyer. Priscilla's mother is a clerk in a clothing store. Priscilla has no brothers or sisters.

Priscilla has come to the community counseling center for help finding a job that will help "pay the bills." As she talks about her situation, she seems to feel hopeless that she could ever get a job she "truly loved." She seems resigned to the fact that she is "trapped in work and love."

## *Response to Priscilla: The Case of the Wandering Hiker*
## *Applications of Career Theory and Assessment Methods*
## *Nancy E. Betz*
## *The Ohio State University*

In terms of the situation in which she finds herself, Priscilla exemplifies the all-too-common case of the single mother who has never obtained the kind of education and/or training necessary to obtain a job/pursue a career that is both economically sufficient, yet also personally satisfying – providing a fit to her vocational interests and talents. On the positive side, though, Priscilla seems to me to be a woman with much potential to profit from career counseling – she has a number of self-expressed interests and seems motivated to improve her life situation. Although she currently lacks hope that she could ever express her interests vocationally, I would begin counseling with the assumption that we can help her find a satisfying, "congruent" occupation as well as one that would provide the economic self-sufficiency that she needs.

Thus, my approach to counseling Priscilla would be two-pronged – helping her meet her immediate needs to support her family yet at the same time encouraging her to both identify and pursue the kind of education and/or vocational training that will enable her to obtain a job that pays adequately and that she also finds satisfying and, ideally, self-actualizing. Thus, our goals are both short- and long-term. Or in another sense, I am using Abraham Maslow's (1954, 1968) hierarchy of needs to guide the timing of our interventions – the lower levels of Maslow's hierarchy, physiological needs (hunger and thirst) and safety needs like shelter, must be satisfied before the highest-level need, self-actualization, can be addressed. Many of our vocational concepts such as Super's (1963) implementation of the self-concept, Holland's (1997) person-environment congruence and even the use of inventories of vocational interests and values, are based on the assumption that we are free to self-actualize, to select careers that fulfill our interests and maximize our potentialities. Yet for many people, including women such as Priscilla, feeding and sheltering oneself and one's family must take precedence over the loftier goal of self-actualization.

Our first focus, then, is the immediate financial needs of Priscilla and her children. Since her welfare benefits have expired, my first question to her concerns how she is currently paying the bills. If she is living with her partner and he is paying the bills, I would want to know how long this situation can realistically continue while she pursues the kind of education/training she needs to obtain a "good" job. Although I do not view permanent economic dependence on her partner as desirable/optimal, it is one temporary option that we will explore.

A second major option we would explore would be community programs/resources supporting educational/vocational training for unemployed/underemployed individuals. Although such programs come in many forms, one type found in many larger communities is workforce reentry programs for single unemployed parents (usually women), battered women, or displaced homemakers. For example the Center for New Directions in Columbus, Ohio provides a full spectrum of support services for women such as Priscilla who need assistance in moving toward economic self-sufficiency. Although such programs usually do not replace career counseling, they often provide useful if not essential support services and systems. Knowledge of community and institutional resources that can be useful to clients is an essential part of the career counselor's repertoire.

Another temporary option is Priscilla's parents, if they have the financial resources to assist her. If providing temporary financial support allows Priscilla to in effect "turn her life around," her parents may be more than willing to provide the temporary financial cushion she needs. A final option would be some type of temporary employment that would permit Priscilla to simultaneously either complete her college degree or obtain the kind of vocational training that she needs.

At the same time as we were addressing the immediate goal of financial self-support, I would be implementing two longer-term interventions, one based on Holland's (1997) concept of person-environment congruence and the other based on Bandura's (1986, 1997) self-efficacy theory.

Trait-factor theory (e.g., see Swanson, 1996), of which Holland's (1997) provides a very useful example, would guide my attempt to help Priscilla identify careers that she would find personally satisfying and meaningful. I would begin this attempt by talking further with Priscilla about her previous patterns and history of likes and dislikes from leisure activities and hobbies to school subjects to occupational daydreams or fantasies. I would ask her the question "If you could be anything you wanted to be, what would you choose?" I would give her an informal introduction to Holland's theory of vocational types (Realistic, Investigative, Artistic, Social, Enterprising, and Conventional) and encourage her to make a self-assessment prior to administering a measure of the themes, as part of the administration of one or more vocational interest inventories. Because I want to ensure a good representation of occupations both requiring and not requiring a college degree, I would administer the Strong Interest Inventory (SII; Harmon, Hansen, Borgen, & Hammer, 1994), which emphasizes the former and the Career Assessment Inventory (Johansson, 1986), which emphasizes the latter. From both inventories Priscilla will gain information about her general occupational orientation (the Holland themes), her basic interests in terms of activities such as science, mechanical activities, agriculture, etc., and numerous specific occupational suggestions. Hopefully, there will be some among these that will provide possible options for her to pursue.

Because she has self-expressed interest in gardening and hiking and her fond memories of her grandfather's farm, I would venture an initial guess that Holland's Realistic Theme would be present in Holland code, perhaps even the high point code. In addition, her previous Biology major might suggest Investigative Interests or perhaps a Realistic Subtheme if the interests in Biology are focused on practical applications of fields such as botany and zoology. Although assessing Priscilla's vocational interests would be essential, it would also be essential to assess her perceptions of her competencies, or self-efficacy, relative to various areas of vocational pursuit. Theoretical statements such as those of Betz (1999) and Lent, Brown, and Hackett (1994) make it clear that both interests and self-perceived competencies, or self-efficacy expectations (Bandura, 1986, 1997), are necessary for individuals to pursue a given career area. Therefore, paralleling my assessment of Priscilla's interests would be an assessment of her self-efficacy, or confidence, with respect to the Holland themes using a measure such as the Skills Confidence Inventory (SCI; Betz, Borgen & Harmon, 1996). (It should be noted that there are other possible measures of both interests and confidence with respect to the Holland themes, as reviewed by Betz, 1999; the SII, CAI, and SCI are discussed for illustrative purposes herein).

Following joint administration of the measures of vocational interests and self-efficacy or confidence, interpretation of the joint profile would begin with Holland theme areas for which Priscilla reported both high interest and high confidence. As suggested in the manual for the SCI (Betz, et al., 1996), areas of high interest and high confidence would be prime targets for serious career exploration.

Second in priority for exploration would be areas for which Priscilla reported high interest but lower confidence. Low confidence may be especially likely to occur for activity areas considered more typical of the other sex. Since Realistic (including building, mechanical, and outdoor activities) is an area traditionally associated with male socialization and on which males consistently obtain higher scores on both interest and confidence measures (Betz, 1993; Betz et al., 1996), Priscilla's postulated interests in Realistic activities may not be accompanied by high levels of Realistic confidence. If low confidence were evident, interventions based on Bandura's self-efficacy theory would be appropriate. These interventions would include one or more of the sources of efficacy information postulated by Bandura – successful performance accomplishments, vicarious learning or modeling, anxiety management, and encouragement from others.

Successful performance accomplishments would be facilitated by enrollment in educational courses or programs geared at a level where Priscilla could make positive learning advances without experiencing failure. As the counselor, I would view myself as a major source of encouragement and support for Priscilla – her "personal cheerleader."

As an example, Priscilla's possible interests in Realistic activities would be compatible with her enrollment in one of the increasingly prevalent programs designed to increase the representation of women in nontraditional trades such as construction, carpentry, plumbing, and electronics. Depending on her interests in these areas, such programs equip women to fill well-paying, generally secure jobs that can lead to considerable personal satisfaction with one's work. Other options In Holland's Realistic area include police officer and firefighter. An occupational area compatible with Realistic and Investigative, as well as Conventional if that is in her Holland Code, is the huge area of information/computer technology and science. Excellent vocational training is available in these areas, or Priscilla could opt to complete her college degree in a technology-related field.

Because I have not yet actually begun career counseling with Priscilla, the above occupational options are only suggestions based on "hints" that came from the initial (and very brief) description of the client. Obviously, we would need skilled interviewing and comprehensive vocational assessment to generate a set of occupational options capable of meeting Priscilla's needs for the economic support of herself and her children as well as for fulfilling work. Although additional discussion might focus on the quality of her relationship with her partner, with an emphasis on how that relationship nurtures and supports her as a worthwhile human being, we assume that her long-term quality of life is best served by the achievement of economic self-sufficiency and self-actualization. These achievements will facilitate not only her quality of life, but the quality of life for her children and the quality of her future relationships.

## References

Bandura, A. (1986). *Social foundation of thought and action: A cognitive theory.* Englewood Cliffs, NJ: Prentice Hall.

Bandura, A. (1997). *Self-efficacy: The exercise of control.* New York: W.H. Freeman.

Betz, N.E. (1993). Issues in the use of ability and interest measures with women. *Journal of Career Assessment, 1,* 217-232.

Betz, N.E. (1999). Getting clients to act on their interests: Self-efficacy expectations as a mediator of the implementation of vocational interests. In M L. Savickas & A.R. Spokane (Eds.), *Vocational interests: Meaning, measurement, and counseling use* (pp. 327-344). Palo Alto, CA: Davies-Black.

Betz, N., Borgen, F., & Harmon, L. (1996). *Skills Confidence Inventory applications and technical guide*. Palo Alto, CA: Consulting Psychologists Press.

Harmon, L., Hansen, J.C., Borgen, F.H., & Hammer, A.L. (1994). *Strong Interest Inventory: Applications and technical guide*. Palo Alto, CA: Consulting Psychologists Press.

Holland, J.L. (1997). *Making vocational choices: A theory of vocational personalities and work environments* (3rd ed.). Odessa, FL: Psychological Assessment Resources.

Johansson, C.B. (1986). *Career Assessment Inventory: The enhanced version*. Minneapolis, MN: National Computer Systems.

Lent, R.W., Brown, S.D., & Hackett, G. (1994). Toward a unifying social cognitive theory of career and academic interest, choice, and performance. *Journal of Vocational Behavior, 45,* 79-122.

Maslow, A.H. (1954). *Motivation and personality*. New York: Harper.

Maslow, A.H. (1968). *Toward a psychology of being*. New York: Van Nostrand.

Super, D.E. (1963). Self-concepts in vocational development. In D.E. Super (Ed.), *Career development: Self-concept theory* (pp. 1-16). New York: College Entrance Examination Board.

Swanson, J.L. (1996). The theory *is* the practice: Trait-and-factor/person-environment fit counseling. In M.L. Savickas & W.B. Walsh (Eds.), *Handbook of career counseling theory and practice* (pp. 93-108). Palo Alto, CA: Davies-Black.

## *Response to Priscilla: The Case of the Wandering Hiker*
### *Norman. E. Amundson*
### *The University of British Columbia*

I would see this case developing at two different levels. At the most basic level the concern for a "survivor" job must be addressed. Unemployment benefits have expired, there is a need to "pay the bills" and not a lot of apparent support from other sources. With this in mind I could see some benefit in proceeding directly with the job search process. It is apparent, however, that there is a lot more here than job search. Priscilla certainly seems to be a candidate for setting short- and long-term goals. Some of the comments about hopelessness and feeling trapped in work and love suggest that there is some desire for a more substantive life/work change.

As a starting point I would begin building a collaborative working relationship (the working alliance) with Priscilla focusing on both short- and long-term goals (Gelso & Carter, 1985). I would also try to connect with her as a person. One of my standard lines is "Before we go further with this counseling business, I would like to find out more about who you are as a person." This more personal approach helps to define some common ground and also often yields some important content and feeling information that becomes part of the counseling process (Amundson, Westwood & Prefontaine, 1995).

In building the relationship it is important to also share some aspects of how I see the situation. As a counselor I have to use my own creativity and positive outlook to encourage and support the client. In many respects Priscilla may have given up on her future and it is important to rekindle the flame of "hope." One of the ways of achieving this end is to challenge her with her strengths (strength challenge), i.e., past educational achievements and abilities. As part of this process it is important to give her an alternate image of herself and her career options and to openly express my willingness to work with her toward these broader goals.

As I examine Priscilla's situation I need to be aware of certain contextual factors (culture, socioeconomic status, gender, age) but not use these to "put her in a box." She is her own person and I need to leave room for her to express that individuality. At the same time I am aware of the power of certain contextual issues and will adjust my counseling to reflect these realities. For example, when working with some aboriginal clients I use more of a group focus to reflect the importance of family and community members (McCormick & Amundson, 1997). I also make use of certain cultural approaches such as the talking stick and the healing circle.

Another integral part of this initial process concerns a discussion about just what is involved when moving beyond job search (the initial counseling goal) to participating in a broader career exploration process. Many clients are unsure about what is involved and appreciate the opportunity for this discussion. I have found it helpful to use the centric wheel (see Figure One) as a way to describe some of the domains that would be covered as part of career exploration.

This counseling structure serves as a foundation for this initial discussion, but also can be used throughout the counseling process to visually organize the information that is being generated. Other issues to be addressed at this point include time availability and commitment to the process.

## Problem Defining

Priscilla has a "story" to tell and I think that it is important to leave room for her to provide her view of the situation. In listening to the story the focus will need to be on the affective as well as the content aspects of the story. In attending to the emotional elements it is important to be aware of some of the dynamics of unemployment and underemployment (Borgen & Amundson, 1987; Borgen, Amundson & Harder, 1988). Priscilla has gone through a significant period of invalidation and some of her feelings of hopelessness may be reflective of that experience.

A certain amount of information has been provided in the case description and I think that it might be interesting to see at this point how that information could fit within the categories from the centric wheel. In making this delineation I will also indicate some of the additional information that I would seek.

*Skills.* Priscilla has achieved an associate degree in biology and that would seem to imply that she has attained some skills in this particular field. I would want to find out more about this program and the skills that she has acquired. Also, she may have developed some additional skills in the variety of jobs that she has been doing.

*Interests.* From the information given it appears that she enjoys gardening, hiking and being on a farm. It would be helpful to elaborate on these interests. What is it about these experiences that make them so positive?

*Values.* The information about her grandfather (a "hero") appears to contain some important clues about her values. Working hard and not complaining would appear to be qualities that she values for herself. Her current state of unemployment would be particularly difficult for her given this outlook on life.

Figure 1

# The Wheel

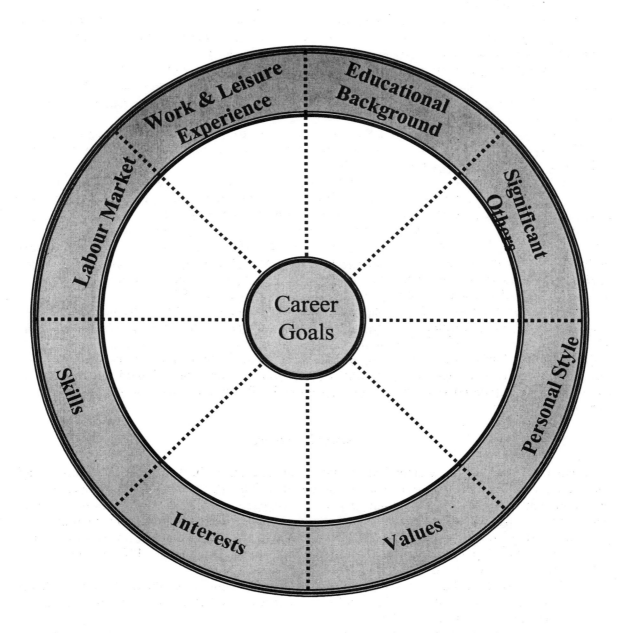

Norman E. Amundson and Gray Poehnell (1996).
Career Pathways 2nd Ed. Richmond BC: Ergon Communications.

*Personal Style.* Again, we can turn to the grandfather and look at his qualities of strength and gentleness. I would suspect that Priscilla tries to reflect similar traits in her relationships with others. Unfortunately, she seems to have translated this approach into some rather detrimental caretaker roles. She seems to be looking for others to nurture and has paid little attention to her own needs.

*Significant Others (Family and Friends).* If one looks at the situation of her current partner (court-ordered substance abuse program) or her parents (father a recovering alcoholic) it would seem that there would be only minimal support. I would like to have some additional information about these relationships and their impact on her career planning. From the information that has been provided it would seem that some connection is being made between work and relationships, i.e., trapped in work and love.

*Educational Background.* Some information is given about her educational background – an associate degree in biology and 35 hours short of a bachelor's degree. Further information about educational programs (and funding options) in her locale would be useful.

*Work and Leisure Experiences.* It would be helpful to have a clearer picture of her previous jobs. I would also like to explore what it was about these jobs that she liked and that she disliked. Very little is known about her leisure experiences. Perhaps there are some connections here to her interest in biology.

*Labor Market.* This section looks at the current labor market conditions in her area as well as identifying her network of career connections. Very little is known about this aspect of the situation and it certainly has an important bearing on the case.

I think that the centric wheel is a very useful tool for categorizing factual information, but it doesn't touch the metaphoric images that also form a part of the client's story. In the information that is provided there is very little attention given to any form of metaphoric imagery. Perhaps the image of being "trapped in work and love" could be explored further. Also I find it interesting that the authors have focused their image on the "Wandering Hiker." Metaphors can be a very important part of the communication process and it is important to train oneself to recognize metaphors and also to work with them as part of the counseling process, i.e., extending the metaphors, changing some aspects of the metaphors, creating new metaphors (Combs & Freedman, 1990).

Metaphors can also be used to examine my own relationship to the client. The image that came to my mind was of a bird with a badly sprained wing coming to the clinic for help. Although this image captures the "helplessness" of the situation, it also puts me in the role of veterinarian (the expert). In thinking further about this I realized that I must be careful to monitor my own behavior so that I would not get pulled into the dependent/caretaker role. It is only through modeling and participating in a more collaborative decision-making process that Priscilla will learn to take control of her own life.

## Problem Resolving

Some of the gaps that have identified through using the centric wheel could be addressed through some initial questioning, but I am reluctant to go too far with the standard "question and answer" procedure. I think that there are more imaginative and effective means of getting at information. Using an "active engagement" counseling approach I would move quickly from hearing the initial problem to using more dynamic methods to encourage additional career exploration and resolution (Amundson, 1998). One of these methods is the Pattern Identification Exercise-PIE (Amundson, 1995). The steps of inquiry associated with the PIE exercise as follows:

1.  I would ask Priscilla to think about an activity (such as hiking) that she really enjoyed. In reflecting on this activity I would want her to identify a specific time when it was very enjoyable and a time when it was less so.

2.  As a next step I would get Priscilla to describe in detail the positive and negative experiences. Using a flip chart (one of my favorite tools) I would write down everything she said

and seek to elaborate the description by asking additional open-ended questions when insufficient details were provided.

3.  After a full discussion of the positive and negative experiences I would ask Priscilla to consider what this information says about her as a person. I believe that there is a form of psychological DNA and if we examine any incident we will see the reflection of some of the basic patterns. At this point it is important to encourage Priscilla to do most of the work in terms of analyzing the information. I will at certain points ask some tentative questions to help with the formulation of patterns, but for the most part it is the client's work.

4.  Once the patterns have been identified it is time to move to application. Again, Priscilla needs to take the lead here and I would be encouraging her to think about how some of these patterns might connect to the career challenges she is facing, i.e., job search, additional educational training..

I have found that the PIE exercise is a great way to open up many additional issues for discussion. Contained within this small framework are often references to family issues, friends, feelings, self-esteem, challenges, and motivations. The PIE activity also has the advantage of being grounded in the client's experiential world.

Many other techniques and strategies (metaphors, drawings, card sorts, career anchors, achievement profiling, information interviewing, journal entries, behavior rehearsal, and so on) can be used to supplement this focus on the resolution process (Amundson, 1998). The selection of strategies would depend on the specific issues that were emerging and the way in which Priscilla was reacting to the various strategies. For some clients the more imaginative methods (art, stories, metaphors) seem more appropriate whereas for others there may be a preference for more systematic methods (library research, behavior rehearsal).

I think that it is important in counseling to maintain an energy level that keeps the client involved and moving forward. This usually means more activity than just the regular counseling sessions. I would want Priscilla to be working between sessions on various homework activities. These activities would be structured so that they would be engaging and relevant to her career exploration needs.

## Problem Closing

With this case I would not be surprised to see some shifts from career exploration to other, more personal issues reflected by the dependent/caretaker roles that she has assumed. In making a shift I would need to be careful not to get ahead of Priscilla. This really requires ongoing vigilance and discussion of the counseling goals. It also requires when appropriate a renegotiation of the counseling contract.

According to brief and solution-focused theory it is important to focus on the goals that have been achieved and also to recognize that further work may be required at a future date (O'Hanlon & Weiner-Davis, 1989; Walter & Peller, 1992). In this case I have made the assumption that there would be an interest in job search and also career exploration. As a counselor in the community counseling center I might also be in a position to do some counseling focusing on personal relationships. The extent to which this sequence developed would depend on the interest of the client, the skills of the counselor, and the mandate of the agency.

## References

Amundson, N.E. (1995). *Pattern identification exercise.* ERIC Digest. Greensboro, NC: ERIC Clearinghouse on Counseling and Student Services, University of North Carolina. (ERIC Document Reproduction Service No. ED 404 585).

Amundson, N.E. (1998). *Active engagement: Enhancing the career counselling process*. Richmond, BC: Ergon Communications.

Amundson, N.E. & Poehnell, G. (1996). *Career pathways* (2nd ed.). Richmond, BC: Ergon Communications.

Amundson, N.E., Westwood, M., & Prefontaine, R. (1995). Cultural bridging and employment counselling with clients from different cultural backgrounds. *Canadian Journal of Counselling, 29*, 206-213.

Borgen, W.A. & Amundson, N.E. (1987). The dynamics of unemployment. *Journal of Counseling and Development, 66*, 180-184.

Borgen, W.A., Amundson, N.E. & Harder, H.G. (1988). The experience of underemployment. *Journal of Employment Counseling, 25*, 149-159.

Combs, G., & Freedman, J. (1990). *Symbol, story & ceremony*. New York: Harper Business.

Gelso, C.J., & Carter, J.A. (1985). The relationship in counseling and psychotherapy: Components, consequences, and theoretical antecedents. *Counseling Psychologist, 13*, 155-244.

McCormick, R.M., & Amundson, N.E. (1997). A career-life planning model for First Nations People. *Journal of Employment Counseling, 34*, 171-179.

O'Hanlon, W.H. & Weiner-Davis, M. (1989). *In search of solutions: A new direction in psychotherapy*. New York: Norton.

Walter, J.L., & Peller, J.E. (1992). *Becoming solution-focused in brief therapy*. New York: Brunner/Mazel.

# SHAHRI: THE CASE OF THE INTERNATIONAL STUDENT

Shahri was a 28-year-old Malaysian student who was attending California State University at Fresno working on his MS in plant science. He presented with a big smile and fast, slightly accented English. He had come to the U.S. six years ago after completing two years of college at a local Malaysian university. He was the third of seven children of Kadisan (father) and Rokiah (mother), who had emigrated from Indonesia to Malaysia. He did not like plant science, but was committed because he had signed a contract with a local company to pay for his education if he would return to work for them for seven years after his graduation.

Shahri traveled each weekend to San Francisco to work as a waiter at a major restaurant and see his many friends at the local gay clubs. He had been doing that for the entire time he had been at Fresno. Being gay in Fresno was not so good, but being gay in Malaysia was even worse. He was getting ready to return to Malaysia when he finished his degree, but he hated his major.

He has come to the university career center to explore his options. He loved dancing and other creative arts. He was quite self-confident and the only member of his family ever to have attended a university. His government had selected him because of his scores and grades for a full scholarship to attend a Malaysian university, but he wanted to come to the U.S. Now that he had studied here for seven years, he was also different from other Malaysians in another way: he spoke English with an American accent while most Malaysians usually had a British accent.

He had promised his parents that he would return after his Master of Science degree was completed, but he had recently met a young man in San Francisco with whom he had fallen in love. He was quite committed to returning to Malaysia, but he was also sad at the impending termination of this new and exciting relationship of six months. He stated that, if he could just marry his new partner, he would gladly stay here.

He had taken the Myers-Briggs Type Indicator previously and had a preference code of ISTJ, and his RIASEC code from the Vocational Preference Inventory was IRC.

## *Response to Shahri: The Case of the International Student*
## *Peter Plant*
## *Royal Danish School of Educational Studies*

This case study is written from the counselor's perspective in the style of stream-of-consciousness, thus illustrating some of the issues, methods, and theoretical underpinnings that could be implemented in this case, covering Image, Plans & Context in Section I. Summary & Rationale follow in Section II.

### Image of Shahri

"Well, Shahri, now that you have told me about your concerns, I'd like to give you some feedback on how I see what you have just said. You know, strangely enough, you don't come across to me as really agonizing. I mean, your problems as your have stated them are evident to me. Let me summarize: you are caught up in dilemmas, cross-cultural pressure, conflicting goals, and sexual preferences. You have signed a company contract that you may be about to break and have promised your parents to come back to Malaysia after your degree. However, then you might decide not to return. You hate your major and you enjoy the liberty of gay lifestyle in San Francisco. Time is running out and you don't want to give up your new relationship. But at the same time you seem quite laid-back and untroubled, as if you are, in fact, putting a distance to your past with some ease. Am I reading this correctly? ... I am. Good. Moreover, your RAISEC Code of from the Vocational Preference Inventory is IRC, which in fact should indicate that you are Realistic and Conventional on top of being Investigative. And judging from your Myers-Briggs Type Indicator with the preference code of ISTJ, you should be Introvert, Sensing, Thinking, and Judging. But I really don't see very much of this conventional, judging, and introvert person in the way you present yourself today. We all change and you have had the opportunity to change a lot during your years in the USA. So perhaps these labels are old stuff. Let's just scrap all this type and code business for the moment and get at the issues from another angle. OK?"

## Plans for Career Counseling

"First of all I'd like to ask you what is the worst that could happen? ....

"Secondly, having mentioned this worst case scenario, what image comes to mind? What metaphor? Please draw it on this flipchart. How big is it in your life space, which is represented by the entire sheet of paper? What else, what other issues or persons are in the picture? Draw them, please. How big are they? How do the different issues and persons fit together? How do they influence each other? Any colors of importance? For instance, what colors are your parents and their expectations; the company contract; the relationship with your gay lover; your self-image; and other issues? Is everything in place now? Is this the situation as it stands at this very moment? Well, how do you feel about it? Illustrate your emotions; make written comments; let them speak like a in a cartoon!"

"Now, are there any changes you would like to make to this picture? What quality do these changes have? Any change of colors? What can you do yourself? What changes are out of your hands? What timeline do you see here? In looking at a timeline: what can be done now; in the short run and what in the long run? Where are your helping forces? Where do you see resistance to your plans? How can you overcome this? What if you can't overcome the obstacles? Any plan B? What does that look like? Draw it in the picture."

## Contextual Factors

"Now, imagine for a moment that you are your parents. What would be their reaction to these plans of yours? And what are the reactions of your extended family? Of the Malaysian University? Of your fellow students? Of your partner here in the USA? What will they say or do (or not say or do) to you? How will you take this? How important is this to you? In short, what is your reaction to their reactions? Do you have any ethical concerns such as letting others down as opposed to walking your own path? Any cultural norms in play here in terms of collective responsibility as opposed to a more individualistic approach? Religious concerns? Financial ones? Other concerns? Rules and regulations in terms of immigration, work permit, study grants, etc?"

## Summary and Rationale

I treat this case with seriousness, empathy, and some humor, as I have hopefully indicated. Shahri is caught up in a multitude of dilemmas that he must disentangle. This is the focal point of the counseling intervention in this case. He wants assistance, i.e., counseling, in this process. Labelling him with types and codes is not much help here. For example, an Introvert and Conventional person would probably go straight home to Malaysia to fulfil societal and parental obligations and expectations. He would most likely not consider for one minute staying in the U.S. and marrying his gay lover! So, the rationale for introducing constructivist approaches (drawing, using flip charts, lifespace, working with metaphors etc) is that he needs to map his dilemmas to be able to handle them. He need to examine how big are they; what their relative positions are, and the importance/color/emotions attached to each, etc? The constructivist approach (see e.g. Sexton & Griffin, 1997) as opposed to testing/matching techniques opens up the possibility of visionary interpretations, new insights, and mapping influences and importance of gender, cultural and religious background, societal and parental expectations, cross-pressures, etc.

The circular questions that I have used ("How would others see this, and what is your reaction to their reactions?") are inspired from systemic counseling (see e.g. Marturana & Varela, 1987). Such types of questions open up reflection on new perspectives, helping the client to consider alternative options, and to anticipate possible responses from significant others. This approach is useful for handling (family-related) dilemmas, which are pivotal in this case. In short, the constructivist and systemic theoretical underpinning of the approaches chosen in this case challenge and question a more testing/labelling based approach with its types and codes.

## References

Marturana, H. & Varela, F.J. (1987): *The tree of knowledge: The biological roots of human understanding*. Boston, MA: Shambhala.

Sexton, T.L. & Griffin, B.L. (Eds.) (1997): *Constructivist thinking in counseling practice, research, and training*. New York: Teachers College, Columbia University.

## *Response to Shahri: The Case of the International Student*
## *Hemla Singaravelu*
## *St. Louis University*

### Image Formed of the Client

There seem to be several issues confronting Shahri as his sojourn in the United States comes to an end. First, it appears Shahri is leading a double life: one as an out gay man in close circles where he can be his true self and another as the son of a Muslim (possibly) family that is proud of his achievements. Second, Shahri cannot disappoint his family by not returning home or revealing his sexual identity and lifestyle, as this would shame his family. In collectivistic societies like Malaysia (Hofstede, 1980; Triandis, 1995), individuals are obligated to maintain the welfare of the family and every action has an impact on the family. Hence, shaming the family name may result in ostracism or exclusion.

Third, resuming his life in Malaysia may be further complicated by having to readjust to his old culture and its traditions. Shahri has experienced acculturation while in the U.S and hence, returning home would cause some level of reverse culture shock. Fourth, he is bound to his sponsoring agency for seven years and as a result must return home and commence his occupation in a field he has no interest or despises.

Fifth, the thought of leaving his new love and returning to a society that is intolerant toward the gay and lesbian population and being isolated is saddening. In Muslim nations like Malaysia, homosexuality is forbidden and illegal. Furthermore, unlike other heterosexual international students who can marry their U.S. partner and acquire permanent residence/citizenship, relationships of gays and lesbians are not legally recognized in this country. Therefore, the option of Shahri marrying his new partner and permanently living in the U.S is currently not possible.

Finally, Shahri's results on the MBTI (ISTJ) and VPI (IRC) seem to be consistent with his chosen field in plant science. However, he has also described liking certain artistic and social events, which can be construed as being inconsistent with his personality style. It is possible these results may reflect his skills and knowledge attained through educational training in plant science and not necessarily his true interest. On the other hand, Shahri could be associating plant science with returning home – and hence, his dislike for the field.

Even though Shahri has come to the career center to receive help in his career indecision, there are several personal issues that are affecting his career path. Expectations to fulfill family, cultural/religious, and sponsoring agency's obligations may be overwhelming Shahri. Furthermore, studies have indicated that sexual identity may play an integral part in a gay person's career identity. This may certainly be true in Shahri's case.

## Other Information to Elicit from the Client

Eliciting his reasons for choosing plant science as an academic major will be helpful. It seems surprising Shahri would complete both his bachelor's and master's in plant science if he disliked it. Was Shahri aware of his sexual orientation before leaving Malaysia? If so was studying in the U.S a way of "escaping" and living free of Malaysian culture, traditions, customs, and laws? Or did Shahri dislike plant science because he associated it with returning home (impending loss of freedom and lifestyle).

It is important to hear more from Shahri about his culture, religion, familial and societal expectations, socioeconomic status, and the political/economic situation in his country. This information will provide the background of the client and will help confirm or correct images the counselor has about the client.

As mentioned earlier, Shahri's career development is closely linked to his sexual identity development. Knowing how "out" Shahri is or where he is in his sexual identity development is important as this addresses the issue of his self-concept. Do his parents suspect/know he is gay? If they are aware then he might not have to deal with a big aspect of his sexual identity, that is, coming out especially to his parents/family.

More information is required about Shahri's sponsoring agency and their agreement. Also, has Shahri inquired about the consequences of not working for his sponsoring agency? Is it possible Shahri will be required to reimburse the amount to the agency if he did not return home? If so, would this be a palatable option for Shahri?

## Proposed Career Counseling Plan (Actions and Interventions)

There are several research findings that confirm the inseparability of career and personal counseling. In fact, a special section in volume 42 of *Career Development Quarterly* (Elliot,1993) was devoted to this issue. I strongly believe that addressing the personal issues confronting Shahri will be the key to identifying his career path. A major aspect of this issue centers on his self-identity in relation to his environment – particularly his sexual identity. Chojnacki and Gelberg (1994), Elliot (1993), Prince (1995), and several others have contended that gay clients' career development and sexual identity development occurs concurrently to form one career identity.

A large portion of an individual's sexual identity entails "coming out." The coming out process is the recognition of sexual orientation and integration of one's identity as a gay man or lesbian woman's into one's personal and social world (Cass, 1979). Furthermore, individuals who self-identify as gay/lesbian and have a positive gay identity are more likely to be well-adjusted (Hammersmith & Weinberg, 1973; Lenna, 1992). Hence, assessing Shahri's awareness of his sexual identity and his degree of being "out" must be addressed. Shahri may be at stage three of Cass's gay identity development where he may be increasingly committed to a gay identity by seeking out the company of other gays to fulfill social and emotional needs. In this stage, gays find social contact a necessity rather than desirable (thus, Shahri's weekly trip to San Francisco, employment as a waiter, and socializing at a gay bar). Disclosure to heterosexuals is extremely limited with the emphasis placed on the maintenance of two separate identities: a public one (straight identity) and a private one (gay), which is exhibited only in the company of other gay people. If Shahri were leading a double life, we would work toward integration and avoid compartmentalization of identities.

Closely related to the issue of sexual identity is Shahri's level of commitment to his new relationship. Exploring the importance of this relationship versus his commitment to his family and sponsoring agency is important. Even though legally marrying his partner is currently not an option, it is, however, possible for Shahri to remain in the U.S. if he can find a sponsor in his field to employ him. First, Shahri (as are all international students) is eligible for a year of practical training after his master's degree. Second, after his practical training Shahri can seek a temporary working permit through the help of an employer and may eventually be able to apply for permanent residency. However, to make the decision to stay in the U.S., Shahri will have to address the issue of not returning to Malaysia and its repercussions. Consequently, discussion should also center on Shahri's relationship and its repercussions as it relates to his home environment.

Fretz and Leong (1982) and Sonnenfeld and Kotter (1982) have given special emphasis to the importance of environmental factors such as social, political, economical, physical, and cultural conditions on career decision making. Additionally, Krumboltz (1981) proposed that family, social policies and procedures, educational system, and community influences, among others, are factors influencing the process of career development. He also noted that the individual might not have control over the influences of some of the environment factors. For Shahri, environmental factors play a large role in his career and sexual identity development. Addressing the reality of these influencing factors and Shahri's perception of them would be the next step.

Because he comes from a collectivistic society, Shahri's self-concept is quite intertwined with the needs of the family. It would be appropriate to review how Shahri perceives his role and identity in relation to the aforementioned environmental factors. Super (1984) had identified six roles individuals play over a life span – the child, student, worker, leisurite, citizen, and homemaker. Assessing his obligation to these roles as it relates to his environment may help in defining his self-concept and identity integration.

Another intervention is to clearly list the consequences of returning home or living in the U.S. Shahri has experienced some level of acculturation while in the U.S. Addressing how he has changed and what impact this will have if he returns home may be appropriate. Additionally, the impact of being gay in Malaysia and how he would handle it if he returned home must also be discussed. Could he see himself coming out to his family or would he have to lead a double life? Here, further discussion on sexual identity and self-concept is appropriate.

There is a certain level of incongruence in Shahri's assessment results (VPI and MBTI) and the description of his preferred activities (waiter- social and dancing - artistic). As contended by Prince (1995), it is possible for a gay man to decide prematurely on a career because of the lack of self-awareness and self-concept. Because Shahri's self-concept is so intertwined with the needs of his family and culture, further exploration and identification of his interests, values, and abilities are needed. Examining the reasons for initially selecting plant science and if he really has some interest in this field is important. Exploring his dislike for plant science and if he is relating it to returning home and losing his freedom and new partner is also appropriate here.

In addition, it is imperative that the degree Shahri has attained is not devalued or unrecognized. Exploring possible careers in the field of plant science might open new avenues and ideas of integrating Shahri's artistic, social side with his investigative, science side. With further information, counseling interventions should move toward identifying a career identity for Shahri and eventually integrating his sexual identity with his self-concept.

## References

Cass, V.C. (1979). Homosexual identity formation: A theoretical model. *Journal of Homosexuality, 4*, 219-235.

Chojnacki, J.T., & Gelberg, S. (1994). Toward a conceptualization of career counseling with gay/lesbian/bisexual persons. *Journal of Career Development, 21*(1), 3-10.

Elliot, J.E. (1993). Career development with lesbian and gay clients. *Career Development Quarterly, 41*, 210-226.

Fretz, B.R., & Leong, F.T.L. (1982). Vocational behavior and career development, 1981: A review. *Journal of Vocational Behavior, 21*, 123-162.

Hammersmith, S.K., & Weinberg, M.S. (1973). Homosexual identity: Commitment, adjustment, and significant others. *Sociometry, 36,* 56-79.

Hofstede, G. (1980). *Culture's consequences.* Beverly Hills, CA: Sage.

Krumboltz, J.D. (1981). A social learning theory of career selection. In D.H. Montross & C.J. Shinkman (Eds.), *Career development in the 1980s: Theory and practice* (pp. 43-66.), Springfield, IL: Charles C. Thomas.

Lenna, H.R. (1992). The outsiders: Group work with young homosexuals. In N.J. Woodman (Ed.), Lesbian and gay lifestyle: *A guide for counseling and education* (pp. 67-85), New York: Irvington.

Prince, J.P. (1995). Influences on the career development of gay men. *Career Development Quarterly, 44*(2), 168-176.

Sonnenfeld, J., & Kotter, J.P. (1982). The maturation of career theory. *Human Relations, 35*(1), 19-46.

Super, D.E. (1984). Career and life development. In D. Brown, L. Brooks & Associates, *Career choice and development* (pp. 192-234). San Francisco, CA: Jossey-Bass.

Triandis, H.C. (1995). *Individualism & collectivism.* Boulder, CO: Westview Press.

# ROBERT: THE CASE OF THE OVERWHELMED HELPER

"I seem to be the main support for everybody, but who is supporting me? I am glad to be able to help my parents, and my wife has been understanding up to now, but the stress is taking its toll on all of us." With this statement, Robert began telling the counselor the story of the last year of his life in Chicago. He is a 28-year-old, Jewish American male who came to see a career counselor initially seeking career transition information. His father recently had a health crisis, and Robert had to take a medical leave to help his parents as his father convalesced and his mother learned to manage his physical needs as well as to handle the financial and other family affairs, of which she had been previously ignorant.

Robert has an engineering degree from a respected school and has had no problems finding employment. He held his first job for two years and the one he left to help his parents for another four. He felt that this job gave him good chances for advancement. Robert's main reason to ask for the leave was his father's health crisis, but during this time he was doing a lot of soul searching. He found himself wondering why he had been so anxious to take the leave and get out of his workplace. He stated that he knows many people who have had family emergencies and that they have been able to accommodate them while remaining employed. Furthermore, he said that although his performance on the job was acceptable, and that he had had no negative feedback, he was very disappointed in his performance, felt he could do better, and worried that his inadequacy would catch up with him soon. Robert is extremely self-critical and stated that he was disappointed in himself in all arenas of his life. He said that he had always been self-critical and that he tended to be a perfectionist. Robert was asking himself not only whether he should look for a different setting in which to work, but also whether he should be considering a different line of work altogether, perhaps in communications or sales, where he could use his people skills and not feel so much pressure to keep up with technological advances.

In a second session, Robert stated that he had been depressed and that he had been seeing a marriage counselor with his wife. Although initially supportive of his decision to take the leave to help his parents, and although she was also actively helping them to stabilize their life, the financial strain of his not working was taking its toll on her and on the marriage. She was eager to start a family and also to buy a house, both of which had to be postponed during this period.

Robert stated that he was overwhelmed with so many issues at the same time, dissatisfaction with work, concern over his father's health and his mother's coping abilities, and the several marital issues. He repeated his initial statement, asking, "Who is going to help *me*?"

## *Response to Robert: The Case of the Overwhelmed Helper*
## *Weaving an Integrative Intervention for Work and Relationships*
### *David L. Blustein, Anna P. Chaves,*
### *Matthew A. Diemer, and Sheila H. Gardner*
### *Boston College*

This case presents many of the complexities and subtle nuances that have long been neglected in much of the career counseling discourse. Consistent with a growing perspective on the integrative nature of treatment modalities (Hackett, 1993; Richardson, 1996), Robert presents his concerns in a way that is not constrained by the artificial boundaries of professional labels. In this case analysis, we explore the complex weave of experiences and issues that form the fabric of Robert's difficult life circumstances. We hope that this case description will introduce readers to the real world of counseling wherein presenting issues and underlying personal strengths and conflicts may often occupy the space between work and relationships.

As in any other sort of counseling or therapy, the first task for the counselor is to develop a genuine, warm, and empathic relationship with the client (Bohart & Greenberg, 1997; Meara & Patton, 1994). Indeed, one of the most powerful ways to learn more about Robert's experiences and provide the comprehensive assessment that is needed is via empathic introspection (Kohut, 1977; Wolf, 1988). Empathic introspection represents a way for the counselor to learn about a client's emotional and psychological life by hovering as close as possible to the client's psychological experience (Wolf, 1988). The use of empathic introspection allows a counselor to convey a deep level of understanding to a client while also learning more about the client's history and concerns (Bohart & Greenberg, 1997). Hence, empathic introspection with Robert would help us to learn about the nature of his presenting problems and how he experiences these concerns.

## Developmental Assessment

The next step in our work would be to assess Robert's full array of issues. We would use two complementary conceptual systems to conduct this assessment. First, we advocate using a domain-sensitive approach wherein both the career and relationship issues can be understood and treated in tandem (Blustein & Spengler, 1995). In brief, the domain-sensitive approach is based on the notion that many (but not all) work and nonwork problems share common space. Given the recursive and often predictable spillover between work and relationship domains (Blustein & Spengler, 1995), we suggest that counselors often need to treat these issues conjointly. Another critical component of the domain-sensitive approach is that the intervention is directed initially within the domain that is most amenable to change. Once a client has some degree of comfort exploring a set of issues within a particular domain, the counselor may be able to traverse the work/relationship space without much resistance. In our view, the domain-sensitive approach offers a meta-perspective that can be used with diverse theoretical orientations while also affirming the critical role of both work and relationships in human experience. (See Blustein & Spengler, 1995, for further details on this perspective.)

Once we determine the overall structure and interconnection of Robert's work and relationship issues, we would then employ a developmentally oriented assessment (Super, 1983). Following the rich tradition of Super's (1980) life-span, life-space perspective, we would attempt to explore Robert's level of self-concept crystallization, the salience of his life roles, and the degree to which he has resolved relevant developmental tasks. Given the case description, it is likely that a thorough developmentally oriented assessment might include some psychometric tools in conjunction with data derived from the counseling sessions and the client's history. It is important to note that our use of a developmental assessment would include exploring Robert's noncareer life roles, including the role of husband and son, both of which are contributing extensively to the depth and scope of his presenting issues. Our analysis of the relational domain would be conducted via information obtained in the initial sessions. It would be critical, however, to consult openly with Robert about including an explicit focus on his relationship issues in our work. This focus, naturally, would be integrated with the marital work and would be directed toward helping Robert to make sense of this difficult time in his life and develop plans to address his concerns.

## Case Conceptualization: Tentative Impression and Needed Information

Our overall impression is that Robert presents as a young man struggling with both work-related and family issues. He is simultaneously unsatisfied with his current employment, is preoccupied with the health and care of his parents, and is experiencing marital discord with his wife. It is clear that Robert is discontented with and unsure about his career in engineering; however, it is less clear why he is struggling with these work-related problems. Some areas to explore further with Robert would be the degree to which he has been able to achieve a successful person-environment fit (Holland, 1997), the degree to which he has engaged in adequate self and environment exploration (Blustein,

1997; Jordaan, 1963), and the degree to which his work-related difficulties result from spillover from family problems (Blustein & Spengler, 1995).

Moreover, Robert reports that he depressed, self-critical, and disappointed in his performance in all domains of his life. As such, we would assess Robert's mental status in greater depth in order to determine if more intensive treatment would be warranted. Most notable is Robert's sense of helplessness within his work and family life. We would ask Robert's permission to consult with the marital therapist, which would be very helpful in learning more about his relational situation as well as in coordinating treatment efforts.

Our initial image of Robert leaves us with considerable gaps of information. The domain-sensitive and life-span, life-space approaches provide some guidance on the sorts of integrative questions that would need to be raised. For example, we are curious about how and why Robert entered into the field of engineering, what he likes and/or dislikes about his current work, what other factors contributed to Robert leaving his job, what are his interests and values, and how other family members would feel about him changing his line of work. Many of these questions would be addressed in the early sessions, given that we typically ask clients to describe their life history in depth, with a particular focus on education and work. We would also want to learn about what is contributing to Robert's lack of self-esteem, what his relationship with his family is like, and why he feels that he alone needs to be responsible for his parents.

## Tentative Directions for Counseling

Working with Robert collaboratively, we would delineate the most salient roles in his "life-space" and explore his expectations for his current and future life goals. Again, the salient issue may be in either the work or nonwork domain or in a psychological space that is shared by the work and nonwork issues. Based on the material detailed in this vignette, we feel that the work and nonwork issues are closely interrelated. As such, we would explore with Robert how to make changes in each domain and how to coordinate these changes. In the work domain, one possibility would be that Robert needs to do more exploration in the new "environment" that he is considering (i.e., working with people). One example of guided exploration would be informational interviews with individuals in person-oriented work environments. Information gained from the interviews could then be processed with the counselor, who would help Robert explore and examine his options about a work transition.

From a life-span, life-space perspective (Super, 1980), we view Robert's transition into a people-oriented field to be an example of recycling through the developmental tasks of career exploration, which can be inherently anxiety provoking (Blustein, 1997). In fact, Robert's ambivalence about initiating exploration may be contributing to his distress. As such, it may be useful to help Robert understand that his need for further exploration is appropriate given his situation, thereby helping to reduce his anxiety. By furnishing Robert with skills in exploration, we would enhance his sense of competence, which may alleviate some of his presenting concerns.

Relatedly, this work transition may affect Robert's personal life in several ways. A new career path may entail returning to college and/or accepting a position with a lower salary than engineering. As such, financial constraints may have further impact on the marital relationship, as the couple is already experiencing distress over finances. In addition, the counseling work would need to address how new career options would affect Robert's family-of-origin; these issues would need to be explored with Robert and with the marital counselor. However, it seems that the overlap of personal issues into his current career transition represents the most challenging aspect of the treatment. By developing a clearer sense of how the personal and work-related issues are interwoven, we would have an opportunity to help Robert construct a new life narrative that will be more consistent with his attributes, interests, and dreams.

## Contextual Issues

Our initial approach to working with Robert, which emphasizes empathic introspection (Kohut, 1977), would allow us to enter Robert's psychological and emotional world and learn more about how he has become the man that he is, facing the difficulties that he faces. We feel it is essential that we develop a clear picture of the contextual factors that have contributed to his development and to his current presentation. The domain-sensitive and life-space, life-span conceptualizations provide an elegant progression from the empathically oriented assessment as they allow for a treatment approach that is also respectful and affirming of contextual issues. Each of these conceptual approaches provides a framework for viewing Robert as a whole person whose psychological space does not fit neatly into a single box.

Among the contextual issues to be explored, understood, and addressed in treatment are Robert's past and current experiences as a man in modern society, the extent to which and the ways in which he identifies with Judaism, and his role and experiences in his family. These contextual issues overlap and are woven in a complex manner such that each has influenced the other (Vondracek, Lerner, & Schulenberg, 1986). Carefully attending to the pattern created may clarify Robert's problem-solving and relational styles and will likely provide insight regarding his emotional life and how we can best help him.

Based on the case vignette, it seems that one of the broadest contextual issues affecting Robert is his experience as a man. His initial statement, in which he asks, "I seem to be the main support for everybody, but who is going to help me," may reflect the painful aloneness and "yearning for connection" (Bergman, 1995, p. 78) that is often experienced by men in our modern culture. Bergman writes poignantly about the simultaneous yearning for and dread of relational intimacy experienced by men, which he argues is a consequence of societal and cultural pressure to separate, disconnect, and become independent in order to "achieve maleness" (p. 74). This early lesson teaches boys that their competence and potential for success lies in what they do with their lives, not in their relationships. The emphasis is on achievement, economic, and intellectual power, not on emotional and relational competence, which may leave many men feeling that in order to be valued and win love they must "become something."

Within the work domain, Robert's selection of a gender-traditional career and the way in which he chose the job (the job gave him good chances for advancement), may provide some indication about the degree to which he is a product of the male developmental process described by Bergman (1995). In the past, Robert's focus seems to have been on achievement and being able to provide sufficiently to meet his wife's desires for a family and home. His current feelings of anxiety and depression may relate to his recent consideration of a new career that would allow him to use previously disavowed relational skills and would take him further away from the traditionally male-oriented world of engineering and technology. Further assessment and discussion with Robert about this issue would certainly help us understand how his experiences as a man have shaped his vocational development and his conflicted feelings around career issues. Such a discussion may also help Robert begin to develop a more flexible idea about what it means "to be a man," and allow him to imagine a life that fits with who he is. Furthermore, addressing how the other potentially relevant contextual issues are interwoven would also seem useful, particularly the complex interrelationship between Robert's masculinity, his family experiences, and his Jewish identity. (See Langman, 1997, for further insights on the cultural context of Judaism in relation to psychotherapy.)

## Conclusion

In closing, our case analysis has emphasized an integrative blend of various theoretical perspectives into a cohesive approach. However, we believe that it is critical not to lose sight of the human being who sits across from us in a counseling session. This case has demonstrated in a compelling way that career issues can also evoke considerable pain in clients, as Robert conveyed so poignantly in this case. Our case report has attempted to give voice to an approach that seeks to affirm client concerns, without regard to their etiology or domain of presentation. Moreover, we have attempted to establish a meaningful understanding of Robert's social, familial, cultural, and historical context, which was critical in our thinking about this case. That Robert twice repeats the refrain "Who is going to help me?" underscores his pain. With the help of the theoretical tools outlined in this report, we hope that counselors will able to respond empathically and effectively to clients such as Robert, whose painful issues are immersed in the muddy waters of contemporary human experience.

## References

Bergman, S.J. (1995). Men's psychological development: A relational perspective. In R.F. Levant & W.S. Pollack (Eds.), *A new psychology of men* (pp. 68-90). NY: Basic Books.

Blustein, D.L. (1997). A context-rich perspective of career exploration across the life roles. *Career Development Quarterly, 45,* 260-274.

Blustein, D.L., & Spengler, P.M. (1995). Personal adjustment: Career counseling and psychotherapy. In W.B. Walsh & S.H. Osipow (Eds.), *Handbook of vocational psychology* (2nd ed., pp. 295-329). Mahwah, NJ: Erlbaum.

Bohart, A.C., & Greenberg, L.S. (Eds.) (1997). *Empathy reconsidered: New directions in psychotherapy*. Washington, DC: American Psychological Association.

Hackett, G. (1993). Career counseling and psychotherapy: False dichotomies and recommended remedies. *Journal of Career Assessment, 1*, 105-117.

Holland, J.L. (1997). *Making vocational choices: A theory of vocational personalities and work environments* (3rd ed.). Odessa, FL: Psychological Assessment Resources.

Jordaan, J.P. (1963). Exploratory behavior: The formation of self and occupational concepts. In D.E. Super (Ed.), *Career development: Self-concept theory* (pp. 42-78). New York: College Entrance Examination Board.

Kohut, H. (1977). *The restoration of the self*. New York: International Universities Press.

Langman, P.F. (1997). White culture, Jewish culture, and the origins of psychotherapy. *Psychotherapy, 34*, 207-218.

Meara, N.M. & Patton, M.J. (1994). Contributions of the working alliance in the practice of career counseling. *Career Development Quarterly, 43*, 161-177.

Richardson, M.S. (1996). From career counseling to counseling/psychotherapy and work, jobs, and career. In M.L. Savickas & W.B. Walsh (Eds.), *Handbook of career counseling theory and practice* (pp. 347-360). Palo Alto, CA: Davies-Black.

Savickas, M.L. (1993). Career counseling in the postmodern era. *Journal of Cognitive Psychotherapy, 7*, 205-215.

Super, D.E. (1980). A life-span, life-space approach to career development. *Journal of Vocational Behavior, 16*, 282-298.

Super, D.E. (1983). Assessment in career guidance: Toward truly developmental counseling. *Personnel and Guidance Journal, 61,* 555-562.

Vondracek, F.W., Lerner, R.M., & Schulenberg, J.E. (1986). *Career development: A life-span, developmental approach.* Hillsdale, NJ: Erlbaum.

Wolf, E.S. (1988). *Treating the self: Elements of clinical self psychology.* New York: Guilford.

# Response to Robert: The Case of the Overwhelmed Helper
## A Life-span Developmental Approach
### David A. Jepsen
### University of Iowa

Based on the case material, I am confident Robert and I could work together toward a "better career" for Robert however he construes "better." Indeed, we would discuss what he likes and wants to keep about his current career and what he dislikes and wants to change. But first, I would do all that I could to make Robert feel comfortable working with me and to inject a feeling of optimism into our initial conversations. My intentions are to form a collaborative relationship by "teaming" with Robert to appraise the problems he presents and to offer interventions to address his career issues.

Early in our conversations, I would check nonverbal indicators of his general mood status and, if warranted, ask about his patterns of sleeping, eating, usual pleasures, and his energy level. (After all, he has described himself as "depressed;" this should be checked.) If he reports considerable "black" material, we would consider together a referral for medical assistance. Furthermore, we would reach an understanding about how to keep our work separate from the marriage counseling.

As part of building a collaborative relationship, I would discuss with Robert our inherent differences, particularly our age and ethnic differences, and ask about how they might influence our communication. At some point, I would ask him to reach me about his family history and traditions. I would ask about family "rules" for finding good work and balancing work and family life, the role models and "black sheep" in the family, his grandparents – especially their work and relationships, and perhaps his early recollections about working and workers in the family.

My perspective is grounded in life-span approaches to career development (Super, 1990). I would employ such robust theoretical constructs as Life Stage, Life Space, and Work Values as lenses through which I would view Robert's career experiences. Cognitive Information Processing (Peterson, Sampson, and Reardon, 1991) constructs describing metacognitive processes would guide my thinking about Robert's self-talk as it affects his decision making.

I would collaborate with Robert to appraise his present problems, his past career development, and his possible future careers. Then we would construct goals for our career counseling. I expect that one goal would be helping Robert to acquire greater comfort with his personal control over career decisions in contrast with his current discomfort with performance and decisions. The issue, at this point, seems to be *comfort* rather than control. We would probably work toward apportioning this time, emotions, and energy among his several roles, and achieving a clearer and more satisfying sense of who he is as a son, husband, worker, and perhaps in leisure and community service roles.

Depending on the final form of our goals, I would offer Robert three kinds of intervention strategies at appropriate times. First, we could work collaboratively to address his disquieting self-talk, the "overwhelmed helper" in the case title, by analyzing how he views himself and the people around hi, and applying cognitive restructuring. The long-range intent is to bolster his efforts to make sense of his work and family life, both past and present, and to stimulate reflection about what he wants his future life to be. The short-range goal is to enable Robert to confront his self-statement (e.g., criticisms, disappointments, doubts about the leave of absence, poor performances) and raise questions about their validity, questions he would probably understand, given his professional training. Perhaps I would ask him, as a homework assignment, to gather evidence supporting and refuting these statements. All the while, I would provide support for his efforts and challenge him to reach his goals.

Second, I would offer to share my version of the stories Robert has presented, to invite his reflection about my stories, and to reconstruct the stories in accord with his own experience. This strategy is sometimes called Describe and Interpret (Jepsen, 1990). More details about applying the strategy are presented later.

Third, we could work together planning direct actions Robert can take toward achieving a more satisfying work and family life. These actions are designed to encourage information gathering and "reality testing." I would offer to supply homework assignments (e.g., ask Robert to write stories illustrating his "people skills"), self-directed activities (e.g., computer-assisted career programs), and scenarios for role playing within the interviews (e.g. role play a discussion with his boss about opportunities to move up in the organization or an initiation to seek outside assistance with his parents' situation.

The collaborative Describe and Interpret intervention strategy would be initiated by offering Robert three stories portraying his current career situation and asking for his modifications. I would say, "Until recently, you were on a career track – perhaps a 'fast track' – of moving ahead with your career when things happened to disrupt or block your movement along that path. Now you must regroup and pause to consider the path and the blocks." After giving Robert an opportunity to think about this interpretation, I would ask, "What do you think about the 'fast track' portrayal? Does it feel like there have been disruptions or blocks? If so, what are they? When did they begin?" This interpretation relies on Super's (Super, 1990) framework of Life Stages and career developmental tasks, in Robert's case the Establishment Stage and the tasks associated with getting ahead in his occupation.

The second story depicts role overload in Robert's Life Space. I would say, "Your life seems to be full of demands and expectations…to be a good husband, to be a good son, to be a good worker. These demands seem to be creating conflicts in your life by pulling you in several different directions at the same time." Again, I would invite his revisions with queries such as, "Does it feel like there are pulls in different directions? What are the forces? How strong are they?" Perhaps a force-field analysis, listing and weighting the forces opposing and propelling him toward his goals, would add clarity by providing a visual representation to his problems.

The third story represents Robert's Work Values, his feelings about what is important in his work and family life. I would pose a series of questions such as, "It is difficult for me to understand what is really important to you and, indeed, if you feel that you must postpone satisfying your personal need until later. What do you want from your work life? Your family life? What keeps you from fulfilling these needs or wants? What values are being fulfilled now?" I would listen for expressions of values and for possible satisfactions he is deriving from expressing the complaints. Perhaps a list of work or family values would simulate this discussion.

After presenting each interpretive story, I would invite Robert's reactions, then ask for his modification, and finally request that he restate the story in his own words. His responses would undoubtedly provide rich material for discussion. Each story contains a metaphor that could be explored: traveling a road or path, pulling and pushing forces, and empty or full vessels. Surely a person trained in engineering will find these metaphorical concepts familiar, although I may need to point out the parallels with his career experiences. We would explore the metaphors for meanings Robert finds difficult to express in words.

We would probably work together for four or five sessions, including homework between sessions, and terminate when Robert left comfortable and confident about a course of action regarding his work life and balancing it with his family life. I would offer to call about six months after termination to check his progress. If the counseling worked out as expected, the "overwhelmed helper" would have found a way to revise his self-criticism and to use the external help he wanted, thus enabling a "better career" to unfold.

## References

Jepsen, D.A. (1990). Developmental career counseling. In W.B. Walsh and S.H. Osipow (Eds.). *Career counseling: Contemporary topics in vocational psychology*. Hillsdale, NJ: Erlbaum.

Peterson, G.W., Sampson, J.P. & Reardon, R.C. (1991). *Career development and services: A cognitive approach*. Monterey, CA: Brooks/Cole.

Super, D.E. (1990). A life-span, life-space approach to career development. In D. Brown, L. Brooks, & Associates. *Career choice and development: Applying contemporary theories to practice* (2nd ed.). San Francisco, CA: Jossey-Bass.

# WILL: THE CASE OF THE "FANCY DANCER"

Will is a 28-year-old gay Cherokee male. He is originally from a small town in Northwest Arkansas. His parents were raised there after his grandparents escaped from the Trail of Tears death march, that was intended to resettle peaceful Cherokee tribes people from the Carolinas to Oklahoma after the U.S. government had stolen their lands. Will is the youngest child of parents who are now in their late 60s. He attended a large state university in California on an Indian scholarship and completed his undergraduate degree in social work. Will has spent the last ten years living in San Francisco where he moved when he found out that he was HIV seropositive. He has a fairly extensive network of friends and lives with his partner of eight years. Will has worked in a number of jobs in social welfare agencies, but is currently unemployed because six months ago he had become symptomatic with recurring pneumocystis. He now is taking a combination of medications that seem to have the pneumonia under control and he is ready to go back to work. He has come to see a career counselor at the One-Stop Center in his city, because he is not sure that he can work a full 40-hour week, and as a social worker he is burned out by having to listen to other people's problems as well as deal with his own. He is at a loss as to what to do.

Will loves nature and being outdoors. He talks about how he used to sleep out in the backyard at his grandparents house all by himself and stay awake all night listening to the insects and feeling the morning dew settle on the sleeping bag. It is his happiest childhood memory. He would love to return to Arkansas to be with his parents and grandparents, but his AIDS condition and the required medical care keep him in the city. Will also loves his Cherokee heritage and is a prize-winning Native American dancer at powwows all over the country. He competes in the "Fancy Dancer" category, which is a highly costumed dance characterized by intricate footwork and rapid spins. Also, his partner has a thriving legal practice and Will is aware of how difficult it is to move such a practice.

Will had been seen by a career counselor previously at his university and that career counselor has mailed the results of his extensive assessment, including the Strong Interest Inventory, Myers-Briggs Type Indicator, California Psychological Inventory, Self-Directed Search, Career Beliefs Inventory, Work Environment Scale, Values Scale, and Career Development Inventory. Each of these inventories was taken eight years ago, but they indicate a preference for Social, Artistic, and Investigative, and Extraversion, Intuition, Feeling, and Perception. At the initial interview Will shares the following results (all scores are as T-scores.)

## Strong Interest Inventory

| | |
|---|---|
| Academic Comfort: | 68 |
| Introversion-Extroversion: | 26 |

*Themes:*

| | | |
|---|---|---|
| Social | Very High | 74 |
| Artistic | Very High | 72 |
| Investigative | Very High | 68 |
| Realistic | High | 62 |
| Enterprising | Very Low | 28 |
| Conventional | Very Low | 23 |

*Basic Interests:*

Very High:

| | |
|---|---|
| Nature | 75 |
| Medical Service | 73 |
| Medical Science | 71 |
| Social Service | 70 |

| Science | 70 |
|---|---|
| Religious Activities | 67 |
| Law/Politics | 65 |

High:

| Mechanical Activities | 59 |
|---|---|
| Business Management | 58 |
| Domestic | 57 |
| Athletics | 57 |

*Occupations:*

| Park Ranger | 65 |
|---|---|
| Psychologist | 64 |
| Physician | 63 |
| YWCA/YMCA Director | 61 |
| University Professor | 60 |
| Minister | 60 |
| Dietician | 59 |
| Public Administrator | 58 |
| Electrician | 57 |

**Myers-Briggs Type Indicator**

| Extraversion | 45 |
|---|---|
| Intuition | 33 |
| Feeling | 11 |
| Perceiving | 47 |

**Values Scale (1 = low, 4 = high)**

| 3.9 | Cultural Identity |
|---|---|
| 3.8 | Altruism |
| 3.8 | Personal Development |
| 3.6 | Autonomy |
| 3.6 | Creativity |
| 3.0 | Working Conditions |
| 2.8 | Variety |
| 2.6 | Life Style |
| 2.4 | Aesthetics |
| 2.4 | Physical Activity |
| 2.4 | Social Interaction |
| 2.0 | Ability Utilization |
| 1.8 | Economic Security |
| 1.8 | Authority |
| 1.6 | Economic Rewards |
| 1.4 | Risk |
| 1.2 | Physical Prowess |
| 1.2 | Social Relations |
| 1.2 | Prestige |
| 1.0 | Advancement |
| 1.0 | Achievement |

## *Response to Will: The Case of the "Fancy Dancer"*
## *Judith Grutter*
## *G/S Consultants*

In the case of Will, my response will follow a Career Development Diagnostic Model that integrates several theoretical perspectives: a person-environment fit typology (Holland, 1985); a developmental stage hypothesis (Super, 1957); a social learning theory approach (Krumboltz, 1979); and an ego identity framework (Marcia, 1966). The model addresses the three primary questions posited for this discussion, as well as other relevant issues.

### Career Development Diagnostic Model

1. Identify career issues.
   - Determine presenting problem (employability vs. suitability).
   - Assess developmental stage (congruence vs. integration issues).
   - Assess vocational identity development (hexagon narrative).
   - Identify barriers to progress.
2. Determine counseling strategies and set contract.
   - Discuss past career exploration activities.
   - Individualize strategies for maximum client motivation.
   - Determine the appropriateness of formal assessment.
   - Reach a mutually agreed-upon exploration plan.
3. Collect self-information as appropriate.
   - Evaluate prior assessments and records of achievement.
   - Administer typical performance assessments (interests, values, self-reported skills, personality).
   - Administer maximum performance assessments (abilities, aptitudes, achievements).
4. Interpret assessments.
   - Integrate assessment results with prior history.
   - Clarify patterns and resolve discrepancies.
   - Explore possibilities.
5. Narrow alternatives and develop action plan.
   - Clarify next steps and long-range goals.
   - Direct toward informational resources.
   - Establish feedback and follow-up procedures.
6. Monitor progress.
   - Evaluate and modify choices.
   - Reassess barriers.
   - Evaluate the outcome.

### Identify Career Issues

Will's stated problem is that he is unemployed and seeking less than full-time employment in a field other than his previous employment of social work. He expresses burnout and less than optimal medical health. He has worked in a number of positions that need clarification. I would want to explore with him the exact nature of his previous professional work experience, the relationship of his dissatisfaction with social welfare work to his own medical concerns, and the circumstances surrounding his job changes. His previous employment appears somewhat congruent with his personality preferences, although there is some possibility that social welfare agency environments drew more upon his inferior Sensing Myers-Briggs Type Indicator (MBTI) preference than upon his dominant Intuition. The extraverted Feeling types, ESFJ and ENFJ, are usually more suited to the paperwork requirements and hands-on caretaking nature of agency work than are extraverted intuitives. It would also have to be explored whether his personality preferences and interest pattern were naturally developed from a freely chosen base of experience or imposed upon him by family, geographic, gender-based, or cultural presses. My initial impression is that he was probably suitably employed, but that other factors intervened. We are probably dealing with a congruence issue – finding a variation of what he was doing previously, rather than an integration issue – considering later-life development of new interests and personality factors.

My initial strategy with career counseling clients is usually to conduct a rather extensive intake interview based on John Holland's typology of personality types and work environments. In many cases this initial information gathering stage of career exploration is more time consuming than the actual action-planning phase. It has been my experience that when this first stage of the process is thorough, the subsequent steps fall into place with fewer roadblocks and barriers. In Will's case, this method would accomplish several objectives: to validate or invalidate prior assessment results, to explore previous congruence, to confirm adequate exposure for vocational identity achievement, and to provide a system for further career exploration.

I would proceed by using a blank hexagon drawing to talk him through the RIASEC model, asking specific questions about previous experiences, societal, gender, and family influences, and reinforcing his understanding of the six personality and work environment categories. I would listen for and note specific positive and negative work, leisure, academic, and family experiences in each corner of the hexagon, and formulate a mental timeline of RIASEC stability. Ultimately I would like to be assured that his college and career choices were a result of his own experiences and not primarily the result of external influences, and to identify when and where his sense of burnout began. I would also listen for evidence that further assessment would or would not be recommended.

There are numerous potential barriers to Will's progress in career counseling, most of which have been noted in his case notes. Briefly, they are related to medical health, physical stamina, "helper's burnout," and potential employer discrimination stemming from attitudes toward HIV, sexual orientation, and/or cultural identity. Less obvious but no less important are the "yes buts" that are likely to arise from employability versus suitability issues. His previously measured interest pattern (SAI), personality type (ENFP), and values (Cultural Identity, Altruism, Personal Development, Autonomy, and Creativity) suggest the potential for a highly idealized concept of work. His past and current health status suggest very practical employability issues. It is likely that he will have to compromise his idealism somewhat in order to meet the reality of his employment needs.

## Determine Counseling Strategies and Set Contract

The only evidence we have of Will's prior career exploration activity is a battery of eight-year-old assessments and at least one meeting with a career counselor at his undergraduate university. Although his career choices seem fairly congruent with his assessment results, I would like to hear directly from him how he went about making his first professional career decisions, locating position possibilities, and actually seeking and finding the jobs he has had. Given his personality preferences and past history, it may be that his various positions have been more a result of intuitive hunches – what felt right at the moment – than an objective evaluation of possibilities. I would want him to develop an objective approach to expanding his knowledge of opportunities, while at the same time capitalizing on his more natural strengths of spontaneity and opportunism.

If our initial discussion verifies his SAI interest pattern and ENFP preferences, I would contract with him to focus on the skill sets that he would like to use in his work and the role that he sees work playing in his current life situation. My primary goal in this stage of counseling is to engage his commitment to a mutually agreed-upon career exploration process. To do that, I would discuss with him various ways to use his creativity and support network to generate a statement of work's meaning, and share it with others for their reactions and feedback. The statement might be written, or musical, or it may even express itself through his greatest talent – Native American dance. Such a process would not necessarily contribute to a lengthy list of job possibilities, but it would honor his strengths and preferences and, it is hoped, gain his willingness to continue with a more objective evaluation of his options.

## Collect Self-information as Appropriate

Although I am a great proponent of the uses of formal assessment in career counseling, I tend to use it more to generate a shorthand for easily understandable personality and work environment vocabulary, and to help to formulate questions to be explored, rather than providing one right answer. With this in mind, it would probably not be helpful to retest Will on the Strong Interest Inventory (SII) or the MBTI, unless his interests have changed significantly as a result of his work experience and his illness, or he indicates that his type preferences are incorrect. We can use the results that he already has to elaborate on helpful, creative, investigative work environments (SAI) where he could make a meaningful difference in others' lives (ENFP). The challenge will be to develop his Judgment preference for Feeling in narrowing down the options generated by his dominant Perception preference for Intuition.

A further assessment of Will's values appears warranted. Life experiences very often alter our needs and values, and a great deal of life has passed under the bridge for him during the past eight years. His current value system and the role that work plays in it will probably be the ultimate determiner of his choices, and so this area will be one of focus and concentration. I would most likely use a values card sort with him, so that we could talk through the values together and force the judgment process of prioritizing. Will's preferred transferable skills also need to be clarified. I often use task element statements from the Strong Interest Inventory® Interpretive Report (Grutter and Hammer, 1994) to do this, and may ask him to retake the Strong primarily for this information (see chapter 1, Grutter, 1998-99). If this isn't possible, a skills card sort would be an appropriate alternative, with a focus on clusters of related skills and the development of an individualized job description, rather than a mere listing of motivated skills.

## Interpret Assessments

In Will's case, there is a compatibility between his MBTI type and his RIASEC code (Hammer and Kummerow, 1966), suggesting a natural development of interests from his genetic predisposition. His work and nonwork history confirm a similar pattern of helping-creating. We will need to confirm his desire to pursue this pattern in the future and resolve any values-skills-interest discrepancies that arise.

## Narrow Alternatives and Develop Action Plan

I am optimistic that Will be able to identify a pattern of skills that he will enjoying using in a helping-creative-investigative work environment. His love of the outdoors and his strong cultural and family identification may prove to be the determining factor in his choices, as well as the barriers identified in our earlier intake discussion. As he resolves the meaning of work in his life, he may find that work is not the primary expression of his identity, but rather what makes such expression possible in his primary relationship, his dance, and other areas of his life. His action plan will most likely include first steps to try out his physical stamina and tolerance for helping others, as well as ideas for the future. Given his SII results on Academic Comfort and Investigative, it would not be unlikely for him to redirect his helping and creative interests through formal continuing education.

## Monitor Progress

One of Will's greatest strengths is his support network, which he has now expanded to include a career counselor. Frequent checkpoints will need to be established to evaluate progress and monitor his presenting barriers. It will not be difficult for him to recognize that careering is a process, not a choice that one sticks with for all time, and as such the direction will bring joys and sorrows, and changes and mindless repetitions that will all piece together in a beautifully unique picture of Will.

## References

Grutter, J. and Hammer, A.L. (1994). *Strong Interest Inventory interpretive report*. Palo Alto, CA: Consulting Psychologists Press.

Grutter, J. (1998-99). *Making it in today's organizations: Taking control of your career enrichment/advancement/transition using the Strong and MBTI*. Palo Alto, CA: Consulting Psychologists Press. (Facilitator's Guide and three booklets).

Holland, J.L. (1985). *Making vocational choices: A theory of vocational personalities and work environments*. Englewood Cliffs, NJ: Prentice Hall.

Hammer, A.L. and Kummerow, J.M. (1996). *Strong + MBTI career development guide* (Revised.) Palo Alto, CA: Consulting Psychologists Press.

Krumboltz, J.D. (1979). A social learning theory of career decision making. In A.M. Mitchell, G.B. Jones, and J.D. Krumboltz (Eds.), *Social Learning and Career Decision Making*. Cranston, RI: Carroll Press.

Marcia, J.E. (1966). Development and validation of ego-identity status. *Journal of Personality and Social Psychology, 3*, 551-558.

Super, D.E. (1957). *The psychology of careers*. New York: Harper & Row.

## *Response to Will: The case of the "Fancy Dancer"*
## *Roger Herring*
## *University of Arkansas-Little Rock*

### The Client's Image

Will appears to be caught in several dualistic situations. On one hand, he physically lives in mainstream society; on the other hand, he continues his Native American heritage through his fancy dancing. In addition, Will is torn between living in the city and wanting to return to his country roots. His gay lifestyle also pits him against mainstream society, albeit he lives in San Francisco. Another conflict exists in his educational background and his current career aspirations.

Additional information would be helpful in delivering an intervention for Will. For example, to what degree has Will been acculturated into mainstream society? Does he have an enrollment card to avail himself of financial assistance and health benefits? What contacts does he have with his tribe other than dancing? What is his partner's perspective? How is he financing his lifestyle and illness? Who are friends and are they supportive of him? How valid and reliable are his test scores? Individuals often change their career interests over time.

## Intervention Plan

Helping professionals who work with Native American clients have to initially assess the client's degree of acculturation. They need to be cautious in making assumptions about the cultural orientation of Native American Indian adult clients. The continuum of acculturation found in Native American Indian families can be generally described as comprising the following five types (Herring, 1997, 1999; Garrett & Garrett, 1994; LaFromboise, Trimble & Mohatt, 1990): pan traditional, traditional, transitional, bicultural, and assimilated. Will reflects characteristics of the last two, especially considering his present residence and his years away from home. Which family pattern Will identifies will determine the path of his counseling. Any suggestions for intervention will include examples that have been effective with Native American Indian adults.

Will's choice of family pattern is of utmost importance because of the Native American Indian view of health and wellness. If Will is completely immersed into mainstream society, the traditional forms and choices of helping would not be incorporated in his intervention. If he presents himself as bicultural, traditional treatment modalities could be utilized.

The role of social influences in the counseling process as perceived by Will also needs to be considered. For example, the underuse of mental health services by Native American Indian adults is often associated with tension surrounding power differentials in counseling relationships and perceived conflicting goals for acculturation between professionals and Native American Indian clients (LaFromboise et al., 1990).

Some practical, synergistic recommendations that may help create a culturally affirmative environment for Native American Indian adults, but which do not require the helping professional to deny his/her own culture include the following (Herring, 1997; 1999):

1. Address openly the issue of dissimilar-ethnic relationships rather than pretending that no differences exist.
2. Evaluate the degree of acculturation of the client.
3. Schedule appointments to allow for flexibility in ending the session.
4. Be open to allowing other family members to participate in the counseling session.
5. Allow time for trust to develop before focusing immediately on deeper feelings.
6. Use counseling strategies that elicit practical solutions to problems.
7. Maintain eye contact as appropriate.
8. Respect the uses of silence. Listen carefully.
9. Demonstrate honor and respect for the client's culture.
10. Maintain the highest level of confidentiality.

The initial session or contact is also vital to developing the counseling relationship with Will, because Native American Indian clients will evaluate the total presentation of the professional (e.g., manner of greeting, physical appearance, ethnicity, nonverbal behavior, and communication). The first few minutes are very important to the success or failure of the session. The professional needs to demonstrate content knowledge of Native American Indian culture to gain respect (e.g., awareness of tribe and familial pattern). Such an acknowledgment will convey the attitude of the professional toward understanding of Will's heritage. Appraisals of cultural commitment and tribal structure, customs, and beliefs will provide useful information on how to proceed (Garrett & Garrett, 1994). But remember, every Native American Indian client should be approached as an individual first.

Group work is becoming the treatment of choice for a number of agencies with programs serving Native American Indian clients (LaFromboise, Berman, & Sohi, 1994). Group social skills training is an effective intervention, especially with social cognitive interventions (LaFromboise & Bigfoot, 1988). Social cognitive strategies reduce the emphasis on individual disclosure, which is difficult for some, and introduces collective responsibility, which responds to the collective approach characteristic of some tribes (LaFromboise & Graff Low, 1989).

Manson, Walker, and Kivlahan (1987) and Fleming (1989) suggested two Native American Indian group treatment strategies based on traditional healing practices: the "four circles" and the "talking circle." The four circles structures group exploration around issues related to individuals with each of the four increasingly larger concentric circles representing the Creator at the center, one's partner or spouse at the next level, one's immediate or "blended" family, and in the outermost circle, one's community and tribal members. The talking circle is a form of group therapy that includes elements of ritual and prayer, but does not depend on interaction between the participants.

Network therapy, a form of therapy created by Carolyn Attneave, a Delaware, involves recreating the clan network to mobilize a family's kin and social system to help a client (LaFromboise & Fleming, 1990). The sessions are conducted in the home and involve considerable numbers of people, including members of the intervention team, the extended family, and others unrelated but known to the family. To be effective, the therapists and family members need to be able to review the family problem, facilitate community meetings, and develop strategies of engaging the system in rebuilding connections and healing relationships to help solve the problem.

LaFromboise & Graff Low (1989) noted that when working with Native American Indian clients, the professional must be aware of the influence the dominant culture may have on the client's self-deprecating and irrational belief system. Beliefs that are irrational by standards of the dominant culture may be perfectly legitimate within the specific cultural context (LaFromboise et al., 1990). For example, mistrust of the educational system and even counseling may be rooted in historical mistrust based in assimilationist policy (Locust, 1988).

Another culturally appropriate technique is the use of guided imagery (Peregoy, 1993). For example, Will comes to seek help with presenting concerns related to his career identity. The professional may want to use guided imagery techniques to have Will visualize himself as he perceives himself to be, and then, have Will visualize what he would really like to do. Once this is done, the client then develops steps, with the assistance of the professional, to work toward the goal of what he would like to be doing in the future.

Garrett and Garrett (1994) offered a few basic recommendations for counseling with Native American clients:

- Ask permission whenever possible and always give thanks.
- Never interrupt – allow sufficient time for responding.
- Be patient.
- Use silence whenever appropriate (or even when it is not).
- Use descriptive statements rather than questioning.
- Model self-disclosure through anecdotes or short stories.
- Make use of metaphors and imagery when appropriate.
- Try not to separate the person from the spiritually or from affiliation with the tribal group. Honor those sacred relationships.
- Recognize the relative nature of value judgments such as "right or wrong" and "good or bad."

## Summary

To reiterate, the suggestions are offered with the presumption of Will's involvement with his heritage on more than a superficial level. Will presents multiple "problems" and faces numerous decisions. In addition to previously mentioned suggestions, an effective strategy is found in social learning theories. Often a client's difficulty is not the decision to be made, but the approach path to making that decision, (Krumboltz, 1983). Some of Will's dilemma might be lessened if some time is directed to what factors assist and obstruct his decision-making abilities.

In addition, Will needs more recent assessment data after trust and rapport have been established. Reinforcement of the availability of the available present data could be easily and quickly gained by administering the Self-Directed Search (SDS; Holland, 1994). The SDS has been proven to be particularly effective with Native American Indian individuals (Gade, Fuqua, & Hurlburt, 1988; Herring, 1999). If Will's test results confirm his interests for Social, Artistic, and Investigative, the helping professional can then begin to guide Will to a career area congruent to Will's desire. If the scores are not congruent with previous scores, then, that is another career story.

## References

Fleming, C. (1989, August). *Mental health treatment of American Indian women.* Paper presented at the meeting of the American Psychological Association, New Orleans, LA.

Gade, E.M., Fugua, D.R., & Hurlburt, G. (1988). The relationship of Holland's personality types to education satisfaction with a Native American high school population. *Journal of Counseling Psychology, 35*, 183-186.

Garrett, J.T. & Garrett, M.W. (1994). The path of good medicine: Understanding and counseling Native American Indians. *Journal of Multicultural Counseling & Development (Special Issue), 22*, 134-144.

Herring, R.D. (1997). Counseling indigenous American youth. In C.C. Lee (Ed.), *Multicultural issues in counseling: New approaches to diversity* (2nd ed., pp. 53-70). Alexandria, VA: American Counseling Association.

Herring, R.D. (1999). *Counseling with Native American Indian and Alaska natives: Synergistic strategies for helping professionals.* Thousand Oaks, CA: Sage.

Holland, J.L. (1994). *Self-Directed Search (SDS) form R* (4th ed.). Odessa, FL: Psychological Assessment Resources.

Krumboltz, J.D. (1983). *Private rules in career decision making.* National Center for Research in Vocational Education. Columbus, The Ohio State University. (ERIC Document Reproduction Service No. ED 229 608).

LaFromboise, T.D.Berman, J.S., & Sohi, B.K. (1994). American Indian women. In L. Comas-Diaz & B. Greene (Eds.), *Women of color: Integrating ethnic and gender identities in psychotherapy* (pp. 30-71). New York: Guilford Press.

LaFromboise, T.D. & Bigfoot D.S. (1988). Cultural and cognitive considerations in the prevention of American Indian adolescent suicide. *Journal of Adolescence, 11,* 139-153.

LaFromboise, T.D. & Fleming, C. (1990). Keepers of the flame: A profile of Carolyn Attneave. *Journal of Counseling and Development, 68,* 537-547.

LaFromboise, T.D. & Graff Low, K. (1989). American Indian children and adolescents. In J.T. Gibbs & L.N. Huang (Eds.), *Children of color: Psychological interventions with minority youth* (pp. 114-147). San Francisco, CA: Jossey-Bass.

LaFromboise, T.D., Trimble, J.E., & Mohatt, G.V. (1990). Counseling intervention and American Indian tradition: An integrative approach. *Counseling Psychologist, 18,* 628-654.

Locust, C. (1988). Wounding the spirit: Discrimination and traditional American Indian belief systems. *Harvard Educational Review, 58*(3), 315-330.

Manson, S.M., Walker, R.D., & Kivlahan, D.R. (1987). Psychiatric assessment and treatment of American Indians and Alaska natives. *Hospital & Community Psychiatry, 38,* 165-173.

Peregoy, J.J. (1993). Transcultural counseling with American Indians and Alaska Natives: Contemporary issues for consideration. In J. McFadden (Ed.), *Transcultural Counseling: Bilateral and International Perspectives.* (pp. 163-191). Alexandria, VA: American Counseling Association.

# PEDRO: THE CASE OF THE MUSIC MAN

Pedro is a married 31-year-old male with no children. He is originally from a small town in Southwest Texas. His parents were raised there after his grandparents emigrated from Ecuador. Pedro is an only child whose parents are now in their late 60s. Pedro has spent the last 20 years living in an East Coast suburb. He has a fairly extensive network of friends and relatives (including his parents) living nearby. Pedro has worked in a number of jobs within the home construction industry and is currently employed as a production worker in a union construction company.

Pedro has a high school diploma from a vocational-technical school. His father was a farm worker and his mother went from high school to being a homemaker. Pedro was an average student in school. He decided to enter a vocational-technical school because that is what all his friends chose to do and because he felt that his family could not afford to send him to college. He selected carpentry in high school because of the potential earning possibilities and because his school counselor told him that carpentry would be a good job for him.

Pedro loves music. It is his only hobby. He boasts a collection of over 3,000 records, 2,000 cassettes, and is closing in on 1,000 CDs. He spends his free time going to concerts, attending music festivals, and watching music channels on television. He likes all types of music except classical.

Pedro is unhappy with his present job. He feels "bored" with his work and pessimistic that there are any viable alternatives available, especially "for someone without a college degree." He reports being more irritable at home and work during the last two months. He is afraid to take time off to go on interviews because he needs money to support himself and his wife and help his parents. He is not sure what job he is interested in at this point. Pedro wonders about the possibility of pursuing additional education but discounts this due to limited finances and time. The priest at his local parish suggested that he speak with a career counselor to figure out what type of work Pedro should do next.

## Response to Pedro: The Case of the Music Man
### Lenore W. Harmon
### University of Illinois at Urbana-Champaign

Pedro is certainly a dedicated listener, but there is no evidence that he makes music or that he ever has. I would probably begin my discussion with Pedro by exploring his hobby, because it will be easy for him to talk about. However, I would want to avoid giving him the idea that it is idle talk unrelated to his pressing concerns. So I would ask about his own involvement with music, inquiring about whether he is involved in making or producing music and whether he has any friends who are musicians or producers of music. I would ask if he has ever dreamed of becoming a musician or being involved in the music industry in some way. If he reports having had such dreams, I would ask what keeps him from attempting to fulfill them. By this time I might have learned a great deal about Pedro's talents, dreams, and values, and I hope he would have become comfortable in the counseling setting.

Other questions I would want to explore with Pedro are why his concerns brought him to counseling at this time. I wonder why he has felt the need for a change more keenly in the last few months than he did previously. I suspect that I might find some precipitating family or financial problems that combined with his lack of enthusiasm for his job to bring him first to his priest and now to me. Regardless of what I discovered about his recent personal circumstances, I would want to explore his earlier decision to enter carpentry. Was he really as reactive in making his education and career decisions as he sounds? If he could have pursued any course of education and career choice as a high school student, where would he have headed? What does he wish he could have done at that time? Is he satisfied with the decision-making process he used, or does he wish he had approached the task of educational and career planning differently? I would also want to explore exactly what his current job entails and what aspects of it he finds satisfactory and unsatisfactory.

By this time I would probably know much more than I did initially about Pedro's decision-making style and self-efficacy estimates. However, I think it would be necessary to understand more about Pedro's cultural heritage to set what I have found in perspective. His family and family history suggest that he is Hispanic, but I don't know how big a factor that is now or has been in the past. Consequently, I would inquire about how and why the family moved from Ecuador to Texas and ultimately to New Jersey and what factors influenced these moves. I would hope to get an understanding of his family's social class and economic circumstances from this discussion. Since he has many relatives in New Jersey, I assume the family is somewhat cohesive and that the families have migrated in a similar pattern, but I would need to verify that assumption. I would hope to find out how close to their original culture various generations of the family are and to what extent they maintain the customs and language of their roots. I would want to know if he feels any intergenerational conflict over acculturation to the United States.

Pedro apparently went to high school in New Jersey. Was he a typical eastern suburban student or did his cultural heritage set him apart as different from his peers? I would want to find out who his friends were and what his activities were. I would hope to learn whether he had experienced any discrimination in his school and if he had, how he felt about it and dealt with it.

Assuming that the discussions suggested above convince me that Pedro's problem is truly a vocational problem, or if not, that the problems can be best approached through a discussion of vocational plans, I would invite Pedro to continue in the assessment process by completing some tests and inventories.

### Formal Assessment

Because there is very little indication that Pedro chose his career based on an inability to handle more formal academic work, I would suggest that Pedro take a test of his academic aptitude. Given the fact that he did not follow an academic track in high school and has been out of the educational system for over ten years, I would choose a measure that focuses more on aptitude than on achievement. Even so, I would interpret the results carefully on my knowledge of whether Pedro speaks English as a first language and the length of time since he has engaged in any studies.

I would certainly want Pedro to complete a measure of vocational interests. Because Pedro seems not to have considered his skills very carefully in making his educational and career decisions, I would probably ask him to complete the Strong Interest Inventory (SII, Harmon, Hansen, Borgen & Hammer, 1994) with its accompanying Skills Confidence Inventory (SCI, Betz, Borgen, & Harmon, 1996), so that I might follow up on my hunch that he lacks confidence in his won skills in many areas. In reviewing the results, I would pay particular attention to the General Occupation Theme scores for Realistic (which I assume would shed some light on his interest in the type of career he is in) and Artistic (which would shed some light on his interest in the arts). If he had high scores on other General Occupational Themes (GOT), they would certainly be worth exploring. The Work Styles scales of the SII would be of particular interest, too, because they may contain clues to the type of learning and the type of work environment he prefers. The SII results might shed some light on why he is unhappy in his current position. Perhaps he has been asked to take a leadership role in which he feels uncomfortable, or asked to work alone when he prefers working with others. Comparing his GOT scores with his Confidence scores might suggest some potential interventions. If there are areas where he has high interest but low confidence, the reality basis for his lack of confidence can be explored. If he seems to have the requisite level of learning ability, he might try college courses or volunteer experiences relevant to his interests. These ideas must remain quite vague until a knowledge of his actual interests and abilities is obtained. Perhaps he actually has a great deal of musical talent and needs to find a way to express it. Perhaps skilled and technical fields are actually a good fit for him. Is there a way for him to enter the world of music using those skills as an audio or video technician?

## Making Changes

Because Pedro is an adult with adult responsibilities and concerns, any changes he makes should be tentative and careful. He should not "close doors behind him" by quitting his job and re-signing from his union until he is very certain that he has found a satisfactory alternative. He may need to look realistically at the costs of further education. They may be less that he thinks if community college courses can be used for tryouts or complete programs of study.

If Pedro contemplates any changes in his career goals as a result of an assessment of his interests and abilities, it is important that those changes be explored in light of his family life. If he is to decide to undertake further training or to develop a small music-related specialty as a sideline to his current job, he will need to consider how his family life will be affected. It is worth noting that Pedro is married and childless at age 31. I would want to explore with Pedro what his wife's role and expectations are. Is she a housewife, a career woman, or both? Do they plan to have children? What does Pedro see as the role each of them should play in the family – as breadwinners and child rearers? What level of financial insecurity is comfortable for each of them? How is his wife likely to react to any changes he might want to explore? Does Pedro feel supported in his search for the source of his unhappiness or as though he is creating family problems? It is entirely possible that what might be a good choice for Pedro at age 18 because of his interests and abilities would be a bad choice for him at age 31, even if the interests and abilities are the same. The barriers he faces to making changes may be quite different today than they were when he was younger. If career change is a threat to his family life, then I would try to help him search for ways to gain satisfaction outside of his career. Can he serve as a weekend disk jockey for weddings and parties instead of making a complete career change? It sounds as though he has the record collection for the job. Does he have an interest in Social concerns? How could he use music to help others?

## Answering the Question

Clearly, we do not have enough information to know whether or not Pedro is a music man. Only Pedro himself can answer that question. To do so he will need to consider how his cultural and family roles shape his future choices. He will need to explore his own abilities, interests, and the confidence he has in how own abilities. He will need to assess his own courage for the process of changing his life. At present the best we can do is allow for the possibility that Pedro is, indeed a man who needs to find a way to express the music of his soul. Alternatively, we cannot rule out the possibility that Pedro is listening to music to avoid "facing the music" of the real world.

## How Can the Counselor Help?

In the past, Pedro seems to have been a rather dependent decision maker (Harren, 1979). His choices seem to have been dictated by what others do or need. The counselor has an opportunity to help Pedro look at his own situation, his abilities, his interests, his values, and even his way of making decisions as he searches for a solution to his discontent. In doing so, I would draw upon my background in "trait and factor" psychology (Osispow & Fitzgerald, 1996) looking for a good "person-environment fit" (Swanson, 1996) for Pedro. It is true that many of the aspects of an individual that are important to consider are not strictly psychological traits. There are important cultural and social values that may weigh equally with the more traditional "traits," such as ability and interest. To help Pedro explore, I would need to consider whether aspects of personal (Blustein, 1994) and cultural (Helms & Piper, 1994) identity theory, stress related to ethnic status (Smith, 1985), and family dynamics (Nichols & Schwartz, 1995), as well as decision-making theory (Phillips, 1994) apply. I would explore what Bandura's theory (Bandura, 1986; Betz, 1992) might tell me about his self-efficacy expectations by comparing his scores on skills confidence scales with interest scales.

Pedro is an interesting client because he illustrates very well how broadly trained and intuitive the counselor must be to do good career counseling. The counselor must let theoretical concerns raise questions for the client to answer literally or through his or her behavior. The theory does not dictate the answers; the client does. Helping the client to weave the answers that probe various aspects of the self and the world into a personal solution is a work of art that is based on science but woven in practice. That practice must respect and use the very unique aspects of the client's person and world.

## References

Bandura, A. (1986). *Social foundation of thought and action: A social cognitive theory*. Englewood Cliffs, NJ: Prentice Hall.

Betz, N.E. (1992). Counseling uses of career self-efficacy theory. *Career Development Quarterly, 41*, 22-26.

Betz, N.E., Borgen, F.H., & Harmon, L.W. (1996). *Skills Confidence Inventory: Applications and technical guide*. Palo Alto, CA: Consulting Psychologists Press.

Blustein, D.L. (1994). Who am I? The question of self and identity in career development. In M.L. Savickas & R.L. Lent (Eds.), *Convergence in career development theories*. (pp.139-154). Palo Alto, CA: Davies-Black.

Harmon, L.W., Hansen, J.C., Borgen, F.H., & Hammer, A.C. (1994). *Strong Interest Inventory: Applications and technical guide*. Palo Alto, CA: Consulting Psychologists Press.

Harren, V.A. (1979). A model of career decision making for college students. *Journal of Vocational Behavior, 14*, 119-133.

Helms, J.E. & Piper, R.E. (1994). Implications of racial identity theory for vocational psychology. *Journal of Vocational Psychology, 44*, 128-138.

Nichols, M.P. & Schwartz, R.C. (1995) *Family therapy*, (3rd ed.). Boston, MA: Allyn & Bacon.

Osipow, S.H. & Fitzgerald, L.F. (1996). *Theories of career development*, (4th ed.). Boston, MA: Allyn & Bacon.

Phillips, S.D. (1994) Choice and change: Convergence from the decision making perspective. In M.L. Savickas & R.W. Lent (Eds.), *Convergence in Career Development Theories* (pp.155-163). Palo Alto, CA: Davies-Black.

Smith, E.C. (1985). Ethnic minorities: Life stress, social support, and mental health issues. *Counseling Psychologist, 13*, 537-579.

Swanson, J.L. (1996). The theory is the practice: Trait-and-factor/person-environment fit counseling. In M.L. Savickas & W.B. Walsh (Eds.), *Handbook of Career Counseling Theory and Practice*. (pp. 93-108). Palo Alto, CA: Davies-Black.

# Response to Pedro: The Case of the Music Man
## Dennis Engels and Martin Gieda
## North Texas State University

My colleague, Martin Gieda, and I agreed to collaborate on this project in the hope of getting a comparison of our respective individual approaches to this case and in hopes of continuing our long-standing discussions about career counseling. In addressing the case we each worked independently and then collaboratively. What follows is our mutual approach to working with Pedro. While we have read the brief case material, we bring much curiosity and a firm belief that no one knows Pedro better than Pedro, himself. Because we so greatly prize self-knowledge, we start by holding our knowledge from his case file in abeyance, as we focus intently on Pedro's self-report. After raising many questions in our attempt to get to know Pedro, we then complied with the literal request of this book's editors via our hypothetical approach limited to the minimal information the editors provided.

## Relationship Building

Although reading the brief case introduction affords glimpses and snippets of Pedro's life and career, we want to get to know Pedro by carefully attending to his own words and demeanor. Getting to know Pedro will involve asking him to speak about himself, starting with introductions and then moving to his reasons for coming to counseling and what he hopes to derive from counseling. As rapport develops, counseling will focus on achieving Pedro's informed consent and our mutual agreement to participate in counseling, with concentrated attention to his life-career development. After Pedro articulates what he wants from counseling, and we respond to Pedro's expectations, paying close attention to Pedro's immediate and long-term goals, we then can agree upon counseling goals and objectives.

## Self-knowledge, Insight, and Personal Social Context

We will continue our interaction by asking Pedro to disclose more information about himself so that we can get to know him and he can possibly get to know himself better. Rather than asking Pedro to start by talking about what, if anything, is uncomfortable, distressing, or otherwise wrong in his life, we'll ask Pedro to talk about all the positives in his life as an initial line of discussion to help both of us get to know Pedro better. Counseling will attempt to seek answers to the following questions: Who and what are the loves of his life? What are Pedro's dreams, about life, work, fun, challenge, and self-expression? What matters most to Pedro and why? What does Pedro see as his greatest strengths, interests, values, and desires? What works in Pedro's life? What works best? What works best most often? Why does Pedro see himself and his life in this manner? What does Pedro have to say about experiences of joy and love in his life? Might Pedro's listed love of music constitute a metaphor or vehicle for productive discussion about what Pedro loves about life and living? Is there any possibility that work has some aspects of self-expression and expression of what Pedro loves or enjoys, and, if so, what are some implications for counseling and action?

## Personal Empowerment, Individual Career Ownership and Stewardship

Counseling will further explore what Pedro sees as salient moments and most crucial decision points in his life and how these events might help us get to know him better. What and who does Pedro believe contributed to those events? What was their context? Who does Pedro see as having made and influenced those decisions? How does someone earn Pedro's respect to such an extent that he favorably seeks and considers that person's advice? How many of those current and early influential people are still available and still valuable for Pedro? What lasting advice and counsel have they afforded him? What are some immediate and long-term implications of this advice and counsel

– any absolutes or rules to live by? How does he regularly take responsibility for his development? Might he be able to create or resurrect some additional means of responsible self-governance?

How does Pedro go about solving problems? Is he strongly influenced by family expectations? Is he independent or dependent? Is he a risk taker seeking adventure? How much money does he need to make? Would his wife work if he went to school? Does she support him in making a career change? Is he a conscientious and reliable worker? What kind of a student was/is he? What were his grades, favorite/worst subjects? What is his self-concept? How much self-efficacy does he possess or experience in his work? Are his career goals realistic? He loves music. Might his passion for music have job placement implications? We will ask Pedro about including his wife in counseling at some point. Would she seek or maintain employment as a means to support his pursuit of further training? Could she make enough money to support the family? Does she approve his considering leaving his current job?

## Present and Future Life-Career Development

Discussions will explore what work means to Pedro? What guides his work and what are his expectations of and for work? How is his work ethic compatible with his work situation? What rewards does Pedro get from his current work? What are the best aspects of his current work? What is Pedro's sense of career and career development? How does he describe his personal career development? How does Pedro describe and explain interaction of his work roles and responsibilities with his other life roles and responsibilities? Might balance and integration of these roles be a matter of productive focus for some of our counseling work together?

What does Pedro want from work and how close is his current work to affording him what he wants? What are some gaps between his current work and what he wants? What are some means to what he wants? Which of these means has he pursued, to what effect? What does he see as employment, educational and personal, social and spiritual obstacles and opportunities? What are the primary opportunities and barriers available to or impeding Pedro? Can Pedro see some immediate, long-term and short-term possibilities? What needs to happen to help Pedro exploit these possibilities, to turn possibilities into probabilities?

### One Approach

Seen in light of aspects of Super's (Super, Savickas, & Super, 1996) theory and Hansen's (1997) Integrative Life Planning approach to life-career development, as well as Rothney's and Allport's acute attention to intrapersonal perspective and development, our overall approach is holistic. This holistic emphasis is followed by stricter, more immediate eclectic attention to Pedro's narrative, with attention to aspects of Holland's theory, Super's theory, trait and factor theory, self-efficacy theory, social learning theories and decision theories (Brown, Brooks & Associates, 1996).

### Processing and Decision Making

What did Pedro get from the counseling experience today? Were his expectations fulfilled? What are five next steps for Pedro – for us as Pedro's counselors? What can Pedro do immediately to improve aspects of his personal, social, spiritual, and career life roles?

### Questions to Ponder

What are the main points we attended to today, and what, if any, implications have we discerned for the near- and long-term? How might education best serve Pedro's current, near and long-term needs? What resources might stimulate and facilitate his interest and his decision making regarding education?

## Response

### Our Images of Pedro

Based solely on the furnished narrative, Pedro appears to be a socially interactive and gregarious individual, suggesting that he may enjoy work that has a social outlet such as sales or customer service. He seems responsible in that he cares for his family and may be influenced by them. Pedro's choice of vocational school because that was what his friends chose thus suggesting that he goes along with what others are doing or suggesting rather than deciding for himself.

### Plans for Career Counseling and Information

We will ask Pedro to provide a detailed history of his work experiences. A review of Pedro's medical history could help discern physical or mental limitations that might preclude certain aspects of work and learning. We will assess Pedro's educational history, favorite subjects, academic strengths and limitations, and involvement in extracurricular school activities to determine his level of academic comfort in pursuit of further education. An assessment battery might help measure his current level of intelligence, abilities, aptitudes, values, and interest areas. If English is not Pedro's primary language we will consider referring him to a career assessment professional that specializes in Spanish-speaking clients. We will also recommend a personality assessment using the Myers-Briggs Type Indicator, 16 PF, or NEO PI-R in an attempt to measure personality factors and then work with Pedro to integrate these personality factors with career themes. The personality assessment also may also identify potential psychological factors and personality traits that may inhibit Pedro's work adaptability and performance across a variety of work settings. Because the narrative indicates Pedro became more irritable the past two months, we recommend further evaluation to rule out a mood disorder, substance abuse, or related factors. Is Pedro motivated for further training and does he value further formal education or on-the-job training? Can he find funding for further education or job training and is there other financial support for him to provide for his family while he pursues additional training?

## References

Allport, G.W. (1950). The Nature of Personality: Selected Papers. Cambridge, MA: Addison Wesley.

Allport, G.W. (1937). *Patterns and growth in personality*. New York: Holt, Rinehart and Winston.

Brown, D., Brooks, L, & Associates. (1996). *Career choice and development* (3rd ed.). San Francisco, CA: Jossey-Bass.

Engels, D.W. (1975). John Watson Murray Rothney, Development of His Published Thought in Counseling and Guidance. University of Wisconsin-Madison: Unpublished dissertation.

Engels, D. W. (1986). John Rothney, eminent practitioner, educator, and researcher. *Journal of Counseling and Development, 65*, 131-140.

Hansen, L.S. (1997). *Integrative life planning: Critical tasks for career development and changing life patterns*. San Francisco, CA: Jossey-Bass.

Rothney, J.W.M. (1958). *Guidance practices and results*. New York: Harper and Brothers.

Rothney, J.W.M. (1972). *Adaptive counseling in schools*. Englewood Cliffs, NJ: Prentice-Hall.

# SARAH: THE CASE OF THE GOAL SEEKING ACCOUNTANT

Sarah is a 32-year-old woman of Russian descent who lives in a major city in the northeastern USA. Sarah's first statement to the counselor was, "Everyone else knows what they want to become, what they are working toward; I have no idea." Sarah has a good job as an accountant for one of the major firms. She has progressed rapidly in her career assignments, but she has no clear ambitions and is terribly frustrated by her lack of direction. As the first session continues, her counselor asks her about her likes and dislikes. To each of these questions Sarah answers, "I don't know. Everyone else knows these things, but I don't."

Sarah is a well-dressed attractive woman. She has been married for eight years, and says that she is happy with her relationship with her husband. They have no children, by mutual agreement. She says that her husband is supportive of any decisions she makes but does not offer any help in her decision making. She can afford to go back to school, if that is necessary to meet her goals, but she states again that her problem is that she has no goals!

Sarah is the oldest child in her family and has three younger brothers. Her parents came to the United States from Russia as teenagers, met and married here, and share a common immigrant's perspective of wanting their children to have a "better life" than they had. They always expected Sarah to achieve as much as her brothers. Sarah tells the counselor that she was a "good kid" growing up, often in contrast to her brothers who got in more trouble both at home and at school than she did. Her parents are proud of her achievements in accounting and are puzzled, even angry on occasion, at the thought that she might "throw it up" for what they see as a fantasy of satisfaction. Work is work in their view, and one is supposed to be loyal to one's employer for life. They are also having trouble accepting that their "good girl" is stirring things up.

Sarah's brothers are supportive of her desire to do something different, but they live in distant cities with their wives and families, and do not interact with Sarah very frequently. She has several good friends, but they are all work colleagues and she does not feel she can confide in them since it might have an impact on her future with the accounting firm if she does decide to stay.

When Sarah is asked about dreams from her childhood, she replies that she was not permitted to dream. That was considered a waste of time in her hard-working family, so she learned at a young age not to talk about her dreams, and soon learned not to dream at all. She expresses frustration and irritation when requested to fantasize, imagine, or dream. She continues with her statements that she does not know; that is why she is here.

## *Response to Sarah: The Case of the Goal Seeking Accountant*
### *John D. Krumboltz*
### *Stanford University*

My first impression is that Sarah may be the victim of wanting to be like other people she knows (or thinks she knows). She says, "Everyone else knows what they want to become, what they are working toward; I have no idea." We should examine that belief. Does everyone know what s/he wants to become? We live in a society where there are incredible pressures to state goals. Most people do eventually succumb and state some occupational aspiration, perhaps just to get the questioner off their backs. Remaining undecided about future goals is not a socially approved option.

### Indecision or Open-mindedness?

Elsewhere (Krumboltz, 1992) I have pointed out that in our society, indecision has a bad reputation. Among career counselors, indecision is just about the worst sin. It is so bad that an extensive literature has built up about the phenomenon. In summarizing that literature, Gordon (1998) listed dozens of terms that have been used to describe degrees of indecision, a few of which include the following: undecided-comfortable, undecided-uncomfortable, moderate indecision, serious career indecision-moderate anxiety, serious career indecision-excessive anxiety, informed indecisive, undecided serious, undecided not serious, undecided career-decided major, indecisive, anxious undecided, transitional indecision, chronic indecision, and developmentally undecided.

The reason for this obsession about indecision is easy to understand historically. Parsons (1909) proposed a three-step model of career counseling that has continued to dominate the field. The third step requires "true reasoning" to match individuals with occupations. If the client cannot decide on a match, the process is not complete. Counselors get frustrated if clients do not follow the theory, and the clients get blamed by being labeled indecisive.

A better way of looking at the situation is to give the phenomenon a more attractive name: open-mindedness. If we think about the process calmly, it is nonsense to expect people to make a logical choice about future activities – especially if the expectation is that they will be locked into that choice for the rest of their working days. People change; the work world changes. Better that people remain open-minded about the possibilities that may still unfurl.

Occupational aspirations turn out to be transitory in most cases. My informal surveys show that only a tiny percentage of working adults are employed in the occupation they aspired to in high school. Occupational goals do change as new occupations are created, as new opportunities arise, and as people develop new interests and skills.

### Helping Sarah

So I am inclined to ask Sarah, "What makes you think you have to have goals? Where did you get that idea?" I would validate her for not having goals. I might say something along this line: "Sarah, it is wonderful that you have been able to resist the pressure to state future goals. From childhood people are constantly asked what they are going to do when they grow up. How can a child be expected to predict the future? It is impossible. The world is changing. You are changing. No one can predict the future with any certainty. It is a completely unrealistic expectation that people should declare what they are going to do in the future. Most people give in though and name some occupation. You have had the courage to resist. At some level you have realized that people are asking you to do something that you cannot do. Yet, you see that some of them claim to have goals, and you wonder if something is wrong with you. Nothing is wrong with you, Sara. The trouble is with the world which expects the impossible."

Now she might react to the validation in a variety of ways. She might say, "You are absolutely right. I love my job. I love my husband. Somehow I got this crazy idea that I had to have goals. Now that I know I was just reacting to social pressure, I feel so much better. I'm an OK person after all. I can now go back to work with that burden of guilt removed. Thanks for all your help. Bye."

Or she might have a quite different reaction: "I know what you mean, but there is something that is still not right. I've done well in accounting. I used to enjoy going to work, but now I dread it. I am still successful. My boss likes my work, but I seem to have burned myself out. I don't know what's wrong, and I don't know what to do about it." In this case a different approach is needed.

### The Planned Happenstance Approach

I would begin with the here and now. "Sarah, here you are beginning a counseling process with me today. What would you like to happen as a result?" Suppose she said, "I want you to tell me what my goals should be." I might reply (tongue in cheek), "OK, your goal is to climb Mt. McKinley." "That's ridiculous. I don't want to climb a mountain." "Ah, excellent, then we have just discovered that you do have preferences and that we can eliminate one type of activity from further consideration. I think we can make some excellent progress together."

I would then continue by orienting her to the approach I would take. It might sound something like this: "Sarah, let me explain how I think we might work together on this situation. The first step is to see if we can figure out what is going on with you at work. You're not happy with your work right now. It would be helpful if you were to start monitoring everything you do on the job and the extent to which you like it or dislike it. We will be examining your work situation to see if the problem can be remedied by changing certain aspects of your work situation – the tasks, responsibilities, coworkers, boss, physical environment, allergies, hours, etc. If your current work situation cannot be improved, then we need to progress to the second step: investigation of alternatives. We would try some exercises to see what you are curious about and what fascinates you."

"As a third step I would want to get you actively involved in trying out alternative activities. Depending on what you discovered about your curiosities, we might get you involved in clubs, self-help groups, hobbies, sports, interactive computer activities, or who knows what else. These would be activities that you would choose to try out – not because you were committed to them but because you wanted to see how you would feel while doing them."

"Who knows what opportunities you might be able to generate from all these experiences? You might discover another line of work you would enjoy more than accounting. You might discover a fascinating hobby that you could do while maintaining your present job. I'll be encouraging you to keep an open mind while learning to be increasingly sensitive to your own feelings about the activities in which you are engaged. How would you feel about getting started on a plan like this?"

If Sarah wanted to work with me on this basis, we would get started right away. If she had questions, I would attempt to answer them. If she wanted to negotiate specific conditions, e.g., number of hours, cost, duration, nature of activities, we would discuss them until we reached a mutually satisfactory contract.

## Learning Theory

The theoretical model is the Planned Happenstance Theory (Mitchell, Levin & Krumboltz, 1999) which extends the Learning Theory of Career Counseling (Krumbotz, 1996) which extends the Social Learning Theory of Career Decision Making (Krumboltz, 1979). The fundamental notion is that people learn through countless learning experiences what they enjoy and do not enjoy, what they are good at and poor at, and what they believe and value.

Does the theory have differential applicability for different genders, ethnic groups, and social classes? Each person has a unique learning history, but membership in various subgroups tends to generate some common types of learning experiences. Does being born a male or a female tend to yield a different set of learning experiences on the average? Probably so these days in the United States. Even more so in certain other countries that have radically different expectations for males and females. So the set of learning experiences is probably systematically different in some respects for males than it for females. And these different experiences would lead to different self-observation generalizations, different task approach skills, and interests in different types of occupations.

Different cultures and subcultures (ethnic communities, socioeconomic groups) provide access to widely different institutions and events where learning experiences take place (e.g., schools, libraries, museums, travel opportunities). To the extent that different groups have access (or are denied access) to these institutions, members of the various groups might on average have quite different learning experiences that ultimately result in different career paths.

The theory itself applies to everyone because everyone has a set of learning experiences that affects her/his career path. The fact that the learning experiences tend to be different for different subgroups of people may be a fact of life with which we must deal, but it does not affect the usefulness of the theoretical premise that helping people find career success and satisfaction can best be achieved by arranging better learning experiences.

People learn skills, interests, work habits, and values as a result of countless learning experiences that occur throughout life. That premise applies equally to males and females, blacks and whites, Catholics and Protestants, gays and straights. Different subgroups may, on average, have learned different skills, interests, work habits, and values and may therefore aspire to different types of occupations. The differences are explained as due to the nature of the learning experiences they are exposed to, not because the theory is any less applicable to any group.

## Normalizing Sarah's Condition

Sarah might be curious about why she seems unable to fantasize, imagine, and dream. She may think that there is something drastically wrong with her. I would lead Sarah through a thought process designed to help her see that her condition is perfectly normal for anyone who had been raised the way she was raised. Prompts I might use to stimulate her recall of formative events could include the following:

- Tell me about what your parents meant when they said they wanted their children to have a "better life."
- What does it mean to you to be a "good girl?" How is your notion of a "good girl" different from that of your parents?
- What have your parents told you about their life in Russia before they immigrated to the U.S.?
- Your parents were Russian immigrants so you have grown up in two cultures. Let's talk about the conflicts you have observed between the cultural values you learned from your parents and the American values you learned from your peers.
- Let's explore how you can reconcile the conflicting values you have been taught.
- In what ways do you want to be similar to your parents? How would you want to be different?
- You said your parents don't want you to throw away a good job for a "fantasy of satisfaction." What do they mean by that? What does that mean to you?
- What does a "goal" mean to you? Tell me some examples of possible goals.
- You say you have no goals. What benefits do you derive from not having any goals? How would your life be different if you did have goals?
- If you had a child and wanted that child to have no goals, how would you raise her? How would you raise her differently if you wanted her to formulate her own goals?
- You are now working in accounting. How did you get into accounting? Tell me the story.

I would use her own account of the unplanned events that led her into accounting and the role she played in creating and capitalizing on those events to guide her into activities in which she could create new unplanned events, some of which might lead her in more satisfying directions.

## Conclusion

Sarah has not yet learned how to reexamine her own assumptions and beliefs. She needs a set of learning experiences to challenge her to explore her assumed need for goals, to see that she is responding normally to the conditions that influenced her, to get her engaged in actions that will gradually help her realize that she can discover her own preferences, and to use those preferences to shape a more satisfying life.

## References

Gordon, V.N. (1998). Career decidedness types: A literature review. *Career Development Quarterly, 46*, 386-403.

Krumboltz, J.D. (1979). A social learning theory of career decision making. In A.M. Mitchell, G.B. Jones, & J.D. Krumboltz (Eds.), *Social Learning and Career Decision Making* (pp. 19-49). Cranston, RI: Carroll Press.

Krumboltz, J.D. (1992). The wisdom of indecision. *Journal of Vocational Behavior, 41*, 239-244.

Krumboltz, J.D. (1996). A learning theory of career counseling. In M.L. Savickas, & W.B. Walsh (Eds.), *Handbook of Career Counseling Theory and Practice* (pp. 55-80). Palo Alto, CA: Davies-Black.

Mitchell, K.E., Levin, A.S., & Krumboltz, J.D. (1999). Planned happenstance: Constructing unexpected career opportunities. *Journal of Counseling and Development, 77*, 115-124.

Parsons, F. (1909). *Choosing a vocation*. Boston, MA: Houghton Mifflin.

## *Response to Sarah: The Case of the Goal Seeking Immigrant*
### *Marian Stoltz-Loike*
### *Windham International*

From the description offered, Sarah appears to be a woman who has led her life to please others. When considering her decision about a career change, Sarah speaks with her brothers and her husband and is frustrated that she cannot speak with her friends about the issue because of conflicts that might arise between her personal career issues and her current career position. It also sounds as if Sarah has little confidence in her own feelings. She contrasts herself who does not have answers with everyone else "who know these things."

Sarah reports that she does not know what she likes or dislikes. Information about how she spent her spare time currently and in the past could be interesting and lead directly to other areas of career exploration. Super's (e.g., Blustein, 1997; Herr, 1997; Nevill, 1997; Phillips, 1997; Savickas, 1997; Super, Savickas & Super, 1996) work on life roles would be very applicable to addressing Sarah's career concerns. Super's insights into career adaptability and the life-career rainbow would provide a valuable framework as Sarah attempts to resolve her career challenges and integrate the personal and career-related aspects of her life. Perhaps spending additional time in areas outside of work – as a volunteer or in a professional capacity – might also help her feel more fulfilled. Additionally, it would be useful to know a bit more about areas of aptitude. Information about what things she did well in when she was in high school or college and why she chose not to pursue those areas might be of value.

Reading the case, I found myself wanting to explore Sarah's feelings that she needed to be a "good girl" and do what her parents wanted so that she would continue to achieve and please them. Her feelings about imagining an ideal job and thinking "out of the box," particularly seem to stir up terrible anxiety. It's hard to envision how Sarah could ever truly be satisfied with achieving a realistic goal if she can't even imagine what that goal would be. I would also like to know why Sarah is looking for counseling at the current time. Has there been some change at work? At home? With her parents? Was there a particular precipitating event?

The Adult Career Concerns Inventory (ACCI; Super, Thompson, Lindeman, Jordaan, & Myers, 1988) or the ACCI used with a behavioral format (ACCI-B; Niles, Lewis, & Hartung, 1997) can also be used to explore career identity. Sarah may need to recycle through some of the stages of career development outlined by Super and others in order to reassess her career choices. She had implemented a career choice but would probably find it valuable to again engage in career exploration, collecting information about different careers, as she forms a more complex vocational identity, followed by crystallizing a vocational preference and making a new career choice, or reaffirming her current career choice.

I think that Sarah might benefit by learning to distinguish between a "good thing" and the "right thing" because currently the two appear to be confused in her mind. Being successful in accounting, not making trouble, and providing satisfaction to her parents might be the "right things" for them but do not necessarily constitute the correct choices for her. Sarah may need to identify the various "good choices" about her career. From her parents' definition, the "right thing" to do may involve continuing in accounting. For Sarah, however, there may be a significant variety of good choices that she could make to provide her with a feeling of self-worth and fulfillment.

Sarah also needs some effective dual-career couple counseling. This would involve some counseling for both her and her husband that would allow conjoint planning of her career, but also ideally provide Sarah with an opportunity to see her career as a extension of herself, rather than the choice of her husband or parents. If this counseling were successful, Sarah and her husband might want to plan things like timing for her career changes so that it would be most compatible with any cycles that are anticipated in her husband's work. Information about her husband's employment, as well as whether or not he is currently employed, would be important. As part of this counseling, her husband might even find that he is interested in making some career changes of his own. Some approaches to counseling for dual-career couples are outlined in Spiker-Miller & Kees (1995) and Stoltz-Loike (1992, 1996).

Some additional exploration about Sarah's socioeconomic status (SES) could be helpful. Clearly, if Sarah left her job to return to school, it might affect the SES level of Sarah and her husband and might affect their lifestyle. Depending on her husband's job and whether or not he is employed, any shift on Sarah's part may or may not have a dramatic influence.

As a simple activity, I would also ask Sarah to place a journal next to her bed and write down any thoughts she may have immediately upon waking. As a more applied activity, it would be valuable to have Sarah create a script of her life, highlighting specific themes and their relation to her indecision, as described by Savickas (1995). Particularly because she does not dream, this activity might be especially enlightening for both the counselor and Sarah although it might be a slow process. Savickas (1995) has shown that creating a personal script can be helpful for the career undecided. Sarah may be involved in a career, but her indecision about her future indicates that she can benefit from this activity.

It would be valuable to learn how Sarah feels that contextual factors affect her career plans. Sarah is the child of Russian immigrants and from the case description it seems that she is not an immigrant herself. Nonetheless, Sarah is likely to have grown up living in two worlds simultaneously. In large northeastern cities, there are extensive enclaves of Russian immigrants. Even the American-born children in these areas typically speak Russian as a first language, and, like their parents, often shop at stores that sell Russian products and cater to Russian tastes. In fact, there are a variety of neighborhoods in New York and Boston where the majority of inhabitants are Russian.

If Sarah was raised in one of these neighborhoods, it is likely to have colored her worldview. On the one hand, at school, she was expected to be an American with American values, taste in clothing, and attitudes. This perspective was very likely to have been supported by her parents. On the other hand, her Russian American community may have supported a different set of values and attitudes. Sarah's response to the need to live in two worlds simultaneously or to select one set of values and attitudes over another might provide insight into her current position.

Another aspect of Sarah's life that it would be of interest to explore is the kinds of jobs that her parents hold and the kinds of jobs that her grandparents had prior to coming to the United States. Many of the Russian immigrants in America were professionals who lost their ability to practice their profession after coming to the U.S. Some of these immigrants were quite successful in integrating into American life after some years through training in their professional area of expertise. Others were able to retrain in another area. Many others, however, were unable to integrate successfully into American life. It would be valuable to know more about Sarah's grandparents. Perhaps they had been professionals or businesspeople in Russia who were unable to transition back into a mainstream job in their area of expertise and worked instead in a more generic, perhaps blue-collar job. This might have influenced Sarah's parents so that they were excessively concerned about employment and job security for themselves and their children.

The nature of the immigrant experience cannot be understated. Particularly if Sarah felt that she "owed" her parents something for all of the hardship they went through to provide her with opportunities in America, it might be hard for Sarah to break away and take care of herself.

Perhaps her attitude toward her current job may relate to a fear of success that may have a variety of sources. Career self-efficacy or the belief that one can succeed, can influence career choices (see discussion in Stoltz-Loike, 1996). This "fear of success" may be particularly relevant for Sarah. I would like to know whether Sarah's husband is of Russian descent and whether he is a first- or second- or later-generation American. His background might significantly influence his attitude toward her career and her success. It might also affect the synergy between their career paths, and his comfort with being on parity with her, or having her take the primary or secondary role as a breadwinner and would represent additional areas for exploration in dual-career couple counseling.

Another issue to explore would be Sarah's facileness with English. There is no reason to assume *a priori* that it is not excellent. However, it might be worthwhile to discuss her feelings about her linguistic sophistication both in written and oral forms. She may be reluctant to move up the corporate ladder for fear that linguistic shortcomings may be highlighted. These concerns may be particularly acute if Russian, rather than English, was her first language.

A final contextual issue is that of gender. It seems that Sarah was willing to excel in school and pick a profession where both men and women are well represented and have an opportunity to be successful. A particular question of importance for Sarah is whether or not there are specific gender-related issues that may be influencing her next career step. How does she feel about women being successful in the career arena she has chosen? Does she believe that women should be in the management (and higher) ranks of companies? Would she be bothered if she earned more money than her husband? Is she more successful than her brothers? How does that make her feel?

A variety of these gender-based stereotypes could be explored to see whether they are restricting the opportunities and mobility that Sarah allows herself. Gender has been shown to correlate with both career choices (Gati, Osipow, & Givon, 1995; Mau, Dominick, & Ellsworth, 1995; and Reschly & Wilson, 1995) and career mobility (Anderson & Tomaskovic-Devey, 1995). I would also use the conjoint counseling of Sarah and her husband to validate information that she might provide. Are there subtle or overt cues that he gives her with regard to support or antagonism toward her career achievements? Identifying how she responds would provide great insight for both partners in the couple.

In summary, in addressing Sarah's feelings about her career, I would like to explore the implications of a variety of contextual factors including gender, family, and socioeconomic issues to understand the backdrop for her life roles. Using Super's life-span, life-space theory, I would like to further explore her life roles as they relate to career and other contexts. Additionally, I think that it would be valuable to involve her husband in some form of dual-career couple counseling since their career and life choices are interdependent.

## References

Anderson, C.D., & Tomaskovic-Devey, D. (1995). Patriarchal pressures: An exploration of organizational processes that exacerbate and erode gender earnings inequality. *Work and Occupations, 22*, 328-356.

Blustein, D.L. (1997). A context-rich perspective of career exploration across the life roles. *Career Development Quarterly, 45*, 260-274.

Gati, I. Osipow, S.H., & Givon, M. (1995). Gender differences in career decision making: The content and structure of preferences. *Journal of Counseling Psychology, 42*, 204-216.

Herr, E.L. (1997). Super's life-span, life-space approach and its outlook for refinement. *Career Development Quarterly, 45*, 238-246.

Mau, W.C., Dominick, M., & Ellsworth, R.A. (1995). Characteristics of female students who aspire to science and engineering or homemaking occupations. *Career Development Quarterly, 43*, 323-335.

Nevill, D.D. (1997). The development of career development theory. *Career Development Quarterly, 45*, 288-292.

Niles, S.G., Lewis, D.M., & Hartung, P.J. (1997). Using the Adult Career Concerns Inventory to measure task involvement. *Career Development Quarterly, 46*, 87-97.

Phillips, S.D. (1997). Toward an expanded definition of adaptive decision making. *Career Development Quarterly, 45*, 275-287.

Reschly, D.J., & Wilson, M.S. (1995). School psychology practitioners and faculty: 1986 to 1991 trends in demographics, roles, satisfaction, and system reform. *School Psychology Review, 24*, 62-80.

Savickas, M.L. (1997). Career adaptability: An integrative construct for life-span, life-space theory. *Career Development Quarterly, 45*, 247-259.

Savickas, M.L. (1995) Constructive counseling for career indecision. *Career Development Quarterly, 43*, 363-373.

Spiker-Miller, S., & Kees, N. (1995). Making career development a reality for dual-career couples. *Journal of Employment Counseling, 32*, 32-45.

Stoltz-Loike, M.E. (1996). Annual review: Practice and research in career development and counseling – 1995. *Career Development Quarterly, 45*, 99-140.

Stoltz-Loike, M.E. (1992). *Dual career couples: New perspectives in counseling*. Alexandria, VA: American Counseling Association.

Super, D.E., Savickas, M.L., & Super, C. M. (1996). The life-span, life-space approach to careers. In D. Brown, L. Brooks & Associates, *Career choice and development* (3rd ed., pp. 121-178). San Francisco, CA: Jossey-Bass.

Super, D.E., Thompson, A.S., Lindeman, R.H., Jordaan, J.P., & Myers, R.A. (1988). *Adult Career Concerns Inventory*. Palo Alto, CA: Consulting Psychologists Press.

# CAROL: THE CASE OF THE CLOSETED WOODWORKER

Carol is a 33-year-old Chinese American woman who presented for career counseling stating that she desired to "know herself better." Specifically, she said that she wanted to learn more about her strengths and weaknesses in order to make a decision about her career direction.

Carol was fired from her most recent employment due to a "conflict with the management." Carol reported that this experience "shot holes" in her self-esteem. She had been employed as a buyer for a local health food store. Carol had been doing this type of work for the past 15 years, working in her home state of California prior to her most recent position in a small town in the southeastern United States. She reports a loss of interest in this type of work, but at the same time she notes a real and continuing enjoyment in the activity of designing creative food displays.

Carol has taken approximately two years of coursework at a community college in California and was enrolled in a course to be trained as an emergency medical technician when she presented for career counseling. In addition, Carol was enrolled in a woodworking class at the local vocational-technical school. She talked about being interested in exploring a variety of occupational options. For instance, she stated that she had an interest in acquiring more information about physical therapy and carpentry. Concerning the former, Carol stated that she had a strong dislike for studying science. Her current interests seemed to relate to activities associated with her woodworking class. The instructor of this class has been very supportive of her. Carol feels as though she possesses some skill in this line of work. As a result, Carol started doing carpentry projects for clients her instructor had referred to her. When she considered doing this work full-time, Carol expressed strong apprehension about the male-dominated aspects of this work (for example, would she be accepted? How would she cope with the sexist aspects of the work climate?).

Carol has two brothers and one sister, but she is the oldest. She is the only one in her family not living in California. Carol reports that her relationship with her father is strained. Carol feels that her father is emotionally distant and highly critical.

Her family is unaware of the fact that, in addition to her career concerns, Carol is in the middle of "coming out" as a lesbian. She is very closeted about her sexual orientation with other people. She has never been particularly attracted to men or women, but has recently met a 24-year-old Chicana woman who is a student at a nearby university. Carol mentions this during last five minutes of the third session and is very hesitant in revealing any additional facts. She seems to be waiting to see if you approve or disapprove of her disclosed sexual orientation.

## *Response to Carol: The Case of the Closeted Woodworker*
### *Nadya A. Fouad*
### *University of Wisconsin - Milwaukee*

Carol comes for career counseling to help her make a career decision, stating that she wants to know herself better. Carol has pursued many training opportunities, including community college coursework, emergency medical technician training, and woodworking. Carol is enrolled in both the emergency medical technician training and the woodworking class at the time she seeks career counseling. Carol's interests appear to be in the Realistic area as indicated by the occupations she has mentioned, such as emergency medical technician (EMT), woodworking, carpentry, and physical therapy. Carol is a Chinese American woman, living apart from her family. She grew up as the eldest daughter of four and reports some emotional strain in her relationship with her father. She reveals, at the end of the third session, that she is attracted to a woman and is identifying as a lesbian.

Carol approaches career counseling with a number of strengths. First, she has sought out many educational opportunities. It is not clear why she chose emergency medical technician, nor why she chose to enter a woodworking class. However, the fact that she has sought out these programs and enrolled in them is evidence of her ability to acquire knowledge of these training opportunities and her willingness to pursue her goals. Second, Carol has clearly defined areas that interest her, as well as knowledge of what she does not like. She enjoys creating enticing food displays, she enjoys woodworking and carpentry, but she does not like science. Third, she was able to persevere in her most recent area of work for over 15 years, managing to find employment even after relocation.

## Conceptualizing Carol's Present Situation

Three aspects of Carol's case intertwine: her career concerns, her identity as an Asian-American woman, and her emerging sexual identity as a lesbian. It is impossible to separate these areas, so I will first discuss issues and areas about which I would want more information, then I will discuss the approach I would use in working with Carol as a career counselor.

Carol is the oldest child in a Chinese American family. I would want to know which generation she is, or how many generations her family has been in the United States. This would give some information about level of acculturation, as well as perhaps how closely Carol is identified with traditional Chinese values and traditions. The history of Chinese Americans in the United States shows that time of immigration is highly related to exposure to discrimination and racism, with earlier immigrants more likely to have suffered atrocities and to be kept in lower occupational levels than more recent immigrants (Leong & Gim-Chung, 1995). However, as Sue and Sue (1999) point out, even highly acculturated Asian Americans are subject to racist remarks and are targets of violence, as evidenced by recent shootings in Chicago. Thus, I would want to know how Carol identifies with her Chinese heritage and how she has dealt with racism in her life.

Yang (1991) suggests that Chinese American women are in danger of triple jeopardy. That is, that they are disadvantaged due to cultural norms perpetuating inequality between men and women, racism, and stress due to trying to live in two cultures. Traditional Chinese values include strong filial piety, focus on perfectionism, high value placed on family relationships, having harmonious relations, stress on the group's goals over the individual's goals, respect for authority, and restraint over emotions (Carnevale & Stone, 1995; Leong & Gim-Chung, 1995; Sue & Sue, 1991, 1999). Which of these are important values to Carol, and which are important to her family? For example, did she move far away from her family as a sign of separation from them and from their values? Is she struggling because her own values are different from her family's? This may be an indication that she is more acculturated to mainstream U.S. culture than her family; it may also be related to her sexual orientation and discomfort with being geographically close to her family as she copes with her emerging sexual identity.

I would want to know how Carol decided to go into the EMT program, and how she decided to go into woodworking. What specifically happened to terminate her employment? What has Carol learned from this experience, and what does it say about how she handles interpersonal conflict? Does she feel she needs to be perfect, and is highly self-critical? Does she feel that she needs to live up to others' expectations? If so, what are her family's expectations? And how would her family react to her coming out as a lesbian? She is anxious about others' reactions to her sexual identity, as indicated by her hesitation in disclosing this information and concern with the counselor's approval.

## Using a Culturally Appropriate Career Counseling Model

Carol has a number of concerns that she brings to counseling, and the course of counseling would depend on which of these are most salient to her. It may be, for example, that she entered career counseling to focus on her sexual orientation, and her career concerns are least important. However, this section will focus on her career concerns. In working with Carol as a career counselor, I would use the Culturally Appropriate Career Counseling Model (CACCM; Fouad & Bingham, 1995). The CACCM explicitly addresses the influence of the role of culture in career counseling and is an extension of models originally proposed by Ward and Bingham (1993; Bingham & Ward, 1994). In step 1, we establish a working relationship, and to do so I would be knowledgeable about Chinese American norms and values, but would also be aware that they might not apply to Carol.

In the step 2, I would focus on the areas of concern that Carol brings to career counseling. Carol states that she wants to know herself better, implying that she is not very knowledgeable about her skills and interests. She reports some interpersonal problems in her previous job that led to her being fired and that her self-esteem suffered as a result; she also reports some interpersonal conflicts with her father. By the end of her work as a buyer she was not interested in many aspects of the job. Although pursuing various educational opportunities may be conceptualized as a strength, it was not always clear that each opportunity was carefully thought out. For example, Carol is in an EMT training program, a fairly demanding training program, but also is in a woodworking class. She would appear to be the most interested in woodworking and is spending much extra time doing projects outside of class. This may indicate some impulsivity on Carol's part; it may also indicate that she is undecided about what area to pursue and trying out various options at the same time. I would also determine the role that discrimination, oppression, and sexual harassment have played in her career decisions.

During step 3 of the CACCM, I would work with Carol to assess the influence of traditional Chinese traditions and values on her career choices and decisions. What role has her family played? Her gender? Her identification as a lesbian? Fouad and Bingham (1995) conceptualize a sphere composed of concentric circles to help identify the way that culture influences career development. The innermost circle is the core of the individual, with successive layers including the client's gender, family, culture of origin, and the dominant culture.

Once Carol has identified the career issues she wants to focus on and the influence of culture on those career issues, career counseling would proceed (step 4) with culturally appropriate processes and goals. In step 5 we would determine and implement a culturally appropriate intervention, with steps 6 and 7 implementing and following up on her decisions, respectively.

I would give Carol the Strong Interest Inventory (SII: Harmon, Hansen, Borgen, & Hammer, 1994) and the Skills Confidence Inventory (SCI: Betz, Borgen & Harmon, 1996) to help her identify areas of interest, as well as areas that she is confident in. It may be that her Realistic interests are not accompanied by confidence in her abilities in that area. I would also help Carol clarify the interpersonal issues that occurred in her last job and determine whether there are skills that she wants to work on in this area, such as assertiveness. I would also help Carol explore the role of her sexual identity in her career decision making. For example, what role does potential employment discrimination play in her decision to be protective about disclosing her sexual orientation? As Elliot (1993) points out, the decision to be open is a major issue for lesbian and gay clients.

## References

Betz, N.E., Borgen, F.H., & Harmon, L.W. (1995). *Skills Confidence Inventory: Applications and technical guide*. Palo Alto, CA: Consulting Psychologist Press.

Bingham, R.P. & Ward, C.M. (1994). Career assessment with ethnic minority women. In W.B. Walsh & S.H. Osipow (Eds.), *Career counseling for women* (pp. 165-195). Hillsdale, NJ: Erlbaum.

Carnevale, A. P. & Stone, S. C. (1995). *American mosaic: An in-depth report on the future of diversity at work*. New York: McGraw-Hill.

Elliot, J. (1993). Career development with lesbian and gay clients. *Career Development Quarterly, 41,* 210-226.

Fouad, N.A. & Bingham, R. (1995). Career counseling with racial/ethnic minorities. In W.B. Walsh & S.H. Osipow (Eds.), *Handbook of vocational psychology* (2nd ed., pp. 331-366). Hillsdale, NJ: Erlbaum.

Harmon, L.W., Hansen, J.C., Borgen, F.H., & Hammer, A.C., (1994). *Strong Interest Inventory: applications and technical Guide.* Palo Alto, CA: Consulting Psychologist Press.

Leong, F.T.L. & Gim-Chung, R.H. (1995). Career assessment and intervention with Asian Americans. In F.T.L. Leong (Ed.), *Career development and vocational behavior of racial and ethnic minorities* (pp. 193-226). Mahweh, NJ: Erlbaum.

Sue, D., & Sue, D.W. (1991). Counseling strategies for Chinese Americans. In C.C. Lee & B.L. Richardson (Eds.), *Multicultural issues in counseling: New approaches to diversity* (pp. 79-90). Alexandria, VA: American Association for Counseling and Development.

Sue, D.W. & Sue, D. (1999). *Counseling the culturally different* (3rd ed.) New York: Wiley.

Ward, C.M. & Bingham, R.P. (1993). Career assessment of ethnic minority women. *Journal of Career Assessment, 1*(3), 246-257.

Yang, J. (1991). Career counseling of Asian American women: Are they in limbo? *Career Development Quarterly, 39,* 350-359.

# Response to Carol: The Case of the Closeted Woodworker
## Y. Barry Chung
### Georgia State University

Carol's case is an interesting one for career counseling for it involves a number of personal and contextual factors and their interactions. I will discuss my conceptualization of her situation, followed by my suggestions for counseling interventions.

## Case Conceptualization

Clearly, Carol is in a state of major life transitions. She has recently moved to a small town in the Southeast away from all of her family members in California. Additionally, at the age of 33 she is thinking about leaving her previous career of 15 years and is considering some career options that are nontraditional for her gender. All these transitions coincide with her coming out as a lesbian.

To better understand Carol's situation, I would attempt to find out answers to the following questions. Why did she move across the country, leaving her family behind? What are the Chinese communities like in her hometown and her new residence and what was her involvement? What is the immigration history of Carol's family and what are her racial identity attitudes? How is she adjusting to living in the Southeast? What did she like and dislike about her previous job? What prompted her to make a career transition? What are important factors in her career decision making? What does she want to accomplish in her career? How does she feel about being a woman with nontraditional career interests? What are some barriers she has encountered as a woman? How does she feel about her sexual orientation? How would her coming out as a lesbian influence her career decisions?

Based on the limited information presented, some conceptualizations and hypotheses are cautiously discussed here. At the age of 33, Carol is searching for a career identity. She spent 15 years doing something in which she was not particularly interested, probably because of pragmatic reasons such as financial need and stability. Being fired from her job prompted her to consider a career/life change. Furthermore, Carol is aware of her career interests and realizes that they are nontraditional for women (e.g., emergency medical technician, physical therapist, carpenter). By taking courses and doing woodwork projects, she has started exploring such options. Another major transition concerns Carol's self-exploration into her lesbian orientation. Such hesitation and confusion has prompted her to seek career counseling, in order to better understand herself and gain more control of her life.

Carol's situation should be further considered within her cultural contexts. In a traditional Chinese family, children's career decisions are often made in a collectivistic fashion (Leong & Serafica, 1995). The needs and expectations of the family are important considerations, sometimes even more influential than one's interests and needs. As the oldest of four children, Carol may carry extra responsibilities for the family. The oldest child is often expected to be successful, be a role model for the younger siblings, and provide financial support so that younger siblings are able to further their education and pursue their careers. It is not clear whether Carol's family situation resembles the aforementioned tradition, but her father seems to be a typical Chinese father who is emotionally distant and highly critical. Carol seems to have trouble dealing with authority figures (e.g., her conflict with management in her previous job), resulting in resentment or rebellion against her family and father's expectations. Because Carol was considering nontraditional career options for women, she may have experienced disapproval from her family, especially her father. Moving away from her family may be a means for Carol to escape the strains and expectations of feeling like a disappointment to her family.

## Counseling Interventions

In light of the various personal and contextual factors in Carol's career development, the theory that I would use to guide my interventions is Social Cognitive Career Theory (SCCT: Lent, Brown, & Hackett, 1996), which seems to hold great promise for addressing multicultural issues in vocational behavior. According to this theory, background variables and their related contextual affordances influence one's learning experiences, which in turn affect one's self-efficacy and outcome expectations. These factors then determine one's interests, goals, and choice actions. Contextual factors also moderate the causal relations in this process and may directly influence career goals and decisions.

In working with Carol, I would first help her explore how her background variables (e.g., birth order, gender, ethnicity, socioeconomic status, sexual orientation) may have contributed to her learning experiences. For example, being the oldest child, she may have been given responsibilities of caring for her siblings and managing family matters, which may have strengthened her management skills. On the other hand, being female may have limited Carol's opportunities to pursue nontraditional interests for women. Her ethnic background may have contributed to her sensitivity to oppression and discrimination. Also, Carol's socioeconomic status, although unknown from the case description, may have forced her to enter the labor force early in life and shortened her formal education. Finally, her sexual orientation may be associated with her nontraditional interests and skills for women. Hence, by examining the influences of background variables and contextual affordances, Carol should be sensitized to the implications of contextual factors.

Next, I would help Carol understand how interests are affected by learning experiences, self-efficacy, and outcome expectations. For example, Carol is doing very well in her woodworking class and she already has some customers requesting her projects. This positive learning experience reinforces her self-efficacy in carpentry, as well as positive outcome expectations, which in turn strengthens her interest in carpentry. An understanding of the process of interest development will be helpful while Carol is exploring her vocational interests. The four sources of learning experience – performance, vicarious learning, social persuasion, and physiological states (Bandura, 1986) – may be applied to develop certain interest areas and skills. An important aspect of this intervention is to enhance Carol's self-efficacy and self-esteem. To further assist Carol in understanding her current interests, traditional person-environment fit measures may be used (e.g., Strong Interest Inventory; Harmon, Hansen, Borgen, & Hammer, 1994).

Because of significant contextual influences, the causal relations from interests to goals to choice actions are not simple for Carol. Therefore, the next step would be to examine how contextual factors influence

Carol's career goals and decisions. An exploration of the immigration history of Carol's family, the family's cultural beliefs, and Carol's racial identity attitudes will be necessary. Chung and Chou's (1999) chapter about counseling American-born and overseas-born Chinese Americans provides a good framework for such an exploration. Carol may benefit from value clarifications regarding how she would like to balance family expectations and her own needs. At this time she seems to be escaping from her family in order to explore her career and sexuality. It is important to discuss her needs for family contact and support, in addition to her current social support in the Southeast.

Gender role and sexual orientation are also important contextual factors to explore. Carol has expressed interest in nontraditional careers for women, such as emergency medical technician and carpenter. However, she is also afraid of sexism in such nontraditional fields. Carol seems to be apprehensive about discussing her sexual orientation and yet, she managed to make the disclosure. It is important that the counselor responds to her nontraditional interests and sexual orientation in a supportive and affirmative manner. I would express appreciation for her willingness to share such information, validate how difficult it may have been for her to do so, express my support for her interest and same-sex orientation, and invite her to share her experiences and feelings. Carol may feel validated by learning that many lesbians have nontraditional sex-role behaviors and interests (Chung, 1995; Fassinger, 1995). Her fears regarding sexism and heterosexism may be addressed jointly, in order to help her establish a sense of self-worth as a woman and lesbian. A feminist approach to dealing with such issues may be helpful. Further, Carol needs to be educated regarding the different aspects of work discrimination. Readers may refer to Chung's (in press) models for helping lesbian, gay, and bisexual persons understand work discrimination and develop effective coping strategies.

In facilitating Carol's coming out process, it is important to consider the possible interactions between ethnic identity and sexual identity development (Chung & Katayama, 1998). Being a Chinese American may make it particularly difficult for Carol to come out as a lesbian. Compared with mainstream American culture, Chinese culture is much more intolerant of homosexuality. Due to a lack of lesbian or gay role models and any kind of social affirmation, the concept of positive lesbian or gay identity does not exist in Chinese culture. Consequently, coming out often involves a Westernization process for Chinese Americans – to disengage from Chinese culture/community and immerse oneself into the White gay culture/community. Perhaps this explains Carol's moving across the country to be away from her family. However, according to Chung and Katayama (1998), ethnic minorities may encounter racism in the middle-class White gay community. Such an experience may result in feelings of marginalization – being rejected by two cultures. It is important for the counselor to help Carol deal with her ethnic identity and sexual identity issues, so as to achieve an integrated positive identity as a Chinese American lesbian woman.

## Conclusion

Carol presents a challenging case that involves personal and contextual factors, such as ethnicity, gender, and sexual orientation. Successful counseling interventions call for both traditional theories and techniques, as well as newer theories and frameworks that are more sensitive to such contextual factors. The counseling interventions discussed above are based on Social Cognitive Career Theory (SCCT) and other theories that deal with ethnic and sexual orientation issues. In my discussion of such interventions, it is evident that personal and career issues are intertwined. An integrative counseling approach is critical for successful work with clients like Carol.

## References

Bandura, A. (1986). *Social foundations of thought and action: A social cognitive theory*. Englewood Cliffs, NJ: Prentice Hall.

Chung, Y.B. (1995). Career decision making of lesbian, gay, and bisexual individuals. *Career Development Quarterly, 44,* 178-190.

Chung, Y.B. (in press). Work discrimination and coping strategies: Conceptual frameworks for counseling lesbian, gay, and bisexual clients. *Career Development Quarterly*.

Chung, Y.B., & Chou, D.S. (1999). American-born and overseas-born Chinese Americans: Counseling implications. In K.S. Ng (Ed.), *Counseling Asian families from a systems perspective* (pp. 145-158). Alexandria, VA: American Counseling Association.

Chung, Y.B., & Katayama, M. (1998). Ethnic and sexual identity development of Asian American lesbian and gay adolescents. *Professional School Counseling, 1,* 21-25.

Fassinger, R.E. (1995). From invisibility to integration: Lesbian identity in the workplace. *Career Development Quarterly, 44*, 148-167.

Harmon, L.W., Hansen, J.C., Borgen, F.H., & Hammer, A.L. (1994). *Strong Interest Inventory*. Palo Alto, CA: Consulting Psychologists Press.

Lent, R.W., Brown, S.D., & Hackett, G. (1996). Career development from a social cognitive perspective. In D. Brown, L. Brooks, & Associates, *Career choice and development* (3rd ed., pp. 373-421). San Francisco, CA: Jossey-Bass.

Leong, F.T.L., & Serafica, F.C. (1995). Career development of Asian Americans: A research area in need of a good theory. In F.T.L. Leong (Ed.), *Career development and vocational behavior of racial and ethnic minorities* (pp. 67-102). Mahwah, NJ: Erlbaum.

# RANDALL: THE CASE OF THE CHALLENGE SEEKER

Randall is a 36-year-old African American male with a college degree in criminal justice and biology (received in 1981) entered counseling in the spring of 1995. He has always lived in an urban environment and grew up in New York City. He sought career counseling in order to explore his career options. At the time he entered counseling, Randall was employed as a surgical laboratory technician. Although he initially enjoyed this work, it had become boring and routine for him. He reported that the most enjoyable parts of this job were taking patient case histories and working with trauma cases. He noted that he was interested in pursuing an occupation that would provide him with more challenge and more opportunities for personal development. Randall described himself as "competitive," "creative," "verbally skilled," and a person who wanted "to make a difference."

Randall's work history reflected a variety of positions in different fields. For example, he had worked as a police officer, a salesperson for IBM, and an advertising executive for several national companies. He obtained his current position after first serving as an emergency room volunteer and then being hired as a "lab tech" first in primary care and then in surgery. His current plans were to explore career options within the field of medical service.

His mother, who had been employed as a nurse, first exposed Randall to the field of medicine. His father was a contractor who worked as a homebuilder and developer. Randall's family relationships were very important to him and he placed a great deal of importance on being able to spend time with his children (ages 3 and 7) and his partner, Regina.

## Assessment Results for Randall

### Salience Inventory (SI) 1 = low, 4 = high

|          | Study | Work | Community Activities | Home & Family | Leisure Activities |
|----------|-------|------|----------------------|---------------|--------------------|
| Part.    | 4.0   | 4.0  | 3.9                  | 4.0           | 2.6                |
| Commit.  | 4.0   | 4.0  | 4.0                  | 3.9           | 1.8                |
| Values Exp. | 3.8 | 3.8 | 3.9                  | 3.8           | 2.1                |

### Adult Career Concerns Inventory (ACCI) Number of concerns rated 4 (considerable) or 5 (great)

*Exploration Stage:*
- Crystallization   4
- Specification   3
- Implementation   2

*Establishment Stage:*
- Stabilizing   0
- Consolidating   2
- Advancing   2

*Maintenance Stage:*
- Holding   0
- Updating   4
- Innovating   4

*Disengagement Stage:*
- Deceleration   0
- Retirement Plan   0
- Retirement Living   1

**Occupational Stress Inventory (OSI)** Results in T-scores

*Occupational Roles Questionnaire:*

| | |
|---|---|
| Role Overload | 54 |
| Role Insufficiency | 74 |
| Role Ambiguity | 49 |
| Role Boundary | 68 |
| Responsibility | 64 |
| Physical Environ. | 80 |

*Personal Strain Questionnaire:*

| | |
|---|---|
| Vocational Strain | 53 |
| Psychological Strain | 44 |
| Interpersonal Strain | 48 |
| Physical Strain | 38 |

*Personal Resources Questionnaire:*

| | |
|---|---|
| Recreation | 52 |
| Self-care | 58 |
| Social Support | 38 |
| Rational/Cognitive Coping | 59 |

**Strong Interest Inventory (SII)**

| | | |
|---|---|---|
| *Academic Comfort:* | | 68 |
| *Introversion-Extroversion:* | | 26 |

*Themes:*

| | | |
|---|---|---|
| Social | Very High | 74 |
| Conventional | Very High | 73 |
| Investigative | Very High | 68 |
| Enterprising | High | 62 |
| Realistic | High | 61 |
| Artistic | Average | 50 |

*Basic Interests:*

Very High:

| | |
|---|---|
| Medical Service | 73 |
| Medical Science | 71 |
| Military Activities | 70 |
| Social Service | 70 |
| Science | 70 |
| Public Speaking | 68 |
| Religious Activities | 67 |
| Office Practices | 67 |
| Law/Politics | 65 |

*High:*

| | |
|---|---|
| Nature | 59 |
| Mechanical Activities | 59 |
| Business Management | 58 |
| Domestic | 57 |
| Athletics | 57 |

*Occupations:*

| | |
|---|---|
| Nursing Home Administrator | 65 |
| School Administrator | 64 |
| Nurse, RN | 63 |

| YWCA/YMCA Director | 61 |
| Executive Housekeeper | 60 |
| Dietician | 60 |
| Public Administrator | 58 |
| Minister | 58 |
| Food Service Manager | 57 |

**Values Scale (V1)** 1 = low, 4 = high

- 4.0 Ability Utilization
- 3.8 Altruism
- 3.8 Personal Development
- 3.6 Authority
- 3.6 Autonomy
- 3.6 Creativity
- 3.4 Achievement
- 3.4 Life Style
- 3.4 Advancement
- 3.0 Working Conditions
- 2.8 Aesthetics
- 2.8 Physical Activity
- 2.8 Economic Security
- 2.6 Social Interaction
- 2.6 Variety
- 2.6 Cultural Identity
- 2.4 Economic Rewards
- 2.2 Risk
- 2.0 Physical Prowess
- 1.4 Social Relations
- 1.2 Prestige

## Response to Randall: The Case of the Challenge Seeker
## Developmental Career Assessment and Counseling
## with a Multipotentialed Client
## Paul J. Hartung and Brian J. Taber
## Northeastern Ohio Universities College of Medicine

To guide our work with Randall, mindful of his goal of exploring his career options, we would use the Career Development Assessment and Counseling (C-DAC) model developed by Super (1983) and described in other case studies (see Hartung, Vandiver, Leong, Pope, Niles, & Farrow, 1998; Niles & Usher, 1993; Osborne, Brown, Niles, & Miner, 1997; and Super, Savickas, & Super, 1996). The C-DAC approach focuses us on the range of issues Randall faces as he nears midlife. It keeps us aware as we begin counseling that work represents but one of many possible roles that give Randall meaning in the broader context of his life (Richardson, 1993). We would therefore strive to identify what meaning he ascribes to work relative to life roles in other areas such as home and family, community, school, and leisure. As we proceed, we would also consider the cultural context of Randall's life and specific culturally relevant issues, such as the client-counselor relationship and intervention approaches, that may influence the counseling process (see Leong & Hartung, 1997; Hartung et al., 1998).

The C-DAC approach helps us to structure our work with Randall through four phases. These phases include a preview (initial interview), depth view (career assessment), data assessment (test interpretation), and counseling (integration). Let us consider each of these phases in turn with Randall.

## Randall: A Preview

Developmental career assessment and counseling begins with a preview of the client's career concerns through an initial interview and review of any available information from the client record. If we had the opportunity to interview Randall personally, we would be highly attuned to his opening statement, listening carefully to the words he uses to characterize his problem and situation. What does he say and how does he say it? If we are fully attentive, the preview may tell us the whole story, which formal career assessment may help us to confirm. These initial pieces of content and process would tell us much about Randall's life story and style (Super et al., 1996). As we meet Randall through the case summary, we form an image of a man who has explored and disengaged from positions in law enforcement and business. He now feels bored by work that he "initially enjoyed." Various questions begin to emerge. Did Randall initially enjoy these other positions too? Was this the pattern in his previous jobs? Initial excitement followed by routine and boredom? What were the circumstances of his leaving his previous jobs as a police officer, salesperson, and advertising executive? Answering these questions might better inform us about Randall's career story and style and serve as a starting point for constructing the next chapter of his life.

Randall has tried to find his place in the world of work, yet the story we preview suggests that at age 36 Randall has yet to locate a suitable and satisfying niche. He has become bored with his job as a surgical lab technician and seeks more of a challenge and opportunity for personal development. Here we get a glimpse of two likely core values: challenge and personal development. We also get a glimpse of his self-concept as we hear him describe himself as "competitive," "creative," "verbally skilled," and a person who "wants to make a difference." We would explore these and other dimensions of his self-concept and note their relation to his life roles of worker, father, spouse, and child. During the preview, we would informally assess the degree to which he was able to realize his self-concept through his previous work, and how his self-concept has played a role in his moving from one position to another.

Beginning in the preview, and continuing throughout counseling, we would attend to potential cultural identity issues. For example, Randall is an *African American* man who appears to emphasize family relationships and spending time with his children and spouse. Identifying his cultural value orientation, level of acculturation, and whether he emphasizes family and group goals or his own personal goals and ambitions may be useful to him and us (Leong & Brown, 1995; Triandis, 1995). To assess cultural role orientation, we could administer the INDCOL Scale (Singelis, Traindis, Bhawuk, & Gelfand, 1995) or use the "I am" method (Kuhn & McPartland, 1954; Triandis, McCusker, & Hui, 1990).

## Taking a Depth View

If warranted from our preview, we would assess Randall's life structure and the importance of his life roles using the Salience Inventory (SI; Super & Nevill, 1985a). We especially want to know the level of importance he ascribes to the role of work in his life. This would help us to appropriately assist Randall to design and shape his life structure and not assume that we know which roles are most important to him. If work represents a salient role to Randall, we would proceed with administering and evaluating the results of the other instruments Randall completed for this case study.

Using the C-DAC approach, we also know that we must first determine his level of adaptability and readiness for career choice and exploration (Savickas, 1997). Otherwise, any interventions aimed at match-making would be much less meaningful and lasting (Super, 1983).

## Assessing the Data

Randall's Salience Inventory (SI) results reveal that he has a high degree of commitment, participation, and values expectation in the areas of study (3.8), work (3.8), community service (3.9), and home and family (3.8). Leisure (2.1) appears a much less salient role for him. When discussing these results with Randall we would explore with him the role leisure plays in his life and if he considered whether his level of participation in other roles provides a recreational outlet. For instance, he might consider spending time with his family or studying to be leisure activities. Given that work appears to be a highly salient role for Randall, we would examine the results from the other instruments that he completed.

The Occupational Stress Inventory (OSI; Ospiow & Spokane, 1987) may help us to clarify the nature of Randall's current job dissatisfaction. Randall's OSI scores indicate high levels of stress related to role insufficiency (74), role boundary (68), responsibility (64), and the physical environment (80). He also displays low scores on personal strain and high scores on personal resources especially in the areas of self-care (58) and rational/cognitive coping (59). This suggests that his coping skills have been effective in dealing with job stress. In exploring these results with Randall, we would want to clarify the personal meaning of these scores and how they play a role in his present career concerns and future vocational choices. For example, his high score in role insufficiency may reflect the boredom he reports in his present job by not being able to fully use his abilities. We would also draw his attention to his low social support score. We would ask who provides support for him and if he has social contacts with others outside his family. Additionally, we would explore with him any barriers that may prevent him from eliciting social support.

The Adult Career Concerns Inventory (ACCI; Super, Thompson, Lindeman, Jordaan, & Meyers, R. A., 1988) provides us with a picture of Randall's current career stage and concerns. We scan his results looking for items rated of considerable or great concern. Randall's ACCI scale scores reveal concerns in the Exploration (9) and Maintenance stages (8) of career development and very little concern for the tasks related to the Establishment stage (4). Specifically, the developmental tasks of Crystallization (4 – considerable concern) in the Exploration stage and Updating (4) and Innovating (4) in the Maintenance stage are important to him. Randall is concerned with Crystallizing his vocational identity and exploring occupations through which he can realize his preferences. Concerns with updating (4) and innovating (4) suggest that he seeks to acquire new skills and take on new challenges. Becoming established in an occupation is not a concern for Randall. Rather, it is a question of which occupation would best meet his needs. Indeed, Randall wants to find a better fit between his vocational identity and work environment. Alternatively, it may be that Randall needs to increase his concern to establish in a suitable position rather than moving from job to job. Randall needs to learn how to settle into a position, and this frustrates him because he has potential in many areas. Randall may also be experiencing a period of career renewal in which he has realized that he probably does not want to maintain his current job but prefers to explore and reestablish in a more satisfying occupation (Murphy & Burck, 1976; Williams & Savickas, 1990).

Vocational interest assessment may help to further clarify Randall's self-concept and explore career options that would allow him to implement it. Randall's Strong Interest Inventory results (SII; Harmon, Hansen, Borgen, & Hammer, 1994) indicate a very high degree of interest on many of the Basic and Occupational interest scales. So many high scores may overwhelm Randall who appears multipotentialed and easily bored. He may find choosing just one occupation limiting. His highest General Occupational Themes scores are 74 on Social, 73 on Conventional, and 68 on Investigative. Randall's interest pattern displays an intermediate level of inconsistency (Social-Conventional). According to Holland (1997), the more inconsistent the interest profile the more difficulty a person may have in making a vocational choice, and the less likely that person will be able to realize a level of occupational stability. Indeed, Randall's continuous job changing reflects his difficulty in finding an occupation in which his interests can be fully realized, and thus switches occupations in hopes of finding the perfect work environment. Essentially, Randall's profile indicates a preference for fields in which he can help others, have structure, and be intellectually stimulated. The Basic Interest scales generally confirm these preferences with Medical Services (73), Medical Sciences (71), Military Activities (70), Social Service (70), and Science (70) rounding out the top five.

Randall's Occupational Interest scores on the SII indicate that his interest pattern is similar to those of Nursing Home Administrator (65), School Administrator (64), and Nurse (63). Additionally important to understanding how Randall's preferences can be realized is his Academic Comfort Level of 68, which indicates that he enjoys academic pursuits. Although Randall entered counseling expressing that he wanted to explore careers in medical services, the results of the SII may reveal to him other options that he had never considered. In reviewing the results of the SII, we would want to explore with Randall his personal meaning of these results. Further, we would ask Randall about his occupational daydreams and how they may relate to his results. We would also ask how he uses his interests in his life and how he proposes to make use of them in creating his career (Savickas, 1995).

The Values Scale (VS; Super & Nevill, 1985b) further clarifies Randall's self-concept. Randall places a high value on ability utilization (4.0), altruism (3.8), and personal development (3.8) and places little importance on physical prowess (2.0), social relations (1.4), and prestige (1.2). Essentially, Randall values being all he can be, helping others do the same, and continuing to foster his own sense of self while refining and developing his skills.

## Counseling with Randall

Based upon what we know about Randall, it appears that Randall has not had the opportunity in his life to fully implement his self-concept. Although he seems satisfied for a short time in a new job, he quickly grows bored and seeks new challenges. Randall reported upon entering counseling that he desires to explore options in the medical services field and certainly there are many fields within this occupational cluster that provide a challenge and where he can make a difference. Presuming that his initially stated goal did change through the course of assessment, we would begin to explore areas in the medical field. Given that Randall has a high academic comfort zone and he places a high value on the student role, we may suggest that he explore options within the medical fields that require advanced training such as that for a physician or dentist. We would discuss with Randall how his self-concept fits these occupations by discussing aspects of these careers and to what degree they match his self-concept. We would also discuss the similarities and differences of these occupations so that Randall has a better sense of where he belongs. Additionally, since Randall places a high value on family, we would encourage that he discuss these options with his family in order to get their impressions of how Randall would fit in these occupations. Should Randall decide to pursue one of these occupations, we would discuss how returning to school would affect the other valued areas of his life and how he and his family could find time to be together.

In order to acquire more information on this topic, he may want to discuss with professionals already employed in these fields how they balance work and family. He could also use such an opportunity to gain information on their experiences in going through training and ultimately entering the medical profession. Additionally, we would want to know if he foresaw any barriers to realizing his vocational aspirations.

Should Randall decide to enter one of these professions, there is no guarantee that he will not become bored with the routine of these fields once he is established. Given that Randall's occupational history to this point suggests that he is capable of performing a myriad of tasks and has a wide range of interests, we would want to explore further with him ways he can satisfactorily find outlets that permit him to grow. This may entail further examination of his life roles in order to identify these potential outlets. For example, we may explore with Randall how he could develop his leisure role as an avenue to use his abilities and interests that he may not be able to use in his work role. With this information at hand we can assist Randall in making plans for finding an occupation that would provide the personal fulfillment he is looking for.

# References

Harmon, L.W., Hansen, J.C., Borgen, F.H., & Hammer, A.L., (1994). *Strong Interest Inventory: Applications and technical guide.* Palo Alto, CA: Consulting Psychologists Press.

Hartung, P.J., Vandiver, B.J., Leong, F.T.L., Pope, M., Niles, S.G., & Farrow, B. (1998). Appraising cultural identity in career-development assessment and counseling. *Career Development Quarterly, 46,* 276-293.

Holland, J.L. (1997). *Making vocational choices* (3 rd ed.). Odessa, FL: Psychological Assessment Resources, Inc.

Kuhn, M.H., & McPartland, R. (1954). An empirical investigation of self-attitudes. *American Sociological Review, 19,* 68-76.

Leong, F.T.L., & Brown, M. (1995). Theoretical issues in cross-cultural career development: Cultural validity and specificity. In W.B. Walsh, & S.H. Osipow (Eds.), *Handbook of Vocational Psychology,* (2nd ed. pp. 143-180). Mahwah, N.J.: Erlbaum.

Leong, F.T.L., & Hartung, P.J. (1997). Career assessment with culturally different clients: Proposing an integrative-sequential conceptual framework for cross-cultural career counseling research and practice. *Journal of Career Assessment, 5,* 183-202.

Murphy, P.P., & Burck, H.D. (1976). Career development of men at mid-life. *Journal of Vocational Behavior, 9,* 337-343.

Niles, S.G. & Usher, C.H. (1993). Applying the career-development assessment and counseling model to the case of Rosie. *Career Development Quarterly, 42*(1), 61-66.

Osborne, W.L., Brown, S., Niles, S., & Miner, C.U. (1997). *Career development assessment and Counseling: Applications of the Donald E. Super C-DAC approach.* Alexandria, VA: American Counseling Association.

Osipow, S.H., & Spokane, A.R. (1987). *Manual for the Occupational Stress Inventory.* Odessa, FL: Psychological Assessment Resources.

Richardson, M.S. (1993). Work in people's lives: A location for counseling psychologists. *Journal of Counseling Psychology, 40,* 425-433.

Savickas, M.L. (1997). Career adaptability: An integrative construct for life-span, life-space theory. *Career Development Quarterly, 45,* 247-259

Savickas, M.L. (1995). Examining the personal meaning of inventoried interests during career counseling. *Journal of Career Assessment, 3,* 188-201.

Singelis, T.M., Triandis, H.C. Bhawuk, D.P., & Gelfand, M.J. (1995). Horizontal and vertical dimensions of individualism and collectivism: A theoretical measurement and refinement. *Cross Cultural Research, 29,* 240-275.

Super, D.E. (1983). Assessment in career guidance: Toward truly developmental counseling. *Personnel and Guidance Journal, 61,* 555-562.

Super, D.E., & Nevill, D.D. (1985a). *Salience Inventory.* Palo Alto, CA: Consulting Psychologists Press.

Super, D.E., & Nevill, D.D. (1985b). *Values Scale.* Palo Alto, CA: Consulting Psychologists Press.

Super, D.E., Savickas, M.L., & Super, C.M. (1996). The life-span, life-space approach to careers. In D. Brown, L. Brooks & Associates, *Career choice and development: Applying contemporary theories to practice* (3rd ed., pp. 121-178). San Francisco CA: Jossey-Bass.

Super, D.E., Thompson, A.S., Lindeman, R.H., Jordaan, J.P.,& Myers, R.A., (1988). *Adult Career Concerns Inventory.* Palo Alto, CA: Consulting Psychologists Press.

Triandis, H.C. (1995). *Individualism and collectivism.* Boulder, CO: Westview Press.

Triandis, H.C., McCusker, C., & Hui, C.H. (1990). Multimethod probes of individualism and collectivism. *Journal of Personality and Social Psychology, 59,* 1006-1020.

Williams, C.P. & Savickas, M.L. (1990). Developmental tasks of career maintenance. *Journal of Vocational Behavior, 36,* 166-175.

# Response to Randall: The Case of the Challenge Seeker
## Verneda Washington
## University of Missouri - St. Louis

### Image of the Client

Randall's case presents a wide range of concerns centering on job dissatisfaction with past positions. There is a major discrepancy between what he finds exciting in a career and the type of jobs he prefers. However, his work history reveals that he has had challenging positions in the past. His past positions as a police officer and an emergency room volunteer typically are very challenging and should provide the variety he needs to be satisfied. This discrepancy indicates that further career exploration is needed to obtain information on other careers in the medical field. Typically, when work is not meaningful and important it is not surprising that little career exploration has been done. Therefore, a more comprehensive evaluation of his values is needed to determine a better job match for him.

The analysis of Randall's case is based on the case description for inferences regarding his interests and values. The scores of the Strong Interest Inventory (SII) indicate that Randall's interests were congruent with the occupational options he was considering. Specifically, his scores in the areas of medical service (73), medical science (71), military activities (70) and science (70) were very high. From these results is obvious that Randall needs to engage in more exploration in the medical field.

Also noteworthy in his career assessment are his elevated scores in social and conventional activities (74) in addition to an strong interest in the investigative domain (68). These varied scores are an indication of his diverse needs and interests and are certainly reflected in his work history.

The diversity of career interests presents a challenge in helping Randall clarify his occupational choices. There may be reluctance in committing to one occupation because of the wide range of interests. Considerable time will be needed to explore the pros and cons of each occupation and its feasibility for Randall's situation. The major themes that will emerge should give direction in examining whether this is a realistic career for him. In any event, it is important to discuss with Randall that it may be difficult for him to find an occupation that will allow for expression of these different interests. It maybe useful to explore ways he can meet some of these needs through work and other needs through community service activities.

Scores from the Values Scale (VI) will be important in examining Randall's core values that seem to be driving his interests. His scores on the VI were high on ability utilization (4.0), altruism (3.8), and personal development (3.8). The results indicate a strong desire to use all his skills and knowledge for his own development, but also to use his talents in a career that involves helping people. These core values would be important to address in clarifying his ideas of what would be "making a difference" in his life.

Although the case material provides implicit references to what might be important values for Randall it is not clear how these values align with his current career interests. Additional information regarding Randall's interests may be acquired by exploring his reactions to his current job as a laboratory technician and past positions. Encouraging Randall to explore salient aspects of these jobs that he felt were "challenging" will provide important information for career planning. Thus, examining these scores with Randall could help clarify his current situation and the appropriateness of the medical career options for his current needs.

## Career Counseling Plans and Inventions

The analysis of Randall's case suggests two primary implications for practitioner preparation and practice. His narrative emphasizes the importance of understanding the client's values and interests as well as family influences. One major consideration in working with this client is to help the client gain knowledge about who he is and what he wants out of life. Acquiring this information will make it possible to understand his needs and wants.

Second, I would clarify further his ideas about boredom. What other things does he find interesting? What does he consider as a challenge? A personality test may be helpful in assessing dominant personality traits that influence his likes and dislikes. When that has been determined, it will be easier to figure out what suits his personality.

Third, it would be important to explore what type of work gives him meaning and purpose. (Isaacson & Brown 2000) argue that work has many meanings for different people. Work can be seen as a way to develop self-esteem, strictly for survival, or as a vocation. Further, the authors argue that work has religious meanings for many individuals. Work in this context is driven from a duty to serve God in this manner. Many feel that they are "called" by a higher power to be in a particular vocation and derive meaning in life by serving others.

Religious factors may have an influence on Randall's inability to commit to a career. Randall's SII scores on religion were fairly significant (67) and may be important in understanding the meaning of work for him. His religious upbringing may have some impact on his values and the career decision process. His ideas about "making a difference" may stem from his religious upbringing. Therefore, it would be important for the career counselor to provide the opportunity for exploring religious/spiritual issues as it relates to career development.

The theoretical model used in this case study would endeavor to explain family persuasion on Randall's career development and provide direction in treatment planning. Roe (1956) maintains the concept that early childhood experiences affect career satisfaction. The need framework of the client is influenced greatly by positive and negative experiences engendered during in the early years of life. The innate predisposition of expending energy to satisfy needs combined with childhood experiences shapes the template used in satisfying emotional and career needs in life. Thus, the family has a tremendous impact on one's perception of success and failure in the workplace. This unique family approach stems from inherited and learned traits and behaviors of interacting with objects and significant others that are apparently consequential in career development. It can ultimately affect whether work is satisfactory or whether a person will be unchallenged.

In examining the current case study, it is apparent that family plays an important role in Randall's career decision process. The narrative indicates that his mother who is a nurse introduced Randall to the medical field. Ultimately, his mother's occupation in the medical field may have had a great influence on his career choice. His past experiences with his family of origin have instilled the importance of family relationships with his own family. A challenge for Randall would be to find medical careers that allow time with the family to maintain these relationships. Thus, any feasible career option would need to provide an opportunity for expression of these family values.

There are many qualitative devices that might be used in assessing Randall's career interests and values. A career genogram would be particularly helpful in tracing Randall's family occupations and values surrounding work. Basically, in career counseling the genogram is used first to get a graphic representation of the careers of a client's family. This would include biological relatives as well as significant others that have had an impact on career development. When used appropriately, this information can be used to understand how family values have influenced the career decision process (Brown & Brooks, 1991).

## Contextual Factors

Although the interests and values of the client are important in doing a comprehensive career assessment, contextual factors such as culture and gender would also be critical in the counseling process. Much of the research in multicultural career counseling focuses on understanding the culture of the client and its impact on the worldview of minority clients (McCollum 1998). These cultural attitudes may have an impact on the career development and career maturity of African Americans (Leong, 1995). In Randall's situation, his scores on the Strong Interest Inventory (SII) reflect the interests of many African Americans. Specifically, Randall's SII scores indicate a high interest in social occupations, which historically have been a strong cultural value. Further, the overrepresentation of African Americans in social and behavioral science occupations may be a manifestation of the Africentric value of unity and community service (Leong, 1995). In the past, the community has been important in empowering African Americans to overcome discrimination and achieve success in western society. Thus, the notion of work in this culture may have different meanings for African Americans than their Caucasian counterparts.

Although using a multicultural approach would certainly be an important factor in Randall's case, caution must be used in categorizing him with other African Americans. Ethnicity is likely to influence career development, albeit it is difficult to discern how such attitudes might influence career choice differences (Leong, 1993). Further, Kimbrough & Salomone (1993) argue that on many factors such as ethnicity and socioeconomic status African Americans are quite heterogeneous. Thus, knowing the ethnicity of a minority client is not sufficient to assess the impact of culture. It is more important to understand how he perceives his culture and its ultimate impact on the decision-making process. In this case study, Randall's value score on cultural identity was relatively low (2.6). This may indicate that his culture is not as important to him as his ability to overcome obstacles. Therefore, it would be important to understand how his cultural identity plays a part in his career choice.

## Summary

As Randall moves through the career self-assessment process and examines his values and interests in his life, it is hoped that he will gain a better understanding of himself and the career options that work best for him. Use of the VS, the SII, and the genogram will be helping in clarifying salient family issues that can be useful in identifying a career that meets his various needs.

# References

Brown, D. & Brooks, L. (1991). *Career counseling techniques*. Boston, MA: Allyn & Bacon.

Isaacson, L.E., & Brown, D. (2000). *Career information, career counseling, and career development* (7th ed.). Needham Heights, MA: Allyn and Bacon.

Kimbrough, V. & Salomone, P. (1993). African Americans: Diverse people, diverse career needs. *Journal of Career Development, 19(*4), 265-278

Leong, T. (1995). *Career development and vocational behavior of racial and ethnic minorities*. Mahwah, NJ: Erlbaum.

McCollum, V. (1998). Career development issues and strategies for counseling African Americans. *Journal of Career Development, 25*(1), 41-52.

Roe, A. (1956). *Psychology of occupations*. New York: Wiley.

# RAVEN: THE CASE OF THE RIGHTEOUS PARALEGAL

Raven is a 37-year-old Native American woman (Arapaho/Crow) who works as a paralegal at a small law firm in a medium-sized city in the northwestern United States. The law firm specializes in personal injury. Raven has worked at this law firm for two years. Previously, she has worked at two other law firms in town. She quit both previous jobs very abruptly after her situation was "too much to handle." Prior to moving to this town, Raven had worked at four other law firms as a paralegal in a nearby large city. She also ended all of those previous jobs, except one, abruptly after her frustration level became too high. The one exception was the first paralegal job she had after her two years of college to become trained as a paralegal. At this job she stayed nine years.

Raven explains that her first job, which she "earned" in the 1970s, provided her with the opportunity to be an advocate for people with low incomes or who were taken advantage of by "big business." More recently, she felt the paralegal job in her specialty (personal injury) had become a "sleazy" job in which lawyers do not act in the best interest of the client but only for their own financial gain. Raven feels this change does not fit her value system and is in conflict with why she was motivated to become a paralegal in the first place. As a result, Raven thinks that she no longer wants to work as a paralegal.

In her current job, Raven explains that she has few friends. She gets "fed up" with her coworkers and often disagrees with the actions of lawyers (who are now younger than she). At times, Raven feels so frustrated that she has to leave the workplace because her tension gets to be "too much to handle" and she "shuts down."

Outside of her work Raven is an accomplished artist. She has displayed several paintings at art shows and has been able to sell several of her paintings. She describes herself as a very spiritual person. She has additional interests in astrology and poetry. Her ideal career would be to "work for John Grisham," the accomplished author. Raven is willing to acquire additional training, but she insists on keeping a steady income to remain comfortable and safe.

Raven lives alone, but she lives near her younger sister. Raven's family is scattered around the Northwest and Plains states. Her father abused Raven as a child. She has a poor relationship with her brother, a psychiatrist, who believes Raven fabricated the story about being abused by her father. The only person in the family close to Raven is her sister. She describes one or two "older" lawyers as her only friends.

Raven has been divorced for five years. She married one of her brother's friends shortly after she obtained her first paralegal job. The relationship became physically abusive and divorce happened four years after being married. Since then Raven has had a few relationships, often with the "wrong type of people."

Raven has been in and out of therapy for a number of issues surrounding the past abuse and other personal issues. She has come to career counseling to try to find a new career path.

## Response to Raven: The Case of the Righteous Paralegal
### Jack Watson and Janet G. Lenz
### Florida State University

This analysis of the case of Raven is written from the perspective of Cognitive Information Processing theory (CIP; Peterson, Sampson, & Reardon, 1991; Peterson, Sampson, Reardon, & Lenz, 1996). From this theoretical base, our goal as career counselors is not only to help Raven solve her current career problem, but also to provide her with the skills necessary to improve her future career problem solving and decision making.

Raven would initially be seen as a walk-in client. She would likely present with a problem that would be defined as a "gap" between the value system required by her current job (i.e., make money at the client's expense) and her actual value system (i.e., work to help the underprivileged). The gap is manifesting itself into an erratic employment history and desire to find a new career. An initial assessment of Raven's readiness to use career services would follow. The counselor would make a preliminary assessment of Raven's career problem-solving competencies based upon a discussion of what led her to seek career assistance. Given the complexity of Raven's case (i.e., multicultural, values-based) and her inability to decide upon a specific occupation, she would be asked to complete the Career Thoughts Inventory (CTI; Sampson, Peterson, Lenz, Reardon, & Saunders, 1998). Raven's hypothetical responses to the CTI would probably reveal slightly elevated dysfunctional career thoughts related to other adult women.

Her hypothetical CTI scores would likely indicate the presence of an elevated level of negative thoughts related to career problem solving and decision making. Specifically, these negative thoughts may be the result of external factors (e.g., father, brother, community/tribe) and a history of decision-making confusion. Based upon these CTI scores and the way that Raven would likely discuss these issues with a career counselor, it is likely that she would be considered indecisive and she and her counselor would agree upon individual counseling at a time when one-on-one assistance could be provided. Prior to her individual appointment, Raven would be asked to complete a client information form and an informed consent form. As a follow-up to the CTI, the counselor might in a later session ask Raven to complete the Career Attitudes and Strategies Inventory (CASI; Holland & Gottfredson, 1994) to further clarify Raven's thoughts and feelings regarding her current and future work situations. Specifically, the CASI would provide information on issues associated with Raven's job satisfaction, work involvement, career worries, interpersonal abuse, risk-taking style, geographical barriers, and any perceived career obstacles.

The counselor's working conceptualization of Raven would suggest that she is concerned about her ability and desire to continue working at her current firm. She has a tendency to be impulsive (i.e., history of quitting), which is initially expressed in "tension" and subsequent seclusion. With this history, Raven is probably looking for a quick resolution to her problem and could easily discontinue career counseling if she does not feel that it is helpful. Therefore, the counselor will need to continually summarize the steps that have been taken and the progress that has been made. Furthermore, with her Native American heritage and history of abuse, Raven may work best with a female counselor who possesses good relationship skills.

Because of Raven's multicultural heritage, several steps would be taken to help her better understand herself, her cultural views, and her counseling issues. First, the counselor would not rely completely on written descriptions about Native American (Arapaho/Crow) culture to make assumptions about Raven's history and values. Much of this information would be gained directly from discussions with Raven herself. Because of the importance of family and tribe that is often present in Native Americans, several areas would be explored. The counselor would try to gather information about her view of counseling, issues related to family, and attachment to tribal community.

Considering the severity of the personal/family issues that Raven is dealing with (i.e., parental abuse and poor relationship with brother and family), she would be encouraged to continue individual mental health counseling to work through these issues. As Raven has a desire to gain the skills/training necessary to change her occupation while continuing work in order to "remain comfortable and safe," counseling would likely include basic stress management and communication skills training. These skills would help her in situations when her tension becomes "too much to handle" and she "shuts down." Improving stress management skills could also improve her ability to adapt to a new occupational environment and allow her to be less impulsive in her decisions to quit jobs.

Upon developing a relationship and gaining a better understanding of Raven's problems and concerns, she and her counselor would work together to create an individual learning plan (see Figure 1). The ILP helps clarify the goals of therapy and outlines a treatment strategy. Having a plan often helps to motivate clients, makes progress more visible, helps to monitor progress, and maps out the client's future strategies.

***Goals:***
1. Clarify knowledge about self and values.
2. Improve knowledge about career options.
3. Understand how thoughts about self and others affect career choices.
4. Improve communication/stress management/career problem-solving skills.

| *Goal* | *Priority* | *Activity* | *Purpose/Outcome* | *Time* |
|---|---|---|---|---|
| 3,4 | 1 | Continue career counseling | Gain insight and knowledge | 1 hr/wk |
| 3 | 3 | CTI | Identify career thoughts | 20min |
| 3 | 5 | CTI Workbook | Improve self-talk/reduce negative thinking | ongoing |
| 1 | 7 | Values card sort | Understand value system | 45 min |
| 1 | 6 | Projective occupational card sort | Understand how occupations are organized | 45 min |
| 1,2 | 8 | CACG system | Increase self & occ. knowledge | 2 hrs |
| 1 | 4 | SDS | Improve self-knowledge | 1hr |
| 4,1,3 | 2 | Continue counseling | Deal with past issues of abuse | 1hr/wk |
| 2 | 9 | Read career information | Improve occupational knowledge | 1 hr/wk |
| 4 | 10 | Termination with counselor | Assess status/determine future needs | 1 hr |

Figure 1. Raven's Individual Learning Plan (ILP).

As part of the individual career counseling process, Raven would be introduced to the client versions of both the Cognitive Information Processing (CIP) pyramid and the Communication, Analysis, Synthesis, Valuing, Execution (CASVE) cycle (Sampson, Peterson, Lenz, & Reardon, 1992). These theoretical models are designed to help clients understand the information needed (content) and steps to be followed in making informed career decisions (process). The counselor would lead Raven through each of the stages of these models using discussions and the activities outlined on the ILP. The end goal of these interventions is to remove any gaps that may exist in Raven's knowledge base, to help her make the most informed decision at this time, and to give her the skills to solve career problems and make career decisions in the future.

The CIP approach includes three levels of knowledge that are involved in career choice. The base of the pyramid highlights the need for clients to develop both self and occupational knowledge in order to make good career choices. The second level in the pyramid emphasizes the use of problem-solving and decision-making strategies, specifically the CASVE cycle. In the CASVE cycle, individuals are encouraged to fully explore the nature of their career problem (the gap) during the Communication phase, including their thoughts and feelings; identify self and occupational knowledge and typical ways of making decisions during the Analysis phase; identify potential options during the Synthesis phase; evaluate potential options during the Valuing phase; and develop a plan of action during the Execution phase. The third level of the CIP approach is knowledge of one's metacognitions (i.e., self-talk, self-awareness, control and monitoring) in problem solving.

Because of the impact that dysfunctional metacognitions can have upon career decision-making and the counseling process, the counselor would immediately begin helping Raven identify and change her dysfunctional thoughts. Raven's CTI responses would be used to guide a discussion of her dysfunctional self-talk as it relates to career decision making. Raven would then be given the CTI workbook (Sampson, Peterson, Lenz, Reardon, & Saunders, 1996) to complete as homework. This homework assignment is designed to help Raven reframe her negative self-statements into positive self-statements. The aim of the workbook is to help her learn how to identify, challenge, and alter negative self-talk and take action to maintain more positive career thoughts. The counselor would periodically refer to this homework assignment as well as future metacognitions throughout the counseling process.

As Raven has realized that the requirements of her current occupation do not fit well with her value system and artistic interests, it is important that she be guided in exploring her self-knowledge (Analysis phase of CASVE cycle). To help Raven improve her self-knowledge, she would first be assigned the Self-Directed Search (SDS; Holland, Powell, & Fritzsche, 1994). This instrument would help her to gain a better understanding of her basic personality profile. A hypothetical Holland Code for Raven would be A, C, S. This code reflects her leisure activities, that capture her artistic interests and talents, her "C" competencies and abilities that she has developed through her work, and her interest in helping others. The lack of consistency in her SDS code would indicate the need for increased attention to her occupational aspirations. The counselor would explore her occupational daydreams to learn more about how these reflect her current interests, values, and skills. The summary code from Raven's occupational daydreams could be used to expand her knowledge of options (Reardon & Lenz, 1998).

In order to further clarify Raven's self-knowledge of her values and occupational needs, and for the counselor to gain insight into her personality, the counselor would utilize a card sort task(s). Raven's discussion of "earning" her first job, and reflection that her "value system" was the major reason for the erratic work history and change in occupations, suggests that Raven's values will be a major factor in deciding upon a new occupation. Furthermore, a projective vocational card sort could be used to provide a semi-structured forum for gathering a substantial amount of projective information about personal, occupational, problem-solving, familial, and organizing issues (Peterson, 1998).

A list of occupations with duties and responsibilities congruent with Raven's three-letter Holland Code and daydreams code would be created using the Occupations Finder as well as the *Dictionary of Holland Occupational Codes* (Gottfredson & Holland, 1996). The information learned about Raven's value system and occupational needs would also be used to brainstorm for a list of additional occupations to be considered. This entire list would be shortened by Raven to include only those occupations that are consistent with her current values. The counselor would also work with Raven to help her explore the extent to which she may wish to consider occupations that would use the skills and competencies developed in her past work history versus those occupations that would tap the skills developed through her artistic accomplishments.

To improve occupational knowledge, Raven would be encouraged to briefly research each of the occupational titles that she has included on her list of possibilities. The research would involve finding basic information (e.g., starting salary, educational requirements, skills needed) about these occupations through the use of computer-assisted career guidance systems (CACG) and other occupational resources. Given her interest in John Grisham's work, she may find it interesting to read vocational biographies as part of her occupational exploration. With facilitation from the counselor, Raven would be guided in reducing her list of potential occupations to 3-5 based upon similarities between self-knowledge (i.e., values, interests and skills) and occupational knowledge (Synthesis phase).

Upon shortening her list of potential occupations, Raven would be instructed to begin a larger and more detailed informational search that would help her to make a final decision (i.e., Valuing phase of CASVE cycle). In conjunction with the additional information, Raven would also be instructed to consider the costs and benefits of each occupation as it relates to herself, family, cultural group, community, and society. Many of these categories may be very important to Raven, as Native Americans are often very concerned about their community. Once the costs and benefits of each occupation have been considered, Raven will be encouraged to begin rank ordering her options so as to decide upon a primary course of action and a backup plan.

Once a decision has been made, Raven will be led in creating a plan for obtaining the occupation of her choice (i.e., Execution phase). This plan might include options for obtaining further education as appropriate, reality testing, as well as developing a job search strategy for making the transition to a new field of work. After making a plan, Raven will be encouraged to put the plan that she has developed into action. The counselor will continue to provide Raven with support and discuss any negative thinking that may compromise her ability to make effective use of career resources. While taking steps to attain her goals, Raven would be encouraged to continue assessing her current situation, her feelings about the decision that she has made and be helped in anticipating any new problems that may arise from making a transition (Communication phase of CASVE cycle). She would also be encouraged to generalize what she has learned from this experience to future career choices.

## References

Gottfredson, G.D., & Holland, J.L. (1996). *Dictionary of Holland Occupational Codes* (3rd. Ed.), Odessa, FL: Psychological Assessments Resources.

Holland, J.L., Gottfredson, G.D. (1994). *Career Attitudes and Strategies Inventory: An inventory for understanding adult careers.* Odessa, FL: Psychological Assessments Resources.

Holland, J.L., Powell, A.B., & Fritzsche, B.A. (1994). *Self-Directed Search professional user's guide.* Odessa, FL: Psychological Assessments Resources.

Peterson, G.W. (1998). Using a vocational card sort as an assessment of occupational knowledge. *Journal of Career Assessment, 6*(1), 49-67.

Peterson, G., Sampson, J.P, Jr., & Reardon, R. (1991). *Career development and services: A cognitive approach.* Pacific Grove, CA: Brooks/Cole.

Peterson, G., Sampson, J.P., Jr., Reardon, R., & Lenz, J. (1996). A cognitive information processing approach. In D. Brown, L. Brooks & Associates, *Career choice and development* (3rd ed., pp. 423-475). San Francisco, CA: Jossey-Bass.

Reardon, R.C., & Lenz, J.G. (1998). *The Self-Directed Search and related Holland career materials: A practitioner's guide.* Odessa, FL: Psychological Assessment Resources.

Sampson, J.P., Jr., Peterson, G.W., Lenz, J.G., & Reardon, R.C. (1992). A cognitive approach to career services: Translating concepts into practice. *Career Development Quarterly, 41,* 67-74.

Sampson, J.P., Jr., Peterson, G.W., Lenz, J.G., Reardon, R.C., Saunders, D.E. (1996). *Improving your career thoughts: A workbook for the Career Thoughts Inventory.* Odessa, FL: Psychological Assessment Resources.

Sampson, J.P., Jr., Peterson, G., Lenz, J., Reardon, R., Saunders, D. (1998). The design and use of a measure of dysfunctional career thoughts among adults, college students, and high school students: The Career Thoughts Inventory. *Journal of Career Assessment, 6,* 115-134.

# Response to Raven: The Case of the Righteous Paralegal
## M. Carolyn Thomas and Susan E. Riser
### Auburn University - Montgomery

**Image of Raven**

Raven's life is lacking balance and meaning, and the symptoms are evident in her dissatisfaction with her work. She is experiencing conflict between her beliefs and values, her need for financial security, and the mission of her employers. She is being denied the pleasure of being paid to do what she loves and believes in, and the dissonance may create frustration and inability to cope with stress.

In addition, Raven may be suffering from the incongruence of her present lifestyle with values traditionally held by Native Americans. For example, many Native Americans believe that respect and appropriate use of nature lead to harmony and optimum functioning in human relationships (Axelson, 1999). Raven lives in the city, far from the natural world in which her ancestors lived. For many Native Americans, tribe and extended family needs take precedence over those of the individual, in contrast to values often expressed by those of European descent (Anderson & Ellis, 1995). Raven is estranged from her family, except her sister, was a victim of an abusive father, and reports having few friends.

Raven is at a transitional point in her life. She is presently completing a developmental stage of establishing intimate relationships (Erikson, 1968), and has been unsuccessful in establishing a long-term relationship. Whether she is satisfied with her single state is unknown, but if she has not addressed this issue in counseling, this may contribute to her dissatisfaction. She will soon face the crisis of generativity vs. stagnation (Erikson, 1968), which must be resolved satisfactorily for her life to become balanced. In Raven's first job, which allowed her to be an advocate for disadvantaged people, she was able to guide and assist others. Her subsequent positions have denied her that opportunity, and she has had to sublimate her values to those of her employers.

Finally, Raven is spiritual and creative, and the extent to which these characteristics have provided balance and harmony in her life is unknown. Basic in any counseling plan for Raven would be more opportunities to live her values of ethical behavior, service to others, spirituality, and meaningful creativity. Balancing her need for economic security with increasing outlets for her strong personal values and expanding her sense of community within her culture may provide the harmony necessary for Raven to successfully complete her developmental tasks.

**Counseling Model**

Since Raven is Arapaho/Crow, and Native Americans commonly believe that wellness is harmony and illness is disharmony in spirit, mind, and body (LaFromboise & Jackson, 1996), a holistic counseling model is most appropriate. In such a holistic approach, career and personal counseling cannot be separated. Super's life-span, life-space approach is sufficiently comprehensive and inclusive to provide such a holistic approach (Super, Savickas, & Super, 1996). In adopting a comprehensive approach, the counselor can include interventions for dealing with cultural issues (Ibrahim, 1985), and sequencing approaches to complete Raven's healing from childhood abuse (Thomas, 1999). In combining personal and career counseling, the counselor would include assessment, career exploration, preparation of a treatment plan for the issues affecting Raven's career, and evaluation.

**Assessment**

Assessment is an integral part of career counseling, and a combination of traditional and nontraditional approaches might prove most appropriate for Raven. Recommended areas of assessment with Raven include interests; skills; values; work, leisure, and play history and satisfaction; world-view and ethnic identity with her specific Native-American culture; developmental history and meaning of critical events in her life; support within her community; and stage of healing from childhood abuse. Raven can provide important information about her interests, skills, values, and career history by giving a narrative of activities, achievements, education, and aspirations from childhood to the present. Even daydreams and roles played in childhood games can provide insight into roles she might prefer in adulthood.

Information from her narrative can be compared for consistency with results from the Campbell Interest and Skills Survey (CISS) (Campbell, 1992) and the Self-Directed Search (SDS) (Holland, 1995). Raven's expressed interest in art and poetry can be verified with predicted high CISS orientations in helping and creating and high SDS social and artistic orientations. The CISS and SDS can also be used to show consistencies between Raven's stated life goals and values of helping others in difficulty, contributing to human welfare, providing service to others, creating something meaningful, and believing in equality. Both instruments can augment Raven's self-understanding by helping her become aware of additional interests and values with which she did not previously identify.

Ibrahim's (1985) recommendations for assessing worldview and ethnic identity can be used to discern how closely Raven identifies with her Arapaho/Crow culture, and whether this identification is positive or negative. The diversity among Native Americans precludes counselors from making broad generalizations about the many cultures, but certain values seem to be common (Sue & Sue, 1990). Consequently, assessment of her ethnic identify, the major critical events in her life, and support within her family are crucial in planning subsequent counseling.

Finally, assessment of Raven's healing progress from her childhood abuse is essential for designing a treatment plan for her recovery. She has already received some counseling for the abuse, but the pattern of poor and abusive relationships, breaks with much of her family, and multiple jobs indicate only partial recovery from the abuse. Assessing her stage of recovery can help the counselor plan the most appropriate interventions to counteract the negative effects of the abuse on Raven's career and personal life (Thomas, 1999).

## Career Exploration and Treatment Plan

The two counseling components might best be combined, because Raven's work and life history are interwoven. Traditional career exploration and creating options consistent with Raven's cultural and personal values can be accomplished using the CISS and SDS results and materials, complemented by any other available resources.

Since Native-American healing processes greatly involve the client, significant others, and community helpers (LaFromboise & Jackson, 1996), the counselor can plan a broader, nontraditional approach. Based on Raven's worldview and support system assessment, the counselor can elicit Raven's help in identifying other helpers with practices consistent with her culture.

Based on assessments, the major treatment goals and strategies would be collaboratively chosen by Raven and her counselor, and would likely include (1) identifying other helpers in her community and building her personal resources, (2) improving her ethnic identity evaluations and changing her worldview to include more of her personal and cultural values, (3) completing the healing process from the abuse, (4) beginning the ongoing process of life planning that includes personal and career goal setting, and (5) identifying careers and avocations that will provide more harmony and balance in her life.

The most intensive treatment may well be those strategies used by several professional, familial, and community helpers to help her become an empowered nonvictim. This may also be an ongoing process, requiring counseling for a minimum of one to two years. Behaviors, beliefs, and fears learned during the abuse are often major blocks to a meaningful life and will impede Raven's growth until she fully recovers from the abuse.

## Evaluation and Prognosis

Raven's expressed life satisfaction will provide the best measure of successful treatment, since Native-American achievement indicators are often less material than those of other cultures. Life planning is a lifelong process, so her self-counseling will be continuous. Seeking harmony with the universe is also ongoing, as is healing from the negative effects of critical life events. The treatment plan can begin the process and help Raven learn the mechanisms for creating new paths for herself.

The goal of combined career and personal counseling is not to find a path. Rather, the goal is to create new paths. When Raven has created new paths for herself, and those paths lead to increased harmony, creativity, spirituality, and sense of community, her counseling will be positive.

## References

Anderson, M.J., & Ellis, R. (1995). On the reservation. In N. Vacc, S. DeVaney, & J. Wittmer (Eds.), *Experiencing and counseling multicultural and diverse populations* (3 rd ed., pp. 179-198). Bristol, PA: Accelerated Development.

Axelson, J.A. (1999). *Counseling and development in a multicultural society* (3rd ed.). Pacific Grove, CA: Brooks/Cole.

Campbell, D.P. (1992). *Campbell Interest and Skills Survey*. Minneapolis, MN: National Computer Systems.

Erikson, E.H. (1968). *Identity: Youth and crisis*. New York: W.W. Norton.

Holland, J.L. (1995). *Self-Directed Search (SDS) Form R* (4th ed.). Odessa, FL: Psychological Assessment Resources.

Ibrahim, F.A. (1985). Effective cross-cultural counseling and psychotherapy: A framework. *Counseling Psychologist, 13,* 625-638.

LaFromboise, T., & Jackson, M. (1996). MCT Theory and Native-American populations. In D.W. Sue, A.E. Ivey, & P.B. Pedersen (Eds.), *A theory of multicultural counseling and therapy* (pp.192-203). Pacific Grove, CA: Brooks/Cole.

Sue, D.W., & Sue, D. (1990). *Counseling the culturally different: Theory and practice* (2nd ed.). New York: Wiley.

Super, D.E., Savickas, M.L., & Super, C.M. (1996). The life-span, life-space approach to careers. In D. Brown, L. Brooks & Associates, *Career choice and development: Applying contemporary theories to practice* (3rd ed., pp. 121-178). San Francisco, CA: Jossey-Bass.

Thomas, M.C. (1999, January). *Sequencing theoretical approaches in family abuse issues groups.* Paper presented at the conference of the Association for Specialists in Group Work, Albuquerque, NM.

# BILL: THE CASE OF THE DOWNSIZED FATHER

Bill is 39 years old and has a bachelor's degree in political science. Bill has most recently been employed as a regional senior sales executive with a well-known national consumer product corporation based in Georgia. He worked for the same company since he was 24. He lives with his partner, Patricia, and two children (ages 8 and 11) in their home on the outskirts of the city. They purchased their home shortly after they were married and they put a great deal into what Bill calls their "dream house." Bill presents himself in dress and manner as a well-educated professional. He comments about the importance of appearances especially in his field and at his level.

Recently, Bill's company reorganized and his position was eliminated, resulting in his termination. His company provided Bill with six months of severance pay with benefits and has underwritten the cost of outplacement career counseling. During his 15 years with this company, Bill worked his way up from sales associate to sales office coordinator to regional director in a small region to his present position as regional director of the Northeast. He has been working out of the New York office over the past four years and has had to travel a great deal to the South to be with his family and maintain his home. He does most of this traveling on weekends and occasionally adds a day of vacation to the two-day weekend to extend his time with his family. Bill states that he prefers living in the South but would consider jobs in the Northeast if necessary. Bill's partner is able to be flexible about the location of her job.

Bill worries about the impact of his termination on his family and how his friends will perceive him. Being successful and supporting his family has motivated Bill to work hard and strive for promotion. He says, "I believe in giving my all to the job and being rewarded fairly for my efforts." He admits that he just fell into his first job with this company and has never really explored any other jobs, nor has he ever had to conduct a job search. Bill felt sure that he would never be without a position in this company as long as he was a loyal and productive employee. Bill's spouse is supportive, but does not want to be the sole financial provider for the family.

Although Bill expressed anger over his termination, he wants to move on as quickly as possible. He states that there is no time to waste because he may be losing out to younger job seekers. He approaches the task of finding a new position as an unwelcome hurdle in his career plan. Because of his inexperience as a job seeker, Bill feels at a loss as to what he should do and where he should begin searching.

Currently, Bill puts a lot of time into projects around the house. He enjoys improving the property that he feels he has neglected during the past four years. He admits that he may as well get the home ready for the market in case it has to be sold. He is not pleased with this prospect but feels helpless due to his current situation. Other than caring for the home, Bill has lessened his involvement in social activities and this concerns his spouse. He really does not feel comfortable around the "employed" right now and states that he feels embarrassed about his termination.

Bill is determined to use the outplacement career counseling provided by his company. He feels that they owe him that much. He hopes to get something out of the experience but has no idea what to expect. Bill wants to replace what he has lost in his career as quickly as possible. Because he enjoys sales, he would like to find a similar position, but is willing to make some adjustments.

## *Response to Bill: The Case of the Downsized Father*
### *Martha Russell*
### *Russell Career Services*

### Introduction

Bill, as a 39-year-old professional, is facing a problem that continues to affect many employees, aged 35-55, as they deal with the reality of the newly defined world of work (Bridges, 1994). Senior-level executives, well-educated professionals have devoted years to working for a single company in whatever capacity the company determines. At the same time they deal with dual-career issues, commuter concerns, and the ever-challenging balance of family values, financial needs, and employer demands. Bill's progression from sales associate to his present position as regional director appeared to be a viable path of continued success. He held onto a belief that he would never be without a position in this company as long as he was a loyal and productive employee. Losing his job may have shattered that belief, bruised his self-esteem, disabled his ability to use good problem-solving skills, and promoted an inertia that comes from fear (Lopez, 1983. Bill is displaying many of the behaviors typical to the outplaced person, "feeling helpless with his current situation" and being caught in the behavior of needing support while not wanting anyone to know he is unemployed.

## Career Counseling Process

As Bill begins using outplacement services it is important that the first session be structured yet flexible with combined goals of information gathering as well as information giving. Clients often come into the session with four major issues: they are faced with emotions and situations unfamiliar and distasteful to them, they lack current job-seeking skills, they do not know how to access resources including their own networking systems, and they have often waited too long to seek services. The anxiety about finding a new job builds while clients focus on neglected home projects and isolate themselves from friends, family, and social activities. Therefore, it is important to address the anxiety by outlining the steps of the outplacement process and developing an agreed-upon schedule of activity.

Often the first step is to diffuse the feelings of frustration and anger. Self-assessment, establishing a job search plan, and developing or refining job-seeking skills are the steps that follow. In this process a career management plan is also a desired outcome and can be interwoven in all the steps. Although much of traditional outplacement tends to focus primarily on the job search process, using an integrative career counseling process increases the effectiveness of the time and energy spent in moving toward new employment. It does this by addressing the whole person and integrating career and life planning issues (Hansen, 1997).

Integrative career/life planning includes reviewing Bill's past, identifying values and goals for the future, and understanding what is presently occurring in his situation. An initial step is to acknowledge Bill's anger while at the same time honoring his need to move on quickly. There is often a delicate blend between allowing the client to vent and helping the client deal with the realities of the situation while looking positively toward the future. Developing a system for dealing with emotions is important so that Bill can focus all of his energy on the tasks at hand.

## Confidentiality

A statement about the issues of confidentiality is appropriate here because it is often a prime fear of those in outplacement who assume that all conversation is getting back to the company paying the bill. It may be necessary to address this issue with all the players, making sure that all ethical and professional standards are agreed upon. Often a simple statement outlining confidentiality boundaries is enough to allow honest communication.

## Background Information

Background information provides the foundation for developing a plan only if the client values this part of the process. It may be helpful to put a time limit on this aspect of the session if the client appears excessively anxious about getting on with the job search. "Bill, let's spend the first 30 minutes reviewing your past and the choices that you made or that were made for you. This information can help us later as we begin to focus on the kinds of careers you are seeking or the kinds of employers that might appeal to you." A host of questions might be part of the dialogue: his selection of political science as a degree major, "falling into" a sales position, activities as a student, generational and family expectation issues that might surface, as well as his decision making during his history with the company. Have there been other times when he has had a setback in his career? How did he handle those times and what skills did he develop that could be useful now?

Identifying work motivation and work values will address many of the issues Bill presents. Those include striving for career success, concerns about appearances and social contacts, adjusting personal and family needs when they seem to conflict with stated values, and gender and social conditioning especially as they pertain to his view of age in the marketplace. If the process is valued and trust has been established, Bill can be honest about his values and express his likes and dislikes so that he can benefit from the information.

## Structure

Most outplacement clients need to see a career counseling structure that offers immediate results. What would he like to see by the end of this first session and what can he do in between sessions? It is important to eliminate any unspoken and therefore unmet expectations of the process. Two practical activities can take place during the initial work that can help Bill walk away with usable tools:

- One such activity is the development of statements about accomplishments. The counselor might take notes during the session that reflect skills and successes that are transferable into usable statements. This exercise can help individuals move to the point of reviewing experiences positively. It also provides a concrete example useful for resume development, networking, and rebuilding bruised self-esteem.
- Another exercise involves developing a short comfortable statement that can be used in talking with others about his current situation. Whether Bill uses the term "transition, reorganizing, redirecting, or job searching" is less important than his developing a comfort level in seeking and getting support from others.

## Assessments

This client may already have some knowledge of assessment instruments through team building activities, sales training or organizational development programs. Although this article does not address assessments, many are available and appropriate to the outplaced client. The importance may be in how much Bill can discover about his style in the areas of communication, problem solving, decision making, and prioritizing his values.

## Search Skills Training and Support

As with all outplaced clients, the development and use of effective job search skills and strategies are considered as desired outcomes. In addition to resumes and other job search tools, there are three major areas that are important given Bill's situation.

- Networking continues to be the key for developing job leads and marketplace information as well as helping rebuild confidence levels. Job search mentors are individuals who have already gone through the process and are willing to encourage and support the client. Having a successful model can be effective in reducing the time it takes to get a new position.
- Another area is identifying Bill's problem-solving skills so that they can be used effectively in this unfamiliar situation. How did Bill handle sales problems? How did he develop new markets? How did he approach the tasks of recruiting and selecting the best team for his region? If he finds it difficult to identify those skills, he might focus on the skills he would like to develop and how those can be developed through this process.

- A third area that is important in today's job search market is the ability to use the Internet for research. The Internet can help Bill identify geographic areas, occupational resources and company information as well as possible job listings and resume postings. If Bill has computer skills this avenue can increase his knowledge of the job market.

## Conclusion

Bill approaches the task of finding a new position as an unwelcome hurdle in his career plan. A well-thought out and integrative outplacement process can help Bill approach the hurdle with renewed energy and focus. The counselor can assist by –

- Honoring Bill's feelings
- Helping him regain structure
- Working with him to overcome obstacles and internal barriers
- Developing effective job search skills and
- Offering support and practical solutions throughout the process.

## References

Bridges, W. (1994). *Jobshift: How to prosper in a workplace without jobs*. Reading, MA: Addison-Wesley.

Campbell, S.M. (1995). *From chaos to confidence: Survival strategies for the new workplace.* New York: Simon & Schuster.

Hansen, L.S. (1997). *Integrative life planning: Critical tasks for career development and changing Life patterns*. San Francisco, CA: Jossey-Bass.

Lopez, F.G. (1983). The victims of corporate failures: Some preliminary observations. *Personnel and*
Guidance Journal, 61, 631-632

Schlossberg, N.K., & Leibowitz, Z. (1980). Organizational support systems as buffers to job loss. *Journal of Vocational Behavior*, 18, 204-217.

## *Response to Bill: The Case of the Downsized Father*
### *David Patterson*
### *Simon Fraser University*

Bill is described as a hard-working, loyal, stable, family-oriented person. He indicates feelings of betrayal, helplessness, embarrassment, and concern about his current circumstance. The following counseling plan is designed to assist Bill in forming an accurate and positive view of himself in preparation for his job search. By exploring his strengths, values, attitudes, patterns of living, and beliefs, Bill will deepen his self-understanding and develop action plans. Additional work on normalizing Bill's experience of unemployment may also be of value.

I suspect Bill will enter counseling with a strong need and desire to take action and make concrete plans. It may be important to begin by establishing with him the link between his plans for action and exploratory counseling work. For example, a relationship between counselor and client can be discussed as a first phase "building block" in developing an appropriate level of trust and working alliance. One way for this to happen will be through a focus on Bill's strengths using a series of self-exploration counseling activities. We may also discuss the interrelationship of career and personal planning.

Early in counseling, I might suggest that Bill draw a career timeline of different jobs, roles, and positions he has taken over the years. He would then be asked to identify positive and negative experiences on the timeline. This would be a springboard for rich descriptive information of his strengths and challenges. Counseling skills at this point would include active listening and empathic reflection. In addition to the career timeline, Bill may be coached through the Pattern Identification Exercise (PIE; Amundson, 1998). This exercise involves directed exploration of a single activity that Bill enjoys. Often, the list of strengths, interests, and values that spring from a detailed analysis of one enjoyable activity can have broad application to other areas of a client's life. At its best, the PIE will result in self-discovery and an articulation of client values and strengths.

The Missouri Occupational Card Sort (MOCC; Tyler, 1961) would be another way to clarify both Bill's understanding of occupations and his reasons for interest or disinterest. Because he will be sorting cards listing occupations that may be well outside the realm of possibility, there is an opportunity for novel ideas and "outside of the box" discussion. For example, the idea of becoming a florist may have never occurred to Bill. His reasons for selecting or discarding this occupation may open an area for discussion that would otherwise remain hidden.

Depending on Bill's insight into his situation and expressed need for information, it may be helpful to explore information about occupational trends and unemployment. By discussing the "Roller Coaster of Unemployment" and the "Dynamics of Unemployment" (Borgen & Amundson, 1987), there would be an opportunity for Bill to normalize his experience and situate it within the context of a process. If, for example, he is feeling discouraged, the roller coaster metaphor may validate both a sense of helplessness along with the inevitable ups and downs. This kind of discussion is designed to help Bill integrate his experience with the wider world of people facing similar circumstances. It will be very important to maintain Bill's position as the "expert" on his life, with respect to past experiences, dreams, goals, and aspirations. Information on the experiences of others is only useful with respect to how it is similar/dissimilar to what is going on for Bill.

Clearly, some of Bill's exploratory work could also be conducted in a group setting. There are a number of "Who Am I?" exploratory activities that can be adapted to a group counseling approach with Bill. It is stated that Bill does not feel comfortable around the "employed" right now. A group of clients in similar circumstances would provide him with the opportunity to publicly express these feelings in a context where they may be validated and understood. In addition to validating his experience, a group experience may afford Bill with the opportunity to explore new behaviors in a process such as the 12-step behavioral rehearsal sequence described by Westwood, Amundson, Borgen, Bailey, and Davies (1994). This experience/reflection design will provide Bill with the opportunity to try out new behavior patterns in a safe place before attempting them at a potential workplace.

The role of significant others is clearly important to Bill. The employment status of his spouse, his standing in the community, and the importance he places on the family are all very important components of his counseling treatment plan. It is clearly critical to explore Bill's social support and may be advisable to create a space for formal participation in the counseling sessions for family members. This will be particularly important if Bill begins to feel discouraged or becomes cut off and isolated from his family.

Bill's individual counseling is based on a three-phase model described by Egan (1986) and others. The counseling proves builds from an exploration phase to an understanding phase to an action phase. Client insight and action plans are directly connected to exploratory work in the early phase. Bill may be worried about the impact of the employment termination on his family, and he may feel that he has been betrayed or that his loyalty as an employee has been misplaced. In addressing these specific feelings or beliefs, it is necessary to have a broader picture of Bill upon which to draw the contrast. For example, Bill may have established a pattern of behavior (trusting and hard working), and may now be feeling and acting quite differently (insecure, helpless, and embarrassed). In addition to exploring this shift, tools such as the Individual Style Survey (ISS, Amundson, 1989) may assist Bill in integrating changes in personality styles before and after his job loss. The ISS instrument is transparent in the way that it is scored and provides the opportunity for family and friends to participate in the survey. As such, it is a rich source of material upon which to begin a dialogue.

Contextual factors may also play a role in the approach that is taken to counseling. For example, Bill had been willing and able to maintain his family and employment in different geographical locations. His termination may provide the opportunity to reexamine this arrangement. Is it feasible for Bill to work in a home-based or community-base business? What would be the advantages/disadvantages of this arrangement? This is not a "silver lining" approach to employment counseling where every setback is reframed as an advantage. Instead, from the context of knowing Bill well, the counselor would be able to challenge him to develop a plan that represents a fit for his changing circumstances. Bill may have more time to spend on the job and fewer expenses at a home- or community-based business than was his norm. All options would need to be evaluated carefully for possible advantages that may not be obvious in the absence of a clear perspective and the opportunity for reflection.

The final phase of counseling would be to assist Bill with setting concrete goals and establishing an action plan. Here Bill would be encouraged to explore labor market information, develop a wide network of contacts, and approach the prospect of a formal job search with insight and self-confidence. Goals would be matched to concrete action. There would a focus on the present with specific and achievable steps. These action plans would build upon Bill's strengths and life planning. It is important for the counselor to pay attention to the areas that are within Bill's personal control and to relate current challenges to past success. Specific skills that are needed to proceed with his job search can best be learned when they have relevance and direct applicability to the challenges at hand. It would be a mistake, for example, to provide Bill with a course on using the Internet without first establishing with him why such a course may be of value.

In summary, this counseling approach with Bill would not focus on "solving" the problem of unexpected job termination. Instead, it would be a client-centered model of responding to changing circumstances from the context of a highly personal frame of reference. Bill will be encouraged to self-reflect and take action based upon this experience. It is difficult to say exactly what activities or interventions would be used, as the selection of these would be a collaborative component of the counseling process. Suffice it to say the course of counseling would likely follow the general pattern (exploration, understanding, action), and all three components would be a part of every counseling session.

## References

Amundson, N.E. (1989). *Individual Style Survey*. Edmonton, Alberta: Psychometrics Canada.

Amundson, N.E. (1998). *Active engagement: Enhancing the career counseling process*. Richmond, BC: Ergon Communications.

Borgen, W.A. & Amundson, N.E. (1987). The dynamics of unemployment. *Journal of Counseling and development, 66*, 180-184.

Egan, G. (1986). *The skilled helper: Models, skills, and methods for effective helping* (3rd ed.). Pacific Grove, CA: Brooks/Cole.

Tyler, L. (1961). Research explorations in the realm of choice. *Journal of Counseling Psychology, 8*, 195-201.

Westwood, M., Amundson, N.E., Borgen, W.A., Baily, B., & Davies, B. (1994). *Starting points: Finding your route to employment*. Ottawa: Human Resources Development Canada.

# ROSE ANN: THE CASE OF THE FRUSTRATED HOMEMAKER

Rose Ann is a 39-year-old, slender Caucasian female who presents herself professionally and is very well groomed. She has two other siblings and she is the second oldest. She attended a suburban community college for two years; however, she did not earn a degree. She is currently working her first full-time job in 15 years and is employed as an administrative assistant.

Rose Ann recently left her husband of 15 years, who would not allow her to work outside of the home or pursue further education; he feels that he should be her job. She was referred to career counseling by her personal therapist and is hoping to decide on a field to pursue in college. She is concerned with how she will pay for college and work at the same time.

Rose Ann is seeking a divorce from her husband. She stated he does not want a divorce and he is encouraging her to enter counseling with him. She indicated she is "tired of being poor" and stated that, if she went back to him, he would pay for her education. She is struggling with the decision surrounding the divorce. She has a sister who is very supportive and encouraging of her.

Rose Ann feels her abilities surpass simply keeping house and taking care of her husband. She would like to grow as a person and feels this would be best accomplished by obtaining higher education. She is obviously struggling with her possible divorce and adjusting to the change in lifestyles. As she has not been in the work force for several years, she is not very knowledgeable of the world of work.

Rose Ann often begins the sessions in a very bright mood, excited to explore the world of work and herself further. Typically, by the end of the session, she has turned the focus toward her husband and the possible divorce and she becomes somber and often will cry. She has expressed a great interest in the creative fields and stated she has often edited videotapes for herself and her family. She is investigating educational programs related to this field.

Rose Ann has spent the majority of her life not in the work force; however she is finding great joy and satisfaction in her current administrative position. She feels supporting herself is rewarding and is battling the negative messages she has been receiving from her husband about the meaninglessness of the position she holds. In her hobbies, she tends to take part in creative activities as well as physically active activities.

## Response to Rose Ann: The Case of the Frustrated Homemaker
### A Cultural Ecological Constructivist Approach
### Beverly J. Vandiver
### The Pennsylvania State University

Suspending myself from the objective mindset counselors are trained to assume, my first thoughts about Rose Ann were stereotypical: a dowdy and stout (despite the use of the adjective "slender") white woman who had become dependent on her husband. Although the description I paint is unflattering of Rose Ann and me, my theoretical view of human nature, assessment, and counseling directs me to start with the stereotypical view constructed by society. I embrace a cultural ecological constructivist approach (CECA) to human nature, which is synergistically used in the psychocsocial assessment and treatment of individuals experiencing any number of developmental/phase-of-life problems.

My cultural ecological constructivist view is that we human beings make meaning out of our existence from our cultural and contextual experiences. Whether at a conscious or unconscious level, individuals construct and organize meaning out of life experiences. Although many constructivist models (Gergen, 1985, 1991; Guidano, 1991; Kelly, 1995; Mahoney, 1991; Maturana, 1988; Watzlawick, 1984, 1990) exist, the underlying epistemological belief they share is that "a totally objective reality…can never be fully known" (Rosen, 1996). Constructivists reject the notion that ultimate truth can ever be fully known; rather they hold that knowledge and the meaning attached to it are constructions of the human mind. We as individuals have our personal truths, which cannot be evaluated by objective reality standards (Rosen, 1996). Based on a modified version of Bronfenbrenner's (1979, 1988) developmental/ecological model of human development, I also believe that people grow and develop within the reciprocal interaction of three major cultural contexts or systems: macrosystem, mesosystem, and microsystem. The macrosystem depicts the major cultural, societal, and national beliefs, values, and norms in which the universe and systems are viewed. The mesosystem represents the smaller components of the macrosystem and includes the local communities and institutions within those communities such as schools, hospitals, churches, and the workplace. The microsystem characterizes the individual and his/her relationship to a smaller intimate set of society such as families and friends. Like Bronfenbrenner's, my perspective is sociological, situational or contextual, and it incorporates the individual's psychological and developmental states. The general underpinning of the sociological perspective is that "the social structure represents the context in which each person negotiates her identity, belief systems, and life course" (Herr & Cramer, 1988). It is the situational circumstances in which people develop as human beings. Beyond Bronfenbrenner's model, I also delineate the cultural components of the context from the constructivist lens. To appreciate fully or understand the self, the ecological system must be viewed from the individual's cultural framework.

Across the life span, we experience multiple contexts, sometimes simultaneously, at other times separately. Each context includes the cultural aspects of our society. Within and across cultures (because multiple cultures can be contained within a larger one), sociopolitical aspects define and shape the culture as well. The term sociopolitical is used to emphasize the influence of institutional policies, public or private, that shape the social and cultural structures of society or subgroups of society. For instance, the policies and politics of the United States have shaped society's view and treatment of women, influencing the kind of job held, the amount of money made, and the family and work status held. Because of the changing characteristics of a society's population, societal norms, policies, and politics shift. A reciprocal interaction exits between the social, cultural and political aspects of a society, resulting in an ever-changing and dynamic process. These changes have varying influences on the people of the society depending on their status. Their status is based on numerous aspects, of which many are society's constructions, such as racial/ethnic identification, socioeconomic level, gender, sexual orientation, disability level, and religion, and the degree to which these social constructions have been internalized.

We are all cultural beings, each possessing at the essence of our self-concept a cultural identity. What we do, think, feel, and behave reflect our cultural identity. Our cultural identity starts taking shape at the time of our birth and evolves over our life-span, constructing, deconstructing, and reconstructing, because of our unique biological and psychological characteristics and the sociopolitical and sociocultural context experienced and interpreted during our lifetime. Our cultural identity represents the internalization of those sociopolitical and sociocultural aspects that we have deemed salient and critical in making sense of who we are in the context of what is experienced. For instance, gender becomes salient when told repeatedly by others that this is "women's work." Whether any experience becomes salient is based on the individual's personal construction (interpretation) of it – the significance in relation to other events, the frequency of occurrence, and the context.

Keeping my approach in mind, in working with Rose Ann, as with any client, I would start with myself. To ensure career counseling is culturally relevant and appropriate, Bingham and Ward (1996) have recommended that, as part of the counselor's preparatory work for a client, counselors assess themselves. I examine the sociopolitical reality I have experienced over my lifetime and the cultural identity I have at the time of contact with my clients. I encourage myself to consider in as many ways possible, how I might view the client, starting with the culturally stereotyped, prejudiced views espoused by society. As inaccurate and negative stereotypes are, knowledge of their presence highlights the possible barriers I potentially would erect about a client during the counseling process.

Women who have lived the early part of their adulthood as "traditional housewives" have not been viewed well since the modern era of the Women's Movement. Sensitized to the discrimination women have experienced in society, counselors unknowingly can err on the side of liberalism by encouraging traditional women to take paths they have not internally embraced. This is my concern for Rose Ann.

Rose Ann appears to be in search of an identity, not just a personal or a career one, but a whole Rose Ann identity. I am concerned that Rose Ann was referred for career counseling. I do not view counseling as a dichotomized process. For me counseling is inclusive of both. I am not sure I would accept Rose Ann's case under the circumstances presented. If she had been my client to begin with, I would not have needed to refer her. Based on my construction of counseling, I will address the questions with a minor change: Rose Ann is solely my client. I am working with her to construct an identity she is comfortable with and can live with, recognizing that the process is not static, but dynamic. What she likes about herself will be constantly evolving into a more integrated picture. At the onset of the counseling, I would share with Rose Ann that we will weave back and forth from what are labeled as the personal and the career, but I believe are the same concerns – her view of self and the operationalization of that identity.

Although Rose Ann left her husband of 15 years and is seeking a divorce, she continues to have ambivalent feelings about him. It is not clear whether she wants the divorce or wants him to make substantial changes. It is clear she wants to make significant changes in her life. Her economic status seems salient for Rose Ann, evidenced by her report that she is "tired of being poor," and her husband's use of money as an enticement for her to return "home." Work, achievement, and education are also salient to her identity, but their manifestations have not been fully actualized.

In my initial assessment, I would want to know about the people in her microsystem. Interweaving the cultural aspects with the contextual frame, I would collect information from Rose Ann about her family background. I would ask her to narrate her growing up for me. Who are her parents? What were and are their roles as parents, partners, and workers? I want to know about her two siblings and the nature of their lives and Rose Ann's relationship with them. It is noted that a sister is supportive and encouraging, but no further sibling information is provided. In addition, it is not known whether she has children, and if so, the number, ages, and the nature of their relationship to Rose Ann and their father. It would also be important to know who her friends are and the quality of the friendships. What role have the people in her microsystem served? Have they been and are they supportive of her current identity journey? Who is encouraging besides her sister? Who is discouraging and how does it manifest itself through Rose Ann's attitudes, feelings, and behaviors? I also want to explore her creative side and its expression through videotaping and other ways in the microsystem. What has she constructed about the world of work, education, achievement from her family and friends? In addition, I would want her to narrate her beliefs about Caucasian women's role when growing up, when married, and now when separated. What cultural characteristics, such as race, gender, age, and social status are salient to her? These are some examples of the questions and themes I would want to explore with Rose Ann at the microsystem level.

At the mesosystem level, I would encourage Rose Ann to talk about her current employment as an administrative assistant, likes and dislikes, relationship with colleagues, and the cultural environment of work. Rose Ann's could also be influenced by other mesosystems such as church and other social organizations. Besides her current employment, other settings, knowingly or unknowingly, may be important to her identity. School is, and knowing more about her two-year college stint, the reason for not pursuing more education at the time, and the kind of college experience she is currently seeking is important to the construction of her identity outside of the familial and friendship network. Past mesosystem information such as school, social and extracurricular activities are important and would be explored. Understanding her mesosystem experiences would require its grounding in their cultural characteristics such as the geographical location by region (e.g., North, East), setting (e.g., rural, urban, suburban) of employment, school and other organizations, and the cultural compositions of these environments.

Understanding the influence of the macrosystem can be gleaned through her narration of growing up to the present and exploring what place in society women like her have or are expected to hold. Are these expectations or societal views ones she holds or are they different? If so, how?

Incorporated in the assessment and counseling process would be aspects of the Career-Development Assessment and Counseling (C-DAC) model (Super, 1983), because of its recent revisions to appraise cultural identity (Hartung et al., 1998). Although Rose Ann implicitly has some knowledge and ideas about the world of work as well as her interests, aptitudes, and abilities, she does not consciously view herself as knowledgeable enough. To moderate some of her anxiety and frustration and increase her motivation, the core C-DAC battery (see Super, Osborne, Walsh, Brown, & Niles, 1992; e.g., the Adult Career Concerns Inventory, Super, Thompson, Lindeman, Jordaan, & Myers, 1988; the Strong Interest Inventory, Harmon, Hansen, Borgen, & Hammer, 1994) would be used. The information gleaned would be provided in a narrative and constructivist style by encouraging Rose Ann to consider what she might like to do and then to explore the congruence of the assessment results. Incongruencies would be addressed by exploring how she approached the measures and her construction of what is important.

Two major issues in her life are the relationship with her husband and her financial status. Because a systemic approach undergirds the CECA, the opportunity is available for her husband to be invited into the counseling process if and when Rose Ann and I deem it appropriate and feasible. Equally important, Rose Ann is welcome to invite anyone to counseling she wants to be involved, whether as support or as a forum to address them. In counseling, I would explore with Rose Ann her current financial situation, provide information when she wants it, and support in dealing with the anxiety and distress of managing her finances.

In summary, my counseling approach parallels my theoretical views. I would encourage Rose Ann to tell her story, collaborating with her in knowing the meanings conveyed or the meanings she holds about her life. As she tells her story, I will encourage her to fill me in by providing an historical and current perspective so I can keep pace with her, although it will be seen through the cultural lens and background of an educated African American, single, female, from a southern working-class family raised during the 1960s and 1970s, who is of a similar age and societal generation. My role is to collaborate with her in examining (deconstruction) and reframing (reconstruction) her past and present identity into a more comfortable identity. In addition, I become another support system for her as she struggles to define her existence and to empower her to strengthen the support systems, (e.g., her sister) already in her life, and to create new support systems (e.g., friends, work colleagues). I also would encourage her to continue to be involved in the creative and physical activities she enjoys. These activities provide an outlet for her distress, and also free her to express an identity she enjoys that has been constructed by herself. Her involvement in these activities and the emergence of her identity through them would be used to parallel the possible reconstructions she can make in other aspects of her personal and professional life. By grounding the counseling assessment and process in the cultural ecological constructivist approach described, Rose Ann can construct and own her identity and be more comfortable living and interacting in the diverse cultural/ecological realms we all experience.

## References

Bingham, R.P. & Ward, C.M (1996). Practical applications of career counseling with ethnic minority women. In M.L. Savickas & W.B. Walsh (Eds.), *Handbook of career counseling theory and practice* (pp. 291-314). Palo Alto, CA: Davies-Black.

Bronfenbrenner, U. (1979). *The ecology of human development: Experiments by nature and design.* Cambridge, MA: Harvard University Press.

Bronfenbrenner, U. (1988). Interacting systems in human development. In N. Bolger, A. Caspi, G. Downey, & M. Moorehouse (Eds.), *Persons in context: Developmental processes* (pp. 25-49). New York: Cambridge University Press.

Gergen K.J. (1985). The social constructionist movement in modern psychology. *American Psychologist, 40*, 266-275.

Gergen, K.J. (1991). *The saturated self: Dilemmas of identity in contemporary life*. New York: Basic Books.

Guidano, V.F. (1991). *The self in process: Toward a post-rationalist cognitive therapy*. New York: Guilford Press.

Harmon, L.W., Hansen, J.C., Borgen, F.H., & Hammer, A.L. (1995). *Strong Interest Inventory: Applications and technical guide*. Stanford, CA: Stanford University Press.

Hartung, P., Vandiver, B.J., Leong, F.T.L., Pope, M., Niles, S.G., & Farrow, B. (1998). Appraising cultural identity in career development assessment and counseling. *Career Development Quarterly, 46*, 276-293.

Herr, E.L. & Cramer, S.H. (1988). *Career guidance and counseling through the life span: Systematic approaches* (3rd ed.). Glenview, IL: Scott Foresman.

Kelly, G.A. (1955). *The psychology of personal constructs* (2 vols.). New York: Norton.

Mahoney, M.J. (1991). *Human change processes: The scientific foundations of psychotherapy*. New York: Basic Books.

Maturana, H.R. (1988). Reality: The search for objectivity or the quest for a compelling argument. *Irish Journal of Psychology, 9*, 25-82.

Rosen, H. (1996). Meaning-making narratives: Foundations for constructivist and social constructionist psychotherapies. In H. Rosen & K.T. Kuehlwein (Eds.), *Constructing realities: Meaning-making perspectives for psychotherapists* (pp. 3-51). San Francisco, CA: Jossey-Bass.

Super D.E. (1983). Assessment in career guidance: Toward truly developmental counseling. *Personal and Guidance Journal, 61*, 555-562.

Super, D.E., Osborne, L., Walsh, D., Brown, S., & Niles, S.G. (1992). Developmental career assessment and counseling: The C-DAC Model. *Journal of Counseling and Development, 71*, 74-80.

Super, D.E., Thompson, A.S., Lindeman, R.H., Jordaan, J.P., & Myers, R.A. (1988). *Adult Career Concerns Inventory*. Palo Alto, CA: Consulting Psychologists Press.

Watzlawick, P. (Ed.). (1984). *The invented reality: How do we know what we believe we know? Contributions to constructivism*. New York: Norton.

Watzlawick, P. (1990). *Münchhausen's pigtail or psychotherapy and "reality."* New York: Norton.

# *Response to Rose Ann: The Case of the Frustrated Homemaker*
## *Jan Deeds*
## *University of Nebraska - Lincoln*

As Rose Ann told me her story in our first session I felt as though I was listening to two different women. The first woman reported what she perceived as her shortcomings: her lack of experience, her doubts about her ability to succeed, her fear of being poor, her indecision related to the divorce, her difficult struggle to defend the current job her husband describes as meaningless. The second woman is excited about her recent experiences in the world of work. This woman is looking toward a future full of new ideas and activities. She sees herself as creative, active, and capable of changing her life.

As a feminist therapist who has worked with many Rose Anns, I interpreted this dichotomy as a reflection of the way many women have dealt with the conflicts between societal expectations and their personal aspirations. Despite women's increasing representation in nontraditional occupations and the changes many employers are making to be more "family friendly," there are still many messages women receive about the roles they are expected to fill and what will happen to them if they don't comply.

Born in 1960, Rose Ann was a teenager when the feminist movement of the 1970s in the United States was gaining strength. Upon graduation from high school in 1978 she entered a community college, leaving after two years without completing a degree, and in 1983 she married. There is a lot of important information missing from this time period that I believe is relevant to Rose Ann's current career quest: (1) What were her original career goals upon entering the community college? What did she study? What did she enjoy? Encouraging Rose Ann to remember this period of her life may allow her to reconnect with the aspirations that were purely hers, without the negative messages she's collected for the past 15 years. (2) There is a three-year gap between leaving college and getting married. What did Rose Ann do during this period? Did she have a job? Was she living with her parents? Why did she leave college? I would ask Rose Ann to clarify these experiences and examine the expectations she felt from family and friends, and to look at which of her own dreams she chose to let go at each step. (3) Rose Ann's description of her marriage has many of the symptoms of an emotionally abusive relationship. As a counselor my warning flags went up when I heard about a husband who "won't allow" his wife to work, who says he should be her job, and who belittles the job in which she finds great joy and satisfaction.

Women in relationships like this often become isolated from everyone except their spouse, upon whom they become dependent for everything. The abusive partner reinforces the idea that the woman is helpless or incompetent and therefore can never leave the partner no matter how unsatisfying or even humiliating the relationship becomes. This is the voice of the first Rose Ann, the one who doubts her abilities and fears an uncertain future.

I have heard career counselors express discomfort with addressing relationship issues or other aspects of a client's life, preferring instead to focus on a narrower view of "career." As Rose Ann's career counselor, I would be irresponsible if I ignored the symptoms of a serious power imbalance in the marriage that has shaped her self-image through most of her adult life. "Career professionals and counselors, within the limits of their training and competencies, have a responsibility to help women understand how violence may have affected their career development and to assist them in moving beyond it" (Hansen, 1997).

Rose Ann's husband may not have been physically violent toward her, but belittling her new job and controlling whether or not she works outside the home could be considered forms of emotional and psychological abuse. The "Power and Control Wheel" developed by the Domestic Abuse Intervention Project of Duluth Minnesota (Pence & Paymar, 1993) provides an overview of the continuum of control and violence in relationships. It is my responsibility as a counselor who works with women to have this basic knowledge, because of the pervasiveness of abuse experienced by women.

Having emphasized my concerns about the relationship factors leading up to Rose Ann's current situation, it is important to note that the central task in my sessions with her is to understand her perceptions of the experience. I would explore my interpretation of Rose Ann's situation by asking some of these questions:

1. Who are her friends? Does she have friends outside of her husband's work connections? Do her friends have similar work histories? Are they supportive of her life changes? Helping Rose Ann find a supportive network of women is essential to her success. Spending time with other women who are reentering the work force will help her know she is not the only woman in this situation. Meeting women who are further along in their career journeys will provide Rose Ann with valuable mentors who can warn her about obstacles they've encountered and model that success is possible.

2. What was her mother's work experience? Are her parents still alive? How are they responding to Rose Ann's life change? What is the work history of her sister, who is being supportive and helpful in this situation? The messages Rose Ann receives from her family can help or hinder in the pursuit of her career goals. Understanding the models she observed as a child and throughout her adult life can enhance Rose Ann's awareness of her own approach to the world of work.

3. How did Rose Ann fill her days for the last 15 years? Was she involved in any volunteer activities for her community, religious organization or groups in which her husband was a member? Exploring the skills she developed and used for these activities can boost her confidence and assist her in identifying the next phase of her career path. Adults returning to the work force may downplay the skills and abilities they have developed in unpaid work experiences, and career counselors can encourage people in Rose Ann's situation to identify those tasks as work related.

4. How does Rose Ann perceive her husband's influence on her self-image as it relates to her career goals? I would share the power and control wheel information with Rose Ann to determine if she sees a connection between the messages he has given her over the years and her current self-doubts. What other sources of information can Rose Ann find to provide a more positive view of her skills, abilities, and worth as an individual?

As a feminist therapist I have three major tasks in my work with clients: (1) to identify the social constructs that have influenced her/his situation, (2) to develop together an egalitarian relationship to find solutions that will work within the client's life, and (3) to help the client find her/his own strength to implement the solutions. I would suggest a plan for our counseling sessions that would respect Rose Ann's fears and anxieties about this life change while allowing her to move forward. I would ask her to decide how she wanted to use our sessions for the greatest benefit. As we talk, if she begins to cry and focus on the divorce and her fears, I would ask her to decide how much time she wanted to spend on that focus before returning to her career questions. Acknowledging that life changes of this magnitude are scary affirms that what she is feeling is normal and reassures her that she is in control of her life. She can choose what to focus on in these sessions and work with her personal therapist on these issues. I would encourage Rose Ann to use a career assessment instrument to expand her self-knowledge and open the door to additional career options. I use Holland's Self-Directed Search (SDS) because using the Occupations Finder and the Majors Finder together is an excellent tool for returning students.

I would suggest a visit to the college she is considering and work with her to arrange to meet students and faculty in the areas relevant to her interests. Many schools have a women's center and support programs for nontraditional students, and I would encourage Rose Ann to contact those groups so that she would have her support network in place when she starts taking classes. Volunteering in a women's center or for an organization with a mission that is relevant to her career goals could provide useful experience and contacts with people who can be supportive of her plans. A visit to the financial aid office on campus would give Rose Ann important information about scholarships and other resources to help her achieve her goals.

My task as a feminist career counselor is to empower a client like Rose Ann to learn more about her skills and abilities, to find opportunities to explore the career areas in which she has an interest, and to identify a strong support network to help her work toward her goals. Throughout our sessions I consistently return the power of decision making to the client, who may not be used to being in control of her life. As she takes these initial steps she will find that she is stronger than she thought, and a series of small successes will bolster her for the larger choices she will need to make later.

## References

Hansen, L.S. (1997). *Integrative life planning: Critical tasks for career development and changing life patterns.* San Francisco, CA: Jossey-Bass.

Pence, E., and Paymar, M. (1993). *Education groups for men who batter: The Duluth model.* New York: Springer Publishing.

# TOMOKAZU: THE CASE OF THE RECOVERING CPA

Tomokazu is a 39-year-old Japanese American man who currently works as an accountant. He and his family live in a large city in the southern U.S. He is the oldest of four sons. He has come to career counseling because he is frustrated with his job.

Tomokazu lives in the same town as his family-of-origin. His father is an accomplished businessman who has acquired significant wealth. His father earned a law degree after college and has worked with the government on several important projects. His mother is a homemaker and very protective of Tomokazu. His grandfather who emigrated from Japan was a successful surgeon who helped establish the local university medical school that now bears his name. Tomokazu's entire family was removed to an internment camp in Utah during the Second World War, but returned to their home after being released after the war.

Throughout his undergraduate work in college, Tomokazu was in a fraternity and reports that he really enjoyed the "night life." Tomokazu also reports that he thought very little about a career after college and tended to enroll only in those courses for which he thought his chances of success were high. Tomokazu had several relationships in college and dated his current wife during his last two years of college. At this same time, Tomokazu started attending Alcoholics Anonymous with his future wife. He recognized he had a problem after several incidents with friends and a brush with death in a car accident.

After college, Tomokazu attended a one-year program to earn his CPA. He then started working at an accounting firm and was married shortly after that. After one year, he accepted an impressive job offer from a prestigious accounting firm located in the town where his family-of-origin lived. Although the move has been financially rewarding, it also has created several problems.

Tomokazu and his wife had their first child soon after the move. He has recently found out his wife is pregnant again. Although Tomokazu enjoys his child, he reports that being a father is stressful and that currently he is unhappy with his "home situation." He reports that his wife is also unhappy. She has few friends and also feels the stress of a new baby. Although she is a full-time homemaker, she wants to start working outside the home. She also misses her family, who live in a nearby state and often threatens to move back to them.

Tomokazu enjoys the challenge of his new job but does not find much in common with his colleagues. He had numerous friends at his previous job, but states that this is not the case in his current position where most of the accountants are much older than Tomokazu. Currently, he finds himself becoming overwhelmingly frustrated with small things at work. He has started to attend some AA meetings again, but his wife wants him to spend that time at home helping with their child. Recently, Tomokazu was diagnosed as having bipolar disorder. He refuses to take his medication and disputes the diagnosis.

Tomokazu has come to career counseling at the prompting of his wife. He wonders if he has made the right career choice.

## Response to Tomokazu: The Case of the Recovering CPA
### Chris Reid and Brian T. McMahon
### Medical College of Virginia
### Virginia Commonwealth University

In determining the appropriate evaluation and intervention with Tomokazu, the conceptual framework provided by Person-Environment Correspondence theory (PEC; Dawis & Lofquist, 1984; Loquist & Dawis, 1969, 1991) is very helpful. According to PEC theory, also known as the Minnesota Theory of Work Adjustment, there are two conditions necessary for Tomokazu to experience successful employment on an ongoing basis: job satisfaction and the satisfactoriness of his job performance. Tomokazu's job satisfaction depends upon his relevant interests and needs being met by the occupational reinforcers available in his job. The satisfactoriness of his performance depends upon his ability to successfully meet job requirements. These four components – job requirements, his ability to meet these requirements, his needs, and the job's ability to reinforce these needs – may all change over time. Thus ongoing adjustments are necessary to ensure Tomokazu's job satisfaction and the satisfactoriness of his performance. In simple terms, some realignment of these components appears to be in order. In reality, it is unlikely that the situation is this simple. It is unlikely that the problems are exclusively vocational in character.

Within this case study, Tomokazu's presenting problem was a concern about whether he made the right career choice. This suggests that his level of job satisfaction is inadequate. To address this, we will evaluate the degree to which his interests and needs are being met by what his current job has to offer. To better understand his vocational interests, we turn to the work of Holland (1959, 1992) to examine the fit between his work personality type and the nature of his work environment. We may also apply the constructs and instruments of Super (1957, 1980) such as vocational maturity and job involvement. These will help us frame Tomokazu's interests and needs into a greater life-role perspective, examining the relative importance of various roles (worker, spouse, parent, and the like). All of those roles, as well as the influence of family and culture, need to be considered in developing a holistic view of Tomokazu and his career choices.

Given the information presented in the case study, our first impression is that Tomokazu is a man who is unsure whether he has chosen the right career. Beyond this "presenting problem," he may be struggling with identifying who he is and what he wants from life in general. As a young man he may have experienced considerable pressure to achieve, both academically and in subsequent career activity. We suspect this may reflect the influences of his father and grandfather, and perhaps others. This speculation can be dangerous and may be due to our own stereotypical ideas about Asian Americans. Still, both father and grandfather were very high achievers in occupations involving a higher than average degree of occupational inheritance (medicine and law/business). As long as we are speculating, the parents may have wanted Tomokazu to establish a compelling record of early achievement in order to set an example for his four younger siblings. There also exists evidence that Tomokazu was a *bon vivant*. This may be rooted in an early desire to assimilate to American culture. Perhaps he sought to repudiate his past and establish a more "American" identity as a young man.

These impressions are nothing more that hypotheses, and speculative at best. Nonetheless, we would seek more information about Tomokazu's own identity as a Japanese American. We want to understand *what this means to him* and explore in some detail his sense of belongingness, both in his family as well as in this southern community. We can assess his level of acculturation (Sue, Ivey, & Pedersen, 1996) and the degree to which he ascribes to "traditional" Asian values. These may include a high-status career choice, honor and respect (versus "loss of face"), hierarchical interpersonal relationships, collective versus individual orientation, and the preeminence of family above personal needs (Leong, 1993; Leung, 1993).

We want to learn more about Tomokazu's family system and its impact on his career development. What is his wife's level of acculturation? What is her perspective regarding Tomokazu's roles and priorities? What would happen if his wife worked outside the home? How does Tomokazu's extended family influence his vocational decisions? Did family members have a role in helping him obtain his current job? Might similar opportunities exist elsewhere away from his family, or is Tomokazu geographically restricted? How would Tomokazu's family members react if he moved so that his nuclear family could live more proximate to his wife's extended family?

Equally important to us is the matter of chemical dependency. How are alcoholism and Tomokazu's involvement in AA viewed by family members? Was his wife's past AA involvement in a support role, as per Alanon, or was she in need of AA support herself? How does this affect Tomokazu's sobriety? The history and current status of Tomokazu's own recovery would be keen areas of interest to us even as career counselors (as opposed to therapists). In particular, we want to know the basis for his decision to resume attending AA meetings. Was it for a sense of affiliation, for fear of "slipping," or because he is actively using or abusing alcohol once again? If he is actively abusing alcohol, what is his plan to address this problem? If he is not actively abusing, what is his plan for relapse prevention?

Alcohol abuse has the potential to interfere not only with Tomokazu's overall life satisfaction, but also with his ability to perform at work. Decreased satisfactoriness (diminished job performance) could result in progressive discipline or even termination. Other likely risks to satisfactoriness include those mental health problems that resulted in a diagnosis of bipolar disorder. We want to know how Tomokazu copes with stress and whether his coping strategies have caused problems for him at work or in other life areas. The availability of employee assistance services is worth considering.

As often occurs in counseling, the presenting problem ("Did I make the right career choice?") may be far from the central issue here. This is not a straightforward matter of work adjustment that can in turn resolve matters of chemical dependency or major mental illness. The option of career counseling for Tomokazu is probably a safe, more palatable, less threatening alternative than either marriage or psychiatric counseling, and as such it is an acceptable place to start. It would be professionally irresponsible at best, however to end there.

We would make no plans "for" this client's counseling, career or otherwise, but "with" him, based in part upon the nature of the information obtained as career-oriented evaluations ensue. Given what we do know of Tomokazu's case at this point, we would use an eclectic counseling approach that relies heavily upon the theoretical approaches of Reality Therapy (Glasser, 1984), Rational-Emotive Therapy (Ellis, 1994), and Existential Therapy (May & Yalom, 1995). The intent is to assist Tomokazu in identifying what he really wants from his life and career, and then to plan with him how to effectively attain these goals. We begin by establishing rapport and commending Tomokazu for seeking professional help (even if he required some prodding by his wife). We can work toward building trust so that Tomokazu might be able to openly discuss more aspects of his life than just job-related frustrations.

The next step would be to assist Tomokazu in clarifying for himself what he really wants from life. Tools to help him identify vocationally relevant needs could include the Minnesota Importance Questionnaire (measuring work values), Holland's Self-Directed Search, or other vocational interest tests. It could be, for example, that this man who once so enjoyed college "night life" is now experiencing incongruence between his vocational personality type and that of his work environment, where he is employed as a CPA. Part of clarifying what Tomokazu really wants requires examining the relative salience of different life roles and his perception of their current meaning in his life. Alcohol and psychiatric issues aside, this is still a near-40-year-old man in search of meaning (Frankl, 1963). Existential techniques may assist him in finding a pathway toward that meaning.

The process of clarifying what Tomokazu really wants from his career and other life roles is likely to lead to a discussion of problems in other life areas. As his values are identified, they can be compared to the values of significant others including his wife, parents, and grandfather. Such topics could provide an interesting and safe transition to more serious matters. Marriage, family, psychological, and career issues in this case are clearly interrelated. As career counselors, we could become the trusted professionals who cold help Tomokazu determine for himself that he may require marriage counseling and/or a psychological evaluation to provide a differential diagnosis of his bipolar (or substance abuse, or other) disorder.

After clarifying his career and other life goals, the next step is to examine with Tomokazu what he is currently doing to achieve what he wants and whether those approaches are working for him. It is critical that Tomokazu be the one to evaluate whether his current behaviors are effective; i.e., getting the results he seeks. It may be obvious to us that a particular approach is problematic, but until he determines this for himself, he is unlikely to change anything. In essence, his perceived gap between what he wants and the effectiveness of his approach is the source of motivation for change.

Next, we can assist Tomokazu is developing plans to reach his goals more effectively. These plans should be simple and specific. They should include something started (rather than stopped), something that can be repeated or continued, and something that is independently achievable (versus contingent upon the actions of others). These points are best illustrated in the reverse. A regrettable plan might be to become a millionaire through an elaborate (not simple) scheme. The plan involves purchasing a soybean farm. Then, to stimulate the price of soybeans, a group of people will somehow (not specific) be recruited to participate in a program to prevent (stopping) anyone from drinking milk (contingent upon the actions of others) on the eve of the millennium (not repeatable).

Once Tomokazu develops a plan to meet one of his goals, we can assess his commitment to carrying out the plan. The key question here is, "Will you *really* do it?" If the answer is "probably not," we return to goal clarification and plan development. If the answer is "I don't know," we seek additional information necessary to make a decision. For example, Tomokazu may require verification that he has the knowledge, skills, or abilities required for a given job. Thus we can provide more occupational information or more definitive documentation of his abilities. If Tomokazu's answer to the question "Will you *really* do it?" is "Yes," we may then ask, "What might get in your way?" Our intention would be to help Tomokazu anticipate barriers and develop methods to prevent sabotage of his plans. If these barriers involve irrational beliefs, Rational-Emotive Therapy techniques may be used to dispute them. These techniques must be accompanied by sensitivity to Tomokazu's level of acculturation versus the internalization of traditional Asian values.

As with most career counseling clients, Tomokazu provides us with a complex set of interrelated challenges. In our opinion, an effective approach must begin with the counselor's clear identification of Tomokazu's identity regarding work and other life roles. By serving as a trusted guide while Tomokazu evaluates what he wants from life, develops effective plans to better reach his goals, and implements those plans, the career counselor can have a major impact not only on Tomokazu, but on his coworkers, employer, family members, and others in his community.

## References

Dawis, R.V. & Lofquist, L.H. (1984). *A psychological theory of work adjustment: An individual-differences model and its application*. Minneapolis, MN: University of Minnesota Press.

Ellis, A. (1994). *Reason and emotion in psychotherapy* (revised). New York: Carol Publishing.

Frankl, V.E. (1962). *Man's search for meaning*. Boston, MA: Beacon.

Glasser, W. (1984). Reality therapy. In R. Corsini (Ed.), *Current psychotherapies* (3rd ed., pp. 320-353). Itasca, IL: F.E. Peacock.

Holland, J.L. (1959). A theory of vocational choice. *Journal of Counseling Psychology, 6*, 35-45.

Holland, J.L. (1992). *Making vocational choices* (2nd ed.). Odessa, FL: Psychologist Assessment Resources.

Leong, F.T.L. (1993). The career counseling process with racial-ethnic minorities: The case of Asian Americans. *Career Development Quarterly, 42*, 26-40.

Leung, S.A. (1993). Circumscription and compromise: A replication study with Asian Americans. *Journal of Counseling Psychology, 40*, 188-193.

Lofquist, L. & Dawis, R. (1969). *A theory of work adjustment*. Englewood Cliffs, NJ: Prentice Hall.

Lofquist, L.H. & Dawis, R.V. (1991). *Essentials of person-environment correspondence counseling*. Minneapolis, MN: University of Minnesota Press.

May, R. & Yalom, I. (1995). Existential psychotherapy. In R.J. Corsini and D. Wedding (Eds.), *Current psychotherapies* (5th ed., pp. 262-292). Itasca, IL: F.E. Peacock.

Sue, D.W., Ivey, A.E., & Pedersen, P.B. (1996). *A theory of multicultural counseling and therapy.* Pacific Grove, CA: Brooks/Cole.

Super, D.E. (1957). *The psychology of careers.* New York: Harper & Row.

Super, D.E. (1980). A life-span, life-space approach to career development. *Journal of Vocational Behavior, 16*, 282-298.

## *Response to Tomokazu: The Case of the Recovering CPA*
## *Michael Shahnasarian*
## *Career Consultants of America*

### Overview

This case study presents many diverse, complex issues that merit investigation and analysis by the career counselor. In addition to the pending question about his occupational choice that ostensibly prompted Tomokazu's referral to career counseling, other pertinent issues relate to his mental health status, potential problems with substance abuse, and marriage and family situation. Embedded in the case are also cultural considerations associated with Tomokazu's Japanese American ancestry and apparent issues related to the influence of his family of origin.

In approaching this case, the career counselor is advised to accomplish the following objectives very early during the counseling relationship: (1) clarify and identify the client's presenting issues, (2) determine the areas in which the career counselor is competent and qualified to intervene, (3) present an analysis of the presenting issues and identify issues that are appropriate for the counselor to address, (4) provide referrals to the client for issues that are beyond the boundaries of competence of the counselor, and (5) provide the client with a realistic time frame and plan for addressing the issues to be addressed during the ensuing career counseling sessions.

There are two ethical standards from the Code of Ethics promulgated by the American Psychological Association (1992) that are particularly relevant to the counselor's consideration at the onset of Tomokazu's case. First, Ethical Standard 1.04 (a) addresses boundaries of practitioner competence and advises counselors to provide only services that are within the limits of their competence, based on their education, training, supervised experience, or appropriate professional experience. With respect to Tomokazu's case, this standard will be relevant to potential counselor intervention in areas other than career development. Second, Ethical Standard 1.08 addresses human differences and notes that in cases where differences of age, gender, race, ethnicity, national origin, religion, sexual orientation, disability, language, or socioeconomic status significantly affect the counselor's work concerning particular individuals or groups, counselors obtain the necessary training or experience, or they make appropriate referrals. With respect to Tomokazu's case, this standard may be relevant if the counselor discovers that client characteristics, such as traditions or customs associated with Japanese American males with which the counselor is unfamiliar, merit special consideration.

## Client Analysis

Tomokazu is a Japanese American male approaching middle age (age 39). Apparently, he has emanated from an established, high-achieving, and successful family who continues to maintain a visible and prominent presence in the urban area in which Tomokazu and his wife and child live.

A superficial analysis of Tomokazu's career profile would suggest that he has attained many correlates of career success. However, although Tomokazu has successfully earned a college degree, became a CPA, and secured employment with "a prestigious accounting firm," he is questioning the appropriateness of his career choice. Further analysis of his career and personal situations reveal numerous symptoms of discontentment. As an accountant, Tomokazu has pursued an occupation within the Conventional occupational theme (Holland, 1992). He is in the establishment phase of his career development (Super, Savickas, and Super, 1996).

The oldest of four sons, Tomokazu has had very successful male role models to emulate. His career development to date appears to have been different than his family members. Tomokazu's family, including his "protective" mother, seems to continue having significant influence over him. The case information alludes to significant responsibility and adjustment to change that Tomokazu's is experiencing due to relocation to a new city, a demanding job, his wife's discontentment, and raising a young child with another child soon to come. Of course, Tomokazu's problem with alcohol consumption and recent diagnosis of bipolar disorder must also be considered.

## Helpful Information to Obtain

After obtaining a general understanding of Tomokazu's presenting issues, the career counselor will need further information to guide the selection of appropriate interventions. The case material is helpful in organizing broad categories from which further questions can be elicited, including career-related questions, mental-health related questions, and family and culturally based questions.

### Career Related Questions

- Why did Tomokazu choose to pursue accounting? How committed is he to furthering his career in either a technical or management track as an accountant?
- What does Tomokazu enjoy about his job? What functional areas does he find fulfilling? What transferable skills has he developed?
- What thoughts on career/job change has Tomokazu had to date? How developed are these thoughts?
- What are Tomokazu's standards of success? From where did these standards emanate? How successful has he been in realizing the standards to which he aspires?
- How did Tomokazu obtain his current employment with "a prestigious accounting firm?" Did his family assist him? What are his job responsibilities? Is he meeting his and his employer's performance expectations?
- How well has Tomokazu assimilated into his business community? What, if any, options has he undertaken to further advance his career development within the past 12 months?
- What does Tomokazu hope to obtain from his participation in career counseling?

### Mental Health Related Questions

- What are the reasons that Tomokazu has resumed his participation in Alcoholics' Anonymous? Has his alcohol consumption increased or is there some other reason that he has chosen to resume participation with this organization?
- Who diagnosed bipolar disorder? What are Tomokazu's symptoms? Since he refuses to take his medication and disputes the diagnosis, is Tomokazu adequately familiar with the diagnostic criteria for bipolar disorder? Would he be willing to obtain a second opinion about this diagnosis?

- Has Tomokazu had any experience with psychotherapy?

## Family and Culturally Based Questions
- What, if any, expectations does Tomokazu's family have for him? Does he believe that he has met his family's expectations? How explicit are any familial expectations? To what degree does Tomokazu measure himself in comparison to other males in his family?
- What influence do Tomokazu's family and his wife have on his current disenchantment with his career development?
- To what degree is anxiety that Tomokazu may be experiencing with his wife's pregnancy contributing to his questions about his career development?
- What is the importance of work and career development to Tomokazu's wife? What are the specific reasons that she desires to return to work?
- How does Tomokazu's wife perceive his family's involvement and influence?
- What is Tomokazu's relationship to his siblings and father?
- Would Tomokazu and his wife be amenable to a referral to marriage counseling?
- What resources are available to Tomakazu to facilitate his career development?

## Potential Career Counseling Interventions

The selection of an appropriate intervention strategy will likely be based partially on the career counselor's analysis of information elicited from the preceding questions. For instance, if the counselor's analysis indicates that cultural issues are salient and merit primacy in the intervention strategy, the counselor may choose to adopt models proposed for ethnic minorities by Crites (1981) or Sue (1977). Shahnasarian (1997) outlined a career counseling strategy for an Asian female experiencing a number of career crises in midlife.

Because of the multifaceted and interrelated nature of Tomokazu's presenting problems, a particularly useful theoretical model for the career counselor to consider is the Integrative Life Planning model proposed by Hansen (1997). This model provides a comprehensive framework for integrating identity dimensions (including ethnicity, age, gender, and class), developmental domains (such as social, intellectual, emotional, and career), roles (including family and leisure), and context (including individual, family, organizational, and societal), into the assessment and decision-making process. The holistic approach offered by Integrative Life Planning may be helpful to Tomokazu in examining his life and career situation in concert and working to arrive at decisions that will adequately address the various areas of his life that are unsettled. Tomokazu is a well-educated individual who could potentially respond well to the type of insight-oriented approach that Integrative Life Planning offers.

Of course, as the counseling relationship develops, the counselor will need to determine if appropriate referrals are in order. For instance, an Asian career counselor may better serve Tomokazu. Based upon the available case information, referrals to a marriage and family therapist or a mental health professional, such as a psychiatrist or psychologist, may also be necessary.

A focus on clarifying personal values and work values at the onset of the counseling relationship will likely be helpful to both Tomokazu and the career counselor. This can be accomplished via the counseling process or through formal assessment measures, such as the Minnesota Importance Questionnaire. Self-directed psychoeducational materials may also be useful as homework for Tomokazu. For instance, *Decision Time: A Guide to Career Development Enhancement* (Shahnasarian, 1994) includes structured exercises that challenge clients to consider work and personal priorities, career interests, skills and aptitudes, and life circumstances that relate to critical career decisions.

Because of the potentially adverse affects associated with Tomokazu's noncompliance with taking medication prescribed for bipolar disorder, the career counselor is advised to address Tomokazu's perceptions about his diagnosis early during the counseling relationship. Also, maintain an open mind to the possibility that Tomokazu may be correct about an erroneous diagnosis. Depending on his level of insight and the strength of the therapeutic relationship, the counselor may choose to review with Tomokazu diagnostic criteria from the DSM -IV (American Psychiatric Association, (1994). The counselor may be in a position to interject information that he or she has gathered through interactions with Tomokazu as well as from collateral sources while considering the diagnostic criteria that may pertain to Tomokazu. Client education and mild confrontation may be in order if Tomokazu resists considering that he may be experiencing a mental disorder. However, his acknowledgement of previous problems with alcohol is a positive indicator that he may be receptive to considering that he is experiencing a mental disorder that may be compromising his life and career effectiveness.

## Summary

Tomokazu's case is complex and offers several challenges to career counselors who may lack experience related to mental health counseling, marriage and family counseling, and working with clients from diverse ethnic groups. In approaching this case, it is important that the career counselor refrain from intervening in presenting problems that may be beyond his or her scope of competence. A theoretical framework such as Integrative Life Planning is useful in providing a method for the client to examine presenting problems in a holistic manner and making decisions that offer the potential to reconcile more than one pending dilemma.

## References

American Psychiatric Association (1994). *Diagnostic and statistical manual of mental disorders* (4th ed.). Washington, DC: American Psychiatric Association.

American Psychological Association (1992). *Ethical principles of psychologists and code of conduct.* Washington, DC: American Psychological Association.

Crites, J.O. (1981). *Career counseling: Models, methods and materials.* New York: McGraw Hill.

Hansen, L.D. (1997). *Integrative life planning.* San Francisco, CA: Jossey-Bass.

Holland, J.L. (1992). *Making vocational choices: A theory of vocational personalities and work environment.* Odessa, FL: Psychological Assessment Resources.

Shahnasarian, M. (1994). *Decision time: A guide to career enhancement.* Odessa, FL: Psychological Assessment Resources.

Shahnasarian, M. (1997). The case of Jessica Chang: A business and industry perspective. *Career Development Quarterly, 46,* 161-166.

Sue, D.W. (1977). Counseling the culturally different: A conceptual analysis. *Personnel and Guidance Journal. 56,* 458-462.

Super, D.E., Savickas, M., & Super, S.C. (1996). Life-span, life-space approach to careers. In D. Brown, L. Brooks, & Associates, *Career Choice and Development* (3rd ed). San Francisco, CA: Jossey-Bass.

# CARLOS: THE CASE OF THE DISSATISFIED SEAMAN

Carlos is a 39-year-old Chicano male who has presented for career counseling at an urban career center. At his initial appointment he states that he heard that career counselors do testing on interests and that he would like to take this type of test "to find out what he should do for the rest of his life." He notes that he decided to pursue career counseling now because his wife had been "nagging" him to get some help.

Carlos reported that he had been in the Navy for the past 21 years. He joined the Navy after graduating from high school because there were no jobs in the rural community where he grew up in the southwestern United States. He spent the majority of his naval career on ships and submarines where his expertise was in radar and sonar maintenance, and where he managed crews of 15-50 personnel. He enjoyed his maintenance work but stated that, at times, being a supervisor was "very frustrating." Often, he thought it was just easier to do the work himself rather than relying on others to get the job done. When he was not chosen for a higher rank, he decided to retire from naval service.

After leaving the Navy, Carlos began looking for employment as a "manager," but after eight months of job searching, he has received no offers of employment. Although income from his retirement and his wife's part-time employment have been sufficient to meet the mortgage and basic utility bills, Carlos has borrowed heavily to meet other expenses and he and his wife are rapidly depleting the savings intended for the education of their children. They have two sons, ages 16 and 18, and one daughter, age 12.

Carlos reported that lately he had been feeling tired most of the time. Even his hobbies – gardening and horticulture that have fascinated him since his boyhood days in 4H – are not satisfying now. He confesses that he has been drinking rather heavily for the past month and that there are some days when he just stays at home in his bathrobe watching television. He hopes that the results of an interest test will help him "get back on track."

## *Response to Carlos: The Case of the Dissatisfied Seaman*
## *Rich Feller and Barb Norrbom*
## *Colorado State University*

### Image Formed of the Person

In light of his rural background, family status, and 21-year Naval experience, Carlos appears to be a middle-class, potentially quite traditional male regarding beliefs about how one establishes, moves through, and transitions within career roles. Long-term maritime experience suggests he interacts quite easily with others in close and hierarchical settings. Military leadership, radar and sonar maintenance activities, fascination with gardening, horticulture and 4-H suggests interest and achievement in hands-on, concrete activities (Craft/Career Decision Making System and Realistic/Strong Inventory) and Technical/Manual abilities (Ability Explorer).

We gather that he prefers straightforward, quick and specific answers as opposed to ongoing abstract processes (hence his hope that an assessment will be his magic wand) and that he learns by physically doing things that provide feedback (experiential learning). When unable to independently do things that require him to seek help, it will likely be after exhausting his own possibilities, and/or it may be via pressure from a significant relationship. Now that he has approached a counselor, we suspect he'd like clear parameters, outcomes, and steps to follow so that he can judge results, feel control, and take action.

## Other Information Needed

Interested in his support network, we'd seek definition of his wife's "nagging," what "some help" means, and what meaning he has constructed from his testing experience. Gaps existing between his and his wife's motivation for change and their image of the ideal dual career couple would be explored.

How has he explored with others his job search and present frustration? In leaving the Navy what was lost, what pain/assumptions does he hold, what dream is not fulfilled? What is the gap between his depleting savings and expected educational savings?

What jobs has he applied for and what were his interviews like? How would he change his efforts here? How does he think the "being tired most of the time," losing interest in hobbies, heavy drinking activity, staying home, and watching TV are related? What are his priorities and timeframe for this counseling?

## Career Counseling Plans

Although it would be easy to use diagnostic labels, we are reminded that Carlos' readiness for change, his meaning and urgency applied to the context of this situation, and individuality not confirmed within this written material should make us cautious about labels. We tend to approach this as a learning and skills gap problem needing intervention rather than a clinical model determined to find dysfunction. We are very interested in understanding the role of work in Carlos' life situation. We believe Carlos' coping and resiliency skills as well as his evolving identity and redefinition of life roles upon leaving the military deserve significant attention. In addition, his urgency regarding specific outcomes and time commitment should shape our decisions and plans.

## Direct Actions or Interventions

Assessing the alcohol activity, exercise and diet routine and their relationship to potential discouragement, listlessness, and inactivity is necessary. Referral to a family doctor for a physical and to assess further treatment could be called for should severe depression be confirmed. Referral to an alcohol treatment program, wellness program, and or employment support group might be useful. To the degree Carlos is dependent on alcohol and is physically inactive and isolating himself, his job situation or personal development are unlikely to improve until the situation is holistically addressed.

Confirming one's hypothesis about Carlos' career anchors, achievements, and sense of career success identity using methods compatible with the time available can offer encouragement, hope, and insight to Carlos, as well as deepen our understanding of his goals and commitments.

Teaching gap analysis in terms of his career exploration and transition skills, dual-career motivations, success identity, and life role balance actions is needed. This analysis results in a model that we think he could best identify with, and it could be presented in a diagram form (to take home). Concretely reviewing our intentions, clearly validating Carlos' personal efforts, and rewarding homework seem necessary with what we believe about Carlos' learning and information processing style.

## Theoretical Models

Choice Theory would be the basis for approaching our understanding of Carlos. It supports the concept of "total behavior" (Glasser, 1998) made up of four components: acting, thinking, feeling, and physiological sensations that result from the first three components. Although the four components are interrelated, clients only have direct control over actions and thoughts with feelings and physiology indirectly controlled by the first two components. In summary, clients choose actions, thoughts, and assumptions/worldviews that result in their feelings much like Rational Emotive Behavior Therapy (REBT). From this we hope Carlos would recognize his choices in reacting to his joblessness and its effects on his roles and situation. To the degree his inactivity, depression, and alcohol activity affect his choice making, interventions would shift.

Learning theory provides direction in offering opportunities to assess, observe and develop assets, experiences, and transferable skills intended to close skill gaps. For example, in trying to find a job or new ways to behave, how has he been in this situation before? What did he do? How did that work for him? What's different this time? What might work for him? What has he observed of others in similar situations? How does he think that might work for him? How willing is he to try new choices/options? This may offer tangible results while promoting development and building self-efficacy congruent with his goals.

## Contextual Factors

*Culture*. It would be important to recognize how culture might affect Carlos' priorities for career counseling. It would be important to take into account Carlos' perceived role in a Hispanic family and how he feels he's currently fulfilling that role. Carlos may have grand expectations of himself as the head of the family, or he may play a more egalitarian role, where expectations are flexible. Also, his wife's "nagging" could signify family unrest, economic fear, and feelings of loss of control by Carlos. It would be important to consider the discrimination and oppression that Carlos perceives in his job search as a result of being non-majority and a military manager in an increasingly decentralized workplace. Helping him practice behavioral interviewing responses (Stimac, 1997) can highlight his past performance and verify added value outcomes.

*Socioeconomic Status*. Gaining information about economic resources can clarify the time frame in which Carlos wants to see change and meet goals. Urgency will shape his perception of counseling priorities. Unless aligned with our plan, considerable frustration and misused resources can create resentment. To the degree resources are limited, finding a transition job and government resources to maintain family needs may be most urgent at the expense of development or long-term career exploration.

*Gender*. It would be important to look at the life roles Carlos maintains within this family context and the expectations held for him by significant others. Exploring beliefs about being a male, a male provider, worklife balance, and consumption behaviors tied to male status can lead to greater freedom and choices as well as client resistance.

In working with Carlos these factors will be highly personal based upon his worldview, yet they serve to maintain our respect for the historical context in which we work. Like many problems faced by career counselors, or counselors with additional training in understanding the work of work, clients can benefit from a variety of theoretical disciplines and therapeutic approaches. We hope this response illustrates respect for a wide range of orientations, yet we recognize the need for a rather brief problem-solving approach.

## References

Glasser, W. (1998). *Choice theory: A new psychology of personal freedom*. New York: Harper Collins.

Stimac, J. (1997). *The ultimate job search kit*. Lawrence, KS: Seaton Corporation.

# Response to Carlos: The Case of the Dissatisfied Seaman
## Ellen B. Lent
### University of Maryland

The features of this interesting case are important reminders that clients presenting for career counseling may not segregate their work-related issues in a way that service agencies might sometimes expect. With over 20 years of work behind him, with a spouse and family, and with behavior, mood, and substance abuse problems, Carlos represents an evaluation and intervention challenge to career counselors at any level of experience.

## Initial Impressions

Carlos is in a sudden slide. After 21 years of rising through the ranks of Naval service, he failed to earn promotion and sought retirement. In eight months of job searching, he has failed to land a new job. In the last four weeks, he has failed to consistently get dressed and leave his house. He and his wife are suddenly in deep debt and are quickly draining their teenage children's education funds. His wife is "nagging" him, he has lost pleasure in his prized hobby, and he is drinking heavily. His reasons for seeking counseling lack agency or vitality: interest testing "to find out what (I) should do for the rest of (my) life."

The picture is of a saddened, or angered, man who is alone in new territory and can't find his way around. After many years of extended assignments at sea, he is at home day and night. After managing groups of up to 50 subordinates, he directs no one. His judgment is impaired – exemplified by his excessive spending – and he is socially withdrawn. His wife and teenage children have busy lives and responsibilities that regularly take them out of the house. He is distant from his Southwest U.S. roots and from rural life and the 4-H Club of his childhood.

Carlos appears to have no links to active-duty or retired Navy personnel. Apparently, he received no civilian job assistance from the Navy, since he drifted into this career center after many months of untargeted job seeking. There is no mention of involvement in a radar/sonar maintenance union or association, which might provide career advice after separation from service. He is a high school graduate seeking a civilian management job – literally a fish out of water.

The failure to gain promotion, the absence of active career planning, and the disclosures of reckless spending, heavy drinking, fatigue, and social withdrawal represent a significant reduction from previous functioning. Eight months have elapsed since Carlos retired. Might he have been depressed or traumatized when he was passed over for promotion? Are the present symptoms in direct response to joblessness, or could Carlos be in the midst of a major depressive episode? Are there ethnic and cultural issues that would clarify the picture?

## Person-Centered Evaluation

Approaching this case from a person-centered perspective (see Boy & Pine, 1990; Bozarth & Fisher, 1990, and Lent, 1996) guides the assessment toward understanding the client's unique world and his efforts toward fulfilling valued goals. The client's unique world is perceived by, and reflects, the *self*: "An individual's self-perceptions (which) include one's view of the self as compared to others, one's view of how others see the self, and one's view of how one wishes the self to be" (Boy & Pine, 1990, p. 78). Distortions in self-perception, and resultant barriers to goal achievement, can be understood in relation to the client's level of self-awareness and self-acceptance.

Does the client enhance his development "by fulfilling obligations to the self and others?" Is a basic person-centered principle that aids in career self-assessment (Boy & Pine, 1990, p. 93). This can be addressed by learning about current significant relationships and the client's present goals for himself in the career area and elsewhere. This area of information gathering can prepare the counselor for the next task, which includes probing for interruptions in functioning.

Is the client able to use "openness to the self and others" as a way of developing the self? (Boy & Pine, 1990, p. 98). This can be judged by asking the client what is going well at present, what physical and emotional disruptions he is experiencing, and whether he is speaking openly with important people in his life (besides the counselor) about his progress. His ability to describe his current difficulties, including his lethargy, marital strife, and alcohol use, will give clues as to the extent of his awareness of self.

## Self-Concept and Identity Issues

Spotting self-alienation is an important factor in the initial assessment. This process requires broad awareness of what might contribute to the client's self-concept. Discontinuities between the self and the client's experience should be probed; for instance, why might Carlos not have found work as a manager, after so many years of managerial experience? After a 21-year career with one employer, why is he so abruptly unemployed? After so many years of goal-directed savings, why is he raiding his children's education funds?

Further, as a 39-year-old Chicano male living in the U.S., Carlos' identity or self-concept is in part a function of his ethnic status. The assessment should include questions about how he experiences his ethnic heritage, what culture-based beliefs and attitudes he holds, how he has acculturated to the majority-white society, and whether he has been subjected to negative experiences based upon prejudice or discrimination (Casas & Pytluk, 1995).

Casas and Pytluk (1995) describe five cultural values that may reflect the attitudes of many Hispanic clients and that could have implications for career assessment and counseling in this case: (1) *milismo*, a strong bond to immediate and extended family members; (2) patriarchal family structure, an acceptance of traditional masculine and feminine roles; (3) *respeto*, a respect for one's elders in age and experience; cultural fatalism, a belief that one should resign oneself to events; (4) religiosity, a tendency to be involved in organized religion; and (5) "a belief in folk healing when in crisis, and a tendency not to separate physical from emotional well-being" (p. 161). The counselor, Hispanic or otherwise, should allow these issues to inform the initial assessment.

## Expanded Assessment

In this case, additional evaluation should be completed in the interpersonal, vocational, existential/spiritual, and recreational domains (Boy & Pine, 1990). This includes social, educational, and work history, including religious and cultural-ethnic history, marital and family history, and recreation and leisure history. Also, since Carlos is clearly in emotional distress, there should be a thorough evaluation of physical and mental health symptoms and suicide risk, including family history of emotional problems and mental health treatment and present and past substance use.

Also important is assessing any discrepancies, distorted perceptions, self-alienation, or crises that Carlos may reveal. Was there a trauma or loss experience in the Navy or before? Does he believe he has met with racial discrimination? Does he hint that he feels superfluous in his wife's and children's lives? Does he chafe at the reverse of the patriarchal structure in his own family? Does he state that his drinking is a problem, or does he minimize it? Does he believe that a career counselor will tell him what he should do next, and he will simply follow instructions, as he may have done for much of his career? Is he resigned to whatever fate may bring his way?

## Social and Work History

What are Carlos's socioeconomic status and his parents' livelihoods? What were his parents' career hopes for him? How did he perform in high school? What were his career fantasies? If he has siblings, what were their academic and work choices? Do his cultural values hold that Chicano husbands and fathers are the major financial support of their families?

In the present day, what are the family's expenses that necessitate spending down their savings and incurring heavy debt? What role is Carlos playing in parenting and running the household – including any expressed beliefs about gender roles? What is the level of physical and emotional intimacy with his wife? Besides watching television, what does he do in his spare time? Does he report any friends? Does he have developmental issues related to midlife?

## Vocational Issues

Does he have positive work references from his Naval posts? Did he enjoy being at sea? Does he know of civilian job opportunities related to his radar and sonar expertise? If not, does he wish to transfer his knowledge and job skills into a different content area? Has he been turned down for management positions because he lacks postsecondary education? Does he suspect racial discrimination? Does he desire further education?

Is he truly interested in management, or would he prefer to be a solo performer? He may have an introverted style, since he stated a preference for completing work himself rather than delegating to his subordinates. Or he may not presently have the interpersonal energy needed in management, especially since his mood may have been depressed since his retirement.

## Intervention Suggestions

An initial counseling focus, after the extended assessment recommended above, should address Carlos' mood and behavior impairments and his substance abuse. If he agrees to remain alcohol free, client-centered counseling could proceed by incorporating ethnic-cultural issues into understanding his fatigue, withdrawal, and inappropriate spending.

For instance, the counselor could learn whether Carlos' reluctance to get dressed and leave the house is based on a belief that the husband of the family should be the primary breadwinner and that he does not wish to be seen unemployed in public. The counselor could probe for spiritual and religious beliefs that God will provide for the family's needs and the children's education; or for expressions of resignation to a predetermined fate, with no strong desire to take new action in the job market. And information about support from the extended family could provide a broader picture of Carlos' behavior.

Career interest assessment could be proposed, to accomplish two objectives: to respond to Carlos' stated counseling goal and to increase client self-awareness. It is likely that Carlos would endorse occupational interests in military, mechanical, horticultural, and similar fields, based on his career and avocational history. Inventory results might reveal a lack of similarity with managers of people, which could encourage Carlos to think less rigidly about his vocational future. Other interests might surface. He could begin to address more directly the content of the work he would enjoy and focus less on job titles in his search.

Establishing an open, authentic relationship with Carlos will include an effort to see the world as he does, a willingness to learn the impact of his cultural and ethnic heritage on his current self, and a belief in his ability to overcome obstacles and express himself fully in his job search and in his intimate relationships. The goals of counseling will be greater self-acceptance in all his roles, improved energy and hopefulness, responsible drinking, and return to congruence between expressed hopes and everyday actions.

## References

Boy, A.V., & Pine, G.J., (1990). *A person-centered foundation for counseling and psychotherapy.* Springfield, IL: Charles C. Thomas.

Bozarth, J.D., & Fisher, R. (1990). Person-centered career counseling. In W.B. Walsh & S.H. Osipow (Eds.), *Career counseling: Contemporary topics in vocational psychology* (pp. 45-78). Hillsdale, NJ: Erlbaum.

Casas, J.M., & Pytluk, S.D. (1995). Hispanic identity development: Implications for research and practice. In J.G. Ponterotto, J.M. Casas, L.A. Suzuki, & C.M. Alexander, (Eds.), *Handbook of multicultural counseling* (pp. 155-180). Thousand Oaks, CA: Sage.

Lent, E.B. (1996). The person focus in career theory and practice. In M.L. Savickas & W.B. Walsh (Eds.), *Handbook of career counseling theory and practice* (pp. 109-120). Palo Alto, CA: Davies-Black.

# TIM: THE CASE OF THE HAPPY HOUSEHUSBAND

Tim is a 42-year-old, Caucasian male who is clean and neatly dressed in casual business wear. He is tall and attractive and lives in a large city. He has been a househusband for approximately the past 15 years, but he has had a number of part-time jobs primarily in the area of automobile reconditioning. He earned an associate's degree in business management nine years ago.

Tim declared that he wanted help in deciding how to obtain work in which he can use the skills he learned in his business management degree program. He expressed very strongly that he does not want to be working on cars for the rest of his life. He also expressed interest in obtaining additional education in the same area that he has begun in business management. He was happy being a househusband but now feels a need to find employment, expand his work experience, and have more intellectual interaction in his life and work.

Tim has not expressed any unhappiness concerning his home life other than his desire for more intellectual stimulation in a job. He stated that his wife and family were supportive of his interests in pursuing a career at this time. Tim seemed happy with himself for achieving his associate's degree yet he felt it was just "not enough."

Tim seemed self-motivated to obtain information, support, and resources about what he wanted to accomplish. When he first began coming to career counseling sessions, he was somewhat timid and unsure about what the job market had to offer. He was not very knowledgeable about the range of opportunities and occupations available for him to become involved with if he chose to. Tim expressed his desire to expand his experiences and develop his skills beyond working on cars.

Tim has been a househusband for the past several years. His activities included taking care of the house, caring for the children, and being a companion and support for his wife. He was quite supportive of her career also. Tim said that he enjoyed carpentry as a hobby that he liked to build things out of wood. Client expressed that in the past he enjoyed going to school and that he looks forward to becoming enrolled again this January to begin working on his bachelor's degree.

Tim stated that he liked a lot of variety in his work environment. He disliked jobs that required him to be confined, doing routine monotonous tasks, and getting dirty. Tim tried two different jobs during the course of the career counseling sessions. The jobs paid well, but required him to do the kinds of tasks he found undesirable and so he quit both of them without informing the counselor that he was going to quit.

## *Response to Tim: The Case of the Happy Househusband*
### *Edwin L. Herr*
### *The Pennsylvania State University*

### Images of Tim

My initial image of Tim is that he is probably quite likable, easy to interact with, and makes a positive appearance in his physical presence and grooming. In specific terms, we know something about Tim from about age 27 to 42, the period during which he has been a househusband. We do not know much about Tim's background or experiences, family influences, or other factors that may have led to his career path of the past 15 years. I would like to have such information and might engage Tim in some form of narrative analysis of his adolescence and young adulthood.

Beyond those images, I sense that, although Tim has apparently stuck to being a househusband for 15 years, I am not clear what this role means to him, what he does in the role (for example, does he actually take care of his children, how many, and what ages), what factors motivated him to be a househusband and to engage periodically in part-time work, what satisfactions he receives from being a househusband or from doing part-time work in automobile reconditioning? In addition, I am ambivalent about Tim's self-discipline and about his career maturity. On the one hand, he has persisted as a househusband for a long time but, on the other hand, he quit two recent jobs because he saw them as undesirable without discussing the factors that led to his action with the counselor. Does his persistence as a househusband relate to the opportunity it provides him to work at his own pace, to be independent, to engage in a variety of tasks rather than to be under close supervision, doing routine tasks or doing tasks that he found undesirable? Among other things it would be helpful to know what he found undesirable in these two jobs. It would also be interesting to know what motivated him to pursue an associate's degree in business management and why, after getting it, he apparently did not use the degree to return to the workforce.

With regard to his rather unique work history, it appears that Tim has had very little opportunity in the past to engage in any type of systematic career exploration or to acquire career maturity. His initial timidity and lack of assurance about what the job market has to offer validates his lack of career maturity, his inability to identify the types of information he needs, and how to acquire and to evaluate it. In addition, there is little evidence available to suggest that Tim has a well-formulated vocabulary of self (e.g., interests, values, aptitudes) that he could use as an evaluative base by which to judge the relevance of job options or relevant career planning skills. Each of these questions and hypotheses represent areas for which I would seek specific information.

## Possible Plans for Career Counseling

After a long period as a househusband, a role that he apparently has found satisfying, Tim is now seeking a career change, particularly to a role that gives him more intellectual stimulation and that would provide him a lot of variety in his work environment, that would not require him to be confined or do routine monotonous tasks and get dirty. Since job criteria like "intellectual stimulation," "a lot of variety," or "routine monotonous tasks" are not normative statements, but rather personal perceptions, I would try to clarify what Tim means by these statements. His interpretations of these criteria, rather than mine as the counselor, are important issues.

As I sought to understand more clearly what he hopes to achieve in the career change he seeks, I would also try to clarify what has motivated his desire to find a new career path. Are his duties as a househusband no longer necessary? Are his children now grown and living independent? Has his wife entered a new stage in her own career that no longer requires his support as a househusband? Are there other psychological or economic factors that underlie his desire to find jobs outside the home?

Against such contexts, I would seek to clarify what Tim's goals for career counseling are at this point in his life. I would try to identify how he thinks I can help him and what outcomes would represent success for him. Depending upon how clear he is about such matters, I would likely suggest a number of interventions that we could pursue to help him increase his "cognitive clarity" (Brown & Brooks, 1991), about himself and about his options. Although I do not routinely administer a battery of assessments to my counselees, in Tim's case there are several instruments that might be very useful to help tailor career counseling to his most pressing needs and to help him develop a vocabulary of self. For the first goal, I would likely use the Adult Career Concerns Inventory (ACCI; Super, Thompson, & Lindeman, 1988) to help him be more explicit about the career issues of immediate concern to him and to identify what developmental tasks he is concerned about or currently negotiating.

To help him become more conscious of his own characteristics and to clarify the personal factors important to his decision making, I would likely suggest that he take the Values Scale (VI; Nevill & Super, 1986), to identify what values are important to him in the work environment; an interest measure, probably the Strong Interest Inventory (SII; Strong, Hansen, & Campbell, 1994), to assess his modal personality type and the types of occupational groups whom he resembles; the Salience Inventory, to assess his participation and commitment to various life roles as a worker, student, leisurite, family person, or participant in community activities. Depending upon what Tim tells me about his academic success in his associate's degree program, I might discuss with him the use of a brief aptitude measure such as the Employee Aptitude Survey (Grimsley, Ruch, Warren, & Ford, 1993). With the exception of the aptitude test suggested, the other instruments are essentially self-report instruments, the discussion of the results of which will help Tim to be clearer about what he wants to accomplish in career counseling, what knowledge and skills he needs to acquire to facilitate his career planning, and on what bases (e.g., values, interests, salience) he will make career decisions.

As we engage in career counseling, I would want to help him inventory the skills he has acquired as a househusband, automobile detailer, carpenter, and student of business management. I would want to help him consider the elasticity of these skills, the future occupations to which they might relate, and the ways they might be combined. For example, if he wishes to pursue business management as a major career goal, what does he want to manage? Would his previous career paths give him credibility as a manager of a day care center, an auto body repair shop, a hardware store, or a furniture manufacturing business? Are there other combinations of skills that might build on his past skills or be more congruent with his modal personality type?

Integral to Tim's career explorations, I would help him to probe how he feels about and reacts to supervision. In his previous role as a househusband and in his part-time work in auto reconditioning, he has performed quite independently. Was that by design? Does he not like or perform well under close supervision? Is the latter related to why he left the two recent jobs? Has he considered self-employment or creating an outsourcing firm in some area of specialization that would amplify his opportunities to be in charge? Depending upon his observations about supervisory styles and how he reacts to them, I might consider suggesting that he take a personality inventory such as the 16PF (Institute for Personality and Ability Testing, 1986) to assess more specifically his personality profile and the types of work environments and supervisory styles with which he likely would be most congruent.

Given what appears to be Tim's minimal career maturity and knowledge of the connections between his self-characteristics and available career options, I would refer Tim to a variety of adjunctive techniques. For example, Tim would likely find participation in a computer-assisted career guidance system such as DISCOVER to be helpful. Such a process would provide him the opportunity to rehearse the outcomes of pursuing different combinations of personal characteristics (interests, values, etc.) in relation to occupations and educational options available. In the process he would learn about his own preferences, increase his knowledge of the world of work, and how these two sets of knowledge can be incorporated in decision making. If Tim were to use a computer-assisted career guidance system, I would want to brief him about how to productively use the system, monitor what he is learning from the system, and debrief him after he uses the system to help him solidify his learning (Sampson, Reardon, & Lenz, 1991). In addition, as we become clearer about Tim's occupational and career aspirations, I would likely suggest that he engage in information interviews with personnel directors or employers who can tell him what they seek in specific workplaces and what opportunities and benefits would accrue to Tim. I would also ask Tim to talk with the career services specialists in the institution in which he hopes to matriculate for his bachelor's degree in business management. I would ask him to clarify what specializations are available in the business management curriculum, where their graduates are employed, and what career and placement services are provided by the institution to facilitate Tim's transition to employment.

As Tim gathers information about himself and his options, I would likely help him consider how to determine the relevance of the information he has, how to evaluate it, and how to incorporate it into a plan of action to which he can commit himself.

## Theoretical Models

As suggested in my perspectives on Tim as a person and on the career interventions I would likely suggest to him, I am basically eclectic in my approach to counselees. The dominant theoretical perspectives from which I would draw to work with Tim would include developmental, person-fit, and cognitive approaches. I would want to know about the influences on his career development to date, including those related to his family background, socioeconomic level, gender issues, and any other contextual factors that might be relevant to him. I would want to know of his previous experiences, if any, with career exploration or career guidance and the outcomes of these. I would be interested in the career developmental tasks that he has achieved and those that he has not. I would be interested in determining how he sees himself developmentally at age 42 compared to his peers and I would want to help him assess the developmental tasks that he needs to accomplish as he moves through this "mini-cycle" of career transition.

Given my hypotheses about Tim's possible issues with direct supervision of his work and his needs to operate independently, I am concerned about his "person-environment fit," the congruence between his abilities, interests, and values and the work environment he chooses. Within this concern, I would want to help him acquire a language of self that is comprehensive and useful to him and that he can apply as an evaluative base to the options available to him.

In cognitive terms, I am concerned that Tim acquires a relevant information base about himself and about the work options available to him that he does not now appear to have. I would want to discuss the relevance and utility of the information he acquires and how he is interpreting its meaning for himself. In that sense, I want to reinforce his "cognitive clarity" and to address any irrational beliefs that he brings to such interpretations about himself or his options.

As our initial goal setting and collaboration unfolds, it is possible that other approaches to Tim's career development may be useful. It may be that much of what Tim's career transition is about is an intense search for meaning that to date has escaped him. If so, concepts from constructivism and techniques such as narrative analysis may be relevant. Or, Tim may have problems with his own feelings of self-efficacy in relation to working fulltime in a competitive work environment under close supervision. If so, cognitive behavioral therapy, anxiety management and, perhaps stress management, may be in order.

## References

Brown, D., & Brooks, L. (1991). *Career counseling techniques.* Boston, MA: Allyn & Bacon.

Grimsley, G., Ruch, F.L., Warren, N.D., & Ford, J.S. (1993). *Employee Aptitude Survey.* Glendale, CA: Psychological Services.

Institute for Personality and Ability Testing. (1986). *16PF – Administrator's manual.* Savoy, IL: the author.

Krumboltz, J.D. (1983). *Private rules in career decision making.* Columbus, OH: The National Center for Research in Vocational Education, The Ohio State University. (ERIC Document Reproduction Service No. ED 229 608).

Nevill, D.D., & Super, D.E. (1986). *The Values Scale: Theory, application, and research manual* (Research ed.). Palo Alto, CA: Consulting Psychologists Press.

Sampson, J.P., Jr., Reardon, R.C., & Lenz, J.G. (1991). Computer-assisted career guidance: Improving the design and use of systems. *Journal of Career Development, 17,* 185-194.

Strong, E.K., Hansen, J.I, & Campbell, D.P. (1994). *Strong Interest Inventory.* Palo Alto, CA: Consulting Psychologists Press.

Super, D.E., Thompson, A.S., & Lindeman, R.H. (1998). *Adult Career Concerns Inventory: Manual for research and exploratory use in counseling*. Palo Alto, CA: Consulting Psychologist Press.

## *Response to Tim: The Happy Househusband*
## *Expanding Sources of Fulfillment*
## *Mark S. Kiselica*
## *The College of New Jersey*

Tim's experience as a "househusband" – that is, as an adult male who serves as the primary caregiver of his children and the supporter of his wife or partner as the primary breadwinner for the family – is representative of a growing number of men in the United States. According to federal survey data summarized by Pleck (1997), the percentage of married, employed mothers who reported fathers as their primary child care arrangement rose from 17% in 1977 to 23% in 1991.

In light of this trend, the consideration of Tim's case is timely because his desire to make the shift from the role of househusband to full-time worker outside of the home is shared by many other househusbands who wish to return to the workforce. Qualitative research findings pertaining to men like Tim suggest that they, too, value their role as caregivers but miss the added fulfillment and stimulation that is typically found in the workplace (Dean, 1992). Therefore, describing the process of helping Tim is likely to be instructive for counselors who assist men with the transition from househusband to full-time wage earner.

In this analysis several aspects of career counseling with Tim are highlighted, with Holland's (1985) career typology model serving as the theoretical underpinning of this analysis. Throughout this discussion, particular attention is devoted to the personal, family, and societal factors that have influenced Tim's career thus far and are likely to affect his career transition to the workforce. This analysis begins with an overview of some key concepts of Holland's theory of career development and counseling, followed by a conceptualization of Tim's case according to Holland's model. Strategies for clarifying Tim's self-knowledge and expanding his information about the world of work are described. The educational implications of his career change are also discussed. Finally, the probable lifestyle and family system changes associated with Tim's career transition are considered.

### Key Concepts of the Holland's Theory of Career Development and Counseling

According to Holland's model of career development and counseling, the most typical way an individual responds to the environment is referred to as the modal personality orientation. There are six such orientations, which correspond to six different work environments: realistic, investigative, social, conventional, enterprising, and artistic. Holland proposed that people will be comfortable and happy in a work environment that is compatible with their personality orientation and uneasy in an environment that is suited to a different personality type. In other words, career satisfaction is largely a function of the congruence between an individual's personal qualities and the characteristics, activities, and demands of the work environment. Achieving such congruence is affected by the adequacy of self-knowledge (i.e., the amount and accuracy of personal information an individual possesses about him- or herself) and occupational information. The greater the amount and accuracy of the information the individual has about each, the more adequate and satisfying the career choice is. If life circumstances prevent an individual from developing a good understanding of his or her interests and values, forming a crystallized personality orientation, or acquiring accurate information about work environments, the individual will encounter difficulty in selecting an occupational environment and will change from one environment to another. Therefore, identifying factors that influence a client's sense of self and understanding about the world of work are crucial in understanding a client's current career dilemmas and providing counseling that promotes self-knowledge and increases occupational information are key activities involved in resolving those dilemmas (Holland, 1985).

## A Conceptualization of Tim's Career Dilemma According to Holland's Model

Several factors appear to have influenced Tim's career development thus far and others are likely to influence him as he struggles with the transition of returning to the workforce full time. In terms of prior influences, Tim's decision to be a househusband, made 15 years ago, has shaped a significant era of his career development. Although serving as the primary caregiver for his children while supporting his wife's role as the main breadwinner has been satisfying for Tim, it appears that the duties of caring for his children, maintaining the house, and going to school to earn an associate's degree in business management curtailed his access to and consideration of information about the world of work. Except for some part-time work "primarily in the area of automobile reconditioning," Tim has had limited experience employed in or learning about different occupations. He is unsure about what the job market has to offer him. Although he would like to attain his bachelor's degree, he has not indicated a choice of college major or a focus to his studies. Although he knows that he dislikes automotive work and activities that are confining or involve his "getting dirty" and he likes carpentry as a hobby, he has not clarified extensively the relationship between his personal values and work and the salary rewards and time demands that would characterize a satisfying career. He has tried two different, well-paying jobs but quit both abruptly. In short, he lacks direction and needs to develop a clearer sense of who he is (that is, clarify his interests and his values), learn about occupations that match his personality, identify education/training that will equip him with the skills to work in potentially satisfying careers, and develop realistic plans for achieving his educational and career goals.

## Fostering Self-Understanding

If I were counseling Tim, I would discuss several personal, family, and societal issues before initiating formal assessment and job-information seeking activities with him. Specifically, I would explore with Tim the range of thoughts and feelings he has about ending his 15-year role as househusband by asking him the following questions: What attitudes and values related to the importance of family, gender roles, masculinity, and fatherhood were expressed by your prior choice about being a househusband? What did you enjoy about your experience of being a househusband? What will you miss when you relinquish this role? Although your wife and children support your plans to return to school and work, to what degree do you feel that you are abandoning them by ending your role as househusband? Who will take on some or all of your prior responsibilities as a houseparent now that you are focusing on this next chapter in your career development? What are your fears and insecurities about returning to school after a nine-year absence from school and to full-time work after a 15-year absence from full-time employment? How do you think people in the workforce will react to your having been a househusband for the past 15 years? That is, what biases about masculine roles are you likely to encounter? How might these many concerns – grieving the end of a prior life role, feeling like you are abandoning your family, and fearing the start of a new chapter in your life as a former househusband – be related, if at all, to your abrupt resignation from two different jobs? Why did you quit those jobs? What are your fantasies about how quickly and easily you can reenter the workforce? How realistic are these fantasies? What excites you about leaving your domestic duties? What appeals to you about returning to school, and, eventually, to full-time work? What type of a schedule do you want to follow in the future? How many hours do you want to spend away from home? Since you want to complete your bachelor's degree, how many hours do you need or want to be employed while you are in school?

Asking these questions would help Tim to identify the ambivalent feelings he has about this chapter in his life and to anticipate the challenges and rewards that await him as he proceeds on his journey. In addition, engaging Tim in discussing these issues is likely to create a strong rapport and trust that will facilitate his self-understanding and his readiness to participate in formal assessment procedures.

In an effort to further clarify his interests and values and how they relate to the world of work, I would instruct Tim to complete the Self-Directed Search (SDS; Holland, 1990b), which is an instrument that will yield a code representing Tim's personality type. The information presented in the case description indicates that Tim has a background in business management and automotive reconditioning and enjoys carpentry work; these indicators suggest that he might be a realistic personality type (i.e., oriented toward activities involving motor skills, equipment, machines, tools, and structure) or an enterprising personality type (i.e., oriented toward activities satisfying the needs for dominance, verbal expression, recognition and power). However, since he also is described as being a bit timid and really enjoys working with wood, I suspect that his dominant orientation is realistic. His performance on the SDS will help to evaluate this hypothesis.

## Acquiring Information About Occupations

Using the personality code yielded by the SDS, I would instruct Tim to use the *Occupations Finder* (Holland, 1990a), which is a tool for matching a list of occupations to particular personality codes. Thus, Tim would use his code to identify the type of occupations that match Tim's personality type. Then, I would guide him through the process of acquiring more information about these occupations. For example, we would visit our institution's Office of Career Services where I would direct Tim to several key resources published by the U. S. Employment Service, such as the *Dictionary of Occupational Titles* (U. S. Employment Service, 1991), the *Occupational Outlook Handbook* (U. S. Employment Service, 1998/1999) and recent issues of the *Occupational Outlook Quarterly*, which collectively contain descriptions and employment trends for hundreds of occupations. (These resources are available in print or online at http://stats.bls.gov/oco/ocodot1.htm.) We would also utilize the *National Trade and Professional Associations of the United States* (Columbia Books, 1997), which lists addresses for approximately 1,000 trade and professional associations. Using this latter resource, Tim could contact associations for information related to careers that tentatively appeal to him.

After reviewing the information acquired via these materials, I would ask Tim to select a handful of careers that most interest him. Then, I would ask him to contact people employed in these careers to arrange for career shadowing experiences, which involve observing the behaviors, responsibilities, and details involved in the model's work (Herr & Watts, 1988). Once this stage is completed, I would conduct decision-making counseling to assist Tim in evaluating the pros and cons pertaining to each remaining career and selecting a career that best suits him.

## Educational Planning

Since we live in a rapidly changing world, particularly in the area of technological advances, most adults returning to school and the workforce will require new training in a variety of skills (Herr, 1999). Therefore, I would assist Tim in developing plans for acquiring the advanced education that will equip him with the tools he needs to enter the workforce in his chosen field. Specifically, we would use computerized career counseling systems, such as DISCOVER II by the American College Testing Service, to identify postsecondary schools that offer training in Tim's preferred career. I would also utilize *College Financial Aid Made Easy* (Bellantoni, 1996) to educate Tim about the process of acquiring sources of financial aid, and then I would monitor his progress in obtaining, completing, and filing applications for financial aid and admission to educational institutions.

## Lifestyle and Family System Considerations

In order for Tim to proceed and succeed with his educational and career plans, he would have to clarify some important lifestyle and family issues. Completing additional training and then working fulltime will require significant adjustments in his lifestyle and by his family. I would invite the family to counseling to explore the shifts in their lives that would be required by Tim's career mission. I would ask Tim, his wife, and their children to consider and resolve the following questions: Which duties will Tim have to give up as he returns to school and work? Who will take on Tim's former duties? What sacrifices is each family member willing to make to support Tim's plans? How will the family handle the potential expenses associated with Tim's additional schooling? What new child care expenses, if any, will the family face once Tim is no longer the primary caregiver? What impact will Tim's devotion to his studies have on his leisure time with his family? How can the family address each family member's needs in the face of Tim's new role in life? Resolving these issues is likely to facilitate Tim's successful return to the workforce while engaging the family in a mutually supportive endeavor.

## References

Bellantoni, P.L. (1996). *College financial aid made easy*. Berkeley, CA: Ten Speed Press.

Columbia Books. (1997). *National trade and professional associations of the United States*. Washington, DC: Author.

Dean. J. (1992, August). Men as primary caretakers. In L.B. Silverstein (Chair), *Redefining fathering in patriarchical culture*. Symposium conducted at the Annual Convention of the American Psychological Association, Washington, DC.

Herr, E.L. (1999). *Counseling in a dynamic society (2nd ed.)*. Alexandria, VA: American Counseling Association.

Herr, E.L., & Watts, A.G. (1988). Work shadowing and work-related learning. *Career Development Quarterly, 37*, 78 - 86.

Holland, J.L. (1985). *Making vocational choices: A theory of vocational personalities and work environments* (2nd ed.). Englewood Cliffs, NJ: Prentice Hall.

Holland, J.L. (1990a). *The occupations locator*. Odessa, FL: Psychological Assessment Resources.

Holland, J.L. (1990b). *The Self-Directed Search*. Odessa, FL: Psychological Assessment Resources.

Pleck, J.H. (1997). Paternal involvement: Levels, sources, and consequences. In M.E. Lamb (Ed.), *The role of the father in child development* (3rd ed., pp. 66-103). New York: Wiley.

U.S. Employment Service (1991). *Dictionary of occupational titles* (4th ed.). Washington, DC: U.S. Government Printing Office.

U.S. Employment Service (1998/1999). *Occupational outlook handbook: 1998-1999*. Washington, DC: U.S. Government Printing Office.

# JAMAL: THE CASE OF THE EMERGING EDUCATOR

Jamal is a 43-year-old, African American male who is pursuing career counseling because he has the goal of obtaining a college education and he is exploring all options. He is currently enrolled part time at a local urban community college, taking general education classes with the thought that he is interested in elementary education. Jamal wanted to explore all of his options before making a firm decision. He works full time as a data processor for a local bank. He is working hard to become debt free so that he can go to school full time.

Jamal completed the inventories on DISCOVER to enhance his self-awareness. Based on his results, he came up strong in regions 1, 2, 3, 4, and 12. He printed out a job list of the occupations contained in these regions. His homework was to narrow his job list to 10 or fewer occupations so during the next appointment he could obtain more detailed information about those occupations. He was able to narrow the job list and received that information. For the third appointment Jamal came with two career choices, elementary education and vocational education. He was then advised to do informational interviews with individuals in these occupations to gain greater insight about the actual job.

Jamal was satisfied with the career search process although he still had some concerns about funding a full-time education. In our last session the counselor used the Internet to generate a book list of literature about financial aid and also tapped into some websites that explained the financial aid process and provided additional resources to contact for further information. The counselor also referred Jamal to the financial aid office of the community college he was attending.

## *Response to Jamal: The Case of the Emerging Educator*
## *Vivian J. Carroll McCollum*
## *University of Missouri - St. Louis*

Jamal appears to be an undecided middle-aged college student who shows a lack of career maturity and who demonstrates career indecision. Career indecision and lack of career maturity are not uncommon among African Americans (Westbrook, Stanford, Gilleland, Fleemor, & Merwin, 1988). According to Bowman (1993) and Dillard (1980), a lack of positive Work-related experiences can hinder the career decision-making process and can be the result of African Americans' early entry into low-paying jobs, discrimination, and other issues related to race (Smith, 1983). Career maturity is linked to a person's ability to make age-appropriate career decisions based on future work experiences, lifestyle needs, family and civic responsibility (Super, 1990).

Though Jamal seems to be ambitious and willing to work, his work history has not however, prepared him for the specific career that he plans to pursue. The lack of related work experience often hinders African Americans in their career development. This is often a result of occupational segregation, choosing jobs based on a history of perceived bias or tolerance (McCollum, 1998).

Occupational segregation limits the occupational choices of career seekers. Further exploration of Jamal's interests according to DISCOVER may be in order to determine if Jamal's initial choice was based upon his needs, values, interests, and lifestyle or the product of occupational segregation. Jamal's choice of elementary education fits into the category of "protected careers," those careers that historically have had high demand, offered job stability, and thought to be less racially discriminatory. Career segregation, lack of career choices or the perceived lack of opportunities available to African Americans may explain why African Americans have lower expectations of achieving their occupational aspirations (Arbona, 1990; Loughead, Liu, & Middleton, 1995) and like Jamal, lack career maturity.

A developmental approach to career counseling can be helpful with African American clients if additional developmental tasks are considered. Smith (1983) warned that minorities may face additional developmental tasks such as integrating the meaning and impact of race into their vocational lives and developing coping strategies for dealing with discrimination. This approach allows both the client and the counselor to understand steps that must be taken to establish career maturity. A culturally sensitive developmental approach can also provide guidelines for tasks that must be completed to promote progression in career development (Smith, 1983; Super, 1990; Super & Thompson, 1981). These additional developmental tasks become career-relevant behaviors necessary for occupational success and may also account for Jamal's delay in career fulfillment.

Jamal appears to be a late bloomer, currently making career decisions and completing career development tasks usually associated with a much younger individual. Other reasons for Jamal's delay may be related to the necessity of obtaining work to support himself, and he may have started with low-paying jobs obtained for the purpose of survival without taking into account his interests and skills. Arbona (1989) found that African American men were over-represented in low-level Realistic jobs. Realistic people, as described by Holland (1973) are individuals who avoid goals and tasks that demand subjectivity, intellectual or social abilities and lack artistic expression. These characteristics accurately describe some early labor force entry positions. In essence, Jamal may have put his educational and career pursuits on the back burner because of a lack of direction and he continues to be plagued with a lack of funds.

The self-efficacy theory has elements that predict academic performance and occupational preference. An important element of self-efficacy theory is outcome expectations. According to Bandura (1977), individuals must believe not only that they can perform a particular task but also that the task will lead to the desired outcome. Because Jamal has had some college success, this theory can be applied to his needs in illustrating to him the importance of following an academic plan and how that plan can lead to the fulfillment of his goal to become an elementary educator. He will be able to see that his academic performance will have a great impact on his occupational and social futures.

As a career counselor I would be interested in knowing if Jamal has any career role models. Smith (1983) indicated that the knowledge of different jobs and knowledge of individuals holding those positions become career development needs for African Americans. I would also inquire about his family and the influence his family may have on his career decisions. African Americans often solicit the aid of relatives and friends whose influence can serve to enhance career development for them (Parham & Austin, 1994) and as a counselor, it is important for me to understand the significance of the family group in the career decision-making processes of my client. Another important issue to consider is the referral source that brought Jamal to see the counselor initially. Knowing if the client is a self-referral or third-party referral can often help in deciding upon the types of interventions the client would be willing to explore.

A multicultural approach to career counseling would be appropriate for Jamal. Korman (1992) and Cheatham (1990) indicated that African American clients in career counseling benefit from understanding their own interests, abilities, and values related to the Afrocentric worldview. African Americans share cultural values that may affect the way they make career decisions and how they respond to counseling. This includes involving the community and providing input from a variety of individuals and contexts to which the client has ties. If I were the counselor, I would encourage Jamal to seek diversified career role models from among the ranks of relatives and others within his community. Kin networks, the church, and social service agencies are three sources of support for African Americans and may serve as resources for job shadowing and mentoring (McCollum, 1998).

In order to obtain information about his chosen career and to gain valuable work experience I would encourage Jamal to volunteer in a classroom, interview teachers, and help out in the school office. This would give Jamal an opportunity to get a personal, hands-on view of the school environment. Additionally, I would use follow-up appointments to discuss Jamal's feelings about his observations and interviews.

In order to continue to encourage Jamal and to build his self-esteem and self-efficacy, I would suggest participation in career group intervention. Career group intervention has been successful with African American clients, possibly due to their sense of interdependence and the value of collective orientation over the individual (Bowman, 1993; Merta, 1995; Sue & Sue, 1990). A career group such as a job club (i.e., teachers' club) may serve both as a problem-solving mechanism and a networking outlet.

The most important goal of the career counselor is to keep Jamal on track and to assist him in relieving some of the stress related to his finances. In addition to using Internet resources, Jamal might approach his current employer to see if he could take advantage of their educational reimbursement plan. He might also try other corporations in the community for grant information or information about community financial assistance. Jamal could communicate his need to family, friends, and his church's pastor for their input and their suggestions of additional scholarship sources.

Providing interventions that respect Jamal's cultural values will assist in trust building as well as ensure that Jamal will be an active participant in the career counseling process. Becoming knowledgeable of the environmental and social handicaps of African Americans in general and those specific to Jamal will be invaluable in understanding the career development needs that Jamal has. Finally, helping Jamal to understand his own interests, abilities, and values relative to his Afrocentric worldview may facilitate the exploration of developmental tasks. By providing systematic career interventions that foster exposure to different employment opportunities, Jamal will be able to make career decision that will assist him in meeting his occupational expectations.

## References

Arbona, C. (1989). Hispanic employment and the Holland typology of work. *Career Development Quarterly, 37*, 257-268.

Arbona, C. (1990). Career counseling research and Hispanics: A review of the literature. *Counseling Psychologist, 18*, 300-323.

Bandura, A. (1977). Self-efficacy: Toward a unifying theory of behavioral change. *Psychology Review, 84*, 191-215.

Bowman, S. (1993). Career intervention strategies for ethnic minorities. *Career Development Quarterly, 43*, 14-25.

Cheatham, H.E. (1990). Africentricity and career development of African Americans. *Career Development Quarterly, 38*, 334-346.

Dillard, J.M. (1980). Some unique career behavior characteristics of Blacks: Career theories, counseling, practice, and research. *Journal of Employment Counseling, 17*, 288-298.

Holland, J. (1973). *Making vocational choices: A theory of careers*. Englewood Cliffs, NJ: Prentice Hall.

Korman, J. (1992). A social learning theory of career selection. *Journal of Career Counseling, 7*, 6-10.

Loughead, T., Liu, S., & Middleton, E. (1995). Career development for at-risk youth: A program evaluation. *Career Development Quarterly, 43*, 274-284.

McCollum, V. (1998). Career development issues and strategies for counseling African Americans. *Journal of Career Development, 25*, 41-52.

Merta, R.J. (1995). Group work: Multicultural perspectives. In J. Ponterotto, J. Casas, L. Suzuki & C. Alexander (Eds.), *Handbook of multicultural counseling* (pp. 567-585). Thousand Oaks, CA: Sage

Parham, T., & Austin, N. (1994). Career development and African Americans: A contextual reappraisal using the nigrescence construct. *Journal of Vocational Behavior, 44*, 139-154.

Smith, E. (1983). Issues in racial minorities' career behavior. In W.B. Walsh & S.H. Osipow (Eds.), *Handbook of vocational psychology* (pp. 161-221). Hillsdale, NJ: Earlbaum.

Sue, D.W., & Sue, D. (1990). *Counseling the culturally different: Theory & practice* (2nd ed.). New York: Wiley.

Super, D. (1990). A life-span, life-space approach to career development. In D. Brown, L. Brooks, & Associates. *Career choice and development: Applying contemporary theories to practice* (pp. 197-261). San Francisco, CA: Jossey-Bass.

Super, D. & Thompson, A. (1981). *Adult Career Concerns Inventory*. New York: Teachers College Press.

Westbrook, B., Stanford, E., Gilleland, D., Fleemor, J., & Merwin, G. (1988). Career maturity in grade 9: The relationship between accuracy of self-appraisal and ability to appraise the career-relevant capabilities of others. *Journal of Vocational Behavior, 21*, 269-283.

## *Response to Jamal: The Case of the Emerging Educator*
## *Diane Kjos*
## *Governors State University*

Jamal presents an interesting problem for a career counselor. Here is a 43-year-old male seeking a college education with the goal of getting a college degree. Is it the career counselor's role to simply offer him some career assessment, suggest informational interviewing, and refer him to financial aid? Or should one be concerned about his chances of actually reaching his educational goal? I know that older adults are often surprised at the amount of time they need to devote to their studies and may be unrealistic about how long it is really going to take to get that degree. As a result, the dropout rate for older college students is high. According to National Center for Education Statistics (1998) data, only about 10% of students 30 and over, who begin to work on a bachelors degree complete that degree in five years or less and more than 50% do not complete any degree program.

My initial image of Jamal is that he is a careful person who wants to consider his choices so as to make the right decision. I also note that he has some financial concerns but he doesn't express concerns about time constraints. Is this because he has a lot of free time? Or, is it because he doesn't know how much time he will need to dedicate to his educational efforts? He is a person who apparently likes both people and data, so I would expect him to be personable and willing to seriously consider possible outcomes. Jamal's position as a computer operator would put him in a low to moderate income bracket, depending on how long he has been in his job. I am not sure if he is seeking a degree because he is dissatisfied with his career or is simply seeking a college degree for his own personal satisfaction.

As he is an African American, I would guess that he has experienced discrimination and he may be somewhat wary of me, a white female. On the other hand, he may also see me as the "expert" and, in spite of our differences, part of him may hope that I can give him the secret to success and future happiness.

I would be interested in working with Jamal because I believe that a few sessions of counseling will enhance the likelihood of his success and increased personal satisfaction no matter what decision he makes about his future. Because of his data/person style I would want to pay attention to both with his interpersonal concerns as well as his need for facts. I would begin by working to build a relationship with Jamal that would allow him to feel comfortable about exploring his concerns and, at the same time, give him encouragement to find his way and make his own decisions. I will be aware that a college education may not be the solution to Jamal's discomfort with his current situation and that our counseling sessions may take a completely different direction.

As with any client, I will want to know why Jamal is seeking counseling, and why he is seeking it at this time in his life. I would also wonder what he actually expects from me and I, in turn, would tell him how I saw my role. As a career counselor, my concern would be that Jamal not just identify a possible career area, but that he also have a clear goal, a reasonable plan of action, and the personal resources to achieve that goal. Thus, there are several other areas that I would want to explore with Jamal. These include a career history, family and living situation, and his perception of his personal strengths and resources.

What is motivating Jamal to make a career change at this time in his life? What is he changing from? Why make the change now? What is it about his current job that he finds satisfying? Dissatisfying? What about previous jobs? Although DISCOVER and other forms of assessment can help him identify areas of interest, I would also be interested in and assess other factors that might influence Jamal's job satisfaction. Among these would be how he sees his job status, how satisfied he is with his compensation and benefits, and how he describes his work atmosphere. Because he scored high in the People/Data areas, I would be particularly interested in how he perceives his interpersonal relationships on the job.

I would want to explore Jamal's thinking concerning his future. It may be that Jamal is primarily interested in a college degree rather than a new career. What does he expect this education will give him? I think this is an important consideration at this point in Jamal's life as almost one-half of his work life is behind him.

Then I would wonder about Jamal's family situation. Is he married or in a long-term relationship? Does he have children? Will his family be understanding and supportive? If Jamal is one of the first in his family to attend college, he may face a special set of problems. Family members may have difficulty understanding how much time Jamal will need to devote to his education. Others might have concerns that he will no longer be part of the family if he gets educated. On the other hand, the fact that at 43 he is just beginning his college career may represent an effort to make up for disappointing his family by not getting a college education when he was younger. I would also wonder if Jamal has children and if one or more of his children are currently in college. Conversely, Jamal may not have a family or long-term relationship or he may have been disappointed in his relationships and this proposed career change and/or college education may be a way of compensating for what he sees as a missing piece in his life.

According to the Riverin-Simard (1990) nine stage model of career development, Jamal is moving in to the fifth stage, which is one of reflection and trying to make sense of one's life. How does Jamal's decision to move to a new career contribute to making sense of his life? What will this change contribute to his ongoing development? What factors might contribute to his desire to establish a new career at this point in his life?

I would be interested in his "career story." How did he come to be a computer operator? What satisfaction, if any, has he found in that job? What part of the job is dissatisfying to him and why? What did he do before that? How was that job? How does he see himself as a worker? How does he view those he works with? I would be listening for some clues to his dissatisfaction. Is it related to his personal development? His work environment? Family or societal issues? How would he see his "career story" as a college student? As a teacher?

I would inquire as to how well he was doing in his current courses and would ask if his current job might contribute in any way to the vocational education option. Would he, for example, want to teach in the area of data processing? And would his employer support his educational efforts?

My plans for career counseling would depend, to a great extent, on what I learned about Jamal. Because Jamal appears to be seeking a major career change at a time in life when many people deal with a sense of dissatisfaction with their careers and at a time when some are beginning to consider retirement options, my thinking would be based on a developmental model. However, I believe Jamal may have a "career story" that is not yet finished or even nearing the last chapter so my approach would be narrative. I would pay attention to Jamal's story to trace developmental strands in Jamal's life including his relationships with others and his ability to make satisfying decisions for himself. At some point, it might be useful to construct a career genogram with Jamal so that he could explore his role in the family and how family patterns and expectations might influence his choices at this point in his life. Finally, I would help him build a future story around his career choice. During this process I would pay attention to what is going on between Jamal and myself and how I am reacting to him. I may use immediacy from time to time to help him gain awareness of his style and approach to others.

I would also challenge Jamal to do some reality testing and suggest he do some homework between sessions to explore issues of time and money that might get in the way of his accomplishing his goals. As a part-time student with limited financial resources, Jamal could expect to take six years or more to finish his degree and get a job teaching. And, although the average salary for teachers is considerably more than the average salary of computer operators, Jamal would be starting out at the lower level of the pay scale. Because I see Jamal as a thoughtful and careful person, I believe that he would consider these issues carefully for himself.

Jamal may be an emerging educator, but first of all, he is an emerging college student. At first, his concerns seem relatively simple. "What should I major in? What are my options?" he asks. However, at 43 years of age, he is not beginning his vocational life. He brings several years of experience in the work world, and quite possibly, a bag of hopes and dreams never fulfilled. As a career counselor, my concern would be to help Jamal find a path that would help him make sense of his life and chart a path that will help him begin to fulfill some of his hopes and dreams whatever they might be. For Jamal, finding success in his career as a college student may be the first step in fulfilling those hopes and dreams.

## References

Riverin-Simard, D. (1990). Adult vocational trajectory. *Career Development Quarterly 39*(2), 129-142.

National Center for Education Statistics. (1998). *The Condition of Education 1998, Indicator 12*, [Online]. Available: http://nces.ed.gov/pubs98/condition98/c9812a01.html.

# DARREN: THE CASE OF THE UNEMPLOYED RUNAWAY

Darren is a 45-year-old Caucasian male who has lived in cities all of his life. He grew up in Chicago. Then when he finished high school, he moved to New York to attend college. Then, when he finished his undergraduate degree, he moved to Houston for graduate school. After completing his MA, he took a job in Los Angeles where he lived for 10 years before moving to Portland, Oregon.

He has entered career counseling because he needed help in identifying a viable career option. He had been unemployed for the past year. Darren possessed a bachelor's degree in architecture and a master's degree in landscape architecture. During his intake interview, Darren reported feeling dissatisfied with his previous jobs. Most recently, he had been employed as a landscape architect and reported enjoying the creative aspects of his work. He also mentioned, however, that he had experienced difficulty in getting along with his supervisor and that this was a pattern for him in his previous employment situations. He also reported a strong dislike for structured work environments. He related that he experienced a high level of anxiety when confronted with challenging tasks. Darren also noted that he was typically very sensitive to criticism. His hobbies included photography, computer-aided design work, and reading in the areas of human potential, spirituality, and psychology.

An additional factor concerning Darren's situation at the time he entered career counseling was that he and his wife were in the process of divorcing. The divorce proceedings were focused on the issues of child support and custody relative to Darren's 4-year-old son.

Darren's father was employed as an engineer and his mother was a clinical psychologist (both retired). Darren has a 37-year-old sister currently working as a homemaker. At the time he entered career counseling, Darren's parents were serving as his sole source of financial support. Despite this financial assistance, Darren stated that he felt that he never received from his parents "what he needed." He perceived his parents as being somewhat distant and his father as being rather critical. His father was especially not supportive of Darren's artistic abilities and emphasized the importance of developing scientific skills and knowledge. Both parents were anxious for him to return to work.

He has taken the Strong Interest Inventory and reports his RIASEC code as ARC and his Myers-Briggs Type Indicator preference code is INFJ.

## Response to Darren: The Case of the Unemployed Runaway
## Career Counseling: Facilitating Exploration, Insight and Action
### Karen M. O'Brien and Linda C. Tipton
### University of Maryland - College Park

Career counseling with Darren must extend beyond the traditional matching of individuals and work environments advocated by Parsons (1909) early in the 20th century. More recently, counselors have recognized the importance of an integrated approach to career counseling that addresses the interplay of vocational, self, and interpersonal concerns (Blustein, 1987; Blustein & Spengler, 1995; Gysbers, Heppner, & Johnston, 1998; Lucas, 1993). The most effective intervention for Darren would enable him to explore his feelings and thoughts, gain insight about his behaviors, and move toward changes that will enrich his life. Hill and O'Brien (1999) developed a helping skills model that can be applied to career counseling and used effectively to promote positive changes in Darren's life.

### The Hill and O'Brien Helping Skills Model

The Hill and O'Brien (1999) model proposes that counselors move through three stages (Exploration, Insight and Action) for each problem presented by the client during counseling. The goals of the first stage, Exploration, are to develop a therapeutic relationship that enables clients to tell their stories and to facilitate the expression of thoughts and feelings. The counselor uses basic helping skills (i.e., active listening, open questions, and reflection of feelings) to assist the client in expressing underlying affect and thoroughly exploring thoughts and feelings.

In the Insight stage, clients gain new and deeper understandings of the factors underlying their thoughts, feelings, and behaviors. Clients examine not only the ways in which they contribute to the difficulties that they are experiencing, but they also identify the strengths and coping mechanisms that they can rely on to implement change. Helping skills used by counselors in the Insight stage include the skills used in Exploration, as well as challenges, interpretations, self-disclosure, and immediacy.

Finally, because expression of affect and increased insight rarely lead to lasting change (Hill & O'Brien, 1999), clients enter the Action stage. Counselors work with clients to brainstorm possible changes, evaluate their ideas, select a plan of action, practice skills, and implement and evaluate changes. Throughout the Action stage, counselors rely on basic helping skills as well as direct guidance and information. The three-stage helping process continues as insights gained in addressing one issue inform clients' understanding of other problem behaviors. Moreover, this model provides flexibility for career counselors to develop creative interventions to affect change with clients (see Heppner, O'Brien, Hinkelman, & Humphrey, 1994).

Several basic assumptions form the basis for career counseling using this model. First, the counselor provides support by creating a caring environment in which the client can explore concerns, improve self-understanding, and take action to change life circumstances. However, this model is predicated on the assumption that change does not occur solely in a supportive context. The client must be challenged to participate actively in counseling (e.g., to struggle to express her feelings, think about his contributions to problems, generate possible action plans, and complete homework assignments). Moreover, the focus of the work includes not only career-related concerns, but also exploration of difficulties in interpersonal relationships and self-identity. Finally, career counseling must assist the client to identify the strengths on which the client can build to compose a healthier life.

### The Application of the Hill and O'Brien Model to Career Counseling with Darren

The complexity inherent in most career cases, including Darren's, necessitates cycling through the stages of Exploration, Insight, and Action with respect to several areas of functioning. We have outlined three interrelated areas to address in career counseling with Darren: interpersonal, self, and career issues. Although the issues are presented sequentially, they overlap in counseling as the interpersonal, self, and career issues have a negative impact on Darren's career development and block him from moving forward, and his difficulties in his career development affect his feelings about himself and others. Prior to implementing the Hill and O'Brien (1999) model with Darren, the counselor would assess his psychological status using a structured interview and, possibly, additional testing to rule out significant depression or anxiety. If clinical depression or anxiety is present, the counselor and Darren would take action to alleviate the depression or anxiety using cognitive-behavioral strategies and/or a referral for a medical evaluation.

#### Interpersonal Issues

Career counseling would commence with an examination of the relationship problems that appear to stymie Darren's growth, both personally and in his career. In the Exploration stage, Darren's relationships, primarily with his parents and wife but also with supervisors, would be explored. The counselor would solicit additional information regarding his interpersonal functioning with his family members, his reason for divorcing, and his reaction to custody issues. The counselor would encourage Darren to express his thoughts and feelings about difficulties committing to a relationship or a place to live. After establishing a therapeutic relationship, the counselor would move toward the

Insight stage to challenge Darren to examine how his moves, divorce, unhappiness, and anxiety relate to relationships with others. The Insight stage provides an opportunity for the counselor and Darren to work together to illuminate unhealthy patterns and obtain an understanding of his positive and negative contributions to relationships. For example, Darren's expectations of self and others may not be realistic. He may view all people as critical and distant like his parents, leading to difficulty with respecting authority and receiving criticism. Despite having the privileges usually attendant with being white, male, and from an upper-class background, Darren perceives himself as powerless and pressured to be something he is not. Furthermore, he has become financially dependent on his parents, but remains angry that they are not supportive. Darren's paralysis and apparent passivity seem to be his way of coping with that anger or hurt. Therefore, it would be highly important to address these issues as he attempts to negotiate a custody and divorce settlement. Otherwise, his feeling toward his wife and possible grief over losing a close connection with his son could lead to more withdrawal and paralysis.

Once Darren explores and gains insight into these issues, he and the counselor could move to the Action stage and identify several ways to improve his interpersonal relationships. For example, he might be encouraged to learn assertive communication skills, set limits with others, identify and change unrealistic beliefs, and attempt divorce/custody mediation.

## Self Issues

Darren's self-esteem, which seems confused or fragile, most likely limits his progress. The counselor would revisit the Exploration stage as Darren would benefit from exploring (through journaling, reading self-help books, and talking with the counselor) his feelings about himself and his current life situation. He would be asked to deeply examine his unhappiness and sensitivity to criticism. In addition, the counselor would encourage Darren to talk about how he felt when his dad discouraged his creative endeavors. The Insight stage also would provide the opportunity to address several key questions, such as how Darren limits himself, copes with disappointments and loss, and nurtures himself. Darren seems to feel neglected, and he may need to work at understanding how to care for himself. Finally, Darren would be asked to identify his strengths (e.g., intelligence, life experiences, interesting hobbies) and the ways in which he has placed limits on defining and developing an integrated sense of self.

In the Action stage, Darren would be challenged to brainstorm how he can express and nurture himself. For example, hobbies, relaxation techniques, and support groups might help Darren solidify a sense of self that could result in more effective personal and professional connections with others. In addition, an enhanced sense of self might boost his confidence in managing difficult or stressful tasks.

## Career Issues

Once self and interpersonal issues have been addressed to the point that Darren could understand how they affect his career development, the counselor would cycle back to the Exploration stage. For example, the counselor might ask Darren to describe his career history and his feelings and thoughts regarding his previous career choice and his current unemployment. Darren's Holland code (1985) of ARC is fairly consistent with the RIASEC code for an architect (AIR; Gottfredson & Holland, 1989) and suggests that he may be well suited to landscape architecture and could have a viable career in the field. However, he felt dissatisfied with his work and thus needs to understand what contributes to his unhappiness. To facilitate exploration, the counselor might ask Darren to develop a timeline of his career history that delineates his educational experiences and each position he held (including responsibilities, relationships with co-workers and supervisors, emotional state, likes and dislikes, why he left).

Using this information, Darren and the counselor would move into the Insight stage to further understand his conflict with supervisors, dislike of structured environments, and anxiety related to pressure. For example, Darren may discover that his behaviors contributed to problems in work environments or that parental criticism and lack of support led him to expect the same at work. To capitalize on these insights, the counselor would encourage Darren to practice assertive communication and stress management in the Action stage. In addition, Darren would learn to take responsibility for work behaviors that are self-sabotaging and identify ways to change unhealthy patterns.

Viewing an overall picture of his career history also might help Darren determine whether he could be happy remaining in landscape architecture or switching to another creative field, such as photography or graphic arts. At this point, Darren might return to the Insight stage to apply his newly gained knowledge about his interpersonal functioning and self-esteem to appreciate how these issues could block future progress in his career.

To deepen Darren's understanding of how he may limit his career development, the counselor might extend the Insight stage to explain that Darren's Myers-Briggs Type Indicator preference code, INFJ, is indicative of people who are insightful, creative, and empathic and who seek meaning from their work (Myers & McCaulley, 1985). However, these individuals may be at risk for failing to pursue their career goals, struggling with career decisions, resenting others, and minimizing their empathic and creative selves (Myers & McCaulley, 1985). Moreover, the counselor would discuss the importance of contextual factors in Darren's life and explore issues related to race and ethnicity (e.g., how being white affects his career decisions and relationships with colleagues), social class (e.g., how having many opportunities may both benefit him and cause stress), parental expectations (e.g., how his parents' successes contribute to their hopes for his future and his feelings about himself), and his role as a father (e.g., how having a child may exacerbate the joys and challenges in his life). Finally, the Insight stage could be a useful time to explore issues that emerged in the therapeutic relationship, as processing these issues could model how interpersonal issues are resolved in work environments.

Guided career imagery might facilitate the transition to the Action stage and would help Darren and the counselor explore his vocational options. Information from the imagery activity and the inventory results could help him identify several possible career directions. For instance, he may be happier self-employed in landscape architecture, or he may want to pursue a career in photography. Darren also would be encouraged to use the resources located in a career center to identify additional careers that seem consistent with his interests and personality. Whatever direction he takes, he would benefit from brainstorming how to increase his enjoyment of his career and develop more satisfaction in his life.

In addition, the counselor could assist Darren in gaining skills that will help him acquire information to use when making career decisions. For instance, Darren might be encouraged to schedule several informational interviews with people employed in a variety of fields of interest to him. Prior to the interviews, the counselor and Darren could role-play and videotape a practice interview to assess his interpersonal interactions and self-presentation and to increase confidence and motivation for this task.

### The Termination of Career Counseling: Helping the Runaway Find His Way Home

Counseling would end once Darren has planned and taken action to move forward in his career, became independent from his parents and gained a satisfactory resolution to his divorce and custody arrangements. The counselor would process with Darren the changes that he made (and the work that needs to be done) to develop healthier relationships with others, enhance his self-esteem, and pursue a career direction. Through the expression of his feelings and thoughts and the discovery of insights, Darren has been challenged to recognize and act on his potential for a healthy, stable, self-sufficient and balanced life.

## References

Blustein, D.L. (1987). Integrating career counseling and psychotherapy: A comprehensive treatment strategy. *Psychotherapy, 24*, 794-799.

Blustein, D.L., & Spengler, P.M. (1995). Personal adjustment: Career counseling and psychotherapy. In W.B. Walsh & S.H. Osipow (Eds.), *Handbook of vocational psychology* (2nd ed., pp. 295-329). Hillsdale, NJ: Erlbaum.

Gottfredson, G.D., & Holland, J.L. (1989). *Dictionary of Holland occupational codes* (2nd ed.). Odessa, FL: Psychological Assessment Resources.

Gysbers, N.C., Heppner, M.J., & Johnston, J.A. (1998). *Career counseling: Process, issues, and techniques*. Boston, MA: Allyn & Bacon.

Heppner, M.J., O'Brien, K.M., Hinkelman, J.M., & Humphrey, C.F. (1994). Shifting the paradigm: The use of creativity in career counseling. *Journal of Career Development*, 21, 77-86.

Hill, C.E., & O'Brien, K.M. (1999). *Helping skills: Facilitating exploration, insight, and action*. Washington, DC: American Psychological Association.

Holland, J.L. (1985). *Making vocational choices: A theory of careers* (2nd ed.). Englewood Cliffs, NJ: Prentice Hall.

Lucas, M.S. (1993). Personal, social academic, and career problems expressed by minority college students. *Journal of Multicultural Counseling and Development, 21*(1), 2-13.

Myers, I.B., & McCaulley, M.H. (1985). *Manual: A guide to the development and use of the Myers-Briggs Type Indicator*. Palo Alto, CA: Consulting Psychologists Press.

Parsons, F. (1909). *Choosing a vocation*. Boston, MA: Houghton Mifflin.

## *Response to Darren: The Case of the Unemployed Runaway*
## *An Existential Approach to Career Counseling*
## *Larry D. Burlew*
## *University of Bridgeport*

Darren has reached midlife without a good sense of who he is and/or he isn't taking action based on what he does know. For example, he knows that his MBTI personality type is INFJ and may recall related INFJ characteristics like "succeed by perseverance, originality, and desire to do whatever is needed or wanted; quietly forceful, and conscientious" (Myers & McCaullery, 1990, p. 21). Similarly, he acknowledges his ARC occupational personality code and may recall related characteristics like being independent, duality of being unconventional and conventional, like to work outdoors, creating things with their hands, and stable, well-controlled, and dependable (Hansen & Campbell, 1985, p. 14). Additionally, he knows that he enjoys "creativity," but "dislikes structured work environments" and is anxious when "confronted with challenging tasks." He even acknowledges "feeling dissatisfied with his previous jobs." The moving around may be symptomatic of this dissatisfaction. I might hypothesize that moving around was Darren's struggle to find meaning in his life and, if so, then the moving strategy hasn't worked.

Additionally, Darren may not be accepting responsibility for his own actions. He talks about "his father being unsupportive of his artistic abilities," as if his ultimate satisfaction depended on his father's approval. This might indicate that he is not living in the moment, nor is he living authentically. More important, he is relying on his parents for his "sole source of financial support." This is another indication that he may not feel responsible for his own life and actions at this time. He seems to lack self-confidence because he gets anxious when "confronted with challenging tasks." This is a likely outcome for someone who is living inauthentically because he must rely on others' appraisal of his abilities and work products.

I would like more information on his beliefs about and his actions around his impending divorce. If he has a pattern of not taking responsibility and not taking action on available choices, then this pattern will affect his child support and custody issues. I would also like more information about (1) his work history, how he made his choices to accept various jobs, as well as to leave them; (2) his current relationship with his parents, soon-to-be ex-wife, and son; (3) any history of emotional disturbance (e.g., depression); (4) any history of counseling and how and when career assessment occurred (including what he recalls about his testing results); and (5) actions taken so far with regard to viable career options, his relationship with his parents, and providing for his son.

## Career Counseling Plan

I will use an existential approach to career counseling with Darren for several reasons. First, he has choices to make about his work and career that affect the immediate issue of child support for his son. He seems stuck and not freely making choices to change the situation since his parents seem "anxious" to see him move on. Therefore, at present, he's living a restricted existence because he's acting helpless, not choosing, and not acting to resolve his immediate situation. Second, as mentioned above, I suspect that Darren's moving around, leaving jobs and domiciles, and still feeling dissatisfied are indicators of his failed attempts to find meaning in his life. Thus, he might be experiencing anomic depression, a term Frank (1999) used to "describe the affective reaction to meaninglessness." Third, at 45 he still seems concerned about the way his parents treated him in the past and his belief that his father has been unsupportive. His perception might be that his parents are somehow responsible for his life situation today. He seems sensitive to criticism and has difficulty getting along with supervisors. Such beliefs might indicate that he is not taking responsibility for his own life and the consequences of the choices he makes, but is relying on the "Crowd's" (i.e., parents, supervisors) approval to feel whole or complete, suggesting that he's living inauthentically. Finally, he might be relating to his parents in "I-It" encounters rather than "I-Thou" because, although they seem to be supporting him, he still believes that he never got "what he needed" from them. Seeing a relationship as only "what it should give me" treats the other person(s) as objects or "Its." Relating to other human beings through "I-It" encounters might explain his divorce, as well as difficulties with supervisors.

The most important action I would take is to create a trusting, "I-Thou" relationship with Darren where Darren sees me as a helper and guide and himself as the "owner" and director of his life (Frank, 1999). Until Darren completely tells me his story, all statements mentioned above are only hypotheses. If they are confirmed, then I can confront the existential anxiety that comes from living a restricted existence, not making choices, living inauthentically, and existing in "I-It" relationships. Then, I would guide Darren in the following ways:

1. Help him live in the moment, not ruminate on the past, and see all the potential "projects" from his environment that he could choose to work on.
2. Help him prioritize the current projects that are having the most impact on his life. The major projects I see right now are being able to support himself and his child; re-examining his career and perhaps making a career transition; examining himself in relationships, with his parents, supervisors, son and perhaps wife; and getting through his divorce. Each project relates to one or more of the existential issues described above.

3. In order to take responsibility for himself and his son, Darren may need to find any job that provides support and allows him to pay child support. I would help him establish a monthly budget that would meet his basic needs, plus pay child support and then help him develop a job search plan to find a job that would support that budget.

4. Working on the larger issue of career options will help Darren reexamine aspects of "who he is" and assist him in his continual struggle to find meaning in his life. I would use Super's "Life-Span, Life-Space" model (Zunker, 1998), having him revisit those aspects of which he seems to be aware, such as personality (e.g., INFJ, ARC), employment practices, etc., and consider those aspects that he may not know as much about, like role self-concepts and peer group influence. From this assessment, I will help Darren develop a career plan involving both career and leisure options. Although he will include 1-year, 3-year, and 5-year goals, I will work with him on achieving the most immediate goals. Much of this work will focus on meaningful choices and supporting Darren while he takes action on his choices. In doing so, we will probably also examine his "failed" attempts at finding meaning in life and anomic depression if my assessment is correct.

5. From our work around getting a job and working on a career plan, we will most likely discuss his relationships with past supervisors. From this discussion, we will most likely get into the general area of how he relates to people, including his parents and perhaps his wife, from an "I-It" perspective rather than an "I-Thou" perspective. It will be important to help Darren "distinguish between a neurotically dependent attachment to another [like to his parents and supervisors] and a life-affirming relationship in which both persons are enhanced" (Corey, 1996, p. 176). Gaining self-awareness of his "I-It" encounters will improve any and all of Darren's relationships. Some strategies to help him accomplish this might be keeping a journal of his contacts with people, reflecting on his skills and behaviors when relating, and writing new scenarios using skills and behaviors leading to "I-Thou" encounters. Eventually, he will try out these new skills and behaviors with his parents and new supervisor(s). Additionally, I will reinforce his actions when he works with me in an "I-Thou" encounter. Finally, I will use some Morita Therapy (Burlew & Roland, 1999) strategies such as not reinforcing discussions about his parents not giving him "what he needed," but rather redirect those comments and ask questions like, "What are your parents giving you now? What can you give them in return?"

6. From the discussion about relationships, we will most likely deal with his tendency to live inauthentically, relying on the Crowd for acceptance of who he is. This is evident in his concern about his father never accepting him and his reaction to supervisors' criticism. Additionally, he has even lost faith in himself, feeling anxious when "confronted with challenging tasks." As Darren explores different facets of himself and different ways of being in relationships, I will help him identify "an internally derived value system that does provide a meaningful life" (Corey, 1996, p. 177). When he accomplishes this, I believe that he will find a meaningful work life, truly establish himself in some occupation, particularly as he develops a better relationship with supervisors, and take responsibility for his own choices.

7. Most likely, Darren's impending divorce will be processed as he becomes aware of his behavior in relationships. However, I will also help him see what choices he has regarding his divorce and continued relationship with his wife and help him take action on these choices. This, most likely, will also lead to discussions about the type of family life he wants to have with his son, thus creating a satisfying balance of the father and worker roles.

## Contextual Factors

Corey (1996) cautions that an existential counseling approach is "excessively individualistic, seeming to suggest that all changes can be made inside" (p. 191). There is a long history of oppression and discrimination in the workplace of ethnic-minority workers, women, homosexuals, and low-income individuals. These factors must be taken into account during the counseling process as realistic barriers to eventual achievement of one's career and life choices. Simply because a client becomes self-aware, is directed by his/her own values, and decides on meaningful directions doesn't mean society can be ignored. Rather, factors like the "glass ceiling" must be considered in action plans to implement choices; the client's skills to manage societal barriers must be assessed; and action plans must include steps to deal with any likely oppression and discrimination faced by the minority worker. The existential approach to career counseling must include a realistic appraisal of the effect that society has had on the client's career choices and progression within various work and life choices. However, this appraisal can easily be considered in existential career counseling through the concept of "Being-in-the-World," which simply means we exist and function in our environment and must realize that the environment, in turn, affects the eventual outcome of our choices.

## References

Burlew, L.D., & Roland, C. (1999). Eastern theories. In D. Capuzzi & D.R. Gross (Eds.), *Counseling & psychotherapy* (2nd ed., pp. 379-412). Upper Saddle River, NJ: Merrill.

Corey, G. (1996). *Theory and practice of counseling and psychotherapy* (5th ed.). Pacific Grove, CA: Brooks/Cole Publishing Co.

Frank, M.B. (1999). Existential theory. In D. Capuzzi & D.R. Gross (Eds.), *Counseling & psychotherapy* (2nd ed., pp. 151-178). Upper Saddle River, NJ: Merrill.

Hansen, J.C., & Campbell, D.P. (1985). *Manual for the Strong Interest Inventory* (4th ed.). Palo Alto, CA: Consulting Psychologists Press.

Myers, I.B., & McCaulley, M.H. (1990). *A guide to the development and use of the Myers-Briggs Type Indicator* (7th ed.). Palo Alto, CA: Consulting Psychologists Press.

Zunker, V.G. (1998). *Career counseling: Applied concepts of life planning* (5th ed.). Pacific Grove, CA: Brooks/Cole.

# MALAIKA: THE CASE OF THE EXPLORING BUS DRIVER

Malaika is a 58-year-old African American woman who works as a bus driver for an urban transit company. She has a high school diploma. She was married for 31 years when her husband requested a divorce 4 years ago. Currently, she does not have a partner and feels that this is a void in her life. She is, however, not sure how to meet people her age and is not interested in pursuing the most common avenues for meeting people (for example, church, civic group). Malaika prefers to dress in casual clothes (for example, jeans and t-shirts) and stated that she "never wears a dress." She is a heavy smoker and has smoked since the age of 15. Malaika has no siblings and her parents are deceased. Her father died 15 years ago from a heart attack and her mother died six years ago from Alzheimer's disease.

Malaika presented for career counseling because she felt as though she was "in a rut" and she was worried about what she would do in her retirement. Malaika stated that she had no other skills than those required to operate her bus. Her hobbies include reading (usually about animals), taking care of her pet, and fly-fishing. She stated, however, that she has recently had little interest in any of these activities. Malaika has limited financial resources and no savings.

Malaika stated that she was also concerned about her job security. Several of her closest friends at work had recently been laid off. Most of her remaining co-workers were significantly younger and Malaika felt as though she had little in common with them. She reported feeling depressed and alone. Although Malaika felt isolated, she also enjoyed the company of those who rode her bus each day. After work, Malaika typically returned home to watch television and spend time with her 12-year-old dog that she describes as her "best friend." She hopes to develop a plan for "the rest of her life."

## *Response to Malaika: The Case of the Exploring Bus Driver*
### *Twinet Parmer*
### *Central Michigan University*

"I have reached some sort of meridian in my life. I had better take a survey, reexamine where I have been, and reevaluate how I am going to spend my resources from now on…that there is a down side to life, a back side of the mountain, and I have only so much time before the dark to find my own truth" (Sheehy, 1976, p. 242).

### The Back Side of the Mountain

At first reading "Malaika: The Case of the Exploring Bus Driver" the above passage from Gail Sheehy's book came to mind. I reflected on the above description as it matched so well the point that Malaika had reached in her life. I imagined that Malaika had also reflected on her life in a similar way as evidenced by her statement that she "hopes to develop a plan for the rest of her life." Her statement provided some idea of how to begin conceptualizing her life in preparation for our meeting. I reflected on Super's words "that counselors should be 'ambiverts' who turn either way or to any point on the compass and meet client needs" (1993, p. 135). Desiring to be a good counselor and thus an "ambivert," I would offer several perspectives to counseling Malaika.

My approach is based on my belief that career is personal and thus would play a critical role in her desire to plan all aspects of her life. As Malaika explores her many life roles and future challenge of constructing new roles, I would work with her in understanding what Savickas (1993) terms her "subjective career, that is life story" (p. 213). Savickas noted as counselors explore meaning with their clients, "career counseling [becomes] much more similar to personal counseling and psychotherapy" (p. 212). In addition to exploring personal meaning in career, I would work with Malaika from a perspective of holistic wellness (Myers, Emmerling, & Leafgren, 1992; Witmer, 1985), which lends itself to an emphasis on her cultural context. Parmer (1996) noted that one's life is contingent upon a number of holistic wellness variables that are very often manifested within the context of culture. This process acknowledges the interdependence of the whole person and a sense of well-being that is manifested in the person's lifestyle (Parmer & Rogers, 1997, p. 58). Betz and Corning (1993) discussed how the concept of the "whole person" is an emphasis in many of the career theories particularly in themes of love, work, friendships, relationships, etc.

Thus, considering that Malaika is at a meridian, and I have my compass, I would explore her lifestyle from a cultural context by attending to her perceptions of her life roles and lifestyle as an African American woman. Lifestyle is significant because as Zunker (1990) noted "incorporating dimensions of lifestyle addresses important career-planning factors that might otherwise be ignored" (p.83). This is significant given that there are no theories of career development that explain Malaika's experiences (Hackett & Byars, 1996; Brown, 1995).

## A Meridian and a Compass

Prior to meeting Malaika I felt somewhat apprehensive as I wondered how she would relate to me. Although we are both African American females, I was cognizant that all counseling is multicultural and thus we bring differing experiences and perspectives to the process. I attempted to anticipate what to expect and visualize what might take place at our first meeting especially as it relates to her affect and demeanor. Information presented in the case caused me to wonder about who she was and how her identities had been formed over the life span. My initial reaction to Malaika was the many personal roles she was grappling with in her life. Super (1980) noted that we play a number of life roles at the same time, each having a different degree of satisfaction. I was struck by her multiple life roles and identities and how these statuses may be affecting her life and career. For example, her status based on her gender, race, divorce, depression, lack of resources, and a job that places her as working class could all potentially be a source for multiple oppressions (Reynolds & Pope, 1991). I was also struck by the fact that Malaika at one time enjoyed hobbies and loved animals. I wondered about her family of origin and extended family relationships – whether she had grieved the death of her parents and her marriage, how her physical features such as her height, skin color, degree of aging, etc., would affect her self-concept (Brown, 1995). How did she want to achieve her life plans? I felt that these lifestyle questions were relative to sculpting a picture of Malaika's career decisions and her life plan.

Initially, I would ask Malaika to tell her life story and career story as a means of making meaning out of her existence. It would be important to ask what she expects to achieve from counseling and how she arrived at the decision to come in at the present time. In working with Malaika, I would be aware that holistic wellness involves examining her background relative to how she explains her life experiences from a social, spiritual, occupational, psychological, emotional, environmental, financial, sexual, and intellectual perspective. For example, some of the lifestyle questions that I might explore with Malaika are as follows:

- Social – Tell me about your family and other social relationships. To whom are you connected? Who would you identify as support systems in your life?
- Spiritual – What is meaningful in your life? What have you done to connect to others?
- Occupational – What jobs have you held? What would be your fantasy job? What type of work would you find meaningful? Who were your role models?
- Psychological – How would you describe yourself? Who are you? If you were to choose an animal that describes you, what characteristics would it possess?
- Emotional – How do you experience sorrow, joy, fear in your life? When was there a happy time in your life? Explain the role of hobbies in your life.

- Sexual – How do you experience and live life as it relates to being a woman? How have the various types of intimacy been demonstrated in your life? In your marriage or other relationships? What is important for you in a relationship?
- Environmental – Where do you live? Where did you grow up? What community resources do you have that lend themselves to your meeting people?
- Physical – Are you in good health? How much do you smoke? Eat? How much do you exercise? How attractive/unattractive do you feel? Did you ever have concerns about your body image?
- Financial – What financial resources do you have? How are you planning for retirement? What are your short- and long-term goals?
- Educational – What is your level of education? What additional training have you had? What skills do you have? Have you considered obtaining additional education or training?
- Intellectual – How well do you think and reason? Do you feel smart? How would you describe your school experiences?

After listening to the holistic themes in Malaika's stories, the goal would be to create a life plan that allows her voice to be heard from multiple perspectives. According to Savickas (1993), "the idea of counseling about life structure accommodates multiple perspectives" (p. 211). The specific goals for this plan would involve the examination of her personal and career issues as follows:

- Assist Malaika in understanding and exploring depression, isolation, and being "in a rut."
- Assist Malaika in exploring the lack of interpersonal relationships, which is indicated by the fact that she has no friends, no partner, retreats from other people, and describes her dog as her "best friend."
- Assist Malaika in addressing issues of grief and loss such as her marriage, recent divorce, and the death of her parents.
- Assist Malaika in exploring the results of the Beck Depression Inventory (Stenhouwer, 1985), and the Optimal Theory Applied to Identity Development Model (OTAID) in order to assess her life identity development (Myers, Speight, Highlen, Cox, Reynolds, Adams, & Hanley, 1991).
- Assist Malaika in exploring common occupations based on the results of the Strong Interest Inventory (Harmon, Hansen, Borgen, & Hammer, 1994).
- Assist Malaika in identifying and selecting occupational alternatives and the necessary educational and training requirements.
- Assist Malaika in evaluating and planning for retirement by assessing her values, skills, and abilities.

## Finding Her Own Truth

Being mindful that the personal is an important aspect of career counseling, the following issues are important in Malaika's life plan. At this point I would engage Malaika in some interpretation of her stories and the assessment tools. In interpreting her stories, it is essential that Malaika understand the question of "Who am I?" relative to being an African American woman. The OTAID will be used as a process to gain self-knowledge in the quest to a positive self-identity. Myers et al. (1991) noted that "with this [self] knowledge, individuals can integrate all aspects of being (e.g., age, color, ethnicity, and size) into a holistic sense of self" (p. 58). As a culturally sensitive therapist, I understand that, in addition to gender and related issues common to all women, African American women are confronted with additional barriers in society and the world of work. Brown (1995) supported this contention for African American women by stating that "skin tone was found to be a stronger predictor of occupation and income than background characteristics such as socioeconomic status" (p. 18).

In interpreting her stories she would find some association between her divorce, the death of her parents, and feeling alone and isolated. I would assist her in understanding that she had not grieved and take her through a process that would help her explore how the pain has bogged her down "in a rut." I would interpret the level of depression on the Beck Depression Inventory as moderate to severely depressed (a score in the range of 20-29). I would inform her that depression in African Americans is likely to go undiagnosed (Mitchell & Herring, 1998). I would find some association in her life between depression, self-esteem, and the lack of relationships. She would understand that to be holistically well she must be in relationships that are at the center of human experiences. Thus, Malaika would learn to meet people and perhaps come to appreciate some of the common avenues for meeting people such as church, book clubs, organizations, or even volunteering. She would also be encouraged to expand her social circle by attending a group for divorced women or a relationship group. I am guessing that after working on self-esteem issues she will want to change her image and be more versatile in her attire. The case specifically stated that Malaika was a heavy smoker. Although not stated, given her sedentary lifestyle, I would be concerned about her diet, nutrition, and weight. Finally, I would encourage her to seek out lost kin or relatives as it is unlikely that she is as alone as she describes herself. It is possible that her perception of aloneness is a function of her recent crises.

Given that I have no idea about where to go with Malaika relative to her specific career goals, the results of the Strong Interest Inventory should provide direction for exploring her interests. This should also be insightful for Malaika given that she probably has never thought of planning and discussing a career, nor has she been exposed to various occupations. I would hypothesize that Malaika would find interest in the R-Theme occupations, but additional information is necessary to determine other score combinations. As we explored her interest and congruency with various occupations, I would expect that Malaika would be able to identify work environments that are consistent with her personality and interests. I would find Super's (1980) decision-making process useful in examining her career behavior. The cyclical nature of the process allows her to achieve maximum benefit in the career exploration process until she has found her interest and stabilized. Further, the process is consistent with the goal of exploring her experiences holistically because the process accounts for various combinations of life roles, lifestyle, life space, and life cycle (Super, 1980). Through the career decision-making process, Malaika may want to prepare for another occupation that satisfies her interests. Once she has settled on several occupations it is necessary to consider if there is a requisite for education and training. She may also be encouraged to volunteer in a setting that reflects her personal or career interest, such as caring for animals.

At this point she may also be encouraged to assess her level of commitment to her current job. She might also be encouraged to talk with the authorities at the transit company regarding her retirement benefits. In this society we often encourage individuals to retire early and even start a second career; however, Malaika may not have that option because of her age, number of years of service, or her financial resources. I was also mindful that if she were to retire at this time, she might potentially be setting herself up for other crises related to finances, isolation, etc. In preparation for future retirement, I would have Malaika assess her abilities and personal goals and outline strategies for how she would want to live out the balance of her life. These strategies may include activities such as attending money management seminars, consulting a financial planner, volunteering, or seeking out career role models.

## The Front Side of the Mountain

At this point both Malaika and I can fully appreciate the meaning of the Sheehy passage. I would imagine that we both would equate the "Front Side of the Mountain" with Malaika finding her own truth. Therefore, as Malaika continues to explore the question of "Who am I?" and remains cognizant of how the associated multiple identities affect her holistically, her own truth will unfold. This process will foster growth and assist her in evaluating strengths and weaknesses, skills and abilities, as she crystallizes her life plan. As a part of this plan her career story will be told, and through a process of exploration she will examine her lifestyle and understand that relationships and work are at the center of one's human existence.

## References

Betz, N.E. & Corning, A.F. (1993). The inseparability of "career" and "personal" counseling. *Career Development Quarterly, 42*, 137-142.

Brown, M.T. (1995).The career development of African Americans: Theoretical and empirical issues. In F.T.L. Leong (Ed.), *Career development and vocational behavior of racial and ethnic minorities*. Mahwah, NJ: Erlbaum.

Hackett, G. & Byars, A.M. (1996). Social cognitive theory and the career development of African American women. *Career Development Quarterly, 44*, 322-323.

Harmon, L., Hansen, J.I., Borgen, F., & Hammer, A. (1994). *Strong Interest Inventory*. Palo Alto, CA: Consulting Psychologists Press.

Mitchell, A. & Herring, K. (1998). *What the blues is all about – Black women overcoming stress and depression*. New York: Perigee Books.

Myers, L.J., Speight, S.L., Highlen, P.S., Cox, C.I., Reynolds, A.L., Adams, E.M., & Hanley, C.P. (1991). Identity development and worldview: Toward an optimal conceptualization. *Journal of Counseling and Development, 70*, 54-63.

Parmer, T. (1996). Holistic model of counseling: Don't go into the room without it. Unpublished manuscript. Columbus, OH: The Ohio State University.

Parmer, T. & Rogers, T. (1997). Religion and health: Holistic wellness from the perspective of two African American church denominations. *Counseling and values, 42*(1), 55-67.

Reynolds, A.L. & Pope, R.L. (1991). The complexities of diversity: Exploring multiple oppressions. *Journal of Counseling and Development, 70*, 174-180.

Savickas, M. (1993). Career counseling in the postmodern era. *Journal of Cognitive Psychotherapy: An International Quarterly, 7*, 205-215.

Sheehy, G. (1976). *Passages*. New York: E.P. Dutton.

Stenhouwer, S. (1980). Beck Depression Inventory. In *Test critiques II* (pp. 83-87). Kansas City, MO: Test Corporation of America.

Super, D.E. (1980). A life-span, life-space approach to career development. *Journal of Vocational Behavior, 16*, 282-298.

Super, D.E. (1993). The two faces of counseling: Or is it three? *Career Development Quarterly, 42*, 132-136.

Witmer, J.M. (1985). *Pathways to personal growth*. Muncie, IN: Accelerated Development.

Zunker, V.G. (1990). *Career counseling: Applied concepts of life planning.* Pacific Grove, CA: Brooks/Cole.

# Response to Malaika: The Case of the Exploring Bus Driver
## Courtland C. Lee
## University of Maryland

### Case Analysis

The image formed of Malaika is of a person approaching the end of a productive work life, in a somewhat nontraditional job for a woman, who is concerned about the next phase of her life-span development – retirement. The nature of her depression appears readily apparent. Although she feels that she is "in a rut," it is evident that she is concerned about what she will do with her life when she leaves the routine of her bus route. The fear of being without a job and alone is very real to Malaika.

Given the number of limitations in her life – education, social relationships, perceived skills, leisure time interests, and financial resources, the routine of her job appears to be the cornerstone of her life. It appears that a significant amount of her current social validation comes from her interactions with the people who ride her bus each day. There is a sense of a real fear on Malaika's part of growing old, with little to do, and her dog her only companion.

In forming this image of Malaika, it is necessary to conceptualize her as an individual within a sociocultural context (Lee, 1997). Malaika is a woman, 58 years of age, African American, with a working-class background. It is important to remember that these multiple and multidimensional cultural realities all have a degree of impact on her identity. Each of these realities, to varying degrees, account for how Malaika thinks, feels, and behaves.

These multiple aspects of culture also make imperative that possible issues of sexism, ageism, racism, and classism be factored into the counseling equation with Malaika. The concept of a culturally responsive career intervention with Malaika rests on understanding her as a person within such a sociocultural context.

### Directions for Career Counseling with Malaika

The challenge for counseling with Malaika becomes how to help her become empowered to develop the plan for the rest of her life that she has stated that she wants. This plan will build on her current interests and possibly expand her social interactions and promote a degree of financial security and physical well-being.

Prior to work on any such plan, however, there are a number of questions I would seek to answer that would provide me with a more complete picture of Malaika and her concerns. First, I would want to assess the depth and extent of her depression. How long has she been feeling depressed? Is her depression the reason she has lost interest in her hobbies? Has her depression interfered with her job? Will her depression interfere with her ability to work on the stated goal?

Second, I would want to know more about her divorce. Was it an amicable one? Is she still in contact with her former husband? If so, what is the nature of that contact?

Third, since she is not sure how to meet people and is not interested in making new contacts through church or civic groups, what has she done up to this point to meet people? I would be interested in any attempts, no matter how minimal, she has made to increase her social interaction.

Fourth, I would be interested in her overall health, given her smoking history and behavior. Since she is a 58-year-old African American woman with a history of heavy smoking who has lost a parent to a heart attack, I would be most interested in knowing whether she is at possible risk for cardiovascular problems. Cardiovascular disease is a major health problem for African Americans.

Fifth, given the current layoffs at the bus company, I would want to know about Malaika's job status. Any indication that she is to be laid off would certainly dictate the focus of any career intervention.

Sixth, in a somewhat related vein, I would want to get some indication of the nature of the retirement benefits that Malaika can expect to receive for her tenure with the bus company. Since she has limited financial resources and no savings, such information will be very important in helping her develop a plan for the rest of her life.

Finally, given its age and the fact that she has proclaimed it to be her "best friend," I would want to know something about the health of Malaika's dog. Pets can play a vital role in the health and well being of their owners. Therefore, it would be important to find out how long she can reasonably expect to have this important source of companionship.

Counseling with Malaika would be framed within a cognitive-behavioral intervention context. My primary goal would be to help Malaika become empowered to get out of her rut and make some post-retirement plans (i.e., a plan for "the rest of her life"). Empowerment is a developmental process by which people who are generally powerless or marginalized in some manner become aware of the power dynamics at work in their lives. They then develop the skills and capacity for gaining a degree of control over their lives (McWhirter, 1994).

From a generational and cultural perspective, it may be important at the outset to gain Malaika's trust and allay her fears about "putting her business in the street." As a 58-year-old women with a limited education and financial resources, Malaika could be representative of a generation and socio-economic strata of African Americans that is often suspicious of mental health and related professionals. This is due, in large measure, to the fact that the only counseling many African Americans in her age cohort have often received has been a forced, rather than voluntary, experience with a culturally insensitive or unresponsive agent of the broad social welfare system (Lee, in press).

I would attempt, therefore, to get Malaika to see me as a person first and a professional second. I would adopt an interpersonal approach, initially focused more on the relationship between the two of us rather then any specific counseling goals (Gibbs, 1980). I would engage Malaika in conversation about a variety of nonthreatening issues (e.g., her dog, fly-fishing, the route her bus travels, etc.).

As Malaika begins to reveal her feelings about her retirement worries, her depression, and loneliness, it would be important for me to allow Malaika to "tell her story." As her story unfolds, I would work to elicit a commitment to counseling from Malaika.

This would be the point at which empowerment work begins. Within an existential framework (Lee, 1999; Pack-Brown, Whittington-Clark & Parker, 1998; Vontress, Johnson, & Epp, 1999), I would begin by encouraging Malaika to explore meaning in her life. I would ask her to consider how she sees herself as a human being, a woman, and an African American. I might ask what meaning being an African American woman has for her. I would encourage Malaika to consider what gives her life meaning as an African American woman.

As meaning and purpose in her life become more focused, I would help Malaika to see the interrelatedness of her challenges. She is concerned about impending retirement because it could bring possible financial insecurity as well as increased loneliness and isolation. She is uncertain, and possibly, unskilled in how to increase her social interactions. All of this contributes to her feelings of depression and isolation.

At this point, it is time to engage Malaika in "taking care of business" by helping her develop a plan of action for the "rest of her life." I would explore with her the possibility of dividing this plan into a series of steps that would create a context for her impending new career – her post-bus driving life. I would want to ensure that Malaika's goal is actually to get out of her perceived rut. I would suggest that her first step is to deal with her job situation. I would encourage her to inquire about her job status with the bus company. It will be important for her to ascertain whether there are plans to lay her off prior to her scheduled retirement. The answer to this will determine whether Malaika and

I engage in long-range planning or a short-term problem-solving process focusing on immediate economic necessities.

The second step would be to help her find a financial consultant who can help her engage in some fiscal planning. This could help her cope with the challenges of her limited monetary resources. It is important to her ongoing life planning that Malaika achieve some peace of mind with respect to money and her future.

Step three in the planning process would involve helping Malaika examine her feelings about filling the void in her life brought about by her divorce. Together, we might explore alternative and creative ways of meeting people given her casual style as well as her interest in animals and fly-fishing. It would be important that I encourage her to take risks in "stepping out" to meet new people in creative ways and venues.

Given that she is a heavy smoker, I would encourage Malaika to make addressing health issues an important priority in her life plan. Because she is African American, over age 55, lost her father to a heart attack, smokes heavily, and appears to be relatively inactive physically, Malaika has a combination of both unchangeable and changeable risk factors for cardiovascular problems. It would be important for me to help her to see that part of becoming empowered and exploring meaning in her life would be to take steps to ensure her physical health. Although she can do nothing to change her race, age, or genetics, an important aspect of her life plan might include developing the skills to address health risk factors that she does have the power to change, such as heavy smoking.

## Conclusion

I would consider my work with Malaika a success if she terminated counseling with a sense of hope about herself and her future. This sense of hope would be manifested in an action plan that would empower her to take the steps to get out of her perceived rut. Her plan should provide her with opportunities to step outside of herself and ensure new and unique social relationships and financial peace of mind for an interesting and active retirement.

## References

Gibbs, J.T. (1980). The interpersonal orientation in mental health consultation: Toward a model of ethnic variations in consultation. *Journal of Community Psychology, 8*, 195-207.

Lee, C.C. (1999). Counseling African American men. In L.E. Davis (Ed*.). Working with African American males*. Thousand Oaks, CA: Sage.

Lee, C.C. (Ed.). (1997). *Multicultural issues in counseling: New approaches to diversity.* (2nd ed.). Alexandria, VA: American Counseling Association.

Lee, C.C. (In Press). Counseling African Americans. In R.L. Jones (Ed.), *Black Psychology* (4th ed.). Hampton, VA: Cobb & Henry.

McWhirter, E.H. (1994). *Counseling for empowerment*. Alexandria, VA: American Counseling Association.

Pack-Brown, S.P., Whittington-Clark, L.E. & Parker, W.M. (1998). *Images of me: A guide to group work with African American women*. Boston, MA: Allyn & Bacon.

Vontress, C.E., Johnson, J.A. & Epp, L.R. (Eds.). (1999). *Cross-cultural counseling: A casebook*. Alexandria, VA: American Counseling Association. (ERIC Document Reproduction Service No. ED 429 246).

# SAMUEL: THE CASE OF THE CONFUSED CEO

The counselor looked up in surprise as Samuel entered the room. An expensively dressed Caucasian man of about 60, he radiated confidence and power. From his haircut to his shoes, this man was the personification of the successful business leader, likely to be the CEO of a major corporation, have his picture in the social pages of the newspaper, and sit on philanthropic boards. Indeed, the counselor thought he looked familiar, perhaps from seeing his picture in the newspaper.

But as Samuel started to speak, the counselor realized that his story was a familiar one. Although he obviously was not desperate for money, he was desperate for something meaningful to do with his life. Samuel had indeed been a CEO of a rather large company. When his company was acquired recently in a hostile takeover, Samuel and most of the rest of the top executives were let go. When Samuel hinted to others he knew in the business world that he was interested in employment, the response was always to enjoy the leisure, travel, and play more golf, "while you are still young."

But that was the problem. Samuel felt that he was too young to stop working. He enjoyed the sense of being productive, of making a difference, of doing. He enjoyed putting on a suit and tie – he never liked the casual Friday trend – and going to an office where he had influence and prestige. He felt that all of that had been lost, and although he still looked the part, he felt like a lost little boy, with nowhere to go and no one to play with. Furthermore, his wife was still working at a job she loved, so extensive travel at least for now was out of the question. The mortgage on their house in an expensive suburb was paid off and they had substantial investments, so money was not an issue.

Samuel's informal network informed him that he was too old and too highly paid to be considered for an average executive position. He had an MBA obtained 35 years ago and no particular technical expertise. Although a man of action, with an optimistic and positive outlook, he was stumped. Coming to a career counselor was an act of desperation for him – asking for help was not in his usual repertoire, but his wife had insisted he do something besides mope and suggest ways for her to better organize her work.

Beyond his work as a manager and a casual interest in current events, Samuel's only outlets were golf and reading. But even these last two had always centered on his work life. He really did not know what he liked to do.

## *Response to Samuel: The Case of the Confused CEO*
## *Vance Peavy*
## *University of Victoria, Canada*

As a counselor responding to Samuel, I am guided by a generally constructivist frame of reference (Sexton & Griffin, 1997; Young, 1997). My constructivist assumptions, descriptions and suggested practical procedures are outlined in *SocioDynamic Counseling: A Constructivist Perspective* (Peavy, 1999).

My first assumption is that Samuel has more knowledge about his own life than I or anyone else will ever have. The most important knowledge I can gain about Samuel will come from him – directly without mediation through testing or other "assessment" devices. I must be willing to be "taught" by him. He is the expert on his own life – even though he may not be able to articulate this knowledge in a coherent and forthcoming manner.

My expertise as counselor lies in my ability to provide a communication framework within which he and I can together investigate, clarify, and reveal the issues he is facing. This communication framework is one that is best described as dialogical in the Bakhtian sense (Wertsch, 1998). This means that I recognize the multi-voicedness of Samuel and that I discern and respond to the voiced selves of Samuel for they are the "primary data" sources with which we have to work. It is an assumption of constructivist thought that we humans are autopoetic or self-creating – we literally author and co-author ourselves. From a constructivist perspective, the self cannot be reduced to here-and-now, observable variables and traits but can be reconstructed through storytelling (assembling memories and projections into patterns of meaning). A perception of life-as-authoring (Kozulin, 1998) helps change the focus of counseling from efficiency and solution seeking to tolerance for ambiguity and problem re-creation. What kind of life has this man authored? What are the leads to future lives that he may wish to author? How can he and I engage in re-authoring?

From a dialogical point of view, I assume that "seed-answers" to these questions already lie in Samuel's life experience. Our counseling conversation must allow and promote the telling and re-telling of his nuance life stories. Our co-investigation of his life-narratives will articulate the various issues that Samuel is facing at this point in his life. Further, our dialogical conversation will be revelatory of many of the assumptions underlying those issues and the implications that the issues singly, and in combination, have for Samuel in his efforts to author forward movement in life and to create a future he prefers.

As a constructivist career counselor, a second assumption that guides me is that Samuel and I must work together in a co-constructive manner. We are partners – although we are almost certainly not equal in all respects. We will have had differing life experiences, hold differing values, lead different lifestyles, and may be guided by differing cultural assumptions. Yet we are most likely to co-construct and locate valuable pathways to the future for Samuel to take if we work hand in hand with respect for each other's ability to make valuable contributions to the counseling process. As a constructivist counselor it is incumbent on me to hold an unwavering attitude of authentic respect for Samuel as the person he is and toward his life experience.

The ways in which Samuel can move forward toward his preferred future is a matter for us to co-construct and not an occasion for me to diagnose, interpret, or recommend plans, choices, options, or impose lifestyles which I hold as preferred from my stance as professional counselor. The following scenario suggests how Samuel and I would proceed in our cooperative efforts to find meaningful ways for Samuel to move forward in his life.

The first step in our counseling encounter is to construct some *common ground*. I must have some credibility in Samuel's eyes and I must see him with "fresh eyes" as the person he presents, and not as I expect or theorize him to be. I do my best to present a *human face* that expresses my preoriginal ethical responsibility for the other. A human face shows care, not officialdom; a sense of "we," not the narcissism of an expert "I"; a sense of moral responsibility to the other, not the alienating force of objectification. Common ground usually arises from the finding of life experiences with which both counselor and other can resonate. It also arises from the felt experience of being in the presence of another who unambiguously listens, who respects another as another *is*, and who extends a cooperative, morally responsible hand to another for the purpose of finding and constructing hopeful futures. Samuel and I find common ground in our shared similarity of lives spanning six decades, in both having had to face difficult and ambiguous situations, and of our common realization that "no man is an island."

With our feet upon common ground, I ask Samuel if he is willing to *map* his *life-space*. The term "life-space" refers to an experiential, symbolic space that an individual inhabits. It "contains" all of the meaningful elements of the person's life. It is also a means of describing the coordination of activities and relationships in a person's life. Inspired by Kurt Lewin's (1948) concept of "social space," I use life-space in place of personality or self.

Mapping refers to the creation of a visual map of the person, the person's concern(s), the other people implicated in the concern together with their relationships with the person, and other meaningful phenomena which the person claims to be in some way connected with the topic of concern (Peavy, 1997). The making (drawing) of a map is a cooperative exercise with the counselor posing meaning-generating questions and the other filling in meaningful life-experience details. Mapping is accompanied by inquisitive dialogue that is at once empathic and deconstructive – uncovering underlying assumptions while building up a taken-as-shared body of meaningful understandings between counselor and other. In a sense a map is a visual form of a person's life story or some portion of it. Dialogue and mapping are the most important tools in the counselor's repertory. These two activities enable counselor and other to teach and learn from each other what is needed to begin formulating projects related to actualizing the other's desires for a future.

When Samuel and I have constructed a life-space map, we can begin to see what possible sources of meaning lie in his future, and we can see how these are grounded in earlier life experiences. What we have done is to cooperatively assess his existential situation, and we have done it in a manner that points to various future options.

The next step in our work together is to identify or invent several "personally meaningful projects" that Samuel is able to carry out and that will move him forward toward one or several futures. As Samuel and I co-examine his map we can see several "rich points" that are meaning-invested for him. We pick out three: (1) a fund-raising venture that a nearby golf club is about to undertake, (2) a horticulture center call for volunteers to work in some new gardens being planned, and (3) worry over prostate cancer. One of Samuel's close friends in seriously ill with advanced prostate cancer. Each of these topics has a clear interest for Samuel so he is interested in forming a project in relation to each.

A fundamental assumption of SocioDynamic Counseling is that people change and move on in life by means of activities that they find meaningful and that they have the capacity to carry out. A person is construed as an actor or agent and action/activity implies meaning, purpose, and motive. As Sartre pointed out, it is by our acts that we become who we are. Samuel selects the golf course and prostate cancer as projects that he would like to undertake immediately. We discuss what he might actually do and make up a working plan. With reference to his personal project on prostate cancer, he agrees on three actions. First he will make an appointment with his own physician and arrange to have a PSA test. Second, he will start an Internet search to find out what kinds of knowledge about prostate cancer he can accumulate by web search. Third, he will then undertake a supporting role with his friend. Together these three actions constitute a *personal project* that has a strong meaning and interest for Samuel.

On the second project, Samuel says that he already knows the members of the golf club committee who are discussing a fund-raising strategy, but he knows them only as fellow golfers. He believes that he might be able to use his ability and help in the formulation of a successful strategy for fund-raising. He says that he can call the secretary of the club and find out when the committee is meeting and what he should do to get involved. We discuss several possible contributions he might make and agree together that this is project which he would find meaningful and which would allow to him to use some of his business acumen. He makes some notes on both projects and we agree to meet in two weeks to see how he is making out on them. He remarks that he will take his "map" home and discuss it with his wife so that she too can understand him.

In this short scenario I have briefly described a portion of the SocioDynamic vocabulary: "common ground," "human face," "life-space," "mapping," "dialogical conversation," "personal project," and "cooperative relationship." Each of these is regarded as a *cultural tool* in SocioDynamic counseling. From this perspective, counseling is viewed as a cultural practice in which counselor and other use sensible cultural tools to explore ambiguities and construct projects that enable movement toward preferred futures. The focus of constructivist counseling is not on therapy – persons experiencing career or work concerns have nothing to be cured of – and is directed toward meaningful activities that increase the person's eligibility to participate in social life.

One final note. You may have noticed that I have not used the term "client." This is in keeping with a desire not to objectify the other. The conventional meanings of client include dependent, one who has someone to lean on; a person under the protection of another; one who gets advice from another; customer. I wish to avoid all of these meanings. Therefore, when referring to persons who are seeking counseling I use terms such as "help-seeker," "other," "another," or "person" since I regard words as extremely important cultural tools and I wish to refer to those seeking counseling in non-pejorative ways.

## References

Kozulin, A. (1998). *Psychological tools: A sociocultural approach to education.* Cambridge, MA: Harvard University Press.

Lewin, K. (1948). *Resolving social conflicts.* New York: Harper and Row.

Peavy, R.V. (1997). A constructive framework for career counseling. In T.L. Sexton & B.L. Griffin, (Eds.), *Constructivist thinking in counseling practice, research and training* (pp. 122-140). New York: Teachers College Press.

Peavy, R.V. (1999). *SocioDynamic counselling: A constructivist perspective.* Victoria, BC: Trafford Publishers.

Sexton, T.L. & Griffin, B.L. (Eds.) (1997). *Constructivist thinking in counseling practice, research and training.* New York: Teachers College Press.

Wertsch, J.V. (1998). *Mind as action.* New York: Oxford University Press.

Young, G. (1997). *Adult development, therapy, and culture: A postmodern synthesis.* New York: Plenum.

# *Response to Samuel: The Case of the Confused CEO*
## *Howard Splete*
## *Oakland University*

In career counseling, I believe the counselor must first assess the current situation of the client. The client's needs should be identified and goals set. In discussing my role and the counseling process, I make it clear to the client that I expect them to be willing to take some action steps to reach their goals as established in our session. I describe my role as one of a questioning and clarifying person who helps the client to identify their strengths and use them as a basis for establishing realistic goals. I am involved in helping them determine possible actions, including providing my own suggestions, yet stress they must choose their actions and take responsibility for them.

Based on the information provided about Samuel, I got an image of a successful confident person based on his physical appearance, clothing, and air of self-importance. From the first part of our conversation, which dealt with his being unemployed, I saw him as a frustrated man with time on his hands and no outlet for his energy. I interpreted his comments about his wanting to be employed as his need to be productive and respected.

After this first sharing of background information, I asked Samuel if we could structure the counseling procedure. I gave him an overview of my qualifications, including professional education and training, credentials as a nationally certified career counselor, and career counseling experience. He was informed of the fee structure and asked if this situation was appropriate for him.

I then outlined what I saw as the process and content of this first session. We began with the statement of his goal and mine for the meeting. Samuel repeated his desire to investigate reemployment possibilities. I said my approach would be to discuss with him his past, including his most satisfying experiences in work, schooling and other activities with a focus on his positive contact with others. This approach reflects Super's (1990) recognition of the importance of various life roles and Krumboltz's Social Learning Theory (Mitchell & Krumboltz, 1990) that speaks to one's positive learning experiences as affecting career choices and activities. After discussing his past experiences, I explained we would come up with some implications for possible action on his part. Samuel agreed that we could outline some action steps and he would choose some to do before our next session.

I suggested that it might be helpful for him to review times and events in his life experiences when he felt productive and meaningful. Some his responses included being recognized as an outstanding student in both his undergraduate and graduate school work, helping a United Fund campaign exceed a projected quota, seeing his company expand their product line and profits through his directives, helping young executives in his firm learn the ropes and mentoring them, discussing business possibilities with colleagues from other companies while playing in a business-affiliated golf league, working on some National Alliance of Business programs, and working with a local university in setting up internships and cooperative educational programs for top students.

After I asked him what he saw as common traits or patterns from these positive experiences, Samuel responded that he still wanted to be involved in the field of business and work with others who would take his advice and direction. I added that he seemed to be interested in helping younger people get established in their positions and companies. He agreed and said he had much knowledge to share from his extensive experience. I felt that my approach throughout the session had been one of positive support (Niles, 1996) that would help Samuel to be more confident about his next steps to return to the working environment.

We then discussed possible actions on his part that would relate to his need for respect and provide an opportunity for him to share his expertise. These possibilities included speaking to others who had also left his company about their desire to form a consulting group to work with similar businesses; contacting university officials with whom he had worked on cooperative projects about involvement with them in coordinating this type of program or possibly teaching some business courses; and speaking to staff from the National Alliance of Business about working as a mentor to new business organizations or as a coordinator of School to Work programs. He agreed these were all possible for him to do.

After reviewing these options, Samuel said his first preference would be to direct his former colleagues in a consulting firm. He also said he would like to explore options at the university. Although the possibilities at the National Alliance for Business seemed interesting to him, he said he would like to pursue the first two options first. I asked him how he would go about doing these things. Samuel planned to call three of his most respected past co-workers and invite them to a luncheon to discuss the consulting firm. I asked when and where and he gave me a projected date and place. He then said he would call the contact he had at the university and set up a meeting with her. Samuel said this would be done by our next scheduled session, which would be in two weeks. We concluded our session with a firm handshake during which Samuel thanked me for my time and said, "You can call me Sam."

## References

Mitchell, L.K, & Krumboltz, J.D. (1990). Social learning approach to career decision making: Krumboltz's Theory. In D. Brown, L. Brooks & Associates. *Career Choice and development. Applying contemporary theories to practice*, (2nd ed., pp. 145-196). San Francisco, CA: Jossey-Bass.

Niles, S.G. (1996). Offering appraisal support within career counseling. *Journal of Employment Counseling, 33*, 163-173.

Super, D.E. (1990). A life-span, life-space approach to career development. In D. Brown, L. Brooks & Associates. *Career choice and development: Applying contemporary theories to practice*, (2nd ed., pp. 197-261). San Francisco, CA: Jossey-Bass.

# APPENDIX A
## GUIDELINES FOR CASE RESPONDENTS

I.    Construct a response to three sets of questions:

    A.    What image did you form of the person? What other information would you seek to learn about the client and his/her problems?

    B.    What plans for career counseling would you propose to the client? What direct actions or interventions would you take if you were the counselor? What theoretical models would be the basis for your interventions?

    C.    Please include in your response relevant comments pertaining to how contextual factors (e.g., culture, socioeconomic status, gender) might influence your responses to A and B above.

II.   Write a summary of your response and supply your rationale.

    A.    The response may be organized in any way as long as the three question sets are addressed.

    B.    Your response should be 5-6 double-spaced typewritten pages in length (not including references) and in APA style.

# APPENDIX B
# AUTHOR BIOGRAPHIES

**Norman Amundson** is a professor of counseling psychology in the Faculty of Education, University of British Columbia. He has written numerous articles and his most recent book, Active Engagement, was named the 2000 Best Counselling Book by the Canadian Counselling Association. This book has also been translated into Swedish and Danish.

**Mary Z. Anderson** is an assistant professor in the Department of Counselor Education and Counseling Psychology at Western Michigan University. Her scholarship interests include vocational psychology and assessment, with a particular emphasis on understanding the career development of individuals from diverse populations.

**Alicia Andujo** has an M.S. Degree in Career Counseling, California State University Long Beach. She is a counselor at Long Beach City College, working with international students, and a career counseling instructor, counselor, and co-coordinator for the Puente Program. She is also President of the California Community College Counselors Association, a member of the Southern California HACER McDonald's Hispanic Educational Advisory Board.

**Consuelo Arbona** is the director of training for the doctoral program in counseling psychology at the University of Houston. She received her doctorate from the University of Wisconsin-Madison in 1986. Her major research interests are in multicultural psychology and career counseling.

**Elizabeth Regnier Beil** holds a PhD and is a licensed counseling psychologist in private practice in Columbia, MD, specializing in career uncertainty and grief/loss. She is also a faculty associate at the Johns Hopkins University. She frequently presents on topics of grief, career counseling, termination issues, and group counseling.

**Nancy Betz,** professor of psychology at The Ohio State University, received a PhD in Psychology from the University of Minnesota. She edited the *Journal of Vocational Behavior* from 1984-1990. Betz has authored nearly 100 publications in the field of counseling psychology. She received the John Holland Leona Tyler Awards for Research and for Distinguished Scholarly Contributions.

**David L. Blustein** is a professor and director of doctoral training in the Department of Counseling, Developmental, and Educational Psychology at Boston College. Professor Blustein has published over 60 journal articles and book chapters on career development, work-based transitions, the exploration process, the interface between work and interpersonal functioning, and the impact of social class in human development.

**Larry D. Burlew** holds an Ed.D., is a LPC, and is a professor in the Division of Counseling & Human Resources at the University of Bridgeport in Connecticut. He has worked as a career counselor, as well as an EAP counselor, and his publications focus on career and adult development issues.

**Anna Chaves** is a doctoral student in the Department of Counseling, Developmental, and Educational Psychology at Boston College. Anna's professional interests include adolescent educational and vocational development, and youth prevention and intervention.

**Stuart Chen Hayes**, PhD, N.C.C., is assistant professor and Coordinator of Counselor Education/School Counseling at Lehman College of the City University of New York. He has published multiple refereed journal articles and book chapters on school, family, lesbian, bisexual, gay and transgender (LBGT), and advocacy and social justice issues in counseling. He has presented over 140 local, state, national, and international presentations. He is a member of the American Counseling Association, American School Counselors Association, the Association for Gay, Lesbian, and Bisexual Issues in Counseling, and Counselors for Social Justice and is on the board of the New York Association for Gender Rights Advocacy. He is the co-author of two LBGT youth counseling videos with Microtraining Associates. He is currently working on a GEAR-UP grant and an Education Trust transforming school counseling grant.

**Y. Barry Chung,** PhD, is an assistant professor at Georgia State University. He received his PhD in counseling psychology from the University of Illinois. His professional interests include career development, multicultural counseling, and sexual orientation issues. He has served on the editorial boards of the *Counseling Psychologist, Career Development Quarterly*, and *Journal of Multicultural Counseling and Development.*

**Ellen Cook,** PhD, is professor of counselor education at the University of Cincinnati. She is the author of numerous articles applying ecological models to career development. Cook is the associate editor of *The Career Development Quarterly.*

**Rocco Cottone**, PhD, is a professor of counseling and family therapy and coordinator of doctoral programs in the Division of Counseling at the University of Missouri-St. Louis. He is the author of *Theories and Paradigms of Counseling and Psychotherapy* and *Ethical and Professional Issues in Counseling* (with Vilia Tarvydas).

**James M. Croteau** is an associate professor in the Department of Counselor Education and Counseling Psychology at Western Michigan University. His scholarship interests concern lesbian, gay and bisexual issues in career development, professional training, and other areas. His newest area of scholarship focuses on racism and racial awareness among white people.

**Carol A. Dahir** holds an Ed.D. and is assistant professor and coordinator of counselor education programs at the New York Institute of Technology. She serves as the National Standards project director for the American School Counselor Association (ASCA) and the project manager for Planning for Life, a program that recognizes exemplary career planning programs in schools across the nation sponsored by the US Army.

**Jan Deeds** is the director of the University of Nebraska-Lincoln (UNL) Women's Center and is gender programs specialist for UNL Student Involvement. She has been a member of the American Counseling Association and the National Career Development Association since 1981, and has chaired the NCDA Women's Issues special interest group.

**Matthew A. Diemer** is a doctoral student in the Counseling Psychology program at Boston College. Diemer's areas of research interest are vocational psychology, critical consciousness, long-term relationships, and the impact of race, class, gender and sexual orientation upon human development.

**Dennis Engels** holds degrees in English from St. Norbert College and the University of Wisconsin (UW) and a doctorate in counseling from UW. He is regents professor of Counselor Education at the University of North Texas, Denton. He is a Licensed Professional and National Certified Career Counselor, has published widely, and presents and consults nationally.

**Rich Feller** holds a PhD, is a professor of Counseling and Career Development at Colorado State University, and an NCDA Trustee who specializes in career and workforce development. A former school and admissions counselor he is co-author of *Career Transitions in Turbulent Times*, the *Tour of Your Tomorrow* video series and contributing author of DISCOVER and GIS.

**Mark Fleming** received his Master's Degree in Rehabilitation Psychology and Counseling from the University of North Carolina at Chapel Hill. He is currently a third year Doctoral Candidate in Counseling Psychology at The Pennsylvania State University. He is currently preparing to begin his clinical internship at the University of California at Los Angeles.

**Nadya A. Fouad** holds a PhD, is a professor in the Department of Educational Psychology at the University of Wisconsin-Milwaukee, and a Fellow in and President of Division 17 (Counseling Psychology) of the American Psychological Association. She has published in the areas of cross-cultural vocational assessment, career development, interest measurement, cross-cultural counseling, and race and ethnicity.

**Sheila H. Gardner** received her PhD from the Department of Counseling Psychology at the University at Albany. Although she has taken a brief hiatus to work as a full-time mom, her primary areas of professional interest include the therapeutic relationship, career development and decision making, and cultural issues as they relate to psychological functioning.

**Martin Gieda** received his doctorate in counseling psychology from The Pennsylvania State University. He works as a counseling psychologist at the University of North Texas Counseling and Testing Center and is an assistant professor in counseling. He is a licensed psychologist, National Certified Counselor, and a Licensed Chemical Dependency Counselor.

**Michael Goh** received his PhD in Counseling and Student Personnel Psychology at the University of Minnesota, Twin Cities where he is currently an assistant professor. His professional interests include: understanding helping systems and preferred sources of help within cultures; mental health issues and career development of Southeast Asian immigrants; and counseling in international contexts.

**Jane Goodman** holds PhD and is associate professor of counseling, Oakland University in Michigan. She is the 2001-2002 president of the American Counseling Association and a past president of the National Career Development Association. She is the author or co-author of several books, many articles and book chapters, primarily in the area of adult career development.

**Steven G. Grimsley** holds a M.Ed. in Education and is currently working toward Counseling Certification at Wichita State University.

**Judith Grutter** holds a M.S. and has incorporated the Myers-Briggs Type Indicator (MBTI) in her career development consulting, teaching, training, and writing for over 30 years. A National Certified Career Counselor, she developed and coordinated the graduate programs in career counseling at California State University, Northridge. Grutter is currently a principal with G/S CONSULTANTS in South Lake Tahoe, California. She is an INTJ.

**Norman C. Gysbers** is a professor in the Department of Educational and Counseling Psychology at the University of Missouri-Columbia. He received his MA and PhD degrees from the University of Michigan. Gysbers' research and teaching interests are in career development, career counseling and school guidance and counseling program development, management, and evaluation.

**Michael E. Hall** holds PhD in counseling psychology and is a Certified Career Management Fellow, the International Board for Career Management Certification's highest designation. He is in independent practice in Charlotte, NC where he provides organizational career development services. Also, he is the director of Executive Career Management (*The Transition Team-Charlotte*) and a University of North Carolina-Charlotte adjunct faculty member.

**Lenore W. Harmon** is professor emerita at the University of Illinois where she taught for over 20 years in the Counseling Psychology program. She received her PhD from the University of Minnesota in 1965. She is a former editor of both the *Journal of Vocational Behavior* and the *Journal of Counseling Psychology.*

**JoAnn Harris-Bowlsbey,** executive director of the Career Development Leadership Alliance, a nonprofit organization specializing in curriculum development and the application of technology to assisting individuals with career planning, is also a faculty member at Loyola College in Baltimore. Bowlsbey previously served as executive director of ACT's Educational Technology Center. In that position she led the development of *DISCOVER..*

**Paul J. Hartung**, holds a PhD, is associate professor of behavioral sciences at Northeastern Ohio Universities College of Medicine, and is associate professor of counselor education at University of Akron. His scholarship centers on work as a context for human development, cross-cultural career psychology, physician career development, and communication in medicine.

**Lynn Haley-Banez**, PhD, LPC, NCC is on the counselor education faculty at Fairfield University, emphasizing multicultural counseling and group work. Her workshops, professional training, keynote presentations, and articles are related to diversity in group work. She is currently producing a video and leader guide that highlights how to facilitate diverse groups from a micro-skill perspective.

**Edwin L. Herr** holds EdD is Distinguished Professor of Education at The Pennsylvania State University. The author of some 30 books and 300 articles in counseling and career development, Herr is the former President of the American Counseling Association, National Vocational Guidance Association, Association for Counselor Education and Supervision, and Chi Sigma Iota.

**Roger D. Herring** holds an EdD, a NCC, and a NCSC. He is professor of counselor education at the University of Arkansas-Little Rock. He has 20 years experience in public schools as a teacher, administrator, and school counselor. He has written four texts, over 50 articles, and 16 book chapters on cross-cultural counseling, emphasizing Native American Indian youth and other ethnic minority adolescents.

**Tyrone A. Holmes** is an LPC and is the president of T.A.H. Performance Consultants, Inc., a full service performance consulting firm specializing in diversity empowerment and multicultural communication skill development. He has served as a corporate human resource manager, and as a counseling faculty member at both Eastern Michigan University and Wayne State University in Detroit, MI.

**Ken Hoyt** is a PhD and university distinguished professor, at Kansas State University. He is a past president of the American Counseling Association (ACA) and the National Career Development Association (NCDA). Awards include: The Hitchcock Professional Service Award and NCDA's Eminent Career Award. He has written 11 books, 53 monographs, and 101 journal articles. His major research projects include directing the Counseling for High Skills Program.

**David A. Jepsen** is professor in the Division of Counseling, Rehabilitation and Student Development at the University of Iowa. He has served NCDA as editor of the *Career Development Quarterly* (CDQ), president, and program chair for two national conferences. Currently he is on the editorial board of the CDQ.

**Dhruvi Kakkad** received her B.A. in Psychology at Swarthmore College (1997) and her MSEd in Counseling Psychology at Fordham University (2001). She is currently a doctoral student in counseling psychology at Fordham University. Her primary research interests are in multicultural counseling, at-risk youth, and international peace/human rights issues.

**Helen H. Kim** is an assistant professor in the Counselor Education program at the University of Virginia. Her research interests revolve around multicultural issues in counseling, Asian American identity development, and group work. She has received her academic degrees from University of California, Harvard University, and Southern Illinois University.

**Mark S. Kiselica** is a PhD, NCC, LPC, and associate professor and chairperson of the Department of Counselor Education at The College of New Jersey. He is the author of over 80 publications and has received numerous awards in honor of his national impact on the professions of counseling and psychology.

**Diane Kjos**, PhD, is Professor Emeritus, Governors State University, University Park, Illinois. Recently retired, she lives in Tucson, Arizona. Dr. Kjos is past president of the National Career Development Association and has co-produced three video series in the areas of brief therapy, psychotherapy, and family therapy.

**John D. Krumboltz,** professor of education and psychology at Stanford University, is a fellow of the American Psychological Association and the American Association for the Advancement of Science. On three occasions he received the Outstanding Research Award from the American Personnel and Guidance Association. He is co-author of *Changing Children's Behavior*. He received the Leona Tyler Award, the nation's foremost award in counseling psychology.

**Courtland Lee** is professor of counselor education at the University of Maryland. He served previously as dean of the School of Education and professor of counselor education at Hunter College of the City University of New York and professor at the University of Virginia. He is the author, editor, or co-editor of four books on multicultural counseling and the author of two books on counseling African American males.

**Ellen Lent** is a PhD, a licensed psychologist, and workplace consultant. She has over 25 years experience in a variety of settings. She is on the adjunct faculty at University of Maryland-College Park and provides adjunct services at Johns Hopkins and Georgetown Universities. She is an experienced supervisor, career counselor, researcher, and writer.

**Robert W. Lent** is a professor in the Department of Counseling and Personnel Services, University of Maryland. He received his PhD in counseling psychology from The Ohio State University in 1979. His research interests include applications of social cognitive theory to career development, counseling, and health behaviors.

**Janet G. Lenz** is the associate director for career advising, counseling, and programming in the Career Center at Florida State University (FSU), and a senior research associate in the FSU Center for the Study of Technology in Counseling and Career Development. She received her PhD in Counseling and Human Systems from Florida State University.

**Darrell Anthony Luzzo** is a PhD and author of over 70 publications (including journal articles, books, book chapters, and monographs) that have focused on the career development of high school students, college students, and adults. Luzzo currently serves as the vice president of product development at National Career Assessment Services, Inc.

**Wei-Cheng Mau** earned a PhD in counseling from the University of Iowa. He is a National Certified Counselor and an associate professor at the Wichita State University. He is an editorial board member of the *Career Development Quarterly* and the *Journal of Vocational Behavior*.

**Vivian J. Carroll McCollum** is a professor of counseling at the University of New Orleans and holds a PhD in Marriage and Family Therapy from St. Louis University. Her professional specialty is multicultural issues in counseling and the effects of client/counselor interaction in school counseling, career counseling, and family therapy.

**Brian T. McMahon** is professor and chair of the Department of Rehabilitation Counseling at Virginia Commonwealth University. A former president of the American Rehabilitation Counseling Association, he is now president of the Virginia Council on Problem Gambling.

**Juliet V. Miller** recently retired as Executive Director of the National Career Development Association. She has been a private-practice career counselor, a lead consultant on the development of the National Career Development Guidelines, and a consultant to high school career development programs. She holds a PhD in counseling from the University of Michigan, is an LPC in Ohio, and is a NCCC.

**Amy Milsom** is assistant professor of counselor education at the University of Iowa. She earned her doctoral degree in counselor education from The Pennsylvania State University. She has served as a school counselor in elementary, middle, and high schools and holds the Supervisor of Pupil Services Certificate in Pennsylvania.

**Kathleen Mitchell** is a career counselor and instructor at City College of San Francisco and has a private career counseling practice. She has presented at numerous conferences and organizations on Planned Happenstance, the theory that recognizes how people can learn to create career opportunities by taking action on chance events.

**Spencer G. Niles** is professor of education and the professor-in-charge of counselor education at The Pennsylvania State University. He served previously as professor and assistant dean at the University of Virginia. He is the editor of the *Career Development Quarterly* and serves on the editorial boards for numerous other journals. Niles is a licensed psychologist and licensed professional counselor.

**Richard Noeth**, PhD, is Director of Policy Research at ACT in Iowa City, Iowa. He was a Senior Program Officer at the National Academy of Sciences where he directed a study of President Clinton's Voluntary National Test. Prior to that he was Vice President for Field Services at ETS in Princeton, New Jersey. His doctorate is in counseling psychology from Purdue University where he was named a Distinguished Alumnus in 1994.

**Barbara Norrbom** is a M.Ed. and a licensed secondary school counselor at Lyons High School in Lyons Colorado. She specializes in adolescent career development. A graduate of Colorado State University's (CSU) Counseling and Career Development program, her experiences include working with a variety of clients at CSU's Career Center and College of Liberal Arts.

**Karen M. O'Brien** is an associate professor at the University of Maryland. Her research interests include investigating the career and life development of women and minorities with attention to psychodynamic and social-cognitive variables. She serves on the editorial board of the *Career Development Quarterly* and the *Journal of Counseling Psychology*.

**Thomas V. Palma,** PhD is an assistant professor at Cleveland State University in Counseling and Urban Education. Dr. Palma secured his doctorate in Counseling Psychology from the University of Missouri - Kansas City, completed his clinical internship at the University of Pennsylvania, and was awarded a post-doctoral appointment in the Cultural Foundations program in Counseling Psychology at the University of Nebraska. He is an officer in the American Psychological Association's Division of Counseling Psychology and has focused his scholarly activity on identity formation among marginalized populations (racial/ethnic minorities, women, gay men/lesbians/bisexuals) and counselor decision making and efficacy.

**Twinet Parmer** is Ph.D., LPC, and associate professor of counselor education in the Department of Counseling and Special Education at Central Michigan University. His research and presentations focus on holistic sexuality, family, and career issues that influence the quality of life for African Americans. In addition, she is in private practice conducting sex, family, and couples therapy.

**David Paterson** is an assistant professor and coordinator of the counselling program in the Faculty of Education at Simon Fraser University. He has recently developed and presented a series of lectures on North American career counseling in collaboration with the Shanghai Education Commission.

**John Patrick** is currently an assistant professor of counselor education at California University of Pennsylvania, California. His research interests include career counseling, college counseling, and rehabilitation counseling.

**Rhonda Paul** is a NCC, NCCC, and adjunct faculty member at Oakland University and Wayne State University. She received her PhD in counseling from Wayne State University. She chairs the Task Force on Multicultural Competencies for NCDA and ACA's Professional Development Committee. She received Wayne State University's Professional Achievement Award and the Certificate of Outstanding Merit from the National Board for Certified Counselors.

**R. Vance Peavy** is professor emeritus, Department of Educational Psychology and Leadership studies, and adjunct professor, School of Child and Youth Care, University of Victoria, Canada. Several books on constructivist-sociodynamic counseling published in English, Finnish, Danish, and Swedish languages. He is also the inventor of a post-industrial, constructivist form of counseling under the name of SocioDynamic Counselling.

**Peter Plant** is an associate professor of career development at the Royal Danish School of Educational Studies, Copenhagen, Denmark. He trains career development staff in Denmark and other, mainly European, countries. He is active in European research and development projects and is currently vice-president of the International Association for Educational and Vocational Guidance.

**Joseph G. Ponterotto** is professor of education and coordinator of counseling programs at Fordham University-Lincoln Center, New York City. His primary teaching interests are in multicultural counseling, career development, psychological measurement, and qualitative research methods. He has written extensively in the area of multicultural counseling and is the co-editor or co-author of eight books on the topic.

**Mark Pope** is an Ed.D., NCC, NCCC, RPCC, MAC, and ACS. He is an educator, consultant, counselor and currently serves as associate professor at the University of Missouri-St. Louis in the Division of Counseling and Family Therapy where his specialties include career counseling, addictions counseling, psychological testing, and multicultural counseling. He has written extensively on careers, specifically on the career development of ethnic, racial, and sexual minorities.

**Jeffrey P. Prince** is director of student counseling at the University of California, Berkeley. He received his PhD from the University of Minnesota and has worked as a practitioner, educator and consultant within a number of universities and organizations. He has authored two books and numerous book chapters and journal articles focused on career assessment and counseling.

**Jack R. Rayman** is director of career services and affiliate professor of counseling psychology and education at The Pennsylvania State University. He taught agriculture and English at Rajang Teachers College as a Peace Corps Volunteer in Sarawak, Malaysia. He was a major architect of DISCOVER. He is the author of more than 30 books, journal articles and book chapters.

**Christine Reid** is a PhD CRC NCC CVE CCM. She is an associate professor and director of doctoral studies for the Department of Rehabilitation Counseling at Virginia Commonwealth University. She has been active as a rehabilitation counselor, educator, researcher, and consultant for more than 15 years and has served in leadership roles for various counseling-related accrediting and professional organizations.

**Lee Joyce Richmond,** professor of counselor education at Loyola College, is a former president of ACA and NCDA. Lee has been Chair of the ACA Insurance Trust, the CDTI Board, and currently serves on CACREP. Her interest in spirituality and career development has resulted in two assessment tools and three co-authored books.

**Susan E. Riser** is assistant professor of counselor education at Auburn University Montgomery in Montgomery, AL. She received her PhD in counselor education from Southern Illinois University in 1999. Her interests include human growth and transition, group and career counseling, research in counseling, and development of multicultural counseling competencies.

**Martha M. Russell** is a M.S. and NCC. She is the owner of Russell Career Services, that has been helping individuals and groups deal with the changes in the world of work and the impact on personal career management plans since 1987. She conducts frequent career decision making, career management, and staff development workshops both nationally and internationally.

**Michael Shahnasarian** is a PhD and founder and President of Career Consultants of America, Inc., in Tampa, Florida. He has authored over 30 publications on career development topics. In 1997-1998, he served as president of the National Career Development Association. He has had appointments by two Florida governors to boards pertaining to vocational rehabilitation.

**Carissa Sherwood** is a graduate student working toward a M.Ed. in school counseling at Wichita State University.

**Hemla D. Singaravelu** is a PhD, NCCC, and an assistant professor in the Department of Counseling and Family Therapy at St. Louis University, Missouri. She worked as a career counselor at Southern Illinois University-Carbondale while completing her doctoral program. Her research interests include issues in career development; culture/diversity; and the gay, lesbian, bisexual, and transgender community.

**Howard H. Splete** is professor emeritus Oakland University. He has worked in the counseling field at all educational levels. He has been a career counselor in schools and in private practice and has coordinated adult career counseling centers. Current consulting interests include training career development facilitators and coordinating school counselor academies.

**Brian J. Taber** is a doctoral candidate in Counselor Education and Supervision at Kent State University. He currently works in the Department of Behavioral Sciences at Northeastern Ohio Universities College of Medicine. He has presented and published in the areas of career development, assessment, counseling, and computer-assisted career guidance systems.

**M. Carolyn Thomas** is a PhD, LPC, AAMFT, and professor and coordinator of counselor education and director of the Counseling Center at Auburn University Montgomery in Montgomery, AL. Dr. Thomas earned her doctorate at the University of Iowa. Her specialties include career development and group work, and she has maintained active involvement in NCDA and ASGW.

**Donald I. Thompson** is professor and dean of the Division of Counseling, Education and Psychology, Troy State University Montgomery, Montgomery, Alabama. He has published two books, 35 journal articles/book chapters/monographs, four book reviews, two standardized tests, eight computer software/hardware reviews, and 38 convention paper presentations/abstracts.

**Linda C. Tipton** is a PhD and a staff psychologist and coordinator of consultation and outreach at the University of Maryland Counseling Center in College Park, Maryland. She is also an affiliate faculty member with the Counseling Psychology Program there. Her clinical and research interests include women's career development and dual-career couples issues.

**Elizabeth Toepfer-Hendey** is the assistant director for counseling and planning at Career Services and affiliate assistant professor of counseling psychology at The Pennsylvania State University. She received her Ed.D. in counseling psychology from Teachers College, Columbia University. Her practice, research, and teaching interests encompass career decision making, training, and diversity issues.

**Beverly J. Vandiver** is a PhD and associate professor of counseling psychology at The Pennsylvania State University. Her research interests are in the areas of cultural identity, scale development, and career development. In the area of career and vocational counseling, she has focused on the infusion of cultural identities in career theories and practice.

**Verneda Washington**, PhD, is a graduate of the doctoral program in counselor education at the University of Virginia. She has served on the faculty at the University of Missouri-St. Louis and is a specialist in career and family counseling.

**Jack Watson** is an assistant professor in sport psychology and has an adjunct appointment within the Carruth Center for Counseling and Psychological Services at West Virginia University. He has a PhD in sport psychology and a post-doctoral respecialization in counseling psychology from Florida State University. He is versed in career development theories and previously worked at the Florida State University Career Center.

**Keith Wilson** received his PhD from The Ohio State University with a concentration in rehabilitation services. Among numerous awards, he was awarded the Outstanding Researcher of the Year Award presented by The Pennsylvania Counseling Association in 2001. Dr. Wilson's research agenda includes vocational rehabilitation outcomes among persons with disabilities.

# INDEX

## Age of Client

## Gender of Client

## Cultural Diversity Represented by Client